AIDS and Rural Livelihoods

T0300344

AIDS and Rural Livelihoods

Dynamics and Diversity in Sub-Saharan Africa

Edited by
Anke Niehof, Gabriel Rugalema
and Stuart Gillespie

from Routledge

First published in 2010 by Earthscan

Published 2016 by Routledge

2 Park Square, Milton Park, Abingdon, Oxon, OX14 4RN
711 Third Avenue, New York, NY 10017

Routledge is an imprint of the Taylor & Francis Group, an informa business

ISBN: 978-1-84971-125-8 hardback
ISBN: 978-1-84971-126-5 paperback

Typeset by JS Typesetting Ltd, Porthcawl, Mid Glamorgan
Cover design by Clifford Hayes

A catalogue record for this book is available from the British Library

Library of Congress Cataloging-in-Publication Data

AIDS and rural livelihoods : dynamics and diversity in Sub-Saharan Africa / edited by Anke Niehof, Gabriel Rugalema, and Stuart Gillespie.
      p. ; cm.
   Includes bibliographical references and index.
   ISBN 978-1-84971-125-8 (hardback) – ISBN 978-1-84971-126-5 (pbk.) 1. AIDS (Disease)–Economic aspects–Africa, Sub-Saharan. 2. AIDS (Disease)–Social aspects–Africa, Sub-Saharan. 3. Rural health–Africa, Sub-Saharan. I. Niehof, Anke, 1948- II. Rugalema, Gabriel. III. Gillespie, Stuart (Stuart R.)
   [DNLM: 1. Acquired Immunodeficiency Syndrome–Africa South of the Sahara. 2. HIV Infections–Africa South of the Sahara. 3. Rural Health–Africa South of the Sahara. 4. Rural Population–Africa South of the Sahara. 5. Socioeconomic Factors–Africa South of the Sahara. WC 503 A28705 2010]
   RA643.86.A357A48 2010
   362.196'979200967–dc22
                                        2010013621

Contents

List of contributors   *vii*
Preface and acknowledgements   *xi*

1   AIDS in Africa: dynamics and diversity of impacts and response   1
    Stuart Gillespie, Anke Niehof and Gabriel Rugalema

2   The longitudinal picture: What does it reveal?   13
    Janet Seeley, Jovita Amurwon and Susan Foster

3   Resilience and (dis)continuity in households afflicted by AIDS:
    Some preliminary insights from a longitudinal case study analysis   29
    Gabriel Rugalema, Kirsten Mathieson and Joseph Ssentongo

4   Impacts of AIDS-related morbidity and mortality on non-urban households
    in KwaZulu-Natal, South Africa   43
    Corrie du Preez and Anke Niehof

5   Sweet cane, bitter realities: The complex realities of AIDS in Mkamba,
    Kilombero District, Tanzania   61
    Carolyne I. Nombo

6   Single women's experiences of livelihood conditions, HIV and AIDS in the
    rural areas of Zimbabwe   77
    Gaynor Gamuchirai Paradza

7   Regional agricultural-consumption regimes and women's vulnerability to
    HIV in Kenya   95
    E. Wairimu Mwangi

8   Multilayered impacts of AIDS and implications for food security among
    banana farmers in Uganda   117
    Monica Karuhanga Beraho

9   Impact of HIV/AIDS on local farming knowledge: differences in the
    cognitive salience of maize crop pests between affected and non-affected
    adults and children in Benin   133
    Rose Fagbemissi and Lisa Leimar Price

10 Adult mortality, food security and the use of wild natural resources in a rural
    district of South Africa: Exploring the environmental dimensions of AIDS   153
    Wayne Twine and Lori M. Hunter

11 Applying the Farmer Life School approach to support women of poor and
    HIV/AIDS-affected households in KwaZulu-Natal, South Africa   171
    Kees Swaans, Jacqueline Broerse and Maxwell Mudhara

12 Agricultural policy response to HIV and AIDS: Lessons learned from East
    and Southern Africa   191
    Michelle Remme, Fadzai Mukonoweshuro and Libor Stloukal

13 AIDS and livelihoods: What have we learned and where are we heading?   209
    Stuart Gillespie, E. Wairimu Mwangi, Anke Niehof and Gabriel Rugalema

Index   *227*

List of contributors

Jovita Amurwon is a health economist working with the Medical Research Council, Uganda. She holds an MSc in International Health Care Management, Economics and Policy. She is currently participating in two studies: Impact of HIV on rural household food availability and consumption, funded by International Foundation for Science (IFS), and Cost-effectiveness of HAART in preventing HIV transmission among HIV uninfected, cohabiting sexual partners of HIV-infected individuals accessing HAART. Email: jovita.amurwon@mrcuganda.org.

Jacqueline Broerse is head of the Department of Science Communication and associate professor at the Athena Institute for Research on Innovation and Communication in Health and Life Sciences, VU University, Amsterdam, The Netherlands. She wrote her PhD thesis on participatory strategies for generating biotechnological innovations in the small-scale agricultural sector of developing countries (1998). Her current research focuses on the development and application of interactive learning and action strategies in health policy and research. Email: jacqueline.broerse@falw.vu.nl.

Corrie Du Preez is a full-time lecturer at the Department of Consumer Sciences of the University of Zululand in the province of KwaZulu-Natal, South Africa. Since October 2008, she has also been acting head of the department. She holds a master's degree from Wageningen University, The Netherlands, and will defend her PhD thesis later in 2010 at the same university. Originally trained as a home economist, her research focuses on household production, consumption, livelihood and care. Email: cdupreez@pan.uzulu.ac.za.

Rose C. Fagbemissi holds a master's degree in development sociology from the University of Lomé, Togo. She was formerly a research assistant at the International Institute of Tropical Agriculture (IITA). She is currently working on her PhD at Wageningen University, The Netherlands (defending in 2010). Her research interests include participatory development of agricultural innovations, ethno-biology and ethno-ecology; gender studies in rural development; youth capacity building and child care. Email: fagbemissi@yahoo.com.

Susan D. Foster is a professor of international health at Boston University School of Public Health, Boston, USA. She has worked as a consultant with the Medical Research Council's MRC/UVRI Uganda Research Unit on AIDS since 1990. She has worked on socioeconomic aspects of the HIV epidemic, infectious diseases, and on pharmaceutical policy, and has a PhD from the London School of Hygiene & Tropical Medicine. In Boston she is Director of Public Policy and Education for the Alliance for the Prudent Use of Antibiotics. Email: suzyf921@gmail.com.

Stuart Gillespie is a senior research fellow at the International Food Policy Research Institute (IFPRI), director of the Regional Network on AIDS, Livelihoods and Food Security (RENEWAL) and coordinator of the Agriculture and Health Research Platform (AHRP). He has a PhD in Human Nutrition from the London School of Hygiene and Tropical Medicine (1988), and is currently based in Geneva. Email: s.gillespie@cgiar.org.

Lori Hunter holds a PhD from Brown University (USA) and is an associate professor of Sociology and Environmental Studies at the University of Colorado at Boulder. Her research links demographic dynamics to environmental settings primarily at the Agincourt Health and Demographic Surveillance Site in rural South Africa. She is currently Editor-in-Chief of the journal *Population and Environment* and recently co-edited a special issue of the journal on AIDS & Environment (Vol. 29:2, 2008). Email: lorimaehunter@comcast.net.

Monica Karuhanga Beraho lectures at the Department of Agricultural Extension Education of Makerere University, Kampala, Uganda. She holds a master's degree in agronomy and farming systems at Adelaide University, Australia. In 2008, she successfully defended her PhD thesis – *Living with AIDS in Uganda: Impacts on Banana-farming Households in Two Districts* – at Wageningen University, The Netherlands. Her research interests include: gender and rural development, livelihood and participatory research. Email: monicakb66@yahoo.co.uk or monica@agric.mak.ac.ug.

Kirsten Mathieson graduated from the University Rome La Sapienza, Italy, with an MA in state management and humanitarian affairs. She has previously worked with UNDP in Kenya and thereafter (since 2007) with FAO, where she is currently working in the Gender, Equity and Rural Employment Division. Her work primarily focuses on vulnerability, diseases in rural society and rural livelihoods. Her research interests include household analysis, gender and the socio-economic burden of disease. Email: kirsten.mathieson@fao.org.

Maxwell Mudhara is the director of the Farmer Support Group, Centre for Environment, Agriculture and Development, University of KwaZulu-Natal, South Africa. He holds a PhD in food and resource economics from the University of Florida, Gainesville (USA). His experience is in farming systems' research and extension, economic modelling of smallholder farming systems, impact assessment and participatory approaches. Email: mudhara@ukzn.ac.za.

Fadzai Mukonoweshuro holds a master's degree in development management and is studying for a PhD in applied social science. As a regional expert for the Food and Agriculture Organization of the United Nations, he has provided technical support to the formulation of HIV strategies for the agricultural sector in countries in southern Africa.

He has presented papers at major conferences and has contributed to several publications focusing on policy issues around HIV and food security. Email: fmukono@hotmail.com.

E. Wairimu Mwangi is a consultant with the International Food Policy Research Institute (IFPRI)'s Regional Network on AIDS, Livelihoods and Food Security (RENEWAL) and the Agriculture and Health Research Platform (AHRP). She holds a PhD in rural sociology from the Ohio State University (2009), with a specialization in global social change, social demography and social epidemiology. Email: e.wairimu.mwangi@gmail.com.

Anke Niehof is a full professor at Wageningen University, The Netherlands, holding the chair of Sociology of Consumers and Households. She was trained as an anthropologist and demographer, and holds a PhD from Leiden University, The Netherlands (1985). Together with Lisa Price, since 2002 she managed the AWLAE Project, in which 19 women from 11 African countries did PhD research on themes relating to HIV and AIDS' impacts on women's roles in food and livelihood systems in Africa. Five of them contributed to this book. Email: anke.niehof@wur.nl.

Carolyne Nombo is a lecturer at the Development Studies Institute of Sokoine University of Agriculture, Morogoro, Tanzania, teaching courses in gender and development, public policies and food security. She is also involved in research and consultancy work, focusing on poverty eradication, HIV/AIDS, livelihood and food security, gender issues and community organizations. In December 2007 she obtained her doctorate at Wageningen University. Email: cnombo@suanet.ac.tz or cnombo@yahoo.com.

Gaynor Paradza is a senior researcher at the Centre for Policy Studies, Braamfontein, Johannesburg, and a PhD student with Wageningen University's Law and Governance Group. She is an experienced university lecturer and a researcher on governance, local government service delivery, gender and land tenure, and HIV and AIDS. She acknowledges the support for the research of AWLAE/Winrock International and the financial support of The Netherlands Government. Email: gparadza@hotmail.com.

Lisa Leimar Price has a PhD in anthropology from the University of Oregon and is an associate professor in the Social Sciences Department of Wageningen University, The Netherlands. She is co-manager of the AWLAE Project (see above). Prior to joining Wageningen University she was a senior scientist at the International Rice Research Institute (IRRI). She specializes in gender, agro-biodiversity, natural resource management and ethno-biology. Email: lisa.price@wur.nl.

Michelle Remme is an outposted officer of the Gender, Equity and Rural Employment Division of the Food and Agriculture Organisation (FAO) of the United Nations. She is based in Malawi, where she is responsible for HIV and gender issues in relation to agriculture and food security. She holds a master's degree in international economics and finance and has worked in the health and AIDS sectors for The Netherlands Ministry of Foreign Affairs, the World Bank and the World Health Organisation. Email: michelle.remme@fao.org.

Gabriel Rugalema is a senior officer in the Gender, Equity and Rural Employment Division of FAO, Rome. His research and professional interests include the social, economic and food security implications of disease on society; institutional analysis; disease ecology; emergency risk analysis and response; rural agricultural opportunities and smallholder dynamics. Email: gabriel.rugalema@fao.org.

Janet Seeley, senior lecturer at the School of International Development, University of East Anglia (UK) and Head of the Social Science Research Programme, MRC/UVRI Uganda Research Unit on AIDS, has been actively engaged in research on the social aspects of HIV and AIDS since the late 1980s. In the last 10 years she has been a principal investigator on 15 research projects, including 8 directly related to the impact of HIV and AIDS on individuals, households and communities. Email: j.seeley@uea.ac.uk.

Joseph Ssentongo recently joined the Gender, Equity and Rural Employment Division at FAO headquarters as a spatial analysis consultant. He holds an MSc degree from Warwick University, UK. He has previously worked for OCHA, the Natural Resources and Environment Division of FAO and with the Gulbenkian Science Institute in Lisbon, focusing mainly on disease impact monitoring, epidemic surveillance and harnessing geographical information systems (GIS). Email: joseph.ssentongo@fao.org

Libor Stloukal graduated from the Charles University in Prague with an MA in human geography and obtained his PhD in demography at the Australian National University. Since joining FAO in 1999, he has been working on the linkages between demographic change, agriculture and food security in low-income countries, with particular focus on mitigating the impacts of human diseases and adapting rural development strategies to age-structural changes such as rural population ageing. Email: libor.stloukal@fao.org.

Kees Swaans is assistant professor at the Athena Institute for Research on Innovation and Communication in Health and Life Sciences, VU University Amsterdam (The Netherlands) and is based in Hanoi, Vietnam. He has degrees in agricultural sciences and the management of agricultural knowledge systems from Wageningen University. In 2008 he successfully defended his PhD entitled '*Transcending boundaries: Interactive Learning and Action at the Interface of HIV/AIDS and Agriculture*' at the VU University, Amsterdam. Email: k.swaans@gmail.com.

Wayne Twine is a senior lecturer in ecology in the School of Animal, Plant and Environmental Sciences, University of Witwatersrand, South Africa. His research focuses on various aspects of socio-ecological systems, particularly in communal rangeland settings. His interest in HIV/AIDS is in relation to the contribution of ecosystem services to household resilience during shocks and stresses. He holds a PhD in resource ecology from the University of KwaZulu-Natal, South Africa. Email: rcrd@global.co.za.

Preface and acknowledgements

HIV is unique among the major epidemics in that it has now been around for about 30 years. When the epidemic first broke out, it was expected that, sooner or later, a medical solution would be found, conveniently consigning AIDS to history. Thirty years later and despite major advances in science and medicine, the disease is still with us. Indeed, we have noted in the first chapter of this book that *'while there have been significant medical advances in understanding and responding to the virus and the disease, the wider set of social and economic drivers of HIV epidemics and the multiple, downstream impacts of AIDS on societies and economies are less well known.'* While the observation is valid, at the same time, we acknowledge that there is a growing body of literature based on recent research addressing these issues. Various perspectives have been presented in literature and they have helped shed some light on how the epidemic has driven, and continues to drive, social, cultural and economic changes. Learning lessons from this multitude of research findings, however, is complicated by the different designs underlying the studies; they can be cross-sectional (mostly) or longitudinal, focused at micro-level mechanisms or macro-level trends, and so on. Researchers also make different choices in handling the ethical and methodological problems that inevitably arise when collecting empirical data on AIDS impacts in situations where the disease is still surrounded by secrecy and stigma. The pervasive role of local and context-specific factors in influencing prevalence and shaping impacts further reduces the comparability of research findings. For this reason the quotation above speaks of HIV epidemic*s*, in the plural, for we argue in this book that there is no one single HIV epidemic. What is referred to as 'the HIV epidemic' is in fact a constellation of epidemics of varying intensity distributed across space and time. Sometimes these epidemics coalesce, sometimes they don't. In this book, we have used the concept of diversity to underline not only the epidemiological diversity of HIV but also the differences one sees when examining how different communities and households have responded to the morbidity and mortality effects of these epidemics.

As we continue to learn more about the impacts of AIDS, notions of 'conventional wisdom' are constantly redefined. Scenarios that emerged in the early years of the epidemic had predicted catastrophe, particularly in East and Southern Africa. Hunger would intensify, thousands of households would dissolve, those that would survive would be headed by children orphaned by the epidemic, according to this narrative. Looking back in time, it is obvious that the worst-case scenarios did not come to pass. Indeed, despite its tenacity, AIDS has exacerbated livelihood problems including poverty, but it has not entirely overwhelmed the social fabric of society. To help understand these effects, we emphasize the need to understand the dynamics through which, over time, society grapples with the impacts of epidemics.

The overarching message we try to convey through this book is therefore that unless we understand the differences and the dynamics that characterize the epidemic at local level, it will remain very difficult to draw firm conclusions on its longer term and wider ramifications. Chapters presented in this book illustrate the various dimensions of diversity and dynamics of HIV and AIDS in various rural settings in Africa. In putting together this volume, we try to show how an epidemic moulds or is moulded by the social context in which it occurs. This line of thinking has benefitted from our comparatively long experience in AIDS research. At Wageningen University, Anke Niehof coordinates the AWLAE (*African Women Leaders in Agriculture and Environment*) Project, in which 19 women scholars from 11 African countries undertook PhD research (2004–2008) on topics relating to AIDS and women's roles in food and livelihood systems in sub-Saharan Africa. Findings were published in a special issue of the *Wageningen Journal of Life Sciences*, NJAS (2008, issue 56/3), in the AWLAE Series of Wageningen Academic Publishers, as well as in PhD theses and international journals. Five AWLAE scholars contributed to this book. Gabriel Rugalema's monograph on AIDS and the crisis of rural livelihoods in Tanzania (1999) was the first of its kind. Since then he has widely published on the subject and has been initiating and supervising research on AIDS and rural livelihoods and agriculture in his work at the Gender, Equity and Rural Employment Division of FAO in Rome. In 1989, while working with FAO, Stuart Gillespie published the first paper on the potential impacts of AIDS on African farming systems. Ten years later, after joining the International Food Policy Research Institute (IFPRI) in Washington DC, he co-founded RENEWAL – the Regional Network on AIDS, Livelihoods and Food Security to promote a networking approach to fusing locally relevant research on HIV and hunger with capacity strengthening and policy communications in eastern and southern Africa.

Publishing a book is a long process. There is always a great number of people behind the project. Some may have clear-cut roles and responsibilities, some may not. However, it takes the effort of all those actors to bring the project to fruition. Indeed, behind this project there are numerous actors without whom the book could not have been written: the anonymous respondents and participants in research projects, many of whom have been given a loud and clear voice by the researchers documenting their plight. They allow us to gain insight into how HIV and AIDS affect people's lives, making it possible to look beneath the surface of the figures and statistics that portray the magnitude of the AIDS problem. Having said this, there are a number of more specific acknowledgements that ought to be made. We would like to acknowledge the funding of The Netherlands Government of the AWLAE Project that yielded such valuable research. We are grateful to the NJAS board for allowing Rose Fagbemissi and Lisa Price to use their article in the special issue for a contribution to this book. We also acknowledge generous funding from Irish Aid and the Swedish International Development Cooperation Agency (SIDA) to RENEWAL that supported the involvement of Stuart Gillespie and E. Wairimu Mwangi, along with three studies reported here (Twine and Hunter, Swaans et al, and Mwangi). Finally, we would like to express our particular gratitude to E. Wairimu Mwangi for her invaluable assistance in the editing process, in addition to writing her own contributions to this volume.

The editors
March 2010

Chapter 1

AIDS in Africa: dynamics and diversity of impacts and response

Stuart Gillespie, Anke Niehof and Gabriel Rugalema

Introduction

In the three decades that have passed since the first cases were reported, AIDS has become one of the most highly studied diseases in history. While there have been significant medical advances in understanding and responding to the virus and the disease, the wider set of social and economic drivers of HIV epidemics and the multiple, downstream impacts of AIDS[1] on societies and economies are less well known.

In 2000, HIV was placed firmly on the global development agenda by UN Security Council Resolution 1308, which stated: *'the spread of HIV can have a uniquely devastating impact on all sectors and levels of society'*. A year later, in July 2001, the UN convened the General Assembly Special Session on HIV/AIDS – the first time such a session has been devoted to a single disease. It has only been during this last decade that we have started to unravel the complexities of epidemics – what drives them, what happens as a result of them, and how people respond in the face of their impacts. AIDS epidemics – and there are many – are long-wave events, and their effects will be felt for decades to come, especially in southern Africa where prevalence is highest. Despite the recent slow decline in the rate of new HIV infections, the number of people living with HIV in Africa slightly increased in 2008, partly due to increased longevity stemming from improved access to treatment.

The purpose of this book is to present an account of how, despite the decline in incidence, AIDS epidemics continue to impact rural agricultural-based livelihoods in

---

[1] In this book, when we are discussing infection, we refer to the virus (HIV); when discussing the disease, the broader epidemic, or its impacts, we refer to AIDS.

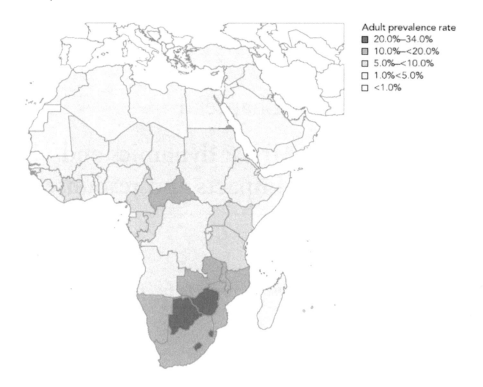

Figure 1.1 *Map of adult HIV prevalence in Africa*

Source: UNAIDS, 2006

Africa and how households and communities respond. Unlike many past analyses, our intention is to bring a number of perspectives into the analysis of impact and responses. First, the critical importance of time has hitherto been neglected, yet historical and recent evidence show that interaction between disease and human society is mediated through time (DeSalle, 1999; Sherman, 2007). We have to recognize that the effects of AIDS are not static, nor is the process through which households and communities respond to impacts. This perspective offers one important advantage: it provides incentive and space for analysing both the impact and responses longitudinally, thus helping to decipher their trajectories through time. Second, the multi-level nature of vulnerability and impact has often been referred to but has remained on the analytical margin. Multi-level here refers both to geographical dispersal of AIDS epidemics across space and time and the various levels of society (micro, meso and macro) at which complex forms of response to AIDS interplay.

This book focuses on Africa for one obvious reason. Since the beginning of the epidemic, sub-Saharan Africa remains the region most affected in the world and is home to two-thirds (67 per cent) of all people living with HIV worldwide. In 2008, 72 per cent of all AIDS deaths occurred in this region. The epidemic is estimated to have orphaned more than 14 million African children. Nine countries in southern Africa – where AIDS is 'hyperendemic' – continue to bear a disproportionate share of the global

AIDS burden – each of them has an adult HIV prevalence greater than 10 per cent and together they represent around one-third of all HIV cases and AIDS deaths globally (see Figure 1.1). With an adult HIV prevalence of 26 per cent in 2007, Swaziland has the most severe level of infection in the world, while South Africa continues to be home to the world's largest population of people living with HIV – 5.7 million in 2007.

By the end of 2008, 44 per cent of adults and children in the region in need of antiretroviral therapy had access to treatment (a huge increase from 2003 when the regional treatment coverage was only 2 per cent). As a result of treatment scale-up, people are living longer in many countries. In Kenya, for example, AIDS-related deaths have fallen by 29 per cent since 2002.

Women and girls continue to be disproportionally affected by HIV in sub-Saharan Africa. Throughout the region, women account for 60 per cent of all HIV infections. Young women between the ages of 15 and 19 are particularly vulnerable to HIV. In Kenya, for example, young women are three times more likely to become infected than their male counterparts.

Outside southern Africa, the epidemic appears to be under control: Uganda has shown how high levels of political commitment and community-led responses can stabilize HIV prevalence. In other locations in eastern Africa, such as Tanzania, infection rates peaked at a lower level than those currently seen in southern Africa. HIV prevalence in West and Central Africa is much lower than in southern Africa, although two countries have significant epidemics (Côte d'Ivoire at 3.9 per cent HIV prevalence and Ghana at 1.9 per cent).

We will shortly turn to discuss the complexity of the causes and consequences of Africa's AIDS epidemics, but first it is important to provide a quick historical perspective of their evolution.

Three decades on – a brief history

1981–1996: Understanding a new disease

The AIDS epidemic was recognized in 1981, initially among gay men in New York and San Francisco (USCDC, 1981). It was officially named Acquired Immune Deficiency Syndrome (AIDS) in July 1982, and in 1983 the human immunodeficiency virus (HIV) was identified as the cause. The number of cases rose rapidly across the USA and was quickly identified in Europe, Australia, New Zealand and Latin America. The main groups at risk in developed countries were gay men, haemophiliacs, blood transfusion recipients, and intravenous drug users. In central Africa, however, health workers were beginning to observe new illnesses such as Kaposi's sarcoma (a cancer) in Zambia; cryptococcosis (an unusual fungal infection) in Kinshasa; and there were reports of 'slim disease' and unexpectedly high rates of death in Lake Victoria fishing villages in Uganda (Bayley, 1984; Hooper, 1999; Iliffe, 2006). These illnesses were occurring in heterosexual adults. By 1982, cases were being seen in the partners and infants of those infected (Shilts, 1988; Iliffe, 2006).

Early responses were biomedical in nature as public health specialists, epidemiologists and scientists struggled to identify what caused AIDS and how it spread between people. This was followed by a focus on how to prevent the spread of HIV by reducing high-risk behaviours (Chin, 2006). At this time there was no treatment available for AIDS and initial hopes of a vaccine faded fast. The World Health Organisation (WHO) led the international response to HIV from the mid-1980s, and national AIDS programmes began to be developed (Mann and Tarantola, 1996).

A handful of academics began to explore the wider implications of AIDS during this time; in 1989, the first paper investigating the potential impact of AIDS on food security in Africa was published, following work commissioned by the FAO (Gillespie, 1989). Yet, denial, underestimation and over-simplification remained rife at all levels in these first 15 years.

1996–2010: The antiretroviral revolution, and new perspectives

By 1996 – the mid-point of the history of AIDS – major changes were underway, as academics and politicians began to take on board the multisectoral, developmental dimensions of the burgeoning AIDS crisis in sub-Saharan Africa. UNAIDS began operations in Geneva in 1996 signalling a realization that AIDS was more than a health issue, requiring better coordination between many UN agencies. At the XIth International AIDS Conference in Vancouver, the arrival of new drugs in developed countries to treat AIDS was announced, and mortality among those being treated plummeted.

In 2000, at the XIIIth International AIDS Conference in Durban, South Africa, Nelson Mandela closed the conference with a call for drugs to be made accessible to all. Since then, the response to AIDS has been dominated by new initiatives for making treatment accessible, especially in developing countries. The price of drugs has fallen dramatically with the manufacture of generic drugs (Graaff, 2007). In 2001, United Nation's Secretary General, Kofi Annan, called for spending on AIDS to be increased tenfold in developing countries, and the Global Fund for AIDS, TB and Malaria was established. The same year, US President George W. Bush announced the Presidential Emergency Plan for AIDS Relief (PEPFAR), targeting 15 developing countries. In 2003, the WHO and UNAIDS proclaimed the '3 by 5' plan, to treat 3 million people in developing countries by the end of 2005.

Over the decade from 1996 to 2006, more financial resources than ever before were made available for the response to AIDS, with emphasis increasingly on making treatment available in the developing world. In 1996 there was about $300 million for HIV/AIDS in low and middle income countries; by 2006 this increased to $8.3 billion. This massive response in recent years – largely a result of treatment becoming available and affordable – led to a remedicalization of AIDS discourse and practice.

New perspectives

Yet the mid-1990s also saw an emergence of a new parallel interest on the part of a broader group of scholars and programme officers in the individual, social and economic environments that underpinned vulnerability to HIV infection.

The role of biological susceptibility linked with chronic malnutrition and ill-health – largely ignored by public health authorities in the early years – was investigated. Detailed social research began to reveal the complex factors that affect behaviour and which extend far beyond the influence of individuals. Academics and programme officers learned how social justice, poverty and inequity conditioned the uneven spread of the virus within and between communities and societies.

The notion of 'risk' – in relation to certain individuals who adopted certain behaviours – became better balanced with a broader focus on *structural drivers* of the epidemic and on social and economic 'risk environments'. The notion of AIDS as a development issue, not purely a health problem, opened the door for many new researchers and development professionals.

Meanwhile, as the impacts of AIDS mounted, a greater focus was also applied to the downstream issues. More questions were being raised about the interaction of AIDS with food and nutrition security. Could AIDS precipitate food insecurity – or even famine? This again brought in the focus on another form of vulnerability – to *impacts* of the disease, not to infection by the virus – and to its converse: resilience.

Biomedical approaches continue to be the basis for the core HIV strategies, but the biomedical hegemony in the scientific study of HIV and AIDS has made way for more contextual approaches and more holistic and interdisciplinary explanatory frameworks (Schoepf, 2001). More attention is now being given to the wider socio-economic, cultural and political ramifications of vulnerability, culminating in widespread recognition that to fully and sustainably address AIDS epidemics, we need to go beyond biomedical and narrowly defined behavioural change solutions.

This realization is reflected in the recent shift away from the 'AIDS exceptionalism' espoused by UNAIDS in the early years of the last decade – to a broader 'AIDS plus' agenda. Climate change, food price hikes, environmental degradation and the emergence of new zoonotic diseases have added to pre-existing livelihood threats, such as poverty. Stillwaggon (2006) places AIDS in a socio-epidemiological framework in which it is one of a cluster of factors that both reflect the conditions of poverty and can lead to further impoverishment. AIDS is but one of several 'multiple stressors' – hugely important, but not the only one threat, and – moreover – one that does not work in isolation. This synergy of factors impacting on rural livelihoods poses several methodological challenges in disentangling the particular effects of AIDS from other poverty-related effects; we will discuss these challenges in the final chapter.

To understand people's responses to the reality of having to live with AIDS in their communities and families, to help them mitigate the impacts of AIDS and curb the spread of HIV infection, one has to pay attention to their perceptions of its causes and the meanings they attach to it. Such emic pictures can be elicited by qualitative anthropological research. AIDS is the kind of affliction of which Susan Sontag (1978, p.58) once said: 'Any important disease whose causality is murky and for which treatment is ineffectual tends to be awash in significance.' AIDS then becomes a metaphor for evil and adversity as is, for example, apparent from its association with declining soil fertility (Misiko, 2008), pests in crops (Githinji, 2008) or witchcraft (Nombo, this volume). The fear that HIV inspires as a condition that is hidden until the infection develops into AIDS, is expressed by the following statement documented in research among the Azande: 'Witches, like HIV positive people, may look like everybody else, but are secretly killing those around them' (Allan, 2007, p359).

AIDS epidemics are thus complex, diverse and dynamic – in terms of what drives them, their effects and the way people perceive them and respond to them. In the face of such complexity and context-specificity we need to continue to develop and refine the evidence base. Only in this way can appropriate, comprehensive, multisectoral responses be developed and sustained. This book is one contribution to this growing evidence base, and to the developing policy discourse on AIDS and livelihoods.

Diversity

HIV is diverse in terms of the factors and conditions that determine its spread, its impacts and the types of responses that people make to these impacts. Early fears the virus would spread rapidly outside Africa have not materialized. Even within sub-Saharan Africa, there are several epidemics with widely differing national prevalences – ranging from less than 1 per cent in some western African countries to 26 per cent in the case of Swaziland. The hardest-hit countries, where AIDS is considered to be 'hyperendemic', are all in southern Africa.

A good survey of the diversity of AIDS epidemics in Africa is offered by John Illife in his seminal work entitled, 'A history of the African AIDS epidemic' (2006). There is no point in repeating that discussion in detail here, but we agree with Iliffe's analysis on the epidemic drive from its epicentre in central Africa to eastern and southern Africa. The critical drive was and remains the movement of people. Thus, locations closer to highways, rapidly expanding trading posts, and some parts of urban centres have been and continue to be hardest hit by AIDS simply due to their geography – places where people and goods converge. It follows that there is no single national or regional epidemic. A national epidemic is often comprised of small subepidemics of varying intensity. A good example is offered by the 2003–2004 Tanzania HIV/AIDS Indicator Survey conducted by MEASURE DHS. The data clearly indicate that HIV prevalence among adults at the time ranged from less than 2 per cent in remote regions with little degree of human mobility and migration to over 10 per cent in some parts of the capital, Dar-es-Salaam, and the southern highland region (characterized by high mobility, migration and trade within Tanzania and to Zambia and Malawi and beyond). Yet, had that study been conducted in the early 1990s, the highest HIV prevalence would have been found in the northwestern region. This tells us that epidemics are not only diverse, they are also dynamic. Areas with high HIV prevalence 20 years ago may not have high prevalence today. The twin aspects of diversity and change are given a sharp focus in this book because they shed light on the diverse and dynamic community and household responses to the onslaught of the epidemic.

Dynamics

AIDS has been described as a 'long wave event' (Barnett and Whiteside, 2002). It takes years for an epidemic to spread through the society and generations for the full impact to be felt.

During the evolution of AIDS epidemics, it's useful to distinguish three sequential phases of vulnerability – upstream (relating to risk of an individual becoming exposed to, and infected with, HIV), midstream (individual risk of developing opportunistic infections after HIV infection) and downstream (risk of serious impacts in households or communities living with HIV) (Gillespie 2008; Edstrom and Samuels 2007). These are depicted in the 'HIV timeline' in Figure 1.2, along with the three core HIV strategies of prevention, care and treatment, and mitigation.

We can view this timeline through the lens of individuals, households and/or communities. Each of these phases of vulnerability have particular drivers and consequences. It is also important to recognize the potentially *cyclical* nature of this

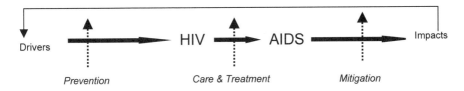

Figure 1.2 *The HIV timeline showing core strategies and stages of vulnerability*

timeline in that impacts of AIDS may increase vulnerability to HIV infection – or the converse, effective mitigation may be preventive. Among poor southern African households, vulnerability is also dynamic as its multiple ingredients are in constant flux – and because people proactively respond to try to reduce their vulnerability. Such responses determine their resilience in the face of concurrent shocks and stresses.

As for *upstream* vulnerability – to the left of Figure 1.2 – research in the last five years or so has shown the importance of various inequalities (socio-economic, gender, age), mobility, food insecurity (especially of young women), and low community-level social cohesion (Gillespie et al., 2007). Such structural drivers will affect the way that more immediate determinants play out (such as long-term concurrent partnerships, the lack of male circumcision, malnutrition and the prevalence of co-infections). Taken together, these interacting factors will condition the effectiveness of classic HIV prevention strategies.

With regard to *midstream* vulnerability, an individual's nutritional status is critically important – given the significantly higher energy requirements following infection. Coexisting sexually transmitted infections (especially HSV-2), household food security, and the time and capacity of the household to care for the individual with HIV, are key too. Such midstream factors will affect access, adherence and effectiveness of care and treatment programmes.

Finally, regarding *downstream* (post-infection) vulnerability – which is the main focus of this book – there are numerous factors and processes that will determine how the impacts of AIDS morbidity and mortality play out at different levels. The quality and quantity of assets at household and community levels, and the local institutional context and processes are important factors.

The particular dynamics relating to the causes and consequences of epidemics also need to be viewed against the wider landscape, which also changes over time. AIDS epidemics coexist (and interact) with chronic and seasonal hunger and with other slow-burn, long-wave dynamics such as climate and environmental change.

In this book, we aim to shed light on the various impacts of – and responses to – HIV and AIDS for different people in different African contexts. In this way, and referring to Figure 1.2, we aim to better understand the types of approaches needed for *mitigation*.

The epidemic may be three decades old but its wider effects are still unfolding. Looking back at what has happened in the past, using a variety of tools and methods, social science faces problems in addressing the phenomenon of HIV and its consequences. The study of HIV and AIDS impacts is fraught with methodological complexities. Cross-sectional research is confronted with the problem of disentangling AIDS effects from the effects of other poverty-related factors, referred to as the problem of attribution (Murphy et al., 2005). Longitudinal research that follows cohorts of people or households over a longer period of time can circumvent attribution. Such research can yield a picture of the dynamics of effects, impacts and responses in a specific group. However, building longitudinal data sets (panel data) is often not feasible because it requires long-term commitment to research funding. The PhD research carried out in the framework of the AWLAE project[2] was faced with the time-frame limitations of a PhD research project (four years), but some of the scholars successfully managed to incorporate a longitudinal perspective by including retrospective questioning and collecting life histories. Five of them (Du Preez, Fagbemissi, Karuhanga Beraho, Nombo and Paradza) contribute to this book. The diversity and contextuality of impacts and dynamics is another problem, which should induce caution with generalizing research findings. Nevertheless, it is through longitudinal and cross-sectional studies carried out in different locations and contexts that we can hope to understand the impact of the disease. The chapters in this volume draw from longitudinal or cross-sectional research conducted in different parts of Africa. They underscore the general conclusion that the impacts of AIDS are still unfolding.

Structure of the book

Following this introductory chapter, the book comprises ten chapters that are based on studies in selected Africa countries, and one regional assessment of agricultural policy and AIDS. We conclude with a synthesis chapter that aims to pull the strands together, assess their collective 'value added' in the context of the existing literature, and frame some recommended steps in research and action.

Geographically, there are five studies from eastern Africa (two each from Uganda and Tanzania, and one from Kenya), four from southern Africa (three from South Africa and one from Zimbabwe) and one from western Africa (Benin). Most studies draw on in-depth household and community-level qualitative and quantitative data to understand the ways in which the different AIDS epidemics have affected people and the livelihoods on which they depend – and how in turn they have responded. The majority of the studies are cross-sectional in design, although the first two (Chapters 2 and 3) are longitudinal and thus capable of shedding light on the dynamics of impact and response over many years.

The contributions in order of their appearance:

Seeley, Amurwon and Foster in 'The longitudinal picture: what does it reveal?' focus on the longitudinal impact of the AIDS epidemic in Masaka District, Uganda. The

---

[2] AWLAE stands for *African Women Leadership in Agriculture and Environment*. The AWLAE project is a joint PhD research project of AWLAE Nairobi, Winrock International and Wageningen University. The project is funded by The Netherlands Ministry of Foreign Affairs. In the framework of the project 19 women scholars from 11 African countries undertake research on themes relating to the impacts of HIV/AIDS on women's role in food and livelihood systems in Africa.

study analyses the changing impacts of the AIDS epidemic on agriculture over a 15-year period (1991/1992–2006/2007) and seeks to understand why agricultural livelihoods in Africa have not collapsed, despite the demographic impacts and the widespread suffering caused by the epidemic. What emerges is a nuanced view of the impact of AIDS in Masaka, highlighting the need to separate the short-term impacts of HIV and AIDS morbidity and mortality at the household level from the longer term impacts aggregated over larger populations.

Rugalema, Mathieson and Ssentongo in their chapter, 'Resilience and (Dis)continuity: Some preliminary insights from a longitudinal case study analysis', examine the impact of AIDS on individuals and households over a period of 15 years in Bukoba district, Tanzania. The chapter analyses what happened to individuals and households over time in terms of sequence of steps and actions that were taken to ensure survival and continuity among households in a community afflicted by AIDS. Using case study analysis, this analysis traces how afflicted households have adapted to the impact of the epidemic. Resilience seems to emanate from social support offered by relatives, an NGO and government.

Du Preez and Niehof in their chapter, 'Impacts of AIDS-related morbidity and mortality on non-urban households in KwaZulu-Natal, South Africa', explore the impact of AIDS on households in a rural setting in KwaZulu Natal, South Africa, through the analysis of changes in living arrangements and mobility of individuals between households. They argue that even in communities hard-hit by the epidemic, households remain in the frontline of response to AIDS by providing moral and material support and personal care. Households try to meet the emergent needs for support and care by adjusting household composition and mobilizing kinship ties. The implication is that despite some holes, the traditional safety nets have not been entirely destroyed by AIDS as originally feared.

Nombo in 'Sweet cane, bitter realities: AIDS in Mkamba, Kilombero District, Tanzania', explores the vulnerability of Mkamba village, Kilombero district, Tanzania – a rapidly urbanizing village whose growth and expansion is influenced by the nearby Kilombero Sugar Company. She points out that the AIDS epidemic reflects the economic, political and social realities of that area. Using a combination of qualitative and quantitative methods, the study examines the extent to which the lives of people in Mkamba, Tanzania, have changed as a result of macro-economic changes such as privatization of the Kilombero Sugar Company. The study shows how the demographic fluidity caused by the migrant workers recruited by the sugar company has compromised the social capital of Mkamba and rendered the society less able to respond to the impacts of the epidemic.

Paradza in her chapter, 'Livelihood decision-making experiences of single women-directed hearth holds in communal farming areas of Zimbabwe', like Nombo argues that to understand the impact of AIDS on communities and how, in turn, communities respond to the impact, one must focus on changes in the macro-environment. To examine this claim, she explores how changes in the economic, social and political context have shaped vulnerability to HIV and AIDS in a communal area in Zimbabwe.

The study focuses on single women (divorced, widowed, never married) in order to try and understand the agency of the women as actors in a changing society characterized by loss of employment, high population mobility, destabilization of livelihoods and high HIV prevalence.

Mwangi in 'Regional agricultural-consumption regimes and women's vulnerability to HIV in Kenya' presents the results of her cross-sectional study that examines how the Kenyan AIDS epidemic intersects with changes in the macro-environment, in particular recognizing that large-scale social and economic factors may constrain opportunities available to individuals and groups to structure their risk to HIV. The chapter advances the literature on the economic sources of vulnerability to HIV by empirically assessing how the regional agricultural context may structure risk for women who are systematically marginalized. The author argues that it is important to pay particular attention to upstream sources of vulnerability (in particular issues related to poverty), because they put people, especially women, at a greater risk of being exposed to HIV.

Karuhanga Beraho in her chapter, 'Multi-layered impacts of HIV/AIDS and implications for food security among banana farmers in Uganda', uses a quantitative approach combined with retrospective questioning to investigate the effects of AIDS on banana farming households in the Masaka and Kabarole districts of Uganda. The chapter highlights the interrelationship between gender and the likely impacts of AIDS on different household types, with their implications for household food security. The main objective is to identify the differential effects of HIV and AIDS by gender of household head, age, life course, wealth status and HIV status.

Rose Fagbemissi and Lisa Leimar Price in their chapter, 'Impact of HIV/AIDS on local farming knowledge: Differences in the cognitive salience of maize crop pests between affected and non-affected adults and children in Benin', examine the extent to which AIDS' deaths in a rural community in Benin have eroded local indigenous farming knowledge. The chapter compares knowledge of adults and children, particularly children orphaned by AIDS, using an ethnobiological approach. The findings show there is a need for rethinking the implications of AIDS for farming knowledge.

Wayne Twine and Lori Hunter in their chapter, 'Adult mortality, food security and the use of wild natural resources in a rural district of South Africa: Is AIDS a unique shock?', investigate the environmental dimensions of the AIDS epidemic in Mpumalanga Province, South Africa. In particular, the authors seek to understand the extent to which natural resource harvesting might mitigate the impacts of HIV on household food security following the death of prime-age adults due to AIDS. The study also investigates how the death of a prime-aged adult intersects with poverty, the use of natural resources, and the state of the local environment, to shape household vulnerability to food insecurity.

Kees Swaans, Jacqueline Broerse and Maxwell Mudhara in, 'Applying the Farmer Life School approach to support women of poor and HIV/AIDS affected households in KwaZulu-Natal, South Africa', present a study on the relevance of the Farmer Life School (FLS) approach for HIV education and increasing the resilience of farm households through agriculture-related activities. The authors note that FLS may be particularly relevant for AIDS mitigation strategies given that the shape of the epidemic is highly dependent on social processes created by people, while consequences of HIV-related illnesses and death are shaped by features of agricultural and livelihood systems. The aim of this study is to gain insight into the strengths and weaknesses of the FLS in the context of AIDS, by implementing an adapted FLS in Msinga, KwaZulu-Natal, a rural and high HIV prevalence area in South Africa.

Remme, Mukonoweshuro and Stloukal in their chapter, 'Agricultural policy responses to HIV and Aids: lessons learned from East and Southern Africa', explore agricultural responses to HIV and AIDS in terms of policy formulation and implementation. It discusses the challenges encountered and the lessons learnt in East and Southern Africa. The authors set the stage by giving a brief background on the evolution of the research on the interactions between agriculture and HIV/AIDS.

Gillespie, Mwangi, Niehof and Rugalema present the synthesis of Chapters 2 to 12 in the concluding chapter entitled, 'AIDS and livelihoods: what have we learnt and where are we heading?'. The chapter seeks to draw lessons from the rich and varied case study material and policy analyses presented in the preceding chapters. It addresses the important subject of the linkages between AIDS, land, rural livelihoods and vulnerability. It looks at the role of social capital and support systems in mitigating AIDS impacts, using a gender perspective in looking at linkages and dynamics. The chapter also reflects again on the methodological challenges in AIDS research (see above). An attempt is made at formulating general conclusions at the end.

References

Allen, T. (2007) 'Witchcraft, sexuality and HIV/AIDS among the Azande of Sudan', *Journal of Eastern African Studies*, vol 1, pp359–396

Barnett, T. and Whiteside, A. (2002) *AIDS in The Twenty First Century: Disease and Globalization*, Palgrave MacMillan, New York.

Bayley, A. (1984) 'Aggressive Kaposi's Sarcoma in Zambia', *The Lancet*, vol 323, issue 8390, pp1318–320

Chin, J. (2006) *The AIDS Pandemic: The Collision of Epidemiology with Political Correctness*, Radcliffe Publishing, Oxford

DeSalle, R. (1999) *Epidemic! The World of Infectious Diseases*, The New Press, New York

Edstrom, J. and Samuels, F. (2007) HIV, Nutrition, Food and Livelihoods in Sub-Saharan Africa: Evidence, debates and reflections for guidance. Report prepared for DfID www.eldis.org/vfile/upload/1/document/0812/DFIDAIDSLivelihoods.pdf

Gillespie, S.R. (1989) 'Potential impact of AIDS on farming systems: A case study from Rwanda', *Land Use Policy*, vol 6, no 4, pp301–312

Gillespie, S. (2008) 'Poverty, Food Insecurity, HIV Vulnerability and the Impact of AIDS in Southern Africa', *IDS Bulletin*, vol 39, no 5, pp10–18

Gillespie, S., Kadiyala, S. and Greener, R. (2007) 'Is poverty or wealth driving HIV transmission?', *AIDS*, vol 21, suppl 7, ppS5–S16

Graaff, P. (2007) Presentation of the HIV/AIDS Department of the WHO to an 'Informal technical consultation on the relevance and modalities of implementation of an observation for HIV commodities in Africa', organized by Health Economics and HIV/AIDS Research Division (HEARD), University of KwaZulu Natal, the World Health Organisation and the Swedish/Norwegian HIV/AIDS Team on 25th June, 2007

Githinji, V. (2008) 'Ethno-cognitive connections between HIV/AIDS and banana plants in the Bahaya agricultural society in north-western Tanzania', *NJAS Wageningen Journal of Life Sciences*, vol 56, no 3, pp191–201

Hooper, E. (1999) *The River: A Journey Back to the Source of HIV and AIDS*, Allen Lane/The Penguin Press, London

Iliffe, J. (2006) *The African AIDS Epidemic: A History*, James Currey, Oxford

Mann, J. and Tarantola, D. (eds) (1996) *AIDS in the World II*, Oxford University Press, Oxford, 1996

Misiko, M. (2008) 'An ethnographic exploration of the impacts of HIV/AIDS on soil fertility management among smallholders in Butula, western Kenya', *NJAS Wageningen Journal of Life Sciences*, vol 56, no 3, pp167–179

Murphy, L.L., Harvey, P. and Silvestre, E. (2005) 'How do we know what we know about the impacts of AIDS on food and livelihood security? A review of empirical evidence from rural sub-Saharan Africa', *Human Organization*, vol 64, pp265–274

Schoepf, B.G. (2001) 'International AIDS research in anthropology: taking a critical perspective on the crisis', *Annual Review of Anthropology*, vol 30, pp335–361

Sherman, I.W. (2007) *Twelve Diseases That Changed Our World*, ASM Press, Washington DC

Shilts, R. (1988) *And the Band Played On: People Politics and the AIDS Epidemic*, Viking, London

Sontag, S. (1978) *Illness as Metaphor*, Farrar, Strauss and Giroux, New York

Stillwaggon, E. (2006) *AIDS and the Ecology of Poverty*, Oxford University Press, Oxford

UNAIDS (2006) *Report on the Global AIDS Epidemic*, UNAIDS, Geneva

USCDC (1981) *Morbidity and Mortality Weekly Reports* of 5th June and 5th July 1981, US Centers for Disease Control, Atlanta

Chapter 2

The longitudinal picture: What does it reveal?

Janet Seeley, Jovita Amurwon and Susan Foster

Introduction

Regina died in 1995, she was 34 years old. Regina had two sisters (Rose and Teddy) and a brother. Rose had died in 1990, her partner, a lorry driver, had died in 1986. When we first met Regina in 1990 she had been living with the 13 year old daughter and eight year old son of her sister Rose and their five year old cousin (the brother's son). The family stayed in the house that had belonged to her father. Regina's father had left his land to his four children. Each of the girls had received four acres but the boy had received more. When Rose died her children inherited her land. When Regina died her land was given to her sister Teddy because she had not had children. Their brother, who lived nearby on his piece of land, did not like this arrangement, saying that he had been given full control of all the land by their father, and sought to reclaim his father's land from his sister and his sisters' children through the local courts. He failed in his attempt. Teddy's son now lives on her portion of land to 'guard' it from his uncle. The bulk of the land is fallow because the son of Rose is in Kampala and his sister, who could have access to the land if she needed it, has married and moved to another village.

Regina's family live in rural South West Uganda, an area that in the late 1980s was often viewed as being at the epicentre of the HIV epidemic (Hudson et al., 1988). Both she and her sister Rose died of an AIDS-related illness, deaths that had a profound influence on the lives of Rose's children and the management of the family homestead and land. The impact on this one family was mirrored in many other places, as described by Barnett and Blaikie (1992) who, based on fieldwork in Rakai, Uganda, in the late 1980s, explained how when adults became sick they could spend less time working the land, with sickness and death leading to a deterioration in the quality of life and livelihood for their families (see Foster, 1993; Rugalema 1999; Feeney, 2001; Urassa et al., 2001; Yamano and Jayne, 2003; Hosegood et al., 2004; Ainsworth, Beegle and Koda, 2005; Beegle et al., 2008; Parker, Jacobsen and Komwa, 2009).

In 2002 the Ministry of Agriculture, Animal Industry and Fisheries in Uganda conducted a study looking at the impact of the epidemic on agricultural production in the country. From a study of 313 households in 4 districts (Rakai, Lira, Iganga and Mbarara) they concluded that the AIDS epidemic had changed family structure because of the multiple deaths of people aged 15–49 years, 'leaving the very young ones and elderly [...] agriculture which absorbs the biggest proportion of the workforce, and constitutes the single most important source of people's livelihood is being threatened by HIV/AIDS' (2002: 4). Jefferis et al. (2007) in their review of the macro-economic impact of HIV/AIDS in Uganda draw the same conclusion:

> *AIDS undermines agricultural systems, affects the nutritional situation and food security of rural families. Families face declining productivity as well as loss of knowledge about indigenous farming methods and loss of assets.* (2007, p.47)

We, and others, have recently called into question this view suggesting that a more nuanced view of the impact of the HIV epidemic is required (Drinkwater et al., 2006; Peters et al., 2008; Seeley et al., 2010). As Chapoto and Jayne (2008) have observed, we believe that there is a need to separate the short-term impacts of HIV and AIDS morbidity and mortality at the household level, which can be severe (as shown in the story at the beginning of this chapter) from the longer term impacts aggregated over larger populations, which are generally less dramatic.

Boerma, Nunn and Whitworth (1998) in a review of 'community studies' of the mortality impact among adults and children described how the large increase in adult and child mortality as a result of the HIV epidemic in the 1980s and early 1990s had led to a dramatic fall in life expectancy in countries (mainly in Africa), even with HIV prevalence levels below 10 per cent. Gregson, Garnett and Anderson, writing in 1994, projected that by year 25 of the epidemic HIV-related disease would account for 75 per cent of deaths among women and men aged 15 to 60 years of age. In some places and for some populations (most notably, women of reproductive age) their projection has proved to be close to the truth (WHO/ UNAIDS/UNICEF 2009). It is not surprising that the longitudinal impact of the HIV epidemic has been a cause of grave concern in government, non-governmental and academic circles for many years.

However, despite the demographic impact and the considerable amount of suffering caused by the epidemic, agriculture and rural livelihoods in Africa have not collapsed to the extent expected as a result of HIV and AIDS. This is what we explore in this paper, focusing on the longitudinal impact of the epidemic on agriculture drawing on research conducted in the area where Regina's family lives.

Background

The research was undertaken in one of the study sites of the Medical Research Council and Uganda Virus Research Institute, Uganda Research Unit on AIDS (MRC/UVRI). There is a General Population Cohort study (GPC) at the site that was established in 1989 in 15 rural villages (expanded to 25 villages in 2000) in a sub-county of Masaka district in south-western Uganda. The main objectives of the GPC are to describe the dynamics of HIV infection within a rural population, to identify the major risk factors for contracting HIV, to quantify the impact on mortality and fertility and to study treatment seeking behaviour. Every year since its inception, the GPC team has conducted annual household censuses of the resident population covering age, sex, education and relationship to household head among other variables. In addition, a medical survey of all willing residents aged 13 and above including collection of blood specimens for HIV testing, and a brief behavioural questionnaire have been administered. The annual surveys are well-accepted by the population, with coverage of 60–70 per cent of the resident population in any given year.

In 1991/1992 an ethnographic study of household coping mechanisms was undertaken that looked at the experience of the members of 27 households selected from 3 of the MRC/UVRI cohort study villages. The findings of that study were presented in Seeley (1993). The study was repeated in the same households in 2006/2007. The focus of the study both in 1991/1992 and 2006/2007 was not only on HIV and AIDS, but on wider aspects of daily life, because we were interested in understanding more about people's lives in general and the challenges as well as the opportunities they face.

The setting

The people living in the study area are largely subsistence farmers who grow maize, beans and plantain bananas, and who also produce small amounts of cash crops such as bananas, coffee and beans. The land is largely fertile. Agriculture is primarily rain-fed and therefore agricultural production is subject to periods of dry weather, which is a major constraint to agriculture in the area (particularly for banana and maize production). The majority of the population are ethnically Baganda (75 per cent), but there is a large representation of immigrants from Rwanda (15 per cent), who have tended to settle over the last 70 years on land at the outskirts of established villages. Four per cent of the population are immigrants from Tanzania. A mixture of other tribes makes up the remainder. The main local language is Luganda, which is spoken and understood by all the tribes. The community is predominantly Christian (Roman Catholic 58 per cent and Protestant 12 per cent) with the majority of the remainder (28 per cent) Muslim. Most households have less than four acres of land. However, there are a small number of sizeable landowners and relatively few households are landless.

Land is arguably the most important resource in this agricultural community. The inheritance of land is determined by three different land tenure systems in Masaka district: customary tenure, *mailo* tenure and leasehold tenure; rules of inheritance vary with each type. Customary tenure, which predates the other forms of land tenure, was mainly in the form of communal land tenure through the chief or ruler, the tribe, the clan and the family. Land was owned corporately but individuals had specific rights to use, and these use rights could be passed on to one's heirs. Women's access to land was only through men in this system. While a woman may be given access to land through her natal family she could not alienate the family property (Barnett and Blaikie 1992). Despite the introduction of other systems, customary tenure remains widespread in Masaka District (Karuhanga, 2008, p118). The second system, *Mailo* tenure, was introduced to Buganda by the British colonial administration.[1] This system introduced individual land ownership, thereby allowing land to be purchased or sold, as well as inherited by those who had been given *mailo* land. The third type of tenure, leasehold, pertains to leases to public land granted by the Uganda Land Commission for 45 or 99 years for specific development activities (Karuhanga, 2008, p120).

The population of the area is very young; just over 50 per cent of the population is under 15 and just 6 per cent are over 60.

Research in the MRC/UVRI cohort found HIV prevalence in the population aged 13 years and over of the original 15 villages to be 8.5 per cent in the annual survey round 1990/1991, 6.2 per cent in 1999/2000 and 7.7 per cent in 2004/2005. By contrast, in the 10 new villages, which include the administrative and trading centre of the sub-county, prevalence also rose from 4.4 per cent in the 1999/2000 survey round to 8.2 per cent in the 2004/2005 survey round.

HIV and AIDS have, therefore, affected many people in the area. When we asked one household head, now in her 80s, for her consent to participate in the study in January 2006, she told us that her household members would have little of interest to tell because 'sickness and losing people are the only changes I know of in this household' over the last 16 years. She said that with good reason because her family had lost 18 children and grandchildren, all but 1 to AIDS-related illness during that period (Seeley et al., 2009). All but 2 of the original 27 households that participated in the 1991/1992 study had lost family members to AIDS and there was no doubt that the epidemic has had a profound effect on people's lives. However, as our detailed findings show much else had happened besides, some of which shows the great resilience of people in the face of adversity, caused not only by illness and death, but also by erratic rainfall, including a severe drought in 1991–1992, and crop and animal disease.

Methods

As noted above, the findings presented in this chapter, are from a longitudinal study of people's livelihoods (the 'trajectory study') conducted in 1991/1992 and 2006/2007, which also drew upon the information collected in the annual GPC survey rounds. The trajectory study had three components. The first component consisted of the restudy of the 27 households included in the 1991/1992 research. The original 27 households were chosen purposively in 1990 to represent a cross-section of different household types (by sex and age of household head, as well as socio-economic status). The socio-economic rankings of the 27 selected households were cross-checked through visits to

---

[1] The *Mailo* (taken from the word 'mile') came in with the 1900 Uganda Agreement. Under the agreement the *Kabaka*, (the King of the Baganda) his family and Baganda Chiefs acquired 8,958 square miles of land as freehold. The remaining land (9000 square miles) was allocated to the protectorate (Karuhanga, 2008, p119).

the households before the main fieldwork began in both 1990/1991 and 2006/2007. In 1991/1992 a team of local people trained in ethnographic research paid monthly visits to the study households assigned to them for the year to record changes in different aspects of the household, such as composition, employment, health, food consumption and social networks. In 2006/2007 when the study was repeated, the same detailed information was collected on day to day life, as well as changes in socio-economic status and household members' memories of what had happened in the intervening 15 years. Life histories of all adult members were collected. The analysis of the data was done manually by the team using thematic content analysis.

The second component focused on 144 households. The methods were based on household questionnaires and both household and individual calendars with household members,[2] including children, from 72 HIV-positive households and 72 HIV-negative control households matched by socio-economic stratum (as defined by ownership of assets and housing attributes) and household structure at the time of enumeration. Index households and matched controls were equally divided between 'early' and 'late' infection, defined respectively as households where HIV infection of one person or more was identified at the time of baseline (1989/1990), the early sub-sample, and those where HIV infection occurred after baseline up to GPC Round 12 (2000/2001), the late sub-sample. This chapter draws on data from components one and two, and focuses primarily on results by HIV status of the household. Of the 144 households, 132 households gave complete individual level calendars of which 55 per cent were HIV-positive households. One hundred and nineteen households gave complete household level information with 52 per cent being HIV-positive. Details are given in Table 2.1.

Overall approval for the study was given by the Ugandan National Council of Science and Technology. Ethical approval was given by the review boards of the Uganda Virus Research Institute and the University of East Anglia. We now present and discuss our findings.

Household demographic change

Twenty-six of the 27 households included in the 1991/1992 study participated in the re-study under component one in 2006/2007. Eleven out of the 26 had remained under

Table 2.1 *Households that gave individual and household level calendars*

Category	No. of individuals (per cent)	No. of households (per cent)
HIV-positive	73 (55)	62 (52)
HIV-negative	59 (45)	57 (48)
Poor	43(33)	38 (32)
Less poor	44 (33)	38 (32)
Better-off	45(34)	43 (36)

[2] Calendars, consisting of a table on which information on different topics is entered for each year for a chosen timespan, have been used as an effective tool for the collection of retrospective data in a number of different settings (see Belli, Shay and Stafford, 2001, for example).

the same head, 5 were under a different head and nine had dissolved. AIDS-related death in immediate or extended families had affected 24 of the households but was blamed for dissolution in only 3.[3] The majority of the 26 households had not experienced a marked change (a noticeable loss or acquisition of assets and income) in their socio-economic status. However, of 8 affected by HIV infection within their households, 4 had experienced some loss of assets or land resulting in a deterioration in their socio-economic status, or these households had dissolved altogether. It was not only factors within these household units that affected the socio-economic status. The loss of a brother or adult child, residing in another household, was in some cases not only an emotional strain but also financially devastating when that person had been providing support or had dependants that now needed a new home. The socio-economic status of 3 of the other 18 households deteriorated while 5 had improved. These 5 households improved largely because younger household heads who actively engaged in agriculture and outside businesses had taken over from elderly parents/grandparents who had died. The household of Regina, with whose story we began this chapter, is a case in point. Regina had taken over the care of Rose's children when she died, as we described. Regina complained to us in 1992 how the family income had suffered while her sister was sick because there was no one to cultivate the land. When Regina was sick, another sister, Teddy, came to stay in the house to care for her and the children, and the crops suffered again. Teddy stayed on after Regina's death to care for the children until they were old enough to leave home. Teddy returned to her husband's home but then her son came to care for the house and cultivate some of the land. He was cultivating the land on behalf of his mother, but he was benefiting from the income made from the crops and built up his livelihood, bringing his wife and child to live with him on the plot.

We looked at household demographic change and the impact on livelihoods for the 144 households in component two. Of these households, calendar data (individual and/or household calendar data) covering a period of 16 years (1990–2006) on mobility, asset ownership and land use, child fostering and education were collected from 139 households (4 refused and 1 was untraceable). Comparisons were done for HIV infection status and wealth category of the households.

Household movement:

Information on household movement is limited, especially for households that dissolved. In the 16-year period we do know that out of 139 households, 36 (26 per cent) moved at least once from their previous location including 10 that dissolved. Households that moved were mostly HIV-positive (6 households), female-headed (21 households), had a small number (no more than 5) of members (29 households), had experienced the death of the household head (16 households) and had a low (poor) socio-economic status (17 households).

Almost all dissolved households were HIV-positive (90 per cent), female-headed (60 per cent), and all were small in size (less than 5 members). Of the dissolved households,

---

[3] In the report of the 1991/1992 study Seeley had predicted that five households were likely to dissolve and disappear because of AIDS. In 2006/2007 we found that only one of those households was among those that had dissolved.

4 were from the poor and less-poor categories, with 2 from the better off socio-economic group.

For the households that did not dissolve, finding work – 15 (58 per cent) – and moving to a new house – 10 (38 per cent) – were the most common reasons for relocation. Eighty-seven per cent of those that moved to find work and 80 per cent of those that moved to new houses were households with at least one person with HIV infection. Of the dissolved households 61 per cent dissolved after the death of a household head.

Movement of individuals below the age of 19 years

Five hundred and four children from 126 households moved house from the component two households. A total of 88 households had children join, and 111 households saw children leave. Fifty-nine per cent of HIV-positive households had children leave, compared with 41 per cent of HIV-negative households. Approximately equal fractions of HIV-positive and HIV-negative households had children moving in. There were no major differences in terms of movement of children by wealth category, although there was a tendency towards children joining the better off households (39 per cent of joining events were to the 20 per cent of households assessed as 'better off'). The children moved for a variety of reasons including birth and death. HIV and socio-economic status did not appear to influence the movement of children: 88 households had children move in and of these 51 per cent were HIV-negative households. One hundred and eleven households had children leave and of these 59 per cent were HIV-positive households.

Figure 2.1, overleaf, shows that the most common reason for joining households was birth, 108 (41 per cent), including in HIV-positive households, although there were fewer births overall in HIV-positive households. In HIV-positive households, other than joining by birth, most children who joined were returning household members, while in HIV-negative households most children were being fostered-in from other households.

Fostering-in is very common, with approximately 30-40 per cent of households reporting fostering in children.[4] More HIV-negative households received children for fostering; this is not surprising since one may expect parents or others making decisions about fostering would choose HIV-negative households as destinations for their children if possible. However, the difference was less marked in the late sample households. There is an increase in fostering in of children among HIV-positive households in recent years in both late and early sample households; this may be the corollary of the reconstitution of the households under a new generation of household head, or it could be because of anti-retroviral therapy, which is sustaining parents and guardians infected with HIV.

Overall, approximately twice as many households reported fostering in children as reported fostering out of children (Figure 2.2).

Children of HIV-positive households were more likely to leave to find work (20 per cent compared to 14 per cent from HIV-negative households), but the differences

---

[4] Fostering of children is widely practised in many parts of Africa. Biological parents may send children to live with other people, often family members, for long periods of time for many different reasons: to strengthen family ties, redistribute child labour, adjust household size because of shortages/surpluses, and schooling (Serra, 2009).

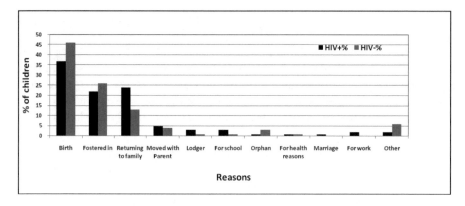

Figure 2.1 *Reason for children joining households by HIV status of the household*

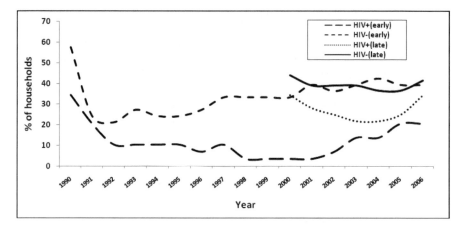

Figure 2.2 *Households fostering in children*

between households by HIV status were not great. Of note is that more children died in HIV-positive households than in HIV-negative households (Figure 2.3).

The picture of household demographic change, given above, is complex even if only child movement is considered. AIDS-related deaths may deplete households, but other family members may move in to take the place of those who died (as Regina and then Teddy did, in the story at the beginning of this chapter), a finding corroborated by Chapoto and Jayne (2008) in their analysis of the impact of 'prime-age death' on household composition in Zambia. Households are not static units. As Jefferis et al. (2007) note, citing a study by Salinas and Hacker (2006), which looked at the impact of HIV on households in Ghana, Kenya, Swaziland and Zambia, the evaluation of the impact of the epidemic at the household level depends on assumptions about labour market efficiency and how quickly workers can be replaced, as well as HIV prevalence and levels of poverty.

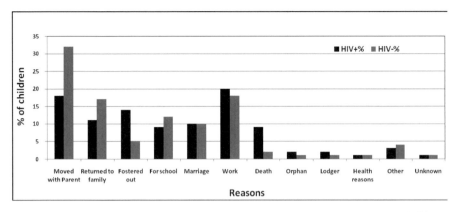

Figure 2.3 *Reason for children leaving households by HIV status of the household*

Impact on land use and cultivation

Land ownership and use

Out of the 119 households that had provided a household calendar (13 gave only individual level calendars), 115 households owned or had owned land. There was a slight difference between HIV-positive and negative households in average acreage of land owned, with HIV-negative households consistently reporting owning between a quarter and a half an acre more land over the period of the study. During the 16-year period, the average amount of land owned by HIV-positive households dropped from 3.4 to 3.1 acres, while that for negative households dropped initially, but they were able to regain their land and stay at the average of 3.6 acres.

For 21 households the reduction in land size was because of sale of land. Fifteen (71 per cent) of these households were HIV-positive. The most common reason given for selling was household and healthcare expenses. More HIV-positive households sold land for healthcare costs (27 per cent) than HIV-negative households (9 per cent).

We then looked at changes in land cultivated. All but one of the 119 households cultivated land during the 16 years. Of the households that cultivated land, 46 households (39 per cent) experienced a reduction in cultivation at least once during the 16 years. Some households experienced multiple reductions over the years.

A comparison of households that had ever had a reduction in cultivation by HIV status and wealth showed a significant difference by HIV status (P=0.049 [Pearson chi2 test]) in households that had a reduction in the amount of land cultivated. By contrast, a comparison by wealth category showed no definite trend.

The death of the household head had a measurable impact on cultivation in many households. Thirty-two household heads died during the period of the study.[5] Of these, 25 occurred in the early sample (1990), and seven in the late (2001). Figure 2.4 shows

---

[5] This excludes heads of ten households that had dissolved. We do not know what happened to cultivation in these households but we know the land was sold or other people inherited the land before the death or soon (1–2 years) after the household head died.

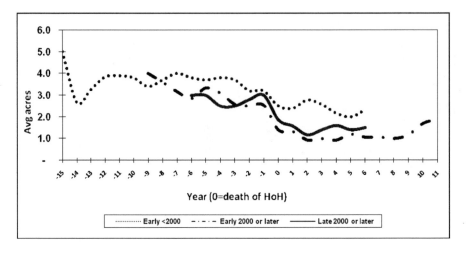

Figure 2.4 *The Impact of the death of the household head on cultivation*

the impact on cultivation of the death of the household head for three groups: first, the 25 households from the early sample whose heads died prior to 2000 (n=14) and those where heads died after 2000 (n=11); the 7 households from the late sub-sample whose heads died from 2000 to the end of data collection in 2006.

Although the trend in the average amount of land cultivated was downward, the slight uptick at the end represents the six households that remained in existence; nine recorded no cultivation at all and appear to have dissolved. Five of these households had the death of the head occur early in the study in 1995 or earlier; only one additional household whose head died in 1999 was still cultivating at the end of the study. This suggests that if the household survives, it takes quite a long time (ten years or more) for the cultivation to regain anything like previous levels. This may be happening as a new generation comes into the picture and takes on the role of household head and begins to cultivate again (as happened in the case of Regina's nephew described in the story at the beginning of this chapter). No such upward trend is seen in the early sample whose heads died after 2000, or in the late sample. We postulate that these households have not had time to reconstitute themselves and resume cultivation. Chapoto and Jayne (2008), whose study on the impact of adult mortality on farming in Zambia noted that their time period was too short for such recovery to take place; they found that male head of household mortality 'generally leads to sizeable reductions in cultivated area'. Our data suggest that if the household does not dissolve completely, it may recover from the loss of the head after a period of time, of up to ten years.

Cultivation of crops

The main crops in this community are maize, beans, matooke (plantain) and coffee, which are grown both for home food and cash. Over the 16-year period there have been changes in the combinations of crops grown.

Maize has become more widely cultivated, rising from about 60 per cent of households in the early 1990s to approximately 80 per cent in the mid-2000s.

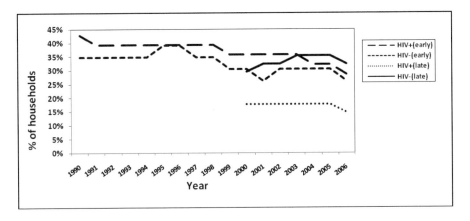

Figure 2.5 *Cultivation of matooke by HIV status of the household*

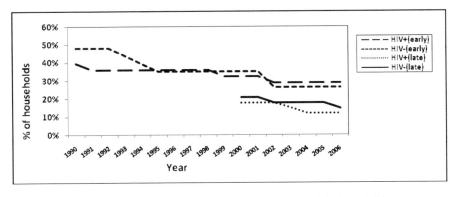

Figure 2.6 *Cultivation of coffee by HIV status of the household*

By 2007, it was the most widely cultivated crop among all income groups, although this appears not to have become a preferred crop of the better off households until recently. Beans were the second most widely cultivated crop, with 70–80 per cent of households cultivating beans, regardless of HIV status or socio-economic status.

However, the trend for matooke and coffee for all household types has been downwards over the 16 years (Figure 2.5).

Cultivation of matooke by socio-economic status shows the same decline over time, with the sharpest decline among the better-off households from the early sample, from about 60 per cent of households to about 30 per cent. Overall, the fraction cultivating matooke by 2007 was less than 30 per cent, with only about 10 per cent of poor households from the late sample cultivating matooke.

The trend for matooke (plantain) was downward in both groups by HIV status, and in most socio-economic groups. Coffee also declined in popularity, especially among HIV-negative households and among the better-off households. Less than 40 per cent of households reported growing coffee, and the trend away from coffee was particularly strong in the late sample households, with less than 20 per cent growing coffee by 2007. This is consistent with findings in the MAAIF (2002) study, which attributes similar changes in their four study districts to HIV/AIDS. The authors write: 'In areas of Mbarara and Rakai, which are matooke growing areas, it is becoming evident that HIV/AIDS has had its toll as only less than half of the households in respective areas reported matooke as their dominant food crop' (p 10). The authors mention labour shortages as the main reason for crop changes, although they say that 'in a few households it was due to pests and diseases as a result of poor management, infertile soils and lack of a market'.

We question the attribution of these changes to HIV and AIDS only. The changes in cropping patterns in our study area were as likely to be said by respondents to be because of pests and diseases rather than just labour shortages, and those labour shortages were not necessarily a result of HIV because there was movement out of households for work (often to a city or town or to become a fisherman or fish trader); this a common reason for the movement of children out of households.

The impact of diseases, prolonged dry spells, changes in food habits (with younger people preferring maize to matooke[6]) as well as changes in the market were findings corroborated in the literature. There have been a series of crop failures due to pests and diseases in recent years, which have been documented. Banana Bacteria Wilt has plagued the banana crop of west and central Uganda for much of the last decade. In 2006 it was thought to have been checked, but there has been a recent resurgence of the disease in Mbarara (west of Masaka).[7] Cassava, a crop upon which many people rely in times of shortage of matooke and maize, has also been severely affected by mosaic disease. This disease was first noticed in Uganda in 1989 and spread to the whole country during the 1990s (Legg and Thresh 2000; Sserubombwe et al. 2008). The varieties of cassava grown in Uganda have been particularly susceptible to this disease; while resistant varieties have been developed and distributed the disease persists in the study area, affecting yields. Coffee has also been affected by disease (Geiser et al.. 2005; Baffes, 2006), but a downturn in the global market price also influenced growers to reduce the amount of coffee. As noted above, many people have turned to maize and beans as staple crops. Unfortunately, these crops are very susceptible to drought and, as we write in 2009 (Seeley et al., 2009), the entire maize crop, which should have been harvested two months ago, stands dried and devoid of cobs, because of a prolonged dry spell (lasting from June to October, reminiscent of the drought of 1992). Sserunkuuma (2005) attributes poor annual yields of maize in Uganda to poor management practices, because even where people have adopted improved varieties they have not been able to afford the inputs those varieties require. He goes on to say: 'The main reasons for the stagnation or decline include extensive use of unimproved maize seeds, depletion of soil fertility, erratic rainfall, prevalence of pests and diseases, little improvement in agronomic and post harvest technologies' (pp 68–69) as well as limited use of fertilizers.

This is not to say that HIV has not had some impact; the division of labour from agriculture to care for sick people has been mentioned by many commentators as a cause

---

[6] Young women in particular were mentioned as preferring maize because it was easier to prepare than matooke.

[7] See 'Banana wilt threatens food basket' at www.freshplaza.com/new_detail.asp?id=40481 (accessed 6th September 2009).

of declines in productivity (Foster, 1993; Chapoto and Jayne, 2008; Parker, Jacobsen and Komwa, 2008). Referring back to our story at the beginning of this chapter, in 1990 when we first met Regina she indeed complained about the neglect of her agricultural land while she had cared for her dying sister Rose. However, as we show above, cultivation has often recovered after the death of the household head; something that Beegle and colleagues (2008) also found in North West Tanzania.

Conclusion

The data from our study present a mixed picture. Major disruption to households and families has been caused by the HIV epidemic in this area. Almost all of the households that dissolved were HIV-positive households. Many households were affected by the loss of adult members, and in households that lost their head of household, the loss of that head brought on a noticeable decline in land cultivation in the years following the death. The story at the beginning of this chapter, illustrates this mixed picture. The family of the three sisters, Rose, Regina and Teddy, was undoubtedly severely affected by HIV; two children lost their mother, father and aunt in a short space of time. However, while the impact of sickness and death took its toll on those left behind and affected cultivation in the medium term, in the long term the family managed to keep their land and pass it on to a new generation to cultivate.

Land size in our study area has declined slightly over time, but population growth is likely to be the reason for this since a fixed quantity of land has to be shared between a growing population and thus more children. Indeed 'land wrangles' are a major source of community discord and even violence. The cultivation of crops and crop mix has changed over time – largely due to drought, pests, disease, world market competition and changing food preferences. While HIV may have played a part in the changes that have occurred, these changes were not easily attributable to the epidemic.

This is not to play down the fact that HIV-related illness and death have undoubtedly made life harder for the many people affected but, when we look at the longitudinal picture it is, as Peters et al. (2008) observe, incorrect to talk of a one-dimensional image of AIDS as a disaster. They observe for the Zomba area in Malawi where they undertook longitudinal research, that 'the HIV epidemic has so far not been associated with an overall decline in agricultural production due to shortages of labour, or major shifts in cropping patterns' (2008, p683). We found the same; these findings point to the need for a more nuanced understanding of the impact of HIV and a sensitivity to a 'locally contingent and differentiated picture' (Murphy et al., 2005, p265) of the longitudinal impact of AIDS.

Acknowledgements

This research was funded by the MRC and ESRC (grant RES-062-23-0051). We are grateful to our colleagues Grace Tumwekwase, Elizabeth Kabunga, Ruth Nalugya, Thadeus Kiwanuka and Dominic Bukenya for data collection and inputs to our thinking and to Brent Wolff, Jim Todd, Pamela Nasirumbi, Oscar Alvarez Macotela and Heiner Grosskurth for their valuable contributions. We are, of course, indebted to the study participants for all the time they have spent with us.

References

Ainsworth, M., Beegle, K. and Koda, G. (2005) 'The impact of adult mortality and parental deaths on primary schooling in North-Western Tanzania', *Journal of Development Studies* vol 41, no 3, pp412–439

Baffes, J. (2006) 'Restructuring Uganda's coffee industry: Why going back to the basics matters'. *Working Paper Series* 4020, The World Bank, Washington DC

Barnett, T. and Blaikie, P. (1992) *AIDS in Africa: Its Present and Future Impact,* Belhaven and Guilford Press, London and New York

Beegle, K., De Weerdt, J. and Dercon, S. (2008) 'Adult Mortality and Consumption Growth in the Age of HIV/AIDS', *Economic Development and Cultural Change*, vol 56, pp299–326

Belli, R.F., Shay, W.L. and Stafford, F.P. (2001) 'Event history calendars and question list surveys: A direct comparison of interviewing methods', *Public Opinion Quarterly*, vol 65, pp45–74

Boerma, J.T., Nunn, A.J. and Whitworth, J.A. (1998) 'Mortality impact of the AIDS epidemic: Evidence from community studies in less developed countries', *AIDS,* vol 12(suppl 1), ppS3–14

Chapoto, A. and Jayne, T.S. (2008) 'Impact of AIDS-Related Mortality on Farm Household Welfare in Zambia', *Economic Development and Cultural Change,* vol 56, pp327–374

Drinkwater, M., McEwan, M. and Samuels, F. (2006) 'The effects of HIV/AIDS on agricultural production systems in Zambia: A restudy 1993–2005', IFPRI/RENEWAL report, Lusaka, Zambia

Feeney, G. (2001) 'The impact of HIV/AIDS on adult mortality in Zimbabwe', *Population and Development Review*, vol 27 no 4, pp771–780

Foster, S. (1993) 'Maize production, drought and AIDS in Monze District, Zambia', *Health Policy and Planning*, vol 8, no 3, pp247–254

Geiser, D.M., Ivey, M.L.L., Hakiza, G., Juba, J.H. and Miller, S.A. (2005) '*Gibberella xylarioides* (anamorph: *Fusarium xylarioides*), a causative agent of coffee wilt disease in Africa, is a previously unrecognised member of the *G. Fujikuroi* species complex', *Mycologia*, vol 97, no 1, pp191–201

Gregson, S., Garnett, G.P. and Anderson, R.M. (1994) 'Is HIV-1 likely to become a leading cause of adult mortality in sub-Saharan Africa?', *Journal of Acquired Immune Deficiency Syndrome,* vol 7, pp839–852

Hosegood, V., McGrath, N., Herbst, K. and Timæus, I.M.(2004) 'The impact of adult mortality on household dissolution and migration in rural South Africa', *AIDS,* vol 18, no 11, pp1585–1590

Hudson, C.P., Hennis, A.J.M., Kataaha, P., Lloyd, G., Moore, A.T., Sutehall, G.M., Whetstone, R., Wreghitt, T. and Karpas, A. (1988) 'Risk factors for the spread of AIDS in rural Africa: evidence from a comparative seroepidemiological survey of AIDS, hepatitis B and syphilis in southwestern Uganda', *AIDS*, vol 2, no 4, pp255–260

Jefferis, K., Nannyonjo, J., Byamugisha, J. and Baine, S. (2007) 'Assessing the macroeconomic impact of HIV/AIDS in Uganda. Phase 1 Report Literature review: the macroeconomic impact of HIV/AIDS' *Final Draft* submitted to Ministry of Finance and Planning and Economic Development/United Nations Development Fund, Kampala, www.econsult.co.bw/, accessed 12th September 2009

Karuhanga, M.B. (2008) *Living with AIDS in Uganda: Impacts on Banana-farming Households in Two Districts,* AWLAE Series 6, Wageningen Academic Publishers, Wageningen

Legg, J.P. and Thresh, J.M. (2000) 'Cassava mosaic virus disease in East Africa: a dynamic disease in a changing environment', *Virus Research*, vol 71, no 1–2, pp135–149

Ministry of Agriculture, Animal Industry and Fisheries (MAAIF) (2002) *The impact of HIV/AIDS on Agricultural Production and Mainstreaming HIV/AIDS Messages into Agricultural Extension in Uganda*, Government of Uganda and FAO, Entebbe, Uganda

Murphy, L.L., Harvey, P. and Silvestre, E. (2005) 'How do we know what we know about the impact of AIDS on food and livelihood insecurity? A review of empirical research from rural sub-Saharan Africa', *Human Organisation*, vol 64, no 3, pp265–275

Parker, D.C., Jacobsen, K.H. and Komwa, M.K. (2009) 'A qualitative study of the impact of HIV/AIDS on agricultural households in southeastern Uganda', *International Journal of Environmental Research and Public Health*, vol 6, no 8, pp2113–2138 (open access http://www.mdpi.com/search/?q=&s_journal=0&s_volume=&s_authors=Komwa&s_section=0&s_issue=&s_article_type=all&s_special_issue=0&s_page=)

Peters, P.E., Walker,P.A. and Kambewa, D. (2008) 'Striving for normality in a time of AIDS in Malawi', *Journal of Modern African Studies*, vol 46, no 4, pp659–687

Rugalema, G.H.R. (1999) *Adult Mortality as Entitlement Failure: AIDS and the Crisis of Rural Livelihoods in a Tanzanian Village*, Shaker Media, Maastricht

Seeley J. (1993) *Searching for Indicators of Vulnerability: A Study of Household Coping Strategies in Rural South West Uganda*, MRC/ODA, London

Seeley, J., Dercon, S. and Barnett, T. (2010) 'The effects of HIV/AIDS on rural communities in East Africa: A twenty year perspective', *Tropical Medicine and International Health* (forthcoming)

Seeley, J., Wolff, B., Kabunga, E., Tumwekwase, G. and Grosskurth, H. (2009) '"This is where we've buried our sons": People of advanced old age coping with the impact of the AIDS epidemic in a resource-poor setting in rural Uganda', *Ageing and Society*, vol 29, pp115–134

Serra, R. (2009) 'Child fostering in Africa: When labor and schooling motives may coexist', *Journal of Development Economics*, vol 88, pp157–170

Sserubombwe, W.S., Briddon, R.W., Baguma, Y.K., Ssemakula, G.N., Bull, S.E., Bua, A., Alicai, T., Omongo, C., Otim-Nape, G.W. and Stanley, J. (2008) 'Diversity of begomoviruses associated with mosaic disease in cultivated cassava (*Manihot esculenta* Crantz) and its wild relative (*Manihot glaziovii* Müll. Arg.) in Uganda', *Journal of General Virology*, vol 89, pp1759–1769

Sserunkuuma, D. (2005) 'The adoption and impact of improved maize and land management technologies in Uganda', *Journal of Agricultural and Development* Economics, vol 2, no 1, pp670–84

Urassa, M., Boerma, J.T., Isingo, R., Ngalula, J., Ng'weshemi, J., Mwaluko, G. and Zaba, B. (2001) 'The impact of HIV/AIDS on mortality and household mobility in rural Tanzania', *AIDS*, vol 15, no 15, pp2017–2023

WHO/UNAIDS/UNICEF (2009) *Towards Universal Access: Scaling Up Priority HIV/AIDS Interventions in the Health Sector. Progress Report* WHO/UNAIDS/UNICEF, Geneva and Paris.

Yamano, T. and Jayne, T.S. (2003) 'Measuring the impacts of working-age adult mortality on small scale farm households in Kenya', *World Development*, vol 32, no 1, pp91–119

Chapter 3

Resilience and (dis)continuity in households afflicted by AIDS: Some preliminary insights from a longitudinal case study analysis

Gabriel Rugalema, Kirsten Mathieson and Joseph Ssentongo

Introduction

With the publication of the *2009 Global Epidemiological Report on HIV and AIDS*, the World Health Organisation (WHO) and UNAIDS have confirmed that the epidemic is finally in decline. Since the beginning of the epidemic, analysis of the impact of AIDS on household demography, livelihoods and food security has captured the imagination of many researchers interested in the social and economic ramification of the epidemic on households and communities. Mostly, studies have shown that the short-term impact of AIDS on households is invariably negative. Information on long-term adaptation mechanisms – what they are and how they work – is still limited. This chapter examines the long-term impact of AIDS on households in a village in Bukoba district, Kagera Region, north-western Tanzania that was hard hit by the epidemic in the late 1980s and much of the 1990s.

Throughout much of the past two decades there has been an intense focus on the analysis of the social and economic impacts of AIDS in Africa, a continent that to date, still bears the heaviest burden of the epidemic. Since 1988, the primary focus has been on rural households deriving their livelihoods from agriculture (Müller, 2004). The intensified focus on rural households was driven by two main factors. First, even though AIDS started as an 'urban disease', it quickly spread in the rural areas. Also rural households could not avoid the burden of caring for their urbanite kinsfolk who contracted the disease in urban areas and returned to the rural areas to seek care or just to die and be buried there. Second, the intensified focus on the impact of AIDS on rural households was the result of the perceived general vulnerability of these households to many social, economic and natural shocks. There was a need to know the extent to which the epidemic would affect the viability of households and local farming systems. There was also a need to know how development policies and programmes would be shaped to mitigate the observed impact of the epidemic.

A fuller analysis of the literature on the impact of AIDS on rural household livelihoods is given by Müller (2004) and Gillespie and Kadiyala (2005). Suffice to mention that the general message projected by these studies was that the impact of AIDS was disastrous and the long-term outlook was, in most cases, rather grim. AIDS was going to disrupt livelihoods significantly mainly due to its adverse effects on household demography and human capital. The knock-on effects of such impact would include increased dissolution of affected households, decrease in social capital and safety nets, changes in cropping patterns, and more generally, higher levels of widespread poverty. Table 3.1 presents a broad overview of the impact of AIDS on rural households.

Some analysts are now arguing that some of the originally observed impacts of AIDS on rural households when the epidemic was at its peak may have dissipated or changed in form as the epidemic has matured and either stabilized or begun to decline

Table 3.1 *Impacts of HIV and AIDS on farming communities and households*

Immediate impacts	Noted* agriculture-related responses by households	Assumed longer term consequences for agriculture and related activities
Loss of labour due to illness, death and caring	Decreases in area cultivated and changes in crop mix; less attention to care of livestock, soil and/or water	Potential decreases in overall food production (food availability, access and stability)
Cutbacks in food availability and consumption	Decreased energy for farm or market tasks	Increased child and adult malnutrition (food utilization and access)
Loss of income and increased medical and funeral expenses	Disinvestment of assets, including sale of livestock and equipment; renting of land; piece-work on other farms	Increased socio-economic inequalities and new or deeper impoverishment for some
Increased dependency, with women and older adults assuming greater household responsibilities	Less time spent on farm production or marketing	Growing gender and age inequalities
Loss of knowledge and skills essential for agriculture	None known	Loss of efficiency, greater stress on natural resource base, increased food insecurity
Loss of access to land and equipment/livestock for widows and children	Female- and child-headed households' dependence on non-farm employment and/or begging	Deepening impoverishment for affected household members

*Noted means cited in at least one study of a localized impact.
Source: Rau et al, 2008

(Rau et al., 2008; Seeley et al., this volume). This makes it all the more necessary to look again at the conclusions made by the old studies and to, where possible, verify if the predicted impact actually did come to pass.

It is now generally accepted that the first generation of studies on AIDS-agriculture nexus had conceptual and methodological limitations. Some of the criticisms have included the fact that almost all studies were cross-sectional and based on very small samples. In addition to this point is the criticism that conclusions drawn from small-scale studies were applied to general populations – a much bigger and complex reality. Subsequent analyses have suggested that the impacts of the epidemic were actually a lot more context-specific than originally assumed (see Gillespie, 2006).

This chapter looks at the longitudinal outcomes of the impact of AIDS on individuals and households over a period of about 15 years. The main objective is to present information about what happened to individuals and households over time in terms of a set and sequence of steps and actions that were taken to ensure survival and continuity among households afflicted by AIDS in the study area. The study area has a very mature epidemic given that the first cases of AIDS were diagnosed in early 1983. For a number of years, AIDS was concentrated in this region to the extent that many people in Tanzania perceived Kagera to be a 'dying place' until the epidemic spread widely and became established in other parts of the country.

Method

The case study material analysed in this chapter originates from the ethnographic study conducted by Rugalema in north-western Tanzania in the early 1990s. The predominant crops then and now are banana, coffee, beans and maize (the last two being seasonal crops). Most households grew their own food and a few sold a surplus. Cattle are still an important livestock although hardly 10 per cent of the village households keep cattle today. Increasingly, piggery and goat keeping are becoming popular.

In 1995, when the first study was conducted, the village had 164 households with a total of 631 inhabitants of which about 90 per cent of the people were Bahaya. The number of households has now grown to 190 and the village population is 845. In this chapter, we analyse the experience of a limited number of households (those that appeared as case studies in the original study cited above). Since the 1990s, the senior author has monitored the changes in the village, particularly those related to the impact of AIDS. It is from this long-term monitoring (about 15 years of observation) that we are able to describe the processes that various case study households or individuals have passed through. The act of monitoring has included observation – specifically yearly visits to the village to assess what is going on and to discuss with the villagers the changes (both positive and negative) they are experiencing. Our aim has generally been to trace how households afflicted by AIDS adapt to the impact of the epidemic but also to assess whether such households do actually recover from the impact. By looking at a very limited number of households and individuals, we are not looking for generalizable trends. Rather we seek to illustrate the differences in outcomes between different households and to discuss the various factors that have contributed to the resilience of the households. In this study, we define resilience as the ability of a unit (individual, household, community) to adjust and recover from the impact of AIDS.

The recovery we are talking about pertains to those who survive. Studies have shown that survivors are often left in bad economic conditions, particularly immediately in the aftermath of the death of the breadwinner. As a result of the death of prime-age adults, often grandparents are left to care for grandchildren in households in what is now known as 'skipped generation households' (Samuels and Wells, 2009). Our interest is to investigate the transition process through which individuals or household pass as they manage to pick up the pieces of their lives and livelihoods.

Results and discussion

In this section we present a narrative of a limited number of households and examine what factors have contributed to the resilience and continuity of either the households or individuals. In two of the cases, the original households dissolved. In one of these cases (Case 1) the children were fostered out and both of them, now in their late teens, are doing relatively well. It is hoped that either both or one of them will, in the years to come, occupy and operate the same land where their parents had lived. In the other case (Case 2), the elderly couple has decided to migrate, leaving behind everything that characterized their past life. Their land will probably remain unoccupied for many years to come. While in these two cases the survivors have survived thanks to the resilience conferred by their extended families, there has been discontinuity in the sense that the original households are no longer there.

On the other hand, cases 3 and 4 illustrate resilience and continuity of households despite the impact of AIDS. In case 3 the widow has worked hard to maintain her farm and bring up the children (now all grown up) while in case 4 the grandmother had to depend on extended family and an NGO for the household wellbeing and the schooling of the children.

Case 1: Going an extra mile to care for orphans: Kabumbilo's family between 1995 and 2009

There is no doubt that different households experience the impact of AIDS differently. Case studies outlined in this section show steps and actions taken (either within a household or outside it) in order to 'pick up the pieces' after the death of key members of a household. Case 1 illustrates the process in which, a household once strong and fairly prosperous had to dissolve because of the death of the two parents. After the death of Kabumbilo the children were first left to stay with their mother even though she was sick. Her mother-in-law and later her own mother moved in to care for the remainder of the household. However, it was already clear to Kabumbilo's relatives that decisions had to be made regarding the welfare of the children in the event of their mother's death. The fostering out of the eldest son was part of this decision making process by Kabumbilo's relatives.

April 1995–July 1996

Kabumbilo, the male head of household, falls ill. His illness is recurrent and every time it becomes more severe. The main complaint is diarrhoea and vomiting. By the time Kabumbilo started falling ill, his wife was in the early stages of her fourth pregnancy.

She was constantly falling ill and so her mother-in-law became the sole care provider for her ill son and her pregnant daughter-in-law. Since Kabumbilo could no longer work, the household had to sell some assets including cattle, timber and a bicycle to generate income for food and medical care. The farm was increasingly being overtaken by weeds as well. In April 1996 the wife delivered a sickly daughter and quickly resumed her roles and responsibilities as mother, wife, carer and provider. Kabumbilo dies in July 1996 survived by four young children, his widow and his elderly mother.

August 1996–June 1998

The widow tries hard to pick up the pieces of her life and that of her children. The biggest pre-occupation is to produce enough food for consumption. The rest of the cattle are transferred from the household for safe keeping, mostly because the household has no (extra) labour to care for the animals. To reduce the number of dependants, the oldest son (then 7) is fostered by the brother of his grandmother who lives some 50km away. Throughout this period the youngest child is in poor health and the mother has to divide her time between farming, household chores and caring for the sick child. The farm is finally no longer productive as it has been overrun by weeds. Food and cash are severely lacking and all three children in the household have signs of malnutrition. The youngest child dies in June 1998 only two months after her second birthday.

July 1998–June 2000

Within a period of two years the size of this particular household has shrunk to only three people. The widow does not recover from the many illnesses afflicting her. The biggest problem is similar to what killed her husband, namely diarrhoea and vomiting. In April 1999, the late Kabumbilo's mother, hitherto a pillar of support, dies suddenly (post-mortem indicates heart attack). The household faces severe scarcity of food and money as the widow and her children show signs of severe malnutrition. Neighbours and extended family members are the only source of support. The widow's mother moves in to care for her daughter and grandchildren but she is elderly and with no economic means. The widow, severely sick throughout 1999, dies in June 2000. The two children are left behind under the care of a severely disabled uncle.

July 2000–May 2002

In August 2000 the extended family decides that one of the children should be cared for by her aunt (father's sister) while the other one should remain with his uncle who has a family of his own. The son who was fostered out immediately after the death of his father, dies suddenly in April 2001, aged 11. The daughter, fostered by her aunt, claims that she is not well treated and comes to stay with the disabled uncle. The uncle falls ill now and then and loses his tailoring business. His wife resorts to casual labour. Life is hard in the household but the extended family does not abandon them.

June 2002–December 2005

Just when all seems to be going the wrong way for this household, the uncle starts to get better at the beginning of 2003. He sells one of his cows to buy a sewing machine. One of his nephews buys another sewing machine for him. With two brand new sewing machines, the business slowly starts to take off. One of the nieces fosters the orphaned girl and takes her to Dar-es-Salaam for secondary school education in 2004. Her young brother remains behind in the village and in December 2005 he passes his primary school exam to join a local secondary school.

January 2006–August 2008

The uncle expands his business by buying two other sewing machines in May 2006. Apart from sewing clothes for his customers, he decided to train young people at a fee. He takes in six apprentices for a course that would last a year. By the end of 2006 he starts a foundation for his new, modern brick house. The house is finished by December 2008. He is now planning to have it electrified and to use electrical power for his sewing business. In the meantime, the girl has finished secondary school and is employed in Dar es Salaam while the boy is expected to finish his secondary studies at the end of 2009. While the farm that the children inherited is not inhabited, some members of the extended family are using it to raise annual crops, the main objective being that it should not be left to turn into a bush. Whenever either of the orphans is ready to occupy it, he or she will find the farm in fair condition.

The case study just presented illustrates one frequent outcome for a household when both parents die leaving behind young children. The most telling aspects of this case are, first, the determined intervention of the extended family members to re-capitalize and stabilize the business of the children's uncle to whom they are most dependent. Without this intervention, it is likely that the orphans would have been once again relocated to one or more households within the extended family. The second aspect is the continued care for the orphan's farm so that it is kept in a productive condition until the rightful owners can settle on it again. The labour to keep the farm in a productive state is provided by relatives other than those who have fostered the children. Both groups – those that have fostered the children and those who are looking after the farm – have a singular objective: to ensure that the orphans survive and will have a smooth landing when they finally return to live on the farm.

Although a lot has been written about AIDS and household dissolution, little is known about the long-term survival of those who are left behind. Certainly a number of possible outcomes are possible. Orphans may be fostered in the extended family system and cared for until they are able to lead independent lives. In some instances they may stay under one roof for a considerable time, in some other instances, they may be forced by circumstances to relocate from one foster household to the other (Fagbemissi et al., 2009; Du Preez and Niehof, this volume). When grown up, the orphans may either establish a new household on their parents' piece of land or they may choose to live somewhere else. Orphans may stay on the land in what has been called an 'orphan-headed household'. Alternatively, they (orphans) may get detached from the family and end up as street children. Although mortality of parents due to AIDS has been cited as contributing to the increasing number of street children in some parts of Africa (Lugalla and Kibasa, 2002), there is no evidence that the majority of the street children today are AIDS orphans. The different outcomes discussed above are important. As demonstrated in Case 1, a child who remains attached to his or her family has some chance to get an education and to grow within a familiar social and cultural system. On the other hand, a child who becomes foot loose and ends up somewhere else is not only denied the comforts of a home but there is the risk that he/she might lose his/her claim on the parental property, particularly land. These dynamics have received little attention in the literature. However, the need to understand the twists and turns of the lives of orphans is critical for any (child) development policy and for the design of social protection programmes for children in countries hard hit by the epidemic.

Case 2: Migration in search of a new beginning: Rutayuga's household between 1992 and 2009

For old parents, losing mature children to AIDS is not easy to accept and more so if those who died were important contributors to the household welfare. Those who are at the highest risk of contracting HIV and dying of AIDS are young adults with living parents. Hitherto, the linkage between grandparents and AIDS has been illustrated in terms of grandparents as carers of their sick children and as having overall responsibility for their grandchildren once their sick children have died. Case 2 highlights another angle in which the death of children may force parents to migrate in search of a new purpose in life.

1992–1997

Rutayuga and his wife lose their eldest son to AIDS in February 1992. Consequently, they take in the widow (daughter-in-law) and her three young children of whom the eldest was born in 1988 and the last one in 1991. The widow is sickly most of the time and so the children are largely dependent on their grandparents. The death of the eldest son is soon followed by the death of his young brother (1996) who had worked and lived in Zanzibar and another son (1996) who had lived in Dar-es-Salaam. Out of the four offspring only one son has survived. He has not been back to the village to see his parents and they do not talk about him, although villagers insist that he works for one of the largest banks in Dar-es-Salaam.

1998–2000

The widow has been through numerous cycles of being ill and being well but in July 1998 she decides to leave her in-laws house for her natal home where she claims she could get better quality care from her parents and kinsfolk. After a few months she feels much better and comes back for her children. Rutayuga and his wife remain in their home, often complaining of loneliness. The widow and her children visit them a couple of times for a few days each time. In January 2000 the widow's health takes a turn for the worst and she dies four months later. She leaves her children in the care of her parents.

2001–2003

Rutayuga and his wife begin construction of a brick house because the mud house they have had since the 1950s is old and the roof is leaking. The bricks had been piled in front of their current house since 1987. The couple had expected to have the house ready in a year or two but the plans had been disrupted by illnesses and the eventual death of their sons. Since money is now tight, Rutayuga decided to build the house using his own labour. After six months of hard labour, he has only managed to build the foundation but not the rest of the edifice. He gives up on the project. In September 2003, Rutayuga and his wife tell their close relatives and friends that they are migrating from the village to settle in Karagwe District on the north-western side of Kagera region. They had acquired a piece of land there and they wanted a new beginning, they claimed. In November 2003, Rutayuga and his wife move to Karagwe and leave behind their two plots of land: the one that Rutayuga had inherited from his father and the one they bought with their own money. Rutayuga informs his relatives that whoever wants to farm the plot of land he had inherited from his father (effectively clan land) is welcome to do so. The second plot of land is left under the guardianship of one of his cousins.

2004–2009

The two plots of land left behind by Rutayuga and his wife are not farmed and so they turn bushy. Rutayuga and his wife have been back to the village a few times either to visit or attend the funeral of a friend or relative. They have indicated that they are happy in Karagwe and have no desire to return to the village they left behind. The couple's old house still stands but is not used. Piles of bricks are everywhere in the front yard, indicating the old couple's dream and intentions that will never materialize. Both farm plots are overgrown with weeds. Every time Rutayuga or his wife visit, they stay with friends or relatives. Last time the senior author saw Rutayuga was in June 2009 when he came back to the village to mourn a cousin who had died. He says life in Karagwe is much better than Bukoba so there is no point him coming back, even though none of his relatives know exactly the village in which the couple has settled.

Rutayuga's household had been what anthropologists call an empty nest for more than ten years. The last child had left the home and established an independent living. For all those years the couple had lived alone. It therefore came as a surprise that after more than 40 years of marriage and living on their own land in the village, they have decided to migrate to a different place. The couple, both in their 70s, could have chosen to stay on their land and continue to farm. They were not wretchedly poor. In fact they were one of the better-off households in the village. They did not migrate either because of stigma because in this area where AIDS has long been seen as a disease that affects everyone (Rugalema et al., 2009), stigma is not an issue. The most important reason for the migration of the couple from Bukoba to Karagwe district is explained by them simply as an attempt to leave behind the painful memories and to start fresh. They wanted to be in a place where landmarks are new, neighbours are new and where there are no gravesites as sad reminders of the tragic death of their children.

This specific type of AIDS-driven migration has largely not been explored. What has been explored widely is the relationship between migration and vulnerability to HIV infection (Gillespie et al., 2007; Hargreaves et al., 2007; IOM, 2007). Regarding migration of adult survivors, we are only aware of two such small studies, conducted in north-western Tanzania (Kessy et al., 2006; Karugendo, 2008). These two studies show that increasingly, widowers and widows whose partners have died from AIDS are migrating from their usual residential areas to fish landing sites on the shores of Lake Victoria or in the many islands in the lake (Rugalema and Mathieson, 2009). The driving force is the desire to leave the old way of life behind, to move to somewhere where one can be anonymous, more generally, to seek new opportunities and a fresh beginning. In some cases, such migrants have assumed aliases so that they cannot be easily traced. Anecdotal evidence indicates that such migrants establish new households and move on with their lives.

While this kind of AIDS-induced migration has been observed in young adults (Karugendo, 2008), Case 2 shows that loss of children may push elderly people to migrate to new areas. To what extent this phenomenon is (becoming) widespread is, at the moment, an open question but one that needs attention and further research.

Case 3: Nyakato's household between 1988 and 2009

1987–1993

The year is 1987 and Nyakato's polygamous husband's health begins to deteriorate. He is in and out of hospital. His business – two retail shops – has nobody to care for them and they are finally closed in early 1988. He dies in October of that year. Each of his wives lived in a different village about 5km apart. Upon the death of the husband, Nyakato just like her co-wife, kept her children, the farm land and the livestock that had been under her care before her husband's death. Nyakato inherited six heads of cattle but by 1993 the number had increased to ten. Nyakato manages to keep all the children in school and to occasionally use hired labour for managing livestock and other 'male' farm tasks. Sometimes she would perform those 'male' tasks herself.

1994–2000

Nyakato's first born son completes primary school education at the local village school in 1994 and joins his mother at the farm. He progressively takes over responsibility for managing livestock. The herd continues to grow and an occasional sale of a beast boosts household income. By 1996 the eldest son feels that farming is not his calling and decides to leave for Dar-es-Salaam to find work or a place where he can be an apprentice to learn a trade. His two young brothers remain with their mother and even though still going to school, they also help their mom with farm work. The second-born finishes his primary education in 1998 and joins his mother on the farm. The third son (last born) completes his education in 2000 and like his elder brother decides to stay on the farm with his mom. The condition of the farm is maintained at the same level as when Nyakato's husband was alive.

2001–2009

Seeing that her young sons are mature enough to be left alone, in May 2001 Nyakato leaves for Dar-es-Salaam to visit her eldest son and stays there for about nine months. The two boys left behind manage well. Nyakato returns to the village in 2002. Her son who lives in Dar-es-Salaam is a mechanic with a stable job and income. Back in the village, the two sons take more responsibility for farm work and care for their mother. In 2007, the second-born asks his mother to let him build his own house. Nyakato consents and a brick house is built. Her youngest son decides to move in with his brother and Nyakato's household becomes an 'empty nest'. Despite moving out, the boys still support their mother. They undertake casual labour to supplement whatever income they get from the sale of crops and animals.

Case 3 illustrates the importance of assets in ensuring long-term survival of households affected by AIDS. Had the household assets been sold during the illness of Nyakato's husband, the outcome would have been different. Also, the survival of one parent, in this case the mother, ensured that the household did not fragment or dissolve and this provided the foundation for continuity. The lesson from this case is that survival of one of the parents is critical for continuity. This observation is supported by evidence from other studies that have shown that survival of the mother has both immediate and intergeneration benefits (Beegle et al., 2008).

At the beginning of the epidemic, when stigma was high and accusation and blame raged, widows were often disinherited because they were often seen as part of the AIDS problem. Recent studies though are beginning to show that the trend of widow disinheritance is, at least in some parts of Africa, declining. In her extensive ethnographic study of widowhood in a village in Kagera Region, north-western Tanzania, Foster (2006 unpublished) took detailed notes about 30 widows living in the village, none of whom had been disinherited or chased away from her land upon the death of a husband. The problem is that many of them were living in poverty (just like many other people not affected by AIDS) and the most pressing issues among widows was how to make the land more productive so as to produce enough food for their children.

As described in Case 3, widow-headed households are not static. They too adapt and change over time. However, the burden of bringing up children single-handedly must be immense. Understanding the needs and challenges facing these households as they move through the impacts of AIDS would be critical for any social protection policy and programmes aimed at widows and their children.

Case 4: Mukagambi's household between 1992 and 2009

1992–1993

Mukagambi's daughter, living and working in Mwanza, begins falling ill in 1992. By 1993, Mukagambi is spending more time nursing her daughter in Mwanza than she is spending on her farm. The farm starts to deteriorate. Some cows are sold while others are relocated to be cared for by friends. By the end of the year, Mukagambi's daughter dies. She leaves behind four orphans, two of whom are left in the care of Mukagambi. The other two are left in the care of their paternal grandparents since their father had died a year before their mother. At the age of 70, Mukagambi becomes responsible for two babies, the oldest two and half years while the youngest just 18 months.

1994–2002

All throughout the illness of her daughter, Mukagambi had known that her son, living and working in central Tanzania, was also sickly. She did not have the opportunity to nurse him, given that she was already caring for her daughter almost full time. Her son dies in August 1994. He leaves no survivors. Mukagambi settles in her new role as caregiver to the two young children. She is often ill and both food and money are in short supply. She sells all the cattle that belonged to her to buy food and other essential needs and services. Despite the difficulties she perseveres. The two orphans start school in 1998. Uniforms and other school materials for the two girls are provided for by some members of the extended family, as well as the Lweru Area Development Programme of World Vision Tanzania. Abolition of school fees at primary and secondary school level has eased the burden that Mukagambi and her relatives would have shouldered in the course of educating the two orphans.

2003–2009

Noting how difficult life has become in Mukagambi's household, extended family members start helping out. According to Mukagambi, she made no request for support but sheer observation has made it obvious to the better-off kinsfolk that the household needs their support. Also, as the two girls slowly become of age, they are helping their granny with household chores, something that has contributed to her improved health. At the time of writing, the two girls are in secondary school. With some support from the extended family, the household is able to feed itself while through government policy on health insurance, the orphans and their grandmother are able to access basic healthcare without paying a fortune.

AIDS has sometimes been dubbed a 'grandmothers' disease (Altman, 2006). The notion emanates from experiences such as the one described in Case 4. The death of young adults due to AIDS has forced grandparents, particularly grandmothers, to resume child upbringing duties. Like Mukagambi, the challenge has been long and hard. In this particular case, the survival of the household depended on Mukagambi's hard work and support from her relatives. Without this support, the household could have collapsed under the weight of the impact of AIDS.

In this case, the other source of support for the household and the orphans in particular has been World Vision Tanzania (WVT), an NGO that some 15 years ago established an office approximately 3 kilometres from the village. Over the years they have provided various forms of support to orphans, but the most important has been what we could call the 'educational subsidy'. By providing school materials to children such as Mukagambi's grandchildren, the NGO has given them a chance to get an education.

Besides the support from the NGO, by abolishing school fees for public schools, the Government of Tanzania has been instrumental in enabling orphans and children from poor households to access education. The case study shows how the interaction between material support by an NGO and the government policy (abolition of school fees) may be fundamental in the building of human capital of orphans. We do not have statistical evidence to show how many orphans have benefited and how effective (in terms of orphan enrolment and retention in the education system) such initiatives have been. As this case shows, orphans have a chance to obtain an education if there are well-targeted policies and programmes.

When we put the four case studies together, we begin to get a semblance of a pattern or picture of the process of resilience. Resilience in this sense is a product of the gravity of the impact of AIDS, particularly household demography as well as the adaptive capacity of that household in terms of the availability of material and social resources essential for a household livelihood. If due to AIDS a household suffers a heavy loss in terms of human lives as well as material and financial resources, the recovery process may take longer and vice versa. The dynamic relationship between AIDS impact, adaptive capacity and resilience at household level is depicted in Figure 3.1.

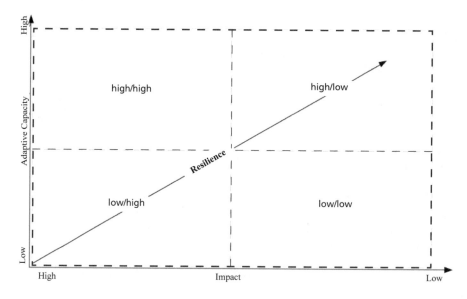

Figure 3.1 *Resilience to AIDS death as a product of impact and adaptive capacity*

A glance at Figure 3.1 shows that over time there is a tendency for impact to lessen provided a household can marshal necessary resources. To illustrate this point, we refer again to the four case studies presented above and their respective location in each of the four quadrants. Case 1 is a typical example of high-impact low-adaptive capacity. When Kabumbilo and his wife died, they left no surviving adult to care for the children *in situ*. Thus the children had to be fostered out. Fifteen years later, the children have grown up and there is every possibility that one of them or both will soon settle on their family land and continue farming. In this household, the social and familial networks have provided the adaptive capacity since assets had been liquidated during the illness of the parents.

A slightly different pattern of resilience is manifested in Case 2. Rutayuga's household experienced low impact in the sense that those who died were not resident in the household, even though they had somewhat contributed to the welfare of their parents. On the other hand most household assets remained intact, giving Rutayuga and his wife a high adaptive capacity. That after a decade or so the household has been able to marshal resources, buy land and settle somewhere else is evidence that over time the impact in this household decreased. Nyakato's household (Case 3) is emblematic of what we have called low-impact high-adaptive capacity. As explained in the text, Nyakato had been a de facto head of household long before the illness and death of her husband. The illness of her husband did not lead to liquidation of assets. Case 4 illustrates a household in which the impact has been high and adaptive capacity low. Mukagambi's children had been the major providers of the household. Their death was a major economic shock to the elderly mother. In addition, she did not have any material resources other than the little piece of land. Needless to say, the adaptive capacity of this household was low. It is important to note that the resilience pattern we have sketched above is, in real life, a lot more complex. Uniformly, when a household experiences AIDS death, there is certainly a psychological and emotional trauma. It takes time to overcome the initial shock. Also, along the way to recovery, a household may shift from one quadrant to another, due to internal and external factors. What we are saying is that given time and some stability, the tendency is to move towards the high-adaptive capacity low-impact quadrant.

In sum, the case studies narrated above show that even in the worst-case scenario (high-impact low-adaptive capacity) time is a very important mitigating factor. Over time, the force of impact moderates, adaptive capacity increases and thus resilience is strengthened. The implication of this analysis is that impact analyses ought to capture the dynamic nature of resilience, particularly the ebb and flow of the adaptive capacity.

Conclusion

Longitudinal studies to track and analyse the long-term impacts of AIDS on individuals and households have only emerged in the last few years (Dinkelman et al., 2007; Seeley et al., this volume). Our analysis is just a small addition, but the need for more longitudinal studies on the impact of AIDS on households cannot be over emphasized. As shown in this paper, the more the epidemic matures (and stabilizes or starts declining), the more the desire to decipher the processes through which individuals and households have passed and what long-term impact the epidemic is having. It will remain impossible to develop a full understanding of the epidemic if we continue to rely on isolated cross-sectional studies.

Back to our study, notwithstanding the limitations of using a few cases to understand a much bigger problem, our analysis and review indicate that there is evidence out there to show how resilient different units (individuals and households) have been to the impact of the epidemic. It is also evident that resilience and continuity are and will continue to be determined by a combination of factors ranging from the support from members of the extended family to government policies on education and health.

Large-scale systematic reviews are required to examine the extent to which interventions by NGOs and government social protection programmes in education and health have contributed and continue to contribute to resilience to the impact of AIDS at household level. Earlier in the epidemic, much was written about the fragility of the African extended family as a social safety net (Rugalema, 1999). There is need to analyse how extended family networks have fared and what lessons can be learned from what was being done through such networks to protect the lives of people affected by AIDS. Evidence presented in this chapter indicates that extended family networks have been resilient and that they did not break down as originally feared.

Looking forward to how the impact of the AIDS epidemic at household level will continue to unfold, what needs to be understood is the general trend in both the epidemiology of the disease and the social and economic factors that drive vulnerability to HIV infection and to the downstream impacts of AIDS. While there are clear signs that the epidemic is finally on the decline, the same cannot be said about poverty trends, particularly in the current climate of a slow global economy. This means that the trends and dynamics of the impacts of AIDS will continue to evolve and this calls for research designs that can capture these dimensions over time.

References

Altman, L.K. (2006) 'Grandmothers rally to raise AIDS orphans', *New York Times*, 12 August

Beegle, K., De Weerdt, J. and Dercon, S. (2008) 'The intergenerational impact of the African orphans crisis: A cohort study from an HIV/AIDS affected area', *International Journal of Epidemiology*, vol 38, no 2, pp561–568

Dinkelman, T., Lam, D. and Leibbrandt, M. (2007) 'Household and community income, economic shocks and risky sexual behavior of young adults: Evidence from the Cape Area Panel Study 2002 and 2005', *AIDS*, vol 21, supplement 7, ppS49–S57

Du Preez, C. and Niehof, A. (this volume) 'Impacts of HIV and AIDS-related morbidity and mortality on non-urban households in Kwa-Zulu Natal, South Africa'

Fagbemissi, R.C., Lie, R. and Leeuwis, C. (2009) 'Diversity and mobility in households with children orphaned by AIDS in Couffo, Benin', *African Journal of AIDS Research*, vol 8, no 3, pp261–274

Foster, V. (2006, unpublished) *Widowhood, HIV/AIDS, and Food Security in Kagera Region, Tanzania: An Ethnographic Analysis*

Gillespie, S., ed (2006) *AIDS, Poverty and Hunger: Challenges and Responses*, IFPRI, Washington DC

Gillespie, S. and Kadiyala, S. (2005) *HIV/AIDS and Food and Nutrition Security: From Evidence to Action*, IFPRI, Washington DC

Gillespie, S., Greener, R., Whiteside, A. and Whitworth, J. (2007). 'Investigating the empirical evidence for understanding vulnerability and the associations between poverty, HIV infection and AIDS impact.' *AIDS*, vol 21, sup 7, pp1–16.

Hargreaves, J.R., Bonell, C.P., Morison, L.A., Kim, J.C., Phetla, G., Porter, J.D.H., Watts, C. and Pronyk, P.M. (2007) Explaining continued high HIV prevalence in South Afrika: Socioeconomic factors, HIV incidence and sexual behaviour change among a rural cohort, 2001–2004.' *AIDS*, vol 21, sup 7, pp39–48.

Karugendo, P. (2008) 'Reasons for migrating to Lake Victoria islands of north-western Tanzania', Paper presented at a seminar on *Researching the Longitudinal Impacts of AIDS*, Imperial Royal Hotel, Kampala, June 2008

Kessy, F., Kweka, J., Makaramba, R. and Kiria, I. (2006) *Vulnerability and Property Rights of Widows and Orphans in the Era of the HIV and AIDS Pandemic: A Case Study of Muleba and Makete Districts, Tanzania*, FAO, Rome

Lugalla, J.L. and Kibassa, C. G. (2002) *Poverty, AIDS and Street Children in East Africa*, Edwin Mellen Press

Müller, T.R. (2004) HIV/AIDS and Agriculture in Sub-Saharan Africa 1: An overview and annotated bibliography. Wageningen Academic Publishers. Wageningen, The Netherlands.

Müller, T.R. (2005) *HIV/AIDS, Gender and Rural Livelihoods in Sub-Saharan Africa*, AWLAE Series No 2, Wageningen Academic Publishers, Wageningen, The Netherlands

Rau, B., Rugalema, G., Mathieson, K. and Stloukal, L. (2008) *The Evolving Contexts of AIDS and the Challenges for Food Security and Rural Livelihoods*, FAO, Rome

Rugalema, G. (1999) 'AIDS Mortality as entitlement failure: AIDS and the crisis of rural livelihoods in a Tanzanian village', *PhD Dissertation*, Institute of Social Studies, The Hague

Rugalema, G. and Mathieson, K. (2009) *Disease, Vulnerability and Livelihoods on the Tanzania-Uganda Interface Ecosystem to the West of Lave Victoria*, FAO, Rome, Italy

Rugalema, G., Muir, G., Mathieson, K., Measures, E., Oehler, F. and Stloukal, L. (2009) 'Emerging and remerging diseases of agricultural importance: Why local perspectives matter', *Food Security*, vol 1, no 4, pp441–455

Samuels, F. and Wells, J. (2009) 'The loss of the middle ground: The impact of crises and HIV and AIDS on "skipped-generation" households', *ODI Project Briefing*, No. 33, Overseas Development Institute, London

Seeley, J., Amurwon, J. and Foster, S. (this volume) 'The longitudinal picture: What does it reveal?'

UNAIDS and WHO (2009) *AIDS Epidemic Update: November 2009*, Geneva

Chapter 4

Impacts of AIDS-related morbidity and mortality on non-urban households in KwaZulu-Natal, South Africa

Corrie du Preez and Anke Niehof

Introduction

This chapter is set in the context of the evolving AIDS epidemic in South Africa. It presents results of research on how non-urban Zulu households in KwaZulu-Natal province deal with emergent care needs because of AIDS-related morbidity and mortality.

In 2007, of South Africa's population of close to 48 million, approximately 18.1 per cent of adults aged 15 to 49 were living with HIV and there were an estimated 1.4 million orphans aged 0 to 17, while approximately 350,000 adults and children died of AIDS (UNAIDS, 2008, pp215–218). Countrywide, 458,951 HIV-infected individuals were receiving antiretroviral treatment, approximately 50 per cent of those in need of treatment (UNAIDS, 2008, p271). Although good quality care cannot replace treatment, well-managed care can improve the quality of life of patients (National Department of Health, 2002).

The epidemic disproportionately affects women; young women aged 15 to 24 years are four times more likely than young men to be infected with HIV (UNAIDS, 2008). According to the 2007 National HIV and Syphilis Prevalence Survey for South Africa, 37.4 per cent of women aged 15 to 49 attending antenatal clinics in the KwaZulu-Natal province of South Africa were infected. Prevalence is highest among women aged 30 to 34 and higher in non-urban than urban areas (National Department of Health, 2008, p11). Women are traditionally the providers of child- and healthcare within the household. The high prevalence of HIV adds to their care burden (Akintola, 2004). The situation in the province is exacerbated by factors such as a high unemployment rate for the KwaZulu-Natal province (41.9 per cent) and the fact that 62.4 per cent of the Black population lives in poverty (KwaZulu-Natal Department of Health, 2005, p14).

The AIDS epidemic increases morbidity (sickness) and mortality (death) at those ages when normally levels of morbidity and mortality of populations are relatively low, which has implications for the epidemic's impacts. Impact can be seen as a continuum between the effect of immediate severe shock and profound long-term changes, occurring at the level of individuals, households, communities and the nation. Because HIV is sexually transmitted, it often clusters in households, resulting in multiple cases of illness and death. The effects of illness and death on households further depend on the composition and resource availability of the household (Barnett and Whiteside, 2006).

The most extreme impact at the household level may be the dissolution of the household. Hosegood et al. (2004) found in their surveillance of more than 10,000 households in non-urban KwaZulu-Natal, South Africa, 2 per cent of households dissolved over a period of 34 months. Households experiencing multiple deaths were significantly more at risk of dissolving. A study conducted in Limpopo province, South Africa, also documents the impact of HIV and AIDS on households, with consistent change in household structure, including an increase in female-headed households, smaller households with fewer children, and more households with orphaned children (Madhavan and Schatz, 2007). Wittenberg and Collinson (2007) reported that although there is an increase in three-generation skip households (comprising grandparents and grandchildren) and households including other relatives, such as stepchildren and nephews/nieces, it was less pronounced in the Agincourt study conducted in Mpumalanga Province than in the national household survey.

Against this background, the present paper looks at HIV/AIDS impacts on non-urban households in a high-prevalence region in South Africa, the province of KwaZulu-Natal. More specifically it aims at providing insights into how afflicted households use their resources to arrange and provide care for the sick and the orphaned, and how that entails changes in living arrangements and in the relations and movements between households.

Conceptual and methodological positioning

There is now a growing body of literature on the effects of HIV/AIDS on households. Based on a review of 32 studies, Naidu and Harris (2005) expressed the need for further multidisciplinary and longitudinal household-level research to assess the full and varied impacts of HIV/AIDS over time. By the research presented in this paper we intend to contribute to meeting this need, especially by showing sequential and multiple impacts of HIV/AIDS on households and living arrangements in response to care needs. Although the research presented here cannot be considered a longitudinal study, it does show AIDS-related impacts on selected households and household responses even over a period as short as six months.

In their study on HIV and AIDS impacts on households in rural Uganda, Seeley et al. (2008) illustrate how in-depth longitudinal research with a small number of households can explain results from quantitative research. While the quantitative analysis of data did not show a significant association between HIV status and poverty indicators, qualitative data on 26 households revealed how AIDS impoverishes households, but that over time AIDS impacts are – to a certain extent – mitigated by the support from kin and members of the local community. Networks of kin and friends and links with people outside the household in general are important for understanding HIV and AIDS impacts. Similarly, Drinkwater et al. (2006) in their study on the effects of HIV and AIDS on agricultural production systems in Zambia identified clusters of households and showed how the links between different households in terms of making their livelihoods were influenced by HIV and AIDS.

For the purpose of this study a household is described as a group of people, related and/or unrelated, sharing a homestead, often consisting of several living units, at a given time. Non-resident members may be included when they are perceived as members by the head and other household members, usually when they spend a significant amount of time at the homestead and contribute to household livelihood generation. In a study on livelihood security in KwaZulu-Natal the author notes that 'the homestead always provides a fallback position for the extended family members who lose employment, need permanent linkage with ancestors and those who retire at the end of their working career' (Mtshali, 2002, p20). Mtshali pictures the patrilineal homestead as a site of continuity amidst ongoing social change, among others caused by labour migration. It is 'home', also to those who live temporarily elsewhere. In our study, the question emerged whether the homestead as a beacon of continuity, family connectedness and social security is crumbling under the impacts of AIDS-related morbidity and mortality through loss of adult homestead members and increased movements of people between homesteads.

In this study, the household (in casu homestead) is not seen as a joint utility-maximizing unit led by an altruistic household head, a notion that gained prominence in the New Home Economics but has been much criticized since (e.g. Kabeer, 1994). Instead, we see it as a (family-based) group that exercises agency to manage resources to provide for its members' daily needs and wellbeing. To this end, households can design and implement strategies (Wallace, 2002). Ceding the point made by Sen (2008) that there is both cooperation and conflict in households, we would like to stress that there should be a certain threshold level of cooperation for households not to fall apart. This threshold is reached when resources to sustain the group are lacking and claims to support and care can no longer be honoured. The latter affects the household's functioning as a 'moral economy' (Cheal, 1989), which is motivated by maintaining enduring social relationships to gain long-term economic security rather than by the rational pursuit of individual interests. AIDS affects the moral economies and resource bases of households. While household boundaries are always more or less permeable and household composition is always subject to change, weakening intra-household ties and deterioration of the household's resource base may lead to the collapse of the household's moral economy and the social group sustaining it. Then, living arrangements become unstable, have to be frequently readjusted to changing circumstances, and earlier strategies no longer apply. Hence, although the household was the unit of analysis in this research, inter-household relations were part of the analysis (Drinkwater, 2003). This is the conceptual background against which the cases presented in this paper were selected and investigated. Additionally, we defined an orphan: as a child 18 years or younger who lost both parents; or lost one parent and the whereabouts of the other parent are unknown to the main caregiver – the latter also sometimes referred to as a 'virtual' double orphan (Case and Ardington, 2006).

The conceptualization of care was guided by Tronto's (1993) framework for the analysis of the adequacy of care, based on both attitude and practice, as underpinned by both morality and resources. Niehof (2004) incorporated Tronto's framework in her micro-ecological approach to health and care by anchoring it to the household. As changes in living arrangements have implications for the household's potential to arrange care and in turn impact on its resources, an adapted version of various livelihoods frameworks was created to assess the livelihoods of the households described in this paper (Carney et al., 1999).

For various reasons HIV/AIDS research is methodologically complex (Wiegers, 2008). A major problem is identifying HIV/AIDS impacts as distinct from other factors that impinge on rural livelihoods. This problem of 'inadequate impact attribution' (Murphy et al., 2005, p270) is particularly urgent in cross-sectional surveys that use proxy indicators for HIV-infection and where control households are lacking. HIV/AIDS research is dominated by the use of survey methods and quantitative data collection. Reviewing 36 impact studies, Booysen and Arntz (2003) only found 11 that also used qualitative methods of data collection, such as focus groups and in-depth-interviews. However, since then several qualitative studies on the socio-economic, socio-cultural and psychosocial impact of AIDS on the living and care arrangements of individuals and households were conducted (e.g. Young and Ansell, 2003; Russell, 2004; Knodel, 2005; Montgomery et al., 2006; Hosegood et al., 2007; Swaans et al., 2008; Ardington et al., 2009). The research findings presented here were obtained by using the case study method and doing in-depth interviews. This approach allowed us to identify and describe impacts of the epidemic as they emerged from the narratives. We did not quantitatively measure impacts. It should be emphasized, however, that the results presented in this paper form part of a broader PhD-research project, which included a survey among 354 households.

Study area and data collection

The study area

The research was conducted in a non-urban area in KwaZulu-Natal province in South Africa. The area is under tribal authority, and 98 per cent of the population is Black African and Zulu speaking. Although only a short distance from a big town, infrastructure is poor; 66 per cent of the households do not have access to piped water at the homestead and 39 per cent have no toilet facility. The average household size is 5.2. The research area is also characterized by unemployment and poverty: only 11.2 per cent of adults are employed, the majority of them in low-paying unskilled or semi-skilled occupations. Many households depend for their income on social grants only or a combination of social grants and part-time or temporary employment. Approximately 25 per cent of the households in the area do not earn any regular monthly income (Statistics South Africa, 2001). HIV prevalence in the area is about 34 per cent (National Department of Health, 2007). Tuberculosis is also a relatively common chronic illness, with at least 60 per cent of those with TB estimated to also be HIV-positive (WHO, 2007). The lack of proper sanitation at many homesteads contributes to poor hygiene, causing additional health problems and making caring for people with AIDS and other chronic illnesses difficult and time-consuming. Unemployment and poverty obstruct access to formal care and support of chronically ill persons and their caregivers (Uys and Cameron, 2003).

Data collection and analysis

Twenty-two case study households were selected from the surveyed households for in-depth assessment of living and care arrangements, and livelihood generation. Selection criteria included sex and age of household head, household size and socio-economic status, and whether and how the household was afflicted and/or affected by AIDS. Afflicted households are those that experienced direct impacts, with at least one household member ill with or having died of AIDS-related illness, while affected households are those that experienced indirect impacts, for example, by having to take in orphans to care for (Barnett and Blaikie, 1992). Due to stigma and secrecy, case study households had to be selected and access gained with the assistance of Community Health Workers (CHWs) working in the study area. Prior to this, the proposed research was presented to local authorities to acquire approval and support for the study and it was on their recommendation that the study was conducted in cooperation with the CHWs. Case study data were collected by means of in-depth interviews with household members, including household heads, caregivers, and when possible, care receivers, and observation of household resources and activities. In addition to data on household structure, and socio-economic and health characteristics of all household members, data were collected on kinship relations, resources, livelihood activities and care arrangements and practices. Initial interviews were guided by a list of predesigned topics and observations by a checklist. Each case study household was visited three times over a period of six months from October 2006 through March 2007. Data on household structure, living and care arrangements, and livelihood generation were updated during follow-up visits. A trained research assistant, fluent in the Zulu language, assisted with interviewing and recording of observations. Qualitative data were analysed by close reading of field notes of the interview responses and documented observations, followed by categorizing, integrating and summarizing the information according to themes.

Results

Six cases were selected for discussion below, based on the changes that occurred in their living arrangements. It should be emphasized that some of the changes occurred prior to the start of the research, while others occurred during October 2006 through March 2007. An overview of selected demographic and socio-economic characteristics of the six case study households is presented in Table 4.1, while changes in living and care arrangements, and livelihoods are described below. All names in the presented cases are pseudonyms.

Case 1

Bongi, the 47-year-old head of the household, initially lived with her daughter, Thobi aged 25, son Philani aged 23, and Thobi's 3-year-old son. Thobi's two older children,

Table 4.1 *Demographic and socio-economic profiles of case study households at commencement of data collection*

Case				Characteristics of Household Head			Selected characteristics of household								
	Sex	Age	Marital status	Level of education	Work status	HH size	Gender distribution		Age distribution			Estimated monthly income in ZAR($)	Number of employed NN members	Main source of income
							M	F	<15	15-64	≥65			
1	F	47	Never married	Some primary school education	Odd jobs, before she got ill	4	2	2	1	3	0	290(39)	0	Government grant [1]
2	F	23	Never married	Some primary school education	Not working, ill	1	0	1	0	1	0	150(20)	0	Private support
3	M	17	Not applicable	Attending secondary school	Not working, at school	2	2	0	1	1	0	200(27)	0	Private support
4	M	46	Married	Some primary school education	Not working, ill	11	4	7	6	5	0	3150(426)	2	Formal employment
5	F	58	Widow	Primary school incomplete	Not working, care for orphans	15	4	11	9	6	0	2190(296)	1	Government grants
6	M	72	Married	No formal schooling	Not working, pensioner	5	3	2	1	2	2	1830(247)	0	Government grants

aged 7 and 5, live with their father at his homestead. Bongi also has another daughter, Nomcebo, aged 23, who lives with her two sons, aged 4 and 2, at the homestead of her partner.

Bongi used to do some sewing, and occasionally worked in a small shop belonging to a family member, which provided her with a small income every month. When she became seriously ill, she could no longer do the sewing or help out at the shop, and neither Philani nor Thobi are working. The only other source of income is the state child support grant received for the 3-year old. Bongi has access to land where she grows some crops and vegetables, but when her health deteriorated she stopped growing maize and neglected the vegetables.

Both Bongi and Thobi are HIV-positive, while Bongi is also treated for TB. Philani is also chronically ill, but has not been tested for HIV. Thobi is asymptomatic, but Bongi became seriously ill and in need of care in October 2006. Nomcebo, with her two children, decided to move in with her mother to help take care of her and to assist with domestic work. Coinciding with this, Thobi's two older children also returned to live with their mother. All four of the children joining the household receive state child support grants, thereby significantly increasing the household income.

In February 2007, after taking treatment for TB, Bongi's condition improved to such an extent that she could take care of herself again as well as do some domestic work. At that time Nomcebo with her children and Thobi's two older children were still residing with her. Bongi was though, no longer willing to be interviewed, claiming that it is because of our visits that her neighbours now know that she has AIDS.

Case 2

Phume, aged 23, has been living on her own since her boyfriend moved out 6 months ago when her HIV-status became known. At the same time Phume sent their 5-year-old daughter, Nomsa, to live with her sister approximately 45 kilometres away. Phume was concerned that she may not be able to take care of Nomsa as her health deteriorates. Her 18-year-old sister, living with distant relatives, is her only remaining close relative since their parents passed away several years ago, the cause of death unknown. In January 2007, Nomsa's father decided that she should go and stay with his family at Mangusi, approximately 200 kilometres away. When Nomsa lived with her aunt, Phume was able to visit her once a month but since she moved to Mangusi she has been unable to visit her as it is too far for her to make the trip and too expensive to travel there.

Phume is HIV-positive and has TB, while the HIV-status of her former boyfriend is not known. Early in 2006 she started displaying symptoms associated with AIDS-related illness. Since then she has been unable to work. Her only source of income is the R150 per month she receives from a distant relative. Phume lives in a small traditional structure and shares a pit latrine with her neighbours. She does most of the domestic work herself and grows some vegetables at her homestead. Her neighbours know that she has AIDS and are very supportive. They assist her with tasks in and around the house when necessary. Twice a month a volunteer home-based carer visits Phume at her home.

Case 3

Themba is 17 years old and lives with his 12-year-old brother. They have been living on their own since their mother died of an AIDS-related illness in 2003. Their father died in 2001 from TB. Themba also has four sisters, aged 20, 15, 12 and 7, living with their maternal grandparents since the death of their mother. Apart from his grandparents and siblings, Themba, to his knowledge, has no other family.

In 2006, Themba was doing grade 10 for the second time and struggling to stay in school. He occasionally missed school and did not give sufficient attention to his schoolwork because of his responsibilities as head of the household. In spite of working as a gardener in Richards Bay on Saturdays and during school holidays, he was not able to pay his school fees every term. As an orphan and still being at primary school, his brother did not have to pay school fees and was progressing well at school.

Themba chose to stay at the homestead he inherited from his parents, rather than with his grandparents and lose the homestead. His younger brother could have gone to live with his grandparents but chose to stay with him. Both grandparents receive state old-age grants, and Themba's grandmother gives him a small amount of money every month, which he mainly uses to buy prepaid electricity and airtime for his mobile telephone. Themba receives food parcels every month as part of a community project and received some money to cover his school fees. The food parcels are delivered by a volunteer home-based carer when she visits Themba and his brother once a month. Themba and his brother have one meal per day, three to four times per week, with their grandparents. Themba tries to grow some vegetables at the homestead, but he does not have much time to tend to the garden as he also does all the domestic work.

In February 2007, two young men aged 17 and 20, both unemployed and hardly known to Themba, apparently attracted by the availability of food, moved in with them. As Themba was not in a position to request them to move out, the volunteer home-based carer, with the assistance of his grandfather intervened and they moved out in March 2007. Themba's grandparents were also not happy that he receives food, while they do not receive anything. At the end of March 2007 Themba left school and started looking for work.

Case 4

Emanuel, aged 46, lives with his wife, Gloria, aged 42, three sons aged 23, 16 and 8 and four daughters aged 19, 13, 11 and 7. Also living with them is their 5-year-old orphaned granddaughter and the 18-month-old daughter of their 19-year-old daughter. They had two older daughters who died of AIDS-related illness in 2004 and 2005, respectively. See Figure 4.1 for Emanuel's kinship diagram.

Emanuel and Gloria's 23-year-old son completed secondary school, while their 19-year-old daughter returned to school in 2006 after the birth of her child, but dropped out before the end of 2006 without completing her secondary school education. Emanuel and Gloria are HIV-positive, but while she is asymptomatic, he is displaying symptoms associated with AIDS-related illness and also has TB. He is not able to work due to his illness, whereas Gloria occasionally does odd jobs in the area as a labourer. Their 23-year-old son started working in September 2006 as a security guard at a local industry while their 19-year-old daughter started working, producing coal, in January 2007.

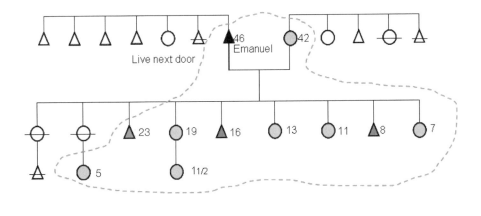

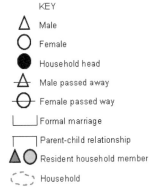

KEY

△ Male

○ Female

● Household head

⊿ Male passed away

⊖ Female passed way

⌐⌐ Formal marriage

⌐⌐ Parent-child relationship

▲◯ Resident household member

(⌐⌐) Household

Figure 4.1 *Emanuel's kinship diagram*

Source: Case studies 2006

Before they started working, the household was dependant on state child support grants and Gloria's small income. Since their daughter started working, the household income increased to R4,150. The family receives child support grants for the four youngest children. The mother of the 18-month-old child applied for a state child support grant, but she is still awaiting a response. Their 5-year-old granddaughter used to receive a child support grant before her mother passed away. Recently, Gloria applied for a state foster care grant, but they are still awaiting a response.

Emanuel recently completed treatment for TB, while he and Gloria take vitamin and mineral supplements which they monthly collect free of charge from the local public health clinic. The children and the 5-year old granddaughter are in good health, except for the 18-month-old granddaughter who shows signs of mental and physical retardation. In January 2007 their 11-year-old daughter went to stay with her aunt in a settlement approximately 30 kilometres away. The aunt offered to take her in to help the family. A sister of Emanuel lives next door. Though she is unable to help financially, she does provide emotional support.

They have access to land where Gloria grows amadumbe (African potato) and a variety of vegetables, while they also have some fruit trees at the homestead. Gloria is also involved in a local community garden, with all produce for household use. Gloria is responsible for most of the domestic work, assisted by Emanuel as far as his illness allows. The daughters of 13 and 11 are responsible for fetching water and collecting firewood. Since the 11-year old left, the 13-year old is occasionally assisted by the younger children. Gloria takes care of the children and grandchildren during the day, and when she works Emanuel takes care of their 18-month-old granddaughter. Although Emanuel can take care of himself most of the time, Gloria is the one to take care of him when necessary. They say they take care of each other. Apart from Emanuel's sister checking on them, they are also regularly visited by a local community health worker and belong to an AIDS support group.

Case 5

Busi, aged 58, is the head of the household since her husband passed away in 2001. She lives with three daughters, Zodwa aged 29, Slindile aged 21 and Bonakelo aged 17, as well as 11 grandchildren, seven of whom are orphaned. Busi had eight children, of whom her two eldest daughters and one son passed away between July 2004 and April 2006, all of them as a result of TB. Her two remaining sons do not live at her homestead. Each of the daughters left three children orphaned, the eldest left two daughters aged 16 and 12 and a son aged 10, and the other, two sons aged 15 and 7 and a daughter aged 1. The whereabouts of the respective fathers and whether they are still alive are not known. The 4-year-old son of Busi's late son has also been living with her since he was 2 months old. The whereabouts of his mother are unknown. Zodwa has three daughters aged 6, 4 and 1, living with her. The 2-year-old daughter of Busi's 23-year-old son, also lives at the homestead, she is occasionally visited by her mother who lives elsewhere. Slindile also had a child, but he passed away in December 2005 when he was 5 months old, while Bonakelo is seven months pregnant. Busi has three sisters living nearby, and although they cannot help financially, they offer emotional support and assist with domestic work when needed. See Figure 4.2 for Busi's kinship diagram.

Although all the children of school-going age are attending school, most of them are in grades below those appropriate for their age. Zodwa is the only employed member of the household, working for a minimum wage as a gardener at a local industry. Busi is not able to work as she is not well, and has to take care of the orphans. Slindile is not working, and according to Busi, not looking for work either.

Busi has been receiving a state disability grant since she had a stroke a few years ago. Zodwa receives state child support grants for each of her three children. None of the orphaned children receive state child support or foster care grants, either because Busi does not have their birth certificates or their parents' death certificates and is therefore unable to apply for state grants. Apart from Busi who had a stroke and has a problem with her eyesight, some other household members are also not healthy; two of the grandchildren have TB.

Apart from Zodwa's mobile telephone, they do not own any assets and live in dilapidated traditional structures without a toilet facility. Once a week they fetch water from a tanker that stops at the main road approximately 500 metres away, being dependent on nearby streams for the remainder of the time. Busi's three daughters and

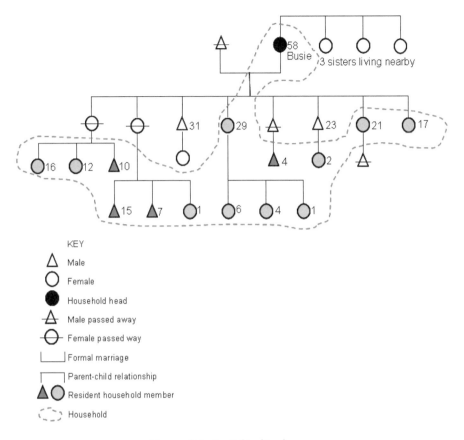

KEY

△ Male

○ Female

● Household head

⊖ Male passed away

⊖ Female passed way

⌷ Formal marriage

⌷ Parent-child relationship

▲○ Resident household member

⌒ Household

Figure 4.2 *Busi's kinship diagram*

Source: Case studies 2006

oldest granddaughter are responsible for fetching water and firewood. The domestic work is shared by Busi and her daughters. When Busi's daughters became ill, she took care of them until they died. Busi and her daughters take care of the small children, but after school and on weekends the older children also have to take care of their younger siblings and nieces.

Case 6

Velaphi, aged 72, lives with his wife Sarah, aged 68, 30-year-old daughter Grace and 2 orphaned grandsons aged 19 and 13, respectively. Their grandsons have been living with them since their father passed away approximately ten years ago while the whereabouts of their mother is unknown. Grace's 12-year-old daughter stays with a sister of Grace in a neighbouring town. The 12-year-old wanted to go and stay there because there are cousins her age. About one kilometre from Velaphi and Sarah, at her own homestead, lives their 39-year-old daughter Nomali, with her five children – four daughters aged 19, 2 and 1-year-old twins – as well as a 16-year old son (Figure 4.3 phase 1). Velaphi

Phase 1, October 2006, Nomali is HIV+, relatively healthy

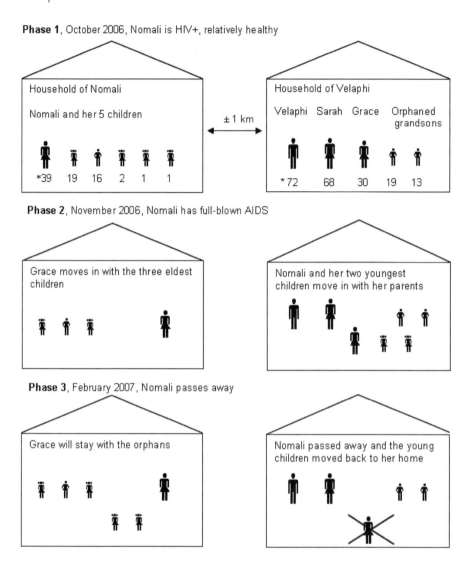

Figure 4.3 *The living arrangements of Nomali and her family*

Source: Case studies 2006

and Sarah have five other children living, with their respective families, in neighbouring towns.

Sarah did not receive any formal schooling, Grace completed secondary school, while their 19-year-old grandson has some primary school education. Their 13-year-old grandson is currently attending primary school and in a grade below that appropriate for his age. Both Velaphi and Sarah receive state old-age grants as well as a state child support grant for their 13-year-old grandson. Neither Grace nor their 19-year-old grandson are working and, according to Sarah, the grandson is not looking for work either. Nomali receives state child support grants for the three youngest children.

In November 2006, Nomali became seriously ill with AIDS-related illness and TB. It is not known when she tested positive for HIV. Initially Nomali's 19-year-old daughter took over her domestic work and the care of the three young children, but soon Nomali became too ill to take care of herself. At first Sarah spent most of the day and occasionally a night at Nomali's place to take care of her, but eventually Sarah decided that Nomali with her two youngest children should move to their homestead so that she could take care of them. At the same time she sent Grace to go and live at Nomali's homestead to take care of the three other children (Figure 4.3 phase 2). At the end of November 2006 Nomali's condition deteriorated and she had to be hospitalized. She passed away in hospital two weeks later. In January 2007 Sarah took the twins back to the late Nomali's homestead, where Grace will now remain to take care of all the children (Figure 4.3 phase 3). In February 2007 Sarah still spent a lot of time at her late daughter's homestead with Grace and the children. The two eldest children did not yet return to school and it was not clear whether they were going to. The whereabouts of the respective fathers of the two oldest and three youngest children are not known. Grace applied to have the child support grants converted to foster care grants, but by the end of February 2007 there was no response.

At Velaphi and Sarah's homestead Grace used to do most of the domestic work, but when she moved, Sarah had to take over the domestic work with some assistance from her two grandsons. Nomali's 19-year-old daughter – already before her mother, became seriously ill – did most of the domestic work and helped to take care of her three young siblings. While Velaphi and Sarah live in a traditional structure with no toilet facility, Nomali's family lives in a brick house with access to electricity for lighting and cooking, as well as a pit latrine.

Discussion

Although changes in living arrangements can be caused by many factors other than morbidity and mortality, the cases described, experienced changes as a direct result of TB and/or AIDS-related illness and death. The time frame of inter-household movements varies between a few months (Case 6) to several years (Case 3). The variation in cases presented illustrates that when movements between homesteads take place, the impact of HIV/AIDS-related morbidity and mortality on the livelihood and resources extends beyond the single household.

From Table 4.1, it is clearly visible that the majority of households depend on social transfers, either grants from government or private grants, as their only or main source of income, emphasizing the strategic importance of grants in coping with poverty. The financial situation of households may even improve when children receiving grants join a household and are 'accompanied' by their grants (Case 1). But when such children move, the gain of income in one household will translate into a loss for another. Furthermore, Cases 4, 5 and 6 show that accessing grants for children is difficult when the status of the child changes and/or the foster parent does not have the required papers. The role of maternal parents or grandparents becomes clear when looking at intra-household cooperation to arrange healthcare or take care of vulnerable or orphaned children (Cases 6 and 3).

All the households are visited regularly by paid community health workers and/or volunteer home-based caregivers, all of them female. These people are well-trained and work closely with the local public health clinic to assist households with care activities, caregivers with emotional support and patients with nutritional advice and traditional treatments to maintain health and relief symptoms. This is very important, as none of the HIV-positive persons in this small sample were on antiretroviral (ARV) treatment at the time of the research. Although treatment is free, to access it means regular blood tests and frequent hospital visits, which translates into indirect costs.

The cases discussed clearly reveal that women are still the main providers of health- and childcare. When the demand on their time to provide care increases (Cases 5 and 6), they have less time to devote to income generating and community activities, which means less time to invest in social networks (Ogden et al., 2006). Research in Tanzania has shown that at some point deteriorating material resources and dwindling social capital reinforce one another (Nombo and Niehof, 2008). This will cause already poor households with weak safety nets 'to fall through' the vulnerability threshold (Donahue et al., 2001; Donahue, 2006). All case households reveal the significance of social capital, the network of kin in particular, as a source of material and immaterial support. Relatives may take in a child to relieve the household's burden (Case 4), may send money (Case 2), or may provide emotional and practical support (Cases 4 and 5). In the case of Phume (Case 2), who is ill and has no relatives living nearby, the neighbours provide the latter kind of support. At the same time, the cases also show 'missing' partners and parents who have opted out and whose whereabouts are sometimes not even known (Case 5).

Although the majority of children in the case study households manage to stay in school, as also found by Kakuru (2006), they are absent from school more often due to HIV/AIDS-related morbidity and mortality. As a result they fall behind. All children aged 10 and older in the case study households were in grades below those appropriate for their respective ages. These children are at risk of eventually dropping out of school, as happened to the 17-year-old Themba.

Some children choose to stay at the homestead of their late parents, with or without adult supervision (Cases 3 and 6), rather than moving in with grandparents or other relatives. They do so in an attempt to retain the homestead and the land they inherited from their parents. But, as can be seen in Case 3, this may make children vulnerable to exploitation. Child migration as a strategy to cope with HIV/AIDS-related morbidity, as described by Ansell and Van Blerk (2004) and Ansell and Young (2004), was employed by two of the households (Cases 2 and 4). Although migration in search of employment has long been common in Southern Africa, migration of ill persons and children seeking care is a much more recent phenomenon (Young and Ansell, 2003).

Conclusion

Inter-household movements are likely to occur when a household affected by HIV/AIDS-related morbidity and mortality does not have the capacity to meet the additional demand for care. The movement of ill persons or vulnerable or orphaned children across household boundaries may make for more efficient use of human, material and financial resources. The cases show a continuous adaptation of living arrangements in response to illness and death. While the homestead and the kinship network still function as important anchors for people's lives, at the same time HIV/AIDS induces flux and instability, changes dependency relations between homesteads, makes 'holes' in safety nets, and undermines relations between partners, in particular those that are not sanctioned by traditional marriage, turning their children into de facto orphans. The homestead also seems to lose its unified and patriarchal character, although more analysis is needed to prove this, and the supportive role and authority of grandmothers and maternal relatives is increasing. Care is not only morally grounded, it can also add to moral authority.

The government should look into ways to facilitate better access to ARV treatment, because this would not only improve and prolong the life of people living with HIV, but also contribute to a better quality of life for household members. Streamlining access to foster care grants will prevent households taking care of orphans or orphans living on their own from living in extreme poverty. Increasing the number of well-trained paid CHWs, and liaising with formal healthcare and social workers, will enhance the much needed support required by households living with the burden of HIV/AIDS-related morbidity and mortality.

Although consisting of a very small sample of households studied over a relatively short period of time, this study reveals significant HIV/AIDS-induced changes in living arrangements, the variation in the time frame of these changes, and the impact of these changes on the livelihoods of households and their potential to arrange health- and childcare. While our findings largely corroborate those of the Africa Centre for Health and Populations Studies, which since 2000 has been conducting similar research in the province at a much larger scale (Hosegood et al., 2004), this study reveals the mechanisms of micro-level social change induced by the AIDS epidemic. It demonstrates the importance of qualitative research to complement cross-sectional survey research that only provides a view of households at one point in time. Although this study already exposes increasing variation in living arrangements and fluidity of household boundaries, more qualitative and longitudinal research is needed to know whether in the wake of the epidemic the cultural and social landscape of rural KwaZulu-Natal is fundamentally changing.

Acknowledgements

The authors wish to acknowledge the support of The Netherlands Ministry of Foreign Affairs for their generous funding of the AWLAE (African Women Leaders in Agriculture and Environment) Project, in the framework of which this research was carried out.

Note

1   Note on government grants at time of data collection: child care grant (age 0 to 14) = R190; old age pension (men age ≥ 65, women age ≥60) = R820

References

Akintola, O. (2004) *A Gendered Analysis of the Burden of Care on Family and Volunteer Caregivers in Uganda and South Africa,* Health Economics and HIV/AIDS Research Division, University of KwaZulu-Natal, Durban, South Africa

Ansell, N. and Van Blerk, L. (2004) 'Children's migration as a household/family strategy: coping with AIDS in Lesotho and Malawi', *Journal of Southern African Studies*, vol 30, no 3, pp673–690

Ansell, N. and Young, L. (2004) 'Enabling households to support successful migration of AIDS orphans in southern Africa', *AIDS Care*, vol 16, no 1, pp3–10

Ardington, C., Case, A., Lam, D., Leibbrandt, M., Menendez, A. and Olgiati, A. (2009) *The Impact of AIDS on Intergenerational Support in South Africa: Evidence from the Cape Area Panel Study*, A Southern Africa Labour and Development Research Unit Working Paper Number 27. Cape Town: SALDRU, University of Cape Town

Barnett, T. and Blaikie, P. (1992) *AIDS in Africa: Its Present and Future Impact*, John Wiley & Sons, Chichester

Barnett, T. & Whiteside, A. (2006) *AIDS in the Twenty-First Century, Disease and Globalization* [3rd edition], Palgrave Macmillan, New York

Booysen, F.l.R. and Arntz, T. (2003) 'The methodology of HIV/AIDS impact studies: A review of current practices', *Social Science & Medicine*, vol 56, pp2391–2405

Carney, D., Drinkwater, M., Rusinow, T., Neefjes, K., Wanmali, S. and Singh, N. (1999) Livelihoods approaches compared: A brief comparison of the livelihoods approaches of the UK Department for International Development (DfID), CARE, Oxfam, and the United Nations Development Programme (UNDP)

Case, A. and Ardington, C. (2006) 'The impact of parental death on school outcomes: Longitudinal evidence from South Africa', *Demography*, vol 43, no 3, pp 401–420

Cheal, D. (1989) 'Strategies of resource management in household economies: moral economy or political economy', in R.R. Wilk (ed), *The Household Economy: Reconsidering the Domestic Mode of Production*, pp11–23, Westview Press, Boulder, San Francisco

Donahue, J. (2006) 'Strengthening households and communities: The key to reducing the economic impacts of HIV/AIDS on children and families', in G. Foster, C. Levine and J. Williamson (eds), *A Generation at Risk: The Global Impact of HIV/AIDS on Orphans and Vulnerable Children*, pp37–65, Cambridge University Press, Cambridge

Donahue, J., Kabbucho, K. and Osinde, S. (2001) HIV/AIDS – Responding to a silent economic crisis among microfinance clients in Kenya and Uganda. Kenya: MicroSave – Market-led solutions for financial services, www.microsave.org, accessed 4 December 2009

Drinkwater, M. (2003) *HIV/AIDS and Agrarian Change in Southern Africa. Presentation for the United Nations Regional Inter-Agency Coordination and Support Office Technical Consultation on Vulnerability in the Light of an HIV/AIDS Pandemic*, Johannesburg, South Africa, www.sarpn.org.za

Drinkwater, M., McEwan, M. & Samuels, F. (2006) *The Effects of HIV/AIDS on Agricultural Production Systems in Zambia: A Restudy 1993–2005*, IFPRI/ RENEWAL report, Lusaka, Zambia

Hosegood, V., McGrath, N., Herbst, K. and Timaeus, I.M. (2004) 'The impact of adult mortality on household dissolution and migration in rural South Africa', *AIDS*, vol 18, no 11, pp1585–1590

Hosegood, V., Preston-Whyte, E., Busza, J., Moitse, S. and Timaeus, I.M. (2007) 'Revealing the full extent of households' experiences of HIV and AIDS in rural South Africa', *Social Science & Medicine*, vol 65, pp1249–1259

Kabeer, N. (1994) *Reversed Realities: Gender Hierarchies in Development Thought*, Verso, London

Kakuru, D.M. (2006) *The Combat for Gender Equality in Education, Rural Livelihood Pathways in the Context of HIV/AIDS*, AWLAE Series No.4, Wageningen Academic Publishers, Wageningen, The Netherlands

Knodel, K. (2005) 'Researching the impact of the AIDS epidemic on older-age parents in Africa: lessons from studies in Thailand', *Generations Review*, vol 15, no 2, pp16–22.

KwaZulu-Natal Department of Health (2005) KwaZulu-Natal Department of Health Strategic Plan 2005–2009/2010, KwaZulu-Natal Department of Health, Pietermaritzburg, www.kznhealth.gov.za, accessed 4 December 2009

Madhavan, S. and Schatz, E.J. (2007) 'Coping with change: Household structure and composition in rural South Africa, 1992–2003', *Scandinavian Journal of Public Health*, vol 35 (Suppl 69), pp85–93

Montgomery, C.M., Hosegood, V., Busza, J. and Timaeus, I.M. (2006) 'Men's involvement in the South African family: Engendering change in the AIDS era', *Social Science & Medicine*, vol 62, pp2411–2419

Mtshali, S.M. (2002) *Household Livelihood Security in Rural KwaZulu-Natal, South Africa*, PhD Thesis at Wageningen University, Wageningen, The Netherlands

Murphy, L.L., Harvey, P. and Silvestre, E. (2005) 'How do we know what we know about the impacts of Aids on food and livelihood insecurity? A review of empirical research from rural sub-Saharan Africa', *Human Organization*, vol 64, no 3, pp265–275

Naidu, V. and Harris, G. (2005) 'The impact of HIV/AIDS morbidity and mortality on households – a review of household studies', *South African Journal of Economics*, vol 73 (special issue), pp533–544

National Department of Health (2002) *Integrated Community-based Home Care in South Africa – A Review of the Model Implemented by the Hospice Association in South Africa*, Government Publishers, Pretoria

National Department of Health (2007) *National HIV and Syphilis Prevalence Survey South Africa 2006*, Department of Health, Pretoria, www.doh.gov.za, accessed 4 December 2009

National Department of Health (2008) *National HIV and Syphilis Prevalence Survey South Africa 2007*, Department of Health, Pretoria, www.doh.gov.za, accessed 4 December 2009

Niehof, A. (2004) 'A micro-ecological approach to home care for AIDS patients', *Medische Antropologie*, vol 16, no 2, pp245–265

Nombo, C.I. and Niehof, A. (2008) 'Resilience of HIV/AIDS-affected households in a village in Tanzania: Does social capital help?', *Medische Antropologie*, vol 20, no 2, pp241–259

Ogden, J., Esim, S. and Grown, C. (2006) 'Expanding the care continuum for HIV/AIDS: bringing carers into focus', *Health Policy and Planning*, vol 21, no 5, pp333–342

Russell, S. (2004) 'The economic burden of illness for households in developing countries: A review of studies focusing on Malaria, Tuberculosis, and HIV/AIDS', *American Journal of Tropical Medicine and Hygiene*, vol 71, no 2 (supplement), pp147–155

Seeley, J., Biraro, S., Shafer, L.A., Nasirumbi, P., Foster, S., Whitworth, J. and Grosskurth, H. (2008) 'Using in-depth qualitative data to enhance our understanding of quantitative results regarding the impact of HIV and AIDS on households in rural Uganda', *Social Science & Medicine*, vol 67, pp1434–1446

Sen, A. (2008) 'Gender and cooperative conflicts', in Janet D. Momsen (ed) *Gender and Development: Critical Concepts in Development Studies*, Volume I, Theory and Classics, pp. 323–360, Routledge, London, New York

Swaans, K., Broerse, J., Van Diepen I., Salomon, M., Gibson, D. and Bunders, J. (2008) 'Understanding diversity in impact and responses among HIV/AIDS-affected households: The case of Msinga', South Africa, *African Journal of AIDS Research*, vol 7, no 2, pp167–178

Tronto, J.C. (1993) *Moral Boundaries: A Political Argument for an Ethic of Care*, Routledge, New York, London

UNAIDS (2008) *Report on the Global HIV/AIDS Epidemic 2008*, UNAIDS, Geneva, www.unaids.org, accessed 4 December 2009

Uys, L. and Cameron, S. (2003) *Home-based HIV/AIDS Care*, Oxford University Press Southern Africa, Cape Town

Wallace, C. (2002) 'Household strategies: Their conceptual relevance and analytical scope in social research', *Sociology*, vol 36, no 2, pp275–292

WHO (2007) TB and HIV country profile, South Africa, World Health Organisation, Geneva, www.who.org, accessed 4 December 2009.

Wiegers, E.S. (2008) *Gendered Vulnerability to AIDS and its Research Implications*, PhD Thesis at Wageningen University, Wageningen, The Netherlands

Wittenberg, M. and Collinson, M.A. (2007) 'Household transitions in rural South Africa, 1996–2003', *Scandinavian Journal of Public Health*, vol 35(Supplement 69), pp130–137

Young, L. and Ansell, N. (2003) 'Fluid households, complex families: the impacts of children's migration as a response to HIV/AIDS in Southern Africa', *The Professional Geographer*, vol 55, no 4, pp464–476

Chapter 5

Sweet cane, bitter realities: The complex realities of AIDS in Mkamba, Kilombero District, Tanzania

Carolyne I. Nombo

Introduction and background to the study area

It is now well-established that AIDS exacerbates existing social and economic problems. In countries hard-hit by AIDS, the epidemic is now regarded as yet another threat to the sustainability of rural communities much like droughts, floods, unemployment and market volatility. From its very beginning, AIDS has been considered a plague of paradoxes (Setel, 2000) mostly because the epidemic reflects the economic, political and cultural characteristics of society so that vulnerability to HIV infection and AIDS impacts varies from one community to another.

HIV prevalence in Tanzania differs from one location to another depending on the social and economic dynamics at play in the spread of HIV like poverty, gender inequality, population mobility, and lack of access to information and essential services. Consequently, some parts of the country have higher levels of HIV prevalence than others, resulting in large prevalence variations by region and even by district, as shown in Figure 5.1.

The study reported in this chapter was conducted in Mkamba village, Kilombero district, Tanzania (cf. Nombo, 2007) in 2004–2005. The overall aim of the study was to analyse how social change including intensive migration into Mkamba area contributes to susceptibility to HIV (likelihood of HIV infection) and vulnerability to AIDS (lack of capacity to deal with the impact of AIDS) at community and household level. The HIV

HIV prevalence

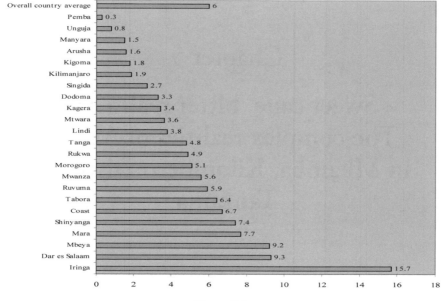

Figure 5.1

Source: TACAIDS et al., 2008

prevalence rate in Kilombero is slightly above the national prevalence rate of 6 per cent.

What causes such differences in prevalence rates? To date, there is little research to help understand the forces that may lead certain communities (villages) or regions to have higher HIV prevalence than others. An effective analysis of both the causes and impacts of high HIV prevalence requires an understanding of contexts of livelihoods and opportunities unique to a given area and/or social group.

The story of Mkamba is intricately intertwined with that of the Kilombero Sugar Company, because the village is situated on the border of the Kilombero sugar estate. For many years, the fortunes or misfortunes of the sugar company have influenced the economy and livelihoods of Mkamba village. Since the late 1990s, Tanzania like many other African countries has adopted privatization, reform measures supported by the World Bank and International Monetary Fund (IMF), which have involved the transfer of all or any of the three kinds of property rights from the state to the private sector: ownership rights, operating rights and development rights (AFRODAD, 2007). Accordingly, ownership of the Kilombero Sugar Company was transferred from the Government of Tanzania to the ILLOVO Sugar Company of Natal, South Africa. The sugar estate occupies 8000 hectares of land. The survey and initial soil test were done in 1957 by experts from The Netherlands. The factory was constructed and started operating in 1960 as a parastatal company under the Sugar Development Corporation (SUDECO). Before privatization in 1998, many Kilombero sugar cane outgrowers lacked the necessary capital, technology and training to take advantage of the improving market. Low capitalization hindered rehabilitation of older farms and the purchase of tools, fertilizers and high-quality cane seed. Inadequate loading services prevented farmers from harvesting and delivering their cane when its sugar content peaks. Poor cane husbandry methods significantly reduced average yields per hectare. These problems have been greatly reduced since ILLOVO purchased the state-owned sugar processing plant and made considerable investments in its rehabilitation. The company's rapid expansion has boosted local demand for raw sugar cane and provided thousands of independent cane outgrowers with new opportunities to expand their production, sales and income. After privatization, more farmers have been attracted to produce sugar cane since the factory offers a reliable market. Sugar-cane outgrowers from 32 groups in Kilombero district, produce cane from about 5203ha, equivalent to 13,007 acres, thereby increasing the area cultivated from 35 per cent in 1997/1998 to 57 per cent in 2003/2004. Sugar cane production from outgrowers increased significantly from 68,000 tons in 2001 to 240,000 tons in 2004.

The company has strengthened the outgrowers cane association (KCGA) responsible for coordinating all the activities pertaining to sugar-cane production and sales in the company as well as defending farmers' interests. The association was established in 1991 with 350 members and its membership has now grown to 2500 members. The company offers extension education and other services such as cane cutting, loading and transport of cane from the field to the factory. The costs related to these services are later deducted from the payments made to the farmers. The existence of the company in the area has stimulated the economy of the area by creating a dependable market for food crops and other items from the adjacent small-scale producers. However, only specific groups such as sugar-cane outgrowers, labourers and a few businessmen, benefited from the privatization; most people had to bear its many costs, such as land shortage and unemployment, at the expense of their overall welfare.

During the peak season (June–December) the sugar cane operations require more labour than is locally available and thus labour is drawn from other regions in the country, mostly Mbeya and Iringa, regions known to have a high HIV prevalence. These regions have traditionally been labour reserves for the industrial agriculture sector of Tanzania. They are also characterized by so-called mobile populations, including traders, migrant labourers and truck drivers. It is well-documented that mobility increases the risk of HIV infection, because the concentration of mostly male migrants potentially increases the demand for commercial sex. Since most of the people in the study area are predominantly poor, engagement in transactional sex is one of the survival strategies (Economic and Social Research Foundation, 2005), and in so doing many are exposed to HIV infection. Once infected, the migrant labourers may spread HIV in their communities of origin. A Tanzanian government study found that migrant farm and plantation workers in Iringa and Morogoro have HIV prevalence rates of about 30 per cent (URT website), which is five times the national average.

Methodology

The research site

Mkamba village is sandwiched between Kilombero Sugar plantations to the east and Udzungwa Mountain National Park to the West, Kidatu village to the South and Kilosa district to the North. Settlements are dense and confined between the foothills of the mountain and the sugar plantation. Though farming employs the majority of the village population, because of its precarious nature, many people have diversified their livelihood portfolios. Most of the inhabitants of Mkamba do not have farming plots near the village; they practice rain-fed farming in land plots very far away from the village. Hence villagers are forced to stay on the farms during the farming season, usually from December to August. In case of a short distance, bicycles are used to go to the fields and to transport farm harvests. The traditional crops produced in distant farms are rice and maize, mostly monocropped. Most cultivation is done manually by hand hoe, using one's own family labour. In the study area a combination of declining farm incomes, increased pressure on land and opportunities created by economic liberalization have given rise to a dynamic informal sector. Mkamba villagers have diversified their livelihood portfolios to include off-farm and non-farm activities.

At the time of the study, the village had a total population of over 12,737 people (Mkamba Village report, 2003). The total area of the village is estimated to be 6.3 square kilometres, resulting in a population density of about 2000 people per square kilometre. The population increases during the sugar cane harvest peak season (May to December) when about 5000 to 6000 casual labourers are recruited from other regions. Though they can live in estate camps, some opt to rent rooms in the village. Other developments such as the establishment of Kidatu hydro-electric power station, partly located in Mkamba village, and the Tanzania and Zambia Railway (TAZARA) line, which passes through the village, have also attracted people to Mkamba. Employment opportunities in sugar-cane estate and in the service sector of the economy as well as easy accessibility to the village have brought people from all corners of Tanzania, resulting in a tremendous population increase and a high degree of ethnic heterogeneity in the village. Most of the incoming population is being squeezed in the limited geographical space. There is no room for extension because the village is surrounded by sugar-cane plantations and protected forest areas.

Research methods

The field-work was conducted in Mkamba village as a case study from August 2004 to July 2005. The study employed a combination of qualitative and quantitative methods. Qualitative methods used included open-ended interviews with key informants, focus group discussions (FGDs) and in-depth interviews with case studies. Nine FGDs were conducted, involving people who represented different groups in the village. The groups were composed of seven to eight people of varied age. There were joint groups as well as separate groups for men and women. Issues discussed included: livelihood, vulnerability, coping with livelihood insecurities, gender differences, social networks and community organisations. The discussions were conducted in Kiswahili. They were all tape-recorded, transcribed and subsequently translated into English for further analysis.

Open-ended interviews were held with key informants, such as government and informal leaders, religious leaders, leaders of community-based organizations in the village, the elderly and influential people in the village, moneylenders, health officers, extension staff and community development workers in order to get general information about the people and situation in the village. The issues explored included: origin of the village, recent history and major events in the village, people's livelihoods in the village, privatization of sugar-cane plantations, social relations and communal activities, witchcraft, AIDS and ways of coping with livelihood insecurities.

For the household survey, from four out of the six hamlets in the village a proportionate sample was drawn, yielding 180 households comprising 903 persons. The households were purposively selected based on AIDS status and household headship, which limits the generalization of the data. Only heads of households were interviewed to provide information on household composition, mortality and morbidity experience, livelihood activities and outcomes, asset ownership, sources of income, household food security, and engagement in mutual exchanges and group activities. The survey was followed up by cases that were purposively selected, based on AIDS status, household headship and economic status for in-depth study.

In-depth interviews with respondents in the case-study households sought to examine perceptions and experiences of households and individuals in coping with insecurities and the challenges of daily life, particularly prolonged illness, death, food insecurity and poverty. A checklist was used to construct life histories in order to examine trends and dynamics related to migration, occupational history, membership in mutual support networks and groups.

Results and discussion

As mentioned earlier, it is not possible to understand the dynamics of AIDS or its impact on livelihoods in Mkamba, without focusing on the Kilombero Sugar Company, particularly in terms of the opportunities and constraints it imposes on Mkamba. Notably the exclusion of people from using company land for farming has been disadvantageous to the majority of Mkamba villagers. As discussed in subsequent sections, most respondents in the study expressed their dissatisfaction with the way privatization has affected their livelihoods and social values.

Land shortage and disruption of smallholder subsistence crop production

Since the Kilombero Sugar Company was privatized, Mkamba has experienced a very high influx of people. It is one of the fastest growing villages in the area, losing its village character and rapidly transforming into a township. This resulted in pressure on available resources, especially land. According to our respondents, before the privatization of the sugar company many households in Mkamba produced food crops on unused company plots. Though legally belonging to the sugar company, local people had access to the land that the company was not utilizing. After privatization, none of the land belonging to the company could be used by the villagers. Even villagers who legally owned plots near the sugar-cane plantation could no longer produce crops other than sugar cane because of the presence of crop vermin like monkeys and rats. Hence, production of crops such as rice, maize and vegetables became difficult; forcing people to resort to utilizing land far away from Mkamba. Farmers who could not get access to virgin land, had to rent plots on a short-term basis at prices of between $11.20 (TShs 15,000/) and $18.5 (Tshs 25,000/) per acre per farming season, which according to the respondents are high prices considering the market value of the produce. Thus the privatization of the Kilombero Sugar Company has meant that men and women of Mkamba have lost access to land. Moreover, the presence of a reliable sugar-cane market has encouraged many people to grow sugar cane at the expense of food crops.

Because of the need to produce food crops as well as other types of commercial crops, the farmers in Mkamba have been compelled to cultivate farm plots located far away from the village and this has come at a price. During the farming period, parents and other adults in households move to the farms, leaving behind school-age children and young ones. Consequently, those left behind get no proper care. They are left with very few resources to live on, leading some of them to seek alternative ways of survival such as engaging in transactional sex. The following case presents an illustration of the problems involved in distant farming, which makes especially young girls susceptible to HIV infection.

Zakia's situation shows how land shortage in the village impacts on household members and increases the vulnerability of children. During the farming season when their parents and other adults go to distant farms, most of the school-going children are left in the village. They have to fend for themselves and when the food situation in the household deteriorates they stop attending school. This case illustrates how distant farming increases a household's vulnerability and jeopardizes the children's future.

Although in other places people may operate farm plots away from their homes, the situation is different for the people of Mkamba. The area is mainly comprised of

Box 5.1 Zakia's story: Left to fend for herself

Zakia is a girl aged 13 years. She lives with her grandmother in Mkamba village. Her parents live in another district with their other six children. Zakia does not want to stay with her immediate family because she can't cope with the farming activities and can't go to school while there. In her grandmother's village she is able to attend a special primary school programme for those who are beyond primary school-age (MEMKWA). She only goes with her grandmother to the distant farm during school holidays. For the past three months her grandmother went back to a distant farm and Zakia was left with about three kilograms of maize flour and about $0.74 (TShs. 1000/) to buy relish to go with the maize meal. She does not know when her grandmother will come back. Zakia's school attendance is sporadic because she goes around peoples' houses in search of housework for food. Usually she is asked to wash the dishes, clean the house or babysit. Although she did not tell me, her neighbour informed me in confidence that she even had to engage in sex in exchange for food. Zakia finally moved from her grandmother's house to a family that took her in as a domestic helper.

migrants who do not necessarily relate well with each other. Hence, those who are left behind when able-bodied people decamp for farming in far-away locations are often left on their own and without family support.

Market monopoly and unemployment

In an environment where there is a single buyer and thousands of suppliers, it is inevitable that monopolistic tendencies arise. This is currently the case at the Kilombero Sugar Company. Despite the fact that the company offers a reliable market, it does not buy more sugar cane from outgrowers once it has reached its production targets. Farmers whose sugar cane is not purchased suffer significant loss. Farmers are forced to sell to the existing sugar mill, because of logistical problems including distances to other sugar mills, the perishable nature of cane and its bulkiness. Another problematic issue is that the majority of the people are employed on a seasonal basis and unemployed for much of the year. In addition, also the employment of those with long-term contracts is dependent on the volatility of the sugar industry. Staff retrenchments are not uncommon. Respondents claimed that the retrenchment policy of the company has caused many people to become unemployed, some of whom are now living in destitute conditions. Many of those who become retrenched are caught by surprise and are unprepared.

Fragility of social cohesion

Increased migration to Mkamba is both an opportunity and a challenge. On the one hand, new arrivals bring in business opportunities and skills. On the other hand, the more multi-ethnic the village becomes the weaker the social fabric and the higher the level of conflict and mistrust. In this subsection, I analyse the implications of migration for social cohesion in Mkamba. Findings of this study reveal that migration has led to tension and conflict among the villagers and that this had a significant impact on the stability of the local community. Lack of mutual support and a proliferation of witchcraft accusations in Mkamba are indicative of a very tenuous state of social cohesion.

Migration imposes further strain on families, which eventually can destroy the family unit (Haour-Knipe, 2008). In Mkamba village, migration has impacted on the way kinship is organized. It has loosened the links between migrants' relatives. Though some kinsfolk may be living in the same area, the kinship support system has been greatly undermined by changing demographic and economic conditions, some of which are due to the privatization of the sugar-cane company. Almost all case-study households revealed that kinship-based arrangements that used to function as a form of social insurance for protection of vulnerable family members have changed. Even though the justification for reciprocal obligations between members of a family is still recognized, implementation is obstructed by economic hardship, self-interest and the general social instability in the village. Informal interviews and focus group discussions revealed that that assistance from kin is nowadays very minimal compared to the past. As one old man said:

'It is not that the sense of brotherhood is dying but the big problem is poor living and economic conditions for many of the families. Life has become very difficult. Even if your relative is sick, you are unable to assist because of lack of income.'

This statement shows that despite the importance of kinship, economic constraints due to various reasons such as climatic problems and increased production costs, privatization and changes in community values have made people more concerned with their immediate family. In the past, food used to be shared among relatives, but as one of the village leaders explained, this is no longer the case:

> 'You know that long ago we used to get plenty of food, but these days, there is harvest decline, we only harvest small amounts of food, which can hardly satisfy one's own family. Thus, the available food is not sufficient. Despite your concern for your relative, it is difficult to offer food assistance. '

Labour exchanges have also declined. Someone's labour is no longer used to secure assistance from kin and neighbours in major undertakings such as harvesting and house construction. Moreover, most of the exchanges are now mediated by cash. Despite the fact that in most informal and formal networks, money contributions have become important, most members have problems getting cash, which limits the support they get from their networks. As a village woman said:

> 'Nowadays people love money more than relatives, if you have no money, then you are nothing. '

Respondents attributed hardship to decrease in agriculture production and changes in economic policies in the country. A lot of them lamented that in the past life was not hard as it is now. One old key informant in the village had this to say:

> 'You know life had changed since *ujamaa* era. Compared with the past, life is very hard now because people cannot even satisfy their basic need for food. And this sugar cane investor has made it even harder by retrenching people from the factory and taking our land.'

The common thread in the statements above is that mutual assistance embedded in kinship groups is functional only when there are resources to share. Once those resources become scarce, people tend to focus inward and to care about survival of themselves only. In Mkamba, the factors that drive such behaviour are many, some external (the economic policy of Tanzania as relates to privatization, hitherto state-controlled enterprises) and some internal (witchcraft beliefs). As already mentioned, the steady inflow of new people in the village has exacerbated the situation.

Ethnic diversity in Mkamba seems to have a negative effect on trust and social interaction. Migration brings in people who are not rooted in the area, who hold different sets of beliefs and who are unlikely, at least in the short-term, to trust the local people or other migrants. Surely, building trust is a process that takes time, but can be hastened and strengthened if there are reputable institutions. Given the weaknesses of institutions of governance in Tanzania in general and Mkamba in particular, it is not surprising that trust among people and institutions is at a low ebb. For example, people interact less frequently with people from other ethnic groups and some women's savings and credit groups dissolved because of ethnic differences in the group (Nombo, 2007). Respondents in the study indicated that overall levels of trust in Mkamba were declining and that for the past ten years or so people had become less trustworthy. In addition to ethnic diversity, economic difficulties also seemed to affect interpersonal trust. There has been a decline in people's incomes due to lack of land in the vicinity, low crop yields and high levels of unemployment. Since many people do not have a reliable means of livelihoods they are not trusted as borrowers and cannot get credit to start a business. Economic hardship, weak institutions and high ethnic diversity were almost always cited as the main reasons for loss of trust and mutual support in the village. This has happened at a critical point when interpersonal trust and reciprocal relations are required to help individuals and households to cope with AIDS and other idiosyncratic shocks.

Witchcraft blame and accusation

Although witchcraft beliefs have probably characterized and modelled social life in Mkamba for centuries, our findings show that these beliefs are now gaining more currency that a few decades ago. As described by an elderly woman respondent, in the past witchcraft accusations were confined among relatives and were easily addressed within the family group. Nowadays, she said anybody can be accused of being a witch and be forced to undergo purification rituals. The following reasons were put forward for the increase in witchcraft accusations in the area. A first one is the growth of the village population and the influx of people from other ethnic groups, allegedly bringing along their own witchcraft techniques. Second, accusations are motivated by jealousy and hatred towards better-off households due to rampant poverty among the people in the area. It was said that economic difficulties as a result of privatization and other socio-economic processes in Mkamba village render people who cannot make ends meet, jealous and hostile towards people who are wealthy. Third, there are many incidences of prolonged illness and deaths for which witchcraft is seen as the main explanation. Diseases such as TB and other prolonged illness have always been seen as witchcraft-induced diseases. To this mix local people have added AIDS. This kind of perception has been observed elsewhere as well (Ashforth, 2001; Sontag, 2001; Allen, 2007).

Deriving from the foregoing discussion, it becomes clear that witchcraft accusations are a form of cultural confrontation and social control. Those who accuse others of witchcraft, gain power over them because the accused, regardless of social or wealth status, are made to undergo degrading cleansing rituals. At worst, the accused may have to leave the area to settle somewhere else. In the end, witchcraft accusations in Mkamba are making people modify their behaviour in ways that would minimize the chances of sparking off suspicion or confrontation. For example, people may not give food gifts for fear of being accused, as stated by a village woman:

> 'Even if I know my neighbours do not have food, I cannot provide them with food for fear of being accused of witchcraft in case a member of that household gets sick, I don't want to be harassed and be taken to the "salon" for shaving.'

Also, relatives accuse each other of witchcraft. For example, during an in-depth interview the woman interviewed claimed that her son, reported to have died of AIDS, was bewitched by her brother. She believed that it is unusual for a person to be sick for so long unless one is bewitched. Although she summoned her brother for cleansing ritual,[1] the son did not get better. Though people claim that the cleansing rituals foster understanding and harmony among people, in the discussions with key informants it transpired that even after being cleansed the relations between accused and accusers are likely to remain strained. Some people I spoke to claimed to have been wrongly accused, but had to go to prove to the community that they were not witches. Especially the newcomers in the area feel humiliated by the ritual. Their relationship with the accuser remains strained, although they keep up appearances. A woman who was once taken for cleansing said:

> 'Do you think I will ever relate well with such kind of person? We agree to go for shaving because people in this area regard it to be a way for reconciliation, so even we newcomers have to live like the natives otherwise you will not live peacefully. It is better to go to prove your innocence.'

Witchcraft accusations are damaging intra-community relations by eroding trust and negatively affecting the viability of social networks.

Full to the brim: Interactions between AIDS, livelihood crises and gender

Beyond the changes brought about by the privatization of Kilombero Sugar Company, Mkamba village is facing many other social and economic problems of which AIDS is the most significant. In this section, I discuss the effects of AIDS on households in Mkamba. Results indicate that AIDS has exacerbated household food insecurity and poverty. Factors such as distant farming, unemployment, poor weather conditions and poor access to markets, all play a part in making life in Mkamba much harder. The AIDS epidemic proved to have wide-ranging implications for the infected individuals and affected households and communities. These are not confined to health status only,

---

[1] A way devised to deal with witchcraft in the area. The accuser and the accused are taken to a specialized place called a 'salon' for cleansing purposes whereby the specialists use a combination of shaving and special medicines to suppress the powers of the witches and protect possible victims against bewitchment.

but extend to the household economy and social organization. The most direct impact of AIDS on households relates to the loss of human capital, which is crucial in pursuing livelihood activities. The impact of AIDS on household labour availability is not only direct but also indirect, because productive time is diverted to taking care of the sick. In the sample of 180 households, 45 households had in total 53 ill young adults who were unable to work. Fifty-three households had experienced the deaths of one or more household members. Though few deaths are attributed to AIDS, one may suspect that many deaths are caused by AIDS-related infections, such as pneumonia and tuberculosis. About 65.2 per cent of all reported deaths were of people in their prime (Nombo, 2007). De Waal and Whiteside (2003) have shown that households that lose young, productive adults are characterized by a high 'effective dependency ratio', implying that, unless able to obtain outside labour, such households are likely to experience labour shortages. Consequently, they cannot produce enough food or earn enough income to meet household needs.

The following case illustrates how chronic illnesses of one or more household members not only reduce food production, but also the household's capacity to generate income to purchase food.

The cumulative impacts of prolonged illness on food production and food access have adverse effects on overall household food security, as is illustrated by Mama Zalima's case (Box 5.2). In the study, affected households reported lack of adequate food and income to buy food as major problems. Such households do not have labour and cash resources for their own food production and cannot purchase enough food because of

---

Box 5.2 Mama Zalima: AIDS-affected,
FOOD INSECURE

Mama Zalima lives with her sister and two children (11) and (8) in a single room. They both came to the village in 1995. Mama Zalima's husband, who worked as a seasonal labourer in sugar plantations, left her and went back to Iringa in 2001. Mama Zalima has a rice plot in a distant farm, but she also sells local brew in the village. Mama Zalima's sister has been suffering from tuberculosis for the past two years. Because of this they could not work in their distant farming plot. Moreover, due to lack of money, Mama Zalima cannot afford to hire people to work on their plot. At the time of interview they had no food stocks left and were buying food from the shops. 'It is not easy to have food stocks for the whole year with all these problems', Mama Zalima says. During her sister's illness she sold six bags of rice to cover for the medical expenses. Mama Zalima could not even engage in income-generating activities and did not get any significant support from her family in Dodoma. Mama Zalima says: 'Our life is miserable but we survive.' Her sister's illness has made her bankrupt and she will have to start all over again. She says, 'Our life will never be the same; imagine, my sister used to do her own business and contribute to household income but now she entirely relies on me.' Many times the family skips meals when Mama Zalima is unable to get food loans from the shops, where she still has debts to pay.

their declining income. The resources needed for food production are severely eroded for households with an individual living with HIV. Especially distant farming becomes difficult for households with sick people. For poor households, use of hired labour is not feasible. When household income is reduced, without any external financial assistance, food intake of the household members will decline. Reduced food intake may also affect the health of non-affected members. The impacts of AIDS on food security observed in this study are similar to what has been reported in other African studies (Loevinsohn and Gillespie, 2003; Wiegers et al., 2006).

The presence of an individual living with HIV in the household creates a financial burden as a result of the direct costs of care and treatment, and indirect costs because of the decline of regular income due to care-giving responsibilities. Households caring for a person with HIV and those who experienced deaths due to AIDS recalled spending between $2.2 (TShs 3000) and $296.6 (Tshs 400,000) per month on medical expenses with an average of $20.3 (TShs 27,186) per month (Nombo, 2007). This is more than the rural Tanzanian average $8.3 (TShs. 11,156) (URT, 2002). During the Focus Group Discussions it became apparent that due to widespread poverty most of the households do not have sufficient income to cater for medical expenses and invest in income-generating activities, which applies especially to households affected by AIDS. Households caring for a person living with HIV have little active labour, cash and time to invest in those activities. Farming depends on household labour and often labour demands are concentrated in specific periods of the year. In case of sickness, most of the farm operations cannot be done on time, which causes poor harvests. Livestock-keeping is also affected because households are forced to sell the animals to meet medical costs. Some households in the study sold pigs, goats and chickens to meet medical and funeral expenses. Affected households were found to have few alternatives to supplement or replenish the low income. Respondents from such households reported using their own savings to pay the costs of medical treatment and funerals, in the end resorting to selling assets such as furniture, a radio, bicycles and livestock. Other households sold food stocks, thereby endangering their food security. Food insecurity may force individuals to adopt livelihood strategies that increase their vulnerability to HIV. In this situation women are more at risk, because they are held responsible for ensuring there is enough food in the household.

This study demonstrates that when a household faces morbidity and mortality due to AIDS, it changes its livelihood activities to adapt to the changing labour demands and declining resources. Most of the affected households withdrew from distant farming and resorted to home-based small-scale activities such as petty trade and gardening, which generally did not yield enough to sustain their livelihoods. Most of the income-generating activities in the area were constrained by the lack of capital and low local purchasing power. A household's ability to offset the impacts of AIDS depends on its assets-base, its capacity to reorganize household resources, and its access to the resources of the extended family. The severity of the impacts is likely to vary according to the economic status of the household, with poorer households suffering more than better-off households. The latter are better able to deal with AIDS effects than poor households, who sometimes have to adopt responses that threaten their livelihood. Since most of the households in the village are already vulnerable due to privatization and other forces, the AIDS epidemic can have devastating effects, because it affects the key assets households need for generating a livelihood and an ability to respond. High levels of morbidity and mortality significantly alter household composition, asset portfolios and livelihood activities. The direct loss of human capital and the diversion of resources and income to caring activities are having a critical impact on livelihood activities on which households depend for securing food and income. Generally, AIDS-affected households require more resources to meet the increasing demands while their production capacity is reduced.

Evidence from this study indicates that the impacts of AIDS are more critical for women than men. Socio-economic factors and cultural values place men in a more favourable position to cope with the impacts. In their roles as mothers and care providers, women are mainly responsible for taking care of individuals living with HIV in the home and for fostering children orphaned by AIDS, in addition to other productive and domestic tasks. Although men do help, women bear the brunt of nursing sick household members. AIDS increases women's workload as they are forced to pursue both productive activities and meet the increasing care demands. As Mama Zalima's case (Box 5.2), shows, when women fall ill they are likely to be abandoned by their partners, while still having to look after children and not receiving the care they need. Caregiving falls disproportionately on women, especially elderly women, who have to do so with minimal resources. Caregivers are at risk of getting infected themselves, because of lack of knowledge about caring for HIV-positive individuals and lack of cash to buy protective gloves. Increased care demands leave women prone to economic insecurity, which may drive them to engage in risky sexual behaviour.

Does social capital help?

In the context of this study, the concept of social capital is used to describe activities in everyday life which involve participation in social networks to meet individual and household needs and the associated norms and values that underlie these networks. The study applies the concept both in terms of its structural aspects (social relations and networks) and its cognitive dimension (trust). Although the family is assumed to be the primary social network for providing care and support to HIV-infected people and others affected by the epidemic, it was found that families are facing increasing social, economic and emotional pressure arising from AIDS and poverty, which affects their coping abilities. The empirical evidence from this study suggests that the social and economic effects of migration and privatization have affected the ability and willingness of extended family members to assist those experiencing AIDS' impacts. Additionally, increased demands for support as a result of the prolonged and unpredictable nature of AIDS-induced illnesses have reduced the extent to which relatives can help each other. It does appear that AIDS is exerting new pressures on many families, who increasingly find it difficult to cope.

AIDS' impacts and other economic stresses influence relationship in the community. Since continual interaction is based on give and take, AIDS-affected and other poor households are unlikely to be able to maintain this exchange. It was explicitly stated by one woman participant during a focus group discussion who reported that:

'No one will be willing to assist someone from January to December knowing that this person will not be able to reciprocate.'

In Mkamba, support networks to deal with AIDS impacts did not evolve. No new groups were formed to deal with this problem. Most of the community groups in the area were established for other purposes, which might indirectly benefit AIDS-affected individuals, but AIDS was not part of their objectives and activities. The assistance by community groups is generally limited and short-term in nature. For example, in the case of sickness, members are entitled to assistance only once. In the event of death, the duration of support is usually limited to the funeral and burial activities. Generally, assistance was not extended to vulnerable and AIDS-affected households faced with prolonged sickness, lack of labour and food insecurity. Such problems, which could have attracted community support, were regarded to be family responsibilities. It was regularly stated that the community was unable to attend to the numerous needs of its members because of poverty and because assistance to those with prolonged illness would require aid for an extended period of time.

Because of widespread poverty in the village, families are often too burdened with their own problems to be of much help to others. Some periods of the year are worse than others for getting assistance. In the focus group discussions it was reported that during the rainy season, known as *masika*, people are fully engaged in farming, but this is also the time when most households experience food insecurity and low income. For the villagers, the term *masika* connotes hardship. In their study in South Africa, Carter and Maluccio (2003) also found that the capacity to cope is weakened in communities that suffer covariant shocks that overwhelm the local social coping mechanisms. Community support is no longer effective to meet the multitude of needs resulting from the AIDS epidemic and other socio-economic problems in the area. Economic stress and hardship seem to affect the community in two nearly opposite ways. As individuals and households struggle to make ends meet, they have little time for other people and communal concerns. People's preoccupation with everyday life activities is dominated by 'getting by'. Many households under stress need material and practical support but such support is not readily available. One of the women during the focus group discussion said:

'Who is there to give you food and money these days? Everyone has to strive for her or his own family'

Another woman commented on the matter by saying that:

'Even if you have friends, it is just "on the mouth". We cannot help each other because our circumstances are the same.'

Vulnerability in the wake of AIDS can foster collective responses among community members, which in turn foster personal empowerment and social change (Haddad and Gillespie, 2001). The epidemic has shown to trigger community responses to help those directly affected (Nnko et al., 2000; Baylies, 2002). In this study, it was assumed that people's realization of sharing the same hardships would motivate collective action to mitigate the problems, but the findings proved otherwise. There was very little community-level mobilization around AIDS' issues related to care and support to those directly affected (Nombo and Niehof, 2008). Although there are several local groups and associations, people in Mkamba so far have not come up with collective initiatives to mitigate AIDS impacts at the community level.

The Mkamba case clearly illustrates how the socio-economic context shapes the dynamics of HIV transmission, as well as the impacts of responses to AIDS. Mkamba village is affected by overlapping and interacting vulnerabilities, among them privatization. The privatization of the Sugar Cane Company created employment opportunities and attracted migrants to Mkamba. Though offering new economic opportunities, privatization also contributed to the impoverishment of the Mkamba community. Generally, the living conditions of many villagers did not improve as a result of the privatization. While there are individuals who have become successful as sugar-cane outgrowers and traders, many more are constantly struggling to survive.The new social environment, in which both migrants and indigenous people live, seems to lack strong community cohesion, rendering people unable to mitigate the impacts of AIDS. High ethnic diversity in the village as a result of in-migration was found to impede trust among the villagers and led to increased tensions. This has contributed to the proliferation of witchcraft suspicions and accusations among community members, thus negatively affecting interpersonal relationships.

Conclusion

Most AIDS' policies are primarily concerned with individual factors associated with the spread and prevention of HIV as well as coping with the impacts of AIDS. Results reported in this chapter highlight the interaction between AIDS and the social and economic context. While AIDS is commonly understood to be a public health problem, this chapter shows that both its causes and consequences are deeply embedded in the social, economic and political processes that shape local communities.

There are factors other than characteristics of individuals that influence vulnerability to HIV and AIDS. Among those, Tanzania's privatization policy seems to have contributed to rising levels of HIV infection and the inability of affected households to cope with AIDS' impacts, because it undermined household subsistence economies, increased migration and put a strain on community cohesion. The message emerging from this discussion is that AIDS' policies and interventions that target behaviour change of individual agents without due regard for the social and economic context in which their behaviour is shaped will produce little result. Therefore, when assessing vulnerability to HIV and AIDS also when designing community-based prevention and mitigation interventions, it is important to take into account the history of the community concerned and its distinctive features. Policy and programme interventions that aim at improving both social and economic environments are necessary to empower community members to protect themselves against HIV and be able to cope with AIDS' impacts.

References

AFRODAD (2007) *Tanzania's Experience with Privatisation Policies. A Case Study*, African Forum and Network on Debt and Development, Harare, Zimbambe

Allen, T. (2007) 'Witchcraft, sexuality and HIV/AIDS among the Azade of Sudan', *Journal of Eastern African Studies*, vol 1, pp359–396

Ashforth, A. (2001) AIDS, Witchcraft, and the problem of power in post-Apartheid South Africa. *The Occasional Papers Number 10* of the School of Social Science, Institute of Advanced Study Princeton University, Princeton, USA

Baylies, C. (2002) 'The impacts of AIDS on rural households in Africa: A shock like any other?' *Development and Change*, vol 33, no 4, pp611–632

Carter, M.R. and Maluccio, J. A. (2003) 'Social capital and coping with economic shocks: An analysis of stunting of South African children', *World Development*, vol 31 no 7, pp1147–1163

De Waal, A. and Whiteside, A. (2003) 'New Variant Famine: AIDS and Food Crisis in Southern Africa', *The Lancet* 362(9391), pp1234–1237

Economic and Social Research Foundation (2005) *The Impacts of HIV/AIDS on Agriculture: The Case of Kilombero and Ulanga District*. A report submitted to EZCORE, ESRF, Ilonga Kilosa, Tanzania

Haddad, L. and Gillespie, S. (2001) 'Effective food and nutritional policy responses to HIV/AIDS: What we know and what we need to know', *Journal of International Development*, vol 13, pp487–511

Haour-Knipe, M. (2008) *Dreams and Disappointments: Migration and Families in the Context of HIV/AIDS*. Joint Learning Initiative on Children and HIV/AIDS, JLICA, Switzerland

Loevinsohn, M., and Gillespie, S. (2003) HIV/AIDS, food security and rural livelihoods: Understanding and responding. Regional Network on HIV/AIDS, Rural Livelihoods and Food Security *Working Paper no. 2*, RENEWAL, Washington DC

Mkamba Village report (2003)

Morogoro Regional Hospital (2009) *Annual Comprehensive Council Health Plans: Annual Implementation Report 2008/09*, Morogoro, Tanzania.

Nnko, S. B., Chiduo, F. Wilson, W. Msuta and Mwaluko, G. (2000) 'Tanzania: AIDS Care – learning from experience', *Review of African Political Economy*, vol 86, pp547–557

Nombo, C. (2007) *When AIDS Meets Poverty: Implications for Social Capital in a Village in Tanzania*, AWLAE Series No 5. Wageningen Academic Publishers, Wageningen, The Netherlands

Nombo, C. and Niehof, A. (2008) 'Resilience of HIV/AIDS-affected households in a village in Tanzania: Does social capital help?', *Medische Antropologie*, vol 20, no 2, pp241–253

Setel, P.W. (2000) *Plague of Paradoxes: AIDS, Culture and Demography in Northern Tanzania (Worlds of Desire)*, The Chicago Series on Sexuality, Gender and Culture, University of Chicago Press, Chicago, USA

Sontag, S. (2001) *Illness as Metaphor and AIDS and its Metaphors*, Picador, New York

Tanzania Commission for AIDS (TACAIDS), Zanzibar AIDS Commission (ZAC) National Bureau of Statistics (NBS), Office of Chief Government Statistician (OCGS) and Macro International Inc (2008), *Tanzania HIV/AIDS and Malaria Indicator Survey 2007–08*, TACAIDS etc., Dar es Salaam, Tanzania

United Republic of Tanzania (2002) *Tanzania Household Budget Survey*, National Bureau of Statistics (NBS), Dar es Salam, Tanzania

United Republic of Tanzania (2009) www.tanzania.go.tz/hiv_aidsf.html, accessed 23 November 2009

Wiegers, E., Curry, J., Garbero, A. and Hourihan, J. (2006) 'Patterns of vulnerability of AIDS impacts in Zambian Households', *Development and Change*, vol 37, no 3, pp1073–1092

Chapter 6

Single women's experiences of livelihood conditions, HIV and AIDS in the rural areas of Zimbabwe

Gaynor Gamuchirai Paradza

Introduction

Although a lot has been written about the impact of AIDS on rural livelihoods, there has been little focus on how women on their own in rural areas of Africa adapt and cope with the knock-on effects of the HIV pandemic and economic challenges. In Zimbabwe, impacts of the HIV epidemic have intersected with economic deterioration and politically volatile conditions to the detriment of the majority of the population who live in rural areas. This study was designed to answer the question of how single women living in the communal areas of Zimbabwe experience these impacts and the macro-economic changes.

Zimbabwe had an estimated 34 per cent HIV infection rate in 2002 (UNDP, 2004a, p 11). The 20–49-year age group accounted for more than 70 per cent of the infected. The death of these economically active people increased dependency ratios as mostly the elderly and children were spared from the epidemic (UNAIDS, 2003). In 2005, 28 per cent of the infected lived in urban areas and the rest lived in rural areas, which included communal areas, commercial farms, growth points, army camps and mining areas. The commercial farms, army camps, mining areas and growth points contained 10 per cent of the population but had a 35 per cent HIV prevalence rate (MOH, 2004; UNDP, 2004b). In addition to the increasing numbers of single women, higher death rates led to increased accusations and preoccupations with witchcraft (Drinkwater, 2003). Widows and women who have lost children are more vulnerable to witchcraft accusations (Schmidt, 1992; Vijfhuizen, 2002).

Zimbabwean rural areas bear the larger burden of the epidemic's morbidity because ill people generally return to the communal areas where life is cheaper and the immediate and extended family can provide care (Mutangadura, 2000; Andersson, 2002). The reduced capacity of the Zimbabwean government to provide healthcare has increased dependence on home-based care for AIDS' patients. Although home-based care has many benefits, it has increased the burden of women who are the majority of the caregivers of the afflicted (Jackson and Kerkhoven, 1995; Hansen et al., 1998). Thus, women living on their own, not only have to secure their livelihoods without men, but are also bearing an increasing burden of care imposed by the pandemic and the regressing economy. The chapter shows, through a series of life histories, the pathways followed by single women as they piece together different kinds of resources to confront (not always successfully) the insecurities of HIV and AIDS, land and livelihood in rural Zimbabwe. It shows that over time the livelihoods of single women hearth-holds have become more vulnerable, although this should not be exclusively attributed to the epidemic. Any attempt to understand the vulnerability of single women should address women's land rights and other fundamental linkages.

Existing studies on the impacts of HIV and AIDS on rural livelihoods and women in rural areas of Africa look at the end of women's marital relationships, through death of the male spouse or divorce. There is a dearth of published research that interrogates the cumulative impact of the various factors on the livelihoods of single women in rural areas beyond the end of the marriage. This chapter focuses on single women in communal areas because they are an increasing proportion of domestic units. The number of single women has been growing because of changes in marital legislation, but also because of women's economic independence following the attainment of the country's independence and the subsequent economic recession that undermined men's ability to marry and sustain families (Scoones et al., 1996; Goebel, 2005). Other factors are Christianity, which affected the institution of marriage by inducing a decline in polygamous marriages, and – in several ways – the AIDS' epidemic. Under the threat of AIDS, women leave their husbands when their behaviour threatens the lives of the rest of the family (Kinsey cited in IFPRI, 1995). The initial gender asymmetry in HIV disease progression led to an increase of single women, as adult male deaths outnumbered female deaths (Gregson et al., 1997; UNAIDS, 1998). The epidemic has also increased the numbers of single women because men are reluctant to marry women whose spouses are suspected to have died from the disease (Muzvidziwa, 2002; Vijfhuizen, 2002). As a result, adult women who do not form an economic unit with a man have become an important category in communal farming areas. These women fall outside the dominant discourse of gendered resource access.

The analysis draws from the life histories of 22 women heads of hearth-holds. In order to place single women in focus, the hearth-hold is used as a unit of analysis (Ekejiuba, 1995). The study was conducted in 2004/2005 in a communal farming area in Zimbabwe. The communal areas are customary tenure areas created by the colonial government to function as a labour reserve. Their internal governance resembles other patrilineal indigenous tenure systems in the world where property and authority are vested in the male head (May, 1983). Although the selling of communal area land is illegal in Zimbabwe (Pankhurst, 1991; Nyambara, 2001a), market transactions in communal area land frequently take place. The governance of resources within the villages remains unclear because of the differential interpretation and application of rules by the various administrators and the specific conditions in each communal area.

Zimbabwean communal areas have been undergoing rapid changes as a result of land redistribution policies (Goebel, 2005; Hartnack, 2005), structural adjustment programmes and economic meltdown (Kanji, 1995), 'Operation Restore Order' (1) (Action Aid International, 2005; UNAIDS, 2005), and HIV/AIDS. This has resulted in the loss of employment opportunities, high population mobility, increased demand for land in communal areas, changing rural–urban resource flows, the destabilization of communal area livelihoods and general uncertainty.

The research context and clarification of concepts

The research focused on 22 single women in the villages of Wasara and Kura in Chikwaka communal area. The site's location offered opportunities to explore the impacts on the communal area of economic change and the influence of factors such as, proximity to the city and growth point, HIV, and commercial farming on local livelihoods. The two villages differ in size, organization, resource access and leadership style, community activity, origin of inhabitants and extent of the informal land market, all significant in shaping hearth-hold vulnerability. To identify homesteads that were hosting single women-headed hearth-holds an inventory of all households was conducted in each village. Twenty-two single women who were divorced, widowed or never married, were selected for the in-depth study. The selected hearth-holds reflect diversity in age, marital status and area of origin of the women, and size and socio-economic status of the unit. The hearth-holds became the subjects of a 12-month in-depth study that comprised life histories, observation and pathway analysis, triangulated with data collected through focus group discussions with village heads.

Wasara is a much larger village than Kura in terms of population and size and has a more heterogeneous population. Wasara continued to grow because of the flourishing illegal land market. It had 68 homesteads at the beginning and more than 90 homesteads at the end of the research period. Kura village with 15 homesteads was much smaller. The Kura village head discouraged selling of land in his village and strictly controlled in-migration. As a result, the population is smaller, has more generous land holdings and is generally more cohesive than Wasara. People gain membership into Kura through birthright and marriage, while in Wasara through kinship, the market, employment and self-allocation. The different village governance systems influenced the way in which single women experienced vulnerability.

The research area has a high HIV prevalence. HIV and AIDS are very sensitive and stigmatized subjects. In this chapter, illness was selected as a distinctive term to also include AIDS-related illnesses. I did not distinguish between AIDS-related illnesses and non-AIDS-related illnesses because what counts are the effects and consequences of illness on livelihoods for choice of strategies.

The hearth-hold refers to a female-directed social unit of consumption and production that is structured on the mother–child bond. It can be independent or interlinked in a household. Female-directed hearth-holds rise out of leviratic unions, intergenerational households of parents and their children, and brothers and their divorced or widowed sisters. A hearth-hold cannot be destabilized by divorce, widowhood or non-marriage. The use of hearth-hold as a unit of analysis enables us to see women as active, often independent, actors who shoulder responsibilities, take risks, strive to maximize livelihood options, to the benefit of their dependents (Ekejiuba,1995, p60). A focus on the hearth-hold facilitates the understanding of the roles of male and female adults better than using the concept of household, because the neoclassical definition of the household assumes a conjugal relationship and a male head unless otherwise stated, which ill fits the African context (Ekejiuba, 1995; Peters, 1995). The household focus on headship renders invisible those single women maintaining families and residing in larger households, such as young single mothers residing in larger families and older un-married women living in households conventionally regarded as male-headed (Varley, 1996; Buvinic and Gupta, 1997).

Research findings

In order to understand the livelihood trajectories of single women, their livelihood portfolios were analysed. The portfolios consist of activities that hearth-holds engage in to secure their livelihoods. The activities comprise reproductive and productive activities, including bearing and raising children, producing and preparing food, and maintaining the home. In order for women to access the village, they had to be recognized as a member. Membership of a village enables women to access land on which to construct a dwelling and/or farm and provides a form of insurance against risks and threats (Scoones et al., 1996, Huisman, 2005, p260). Single women gain access to residence in the patriarchal communal area through kinship, purchasing land on the market, as employees and through using land and homesteads left vacant owing to the high mobility of communal area residents. Once women have secured village membership, they use it as a base from which to negotiate access to other livelihood resources, like land, labour, markets, obligations, assistance and state resources. The pathways of the hearth-holds show that for single women heads of hearth-holds village membership was contingent upon factors that included marital status, age, child-bearing status, child-bearing status, rank and access to non-agricultural income. In the situation of prevailing uncertainty hearth-holds were constantly renegotiating their village membership.

The fast-changing situation in communal areas of Zimbabwe has significantly altered the reproductive responsibilities of hearth-holds. There is a shift from a general trend where women's childcare obligations decline as the children grow older to a situation where hearth-holds are fostering minors whose parents have died or migrated out of the villages. Hearth-holds are also assuming primary care responsibilities for adult children. Some of the single women hearth-holds in the sample lived as dependents in other people's homesteads. Table 1 illustrates the various circumstances leading to the presence of adult children in a hearth-hold. Though hearth-holds are responsible for both young and adult children, the table focuses on the adult children as they have largely been underreported in research that focuses on women's burden of care. The table shows that both young and elderly heads of hearth-holds are caring for adult children. The adult children, aged between 26 and 40, had failed to leave the parental home or moved back into their single mother's residence because of marital breakdown, illness and unemployment. The table also shows that single women hearth-holds have to support children who are employed when their wages are inadequate to set up their own

Table 6.1 *Responsibilities of single women to adult children*

Mother's age and marital status	Adult child's problem	Status of adult child's own household	Estimated length of adult child's dependency
Elderly widow	Ill married daughter (28 years old)	Intact but needs assistance when ill	Whenever the daughter fell ill
	Ill adult son (38 years old)	Dissolved by 'operation restore order' and illness	Ended when he died
	Adult son unmarried (26 years old)	Lost after 'operation restore order'	Indeterminate
Younger divorcee	Divorced daughter (36 years old)	Dissolved	Indeterminate
Elderly widow	Employed son (34 years old)	Lives in work-tied housing	Fallback Life term
	Widowed son (wife was ill) (32 years old)	Dissolved	Indeterminate
Elderly widow	Widowed and divorced daughter whose spouse succumbed to illness (26 years old)	Dissolved: living at growth point	Indeterminate
	Divorced displaced daughter	Dissolved	Indeterminate
Elderly widow	Divorced son who moved back to mother's homestead	Dissolved	
			Indeterminate
Elderly widow	Adult unmarried son	Delayed departure	
Elderly widow	Unemployed married son who has not developed his own homestead	Intact: residing in urban immovable property of the mother	Indeterminate

Source: Fieldwork 2005

homesteads. The table highlights the incidence of marital breakdown due to economic hardship and AIDS-induced illness and mortality. The age cohort of these dependent children shows that they are potentially the most economically active and reproductive group. Their returning to their mother's care represents a loss of remittances for the hearth-hold, an important source of non-agricultural income.

The single women hearth-hold heads are the main providers and decision-makers. The high incidence of opportunistic illnesses among the adult children indicates high HIV prevalence. Some of the adult children who returned to their mother's care also brought a dependent grandchild. The adult children's indeterminate stay could well extend to the duration of the adult child's life. This depends on whether the children remarry and/or manage to secure employment opportunities. Even then, these adult children would only be able to move out of their mother's homestead when they have acquired adequate resources to sustain themselves. This is not easy in an economy where employment opportunities are contracting. The implications of the continued stay of adult children in a hearth-hold's care for the hearth-holds' community membership and livelihood portfolio options and choices of the hearth-hold will be explored in the case studies.

Hearth-holds engage in productive activities to secure food and other basic necessities. Traditionally, rural women relied heavily on agricultural production for subsistence and traded the surplus for other commodities. A hearth-hold's capacity to engage in agriculture used to depend on its ability to secure non-agricultural income for purchasing fertilizer and seed, and hiring labour and draft power. Women secured this income from the wages remitted by their husbands. The decline in marriage, however, negated the reliance of hearth-holds on this institution for income. The hearth-holds increasingly rely on the government, non-governmental organizations and other sources of assistance. Fourteen of the 22 hearth-holds engaged in agricultural production. The case studies illustrate how the combined effects of HIV and AIDS, economic hardship and changing reproductive responsibilities affect the capacities of hearth-holds to engage in agricultural production.

Hearth-hold pathways: typologies of hearth-holds

An examination of the individual women's pathways allows us to illustrate diversity in impact on hearth-holds of a rapidly changing environment. The pathways illustrate the variation in resources, contingency and agency of the single women. An attempt to draw generalizations from the matrix of pathways revealed some common characteristics, which are represented in Table 2. The typology divides hearth-holds into five groups according to their position on a continuum. These ranged from group I, hearth-holds that diversified into accumulation, to group V, hearth-holds that failed to construct viable livelihoods and succumbed to the shocks. The criteria used to stratify the hearth-holds were the viability of their livelihoods, livelihood portfolios, and the capacity of the individual hearth-holds to sustain an independent homestead. The typologies are not fixed. Though generally hearth-holds gradually slipped downwards as they struggled with the increasingly difficult conditions, some progressed to less vulnerable categories with time. Age is important because it relates to experience, accumulation of assets, and possible assistance from children. Women's relationship to the village head was also an important asset for their hearth-holds in negotiating access to other livelihood capitals in the village.

Hearth-holds type I: diversification into accumulation

Type I hearth-holds all headed and controlled independent, well-maintained home-steads. Over time all the hearth-holds had successfully diversified into non-agricultural activities, which reduced their vulnerability to agricultural failure and secured their access to non-agricultural income. They had diverse non-agricultural income sources in their portfolios. The minimum age of the hearth-hold head in this category was 50, meaning that the women had acquired experience and accumulated assets, and that most likely their children had grown and left the house. All single women heads in this category were relatively healthy and were not hosting ill adults. Though some of the hearth-holds had lost family members to AIDS, the accumulated asset base had enabled them to weather the setback. The hearth-holds in category I formed the core of the successful agricultural producers. They were able to mobilize agricultural inputs for their

Table 6.2 *Differentiation of single women hearth-holds*

Characteristics	Assets	Portfolio
CATEGORY I: HEARTH-HOLDS: DIVERSIFICATION INTO ACCUMULATION (4 hearth-holds) Independent, well-maintained homestead, able to save and invest surplus		
Mean age of head 66 No longer child-bearing Single for at least ten years Adult children Healthy No AIDS-related burden	Healthy head Independent, well-maintained homestead Agricultural land Co-resident with family members (labour) livestock Owned agricultural inputs (draught, seed, labour), livestock Kinship, Social networks	Diverse viable activities, Regular receipts of non-agricultural income Surplus agricultural production requirements High capital-high return activities (livestock, pig rearing, beer brewing construction, cross-border trading, pottery) Land baroness
CATEGORY II: HEARTH-HOLDS AT RISK (3 hearth-holds) Independent homesteads. Did not accumulate but get enough to sustain their hearth-holds and meet immediate needs.		
Mean age of head 59 No longer child-bearing Small resident population (max two residents) Healthy Cannot afford to pay for medical care No burden of caring for ill and/or young children	Healthy individuals Independent, poorly maintained homestead Own labour, community, arable land, Social networks	Erratic remittances High reliance on transfers from government and non-governmental agencies for agricultural inputs increases risk of agricultural failure Manage risk by trading their labour in exchange for food and agricultural inputs Depend on NGO activities Pottery, beer brewing, healing
CATEGORY III: VULNERABLE (7 hearth-holds) Independent homesteads poorly maintained who lack resources to sustain livelihoods and rely heavily on transfers		
Mean age of head 54 Child-bearing and post-child-bearing Hosting ill adult and/or young children Cannot afford medical care Losing assets over time	Independent homestead, poorly maintained, Arable land Community membership Heavy burden of care reduces capacity to pursue livelihood activities	Cannot produce subsistence, even if they receive all agricultural inputs on time Rely on transfers and charity (family, church, state) Illegal trading of poached natural produce Commercial farm work
CATEGORY IV: DEPENDENT VULNERABLE HEARTH-HOLDS (7 hearth-holds) Hearth-holds embedded in other people's homesteads lack resources to negotiate access to independent homestead		
Mean age of head 31 Child-bearing and/or ill Dependent children Hearth-hold split between two residences	Lack independent homestead Labour and sometimes Social networks Not accumulating assets to buffer hearth-holds in the short-term	Lack resources to negotiate access to independent homestead High reliance on host (parents, family) Experimental trading; irregular, erratic, low income; high risk-low return activities
CATEGORY V: SUCCUMBED HEARTH-HOLDS (1 hearth-hold) Wholly dependent for food, shelter and care		
Head 32-year old All members ill Dead, dissolved	Kinship support	

Source: Author's Fieldwork 2004/2005

hearth-holds well before the onset of the rains and could produce surplus from their agricultural activities. They had stopped marketing their agricultural surplus, using it instead as a buffer and for negotiating access to labour and other resources. They hired labour from the poorer hearth-holds. The women were able to accumulate some savings, as shown by the capital intensive investments they made. Diversification provided a buffer against short-, medium- and long-term risks. However, the portfolios remained vulnerable in different ways. Riba's story illustrates some of these.

Case 1: Riba: Consolidating a livelihood through opportunistic decision making

Riba was 70 years old in 2005 and the mother of the Wasara village head. She lived with a 36-year-old daughter who had six children. Riba's other children worked and lived in the urban areas and sent her remittances. Riba had two employees aged 11 and 14, who were possibly children orphaned by AIDS. She had a cow, six pigs and some chickens. Riba had a large piece of arable land and had accumulated more by assuming control of land belonging to her sons who had migrated out of the village. She let out some of this land to immigrants in exchange for grain. In 2005, Riba completed the construction of a three-bedroom house and repaired the roof of her thatched kitchen. Riba's husband had lived in town, while she lived in the rural areas and farmed. When her husband died, Riba continued to live in Wasara village. She inherited a house in Harare and the homestead in Wasara. By combining the rental income from the urban property, her deceased husband's pension and proceeds from her pottery and agricultural activities, Riba managed to educate all her children. In 2001, Riba temporarily abandoned her homestead after she was accused of witchcraft following the death of one of her grandchildren. Riba disposed of her livestock and returned to her village of birth, where she lived for two years. She returned to Wasara to take care of her 22-year-old son who was suffering from tuberculosis and chest pains. Riba's son died in 2003. In 2004, Riba disposed of some of her land on the informal land market and used the proceeds to invest in a pig-rearing venture. She purchased all her agricultural seed and fertilizer from the market and hired labour. When the government issued free seed and fertilizer, Riba collected her allocation but put it away for the following year as it was delivered late. She hired extra labour to maintain her homestead and complement her agricultural labour. Riba manufactured clay pots after harvesting her agricultural produce. There was a high demand for the pots from the local village as the Apostolic Church insisted that its members keep 'holy water' blessed by the prophet on their domestic premises to protect them against (HIV/AIDS induced) illnesses, deaths and job losses. The members were encouraged to store the water in clay pots. Riba usually bartered pottery for grain. In the 2004/2005 season she harvested a surplus. She bought more grain on the market, however, to insure her hearth-hold against another drought. One of her sons moved into the urban house after Operation Restore Order, depriving Riba of the rental income from the house.

Riba's life story tells of a hearth-hold that over time has consolidated its position and survived major losses, temporary relocation following the witchcraft allegations, and a heavy load of caring for adult children. Riba's portfolio was robust enough to withstand the AIDS-related death of an adult son, loss of rent of an urban property, the burden of caring for dependent adult children and the loss of remittances due to the continued stay of these adult children in her care. She had accumulated enough assets to tide her over these successive setbacks. Riba's highly diversified portfolio provided a buffer against declining returns to agriculture and the deteriorating economic conditions. Her residence in Wasara and her position as mother of the village head enabled her to accumulate land. Although she suffered a setback when she had to abandon her homestead, she was able to rebuild her livelihood when she returned because of her monopoly of the pottery market and her accumulated land interests. The portfolio of the hearth-hold shows that the unit was accumulating assets and diversifying away from risky activities.

Case 2: Matty: immigrant widow consolidating a successful homestead

At the time of the research, Matty was aged between 65 and 70. She lived in Wasara village with two orphaned grandchildren. The house was a three-bedroom brick-under-tile structure built by her late husband. The property was well-fenced and maintained. Matty purchased all her agricultural inputs and hired labour and draft. Between 2000 and 2005, Matty lost a 32-year-old widowed daughter, a 26-year-old married daughter, and her husband. She had a house in Harare and her only surviving child, a divorced daughter, lived in the United Kingdom. Matty came to live in Wasara in 1976, after her husband retired from his job in town. The couple purchased the land from the village head. Matty's husband died after a short illness. Matty succeeded to the homestead. She also inherited a house in Harare, a plough, a scotch cart and a bicycle from her husband's estate. She collected rent from the house in Harare and received remittances from her daughter in the UK. Matty hired labour for the collection of firewood and the maintenance of her homestead garden.

Matty moved to Makuku early on in life, so that by the time the multiple shocks of Economic Structural Adjustment Programmes, Operation Restore Order and economic decline occurred, her hearth-hold was well enough established to weather the shocks because of the constant receipt of remittances, access to her deceased husband's pension and rental income from the house in Harare. Even when the hearth-hold suffered multiple adult deaths in a short period of time, the remaining income sources were enough to sustain it at above subsistence level. Matty was able to survive in Makuku as an immigrant with limited community support because she obtained services from the market. Her access to foreign currency from her daughter in the UK buffered her hearth-hold against inflation.

Hearth-holds type II: At risk

Although type II hearth-holds managed independent homesteads like those of type I, their homesteads were poorly maintained. Type II hearth-holds were relatively small, having only up to two members. Besides the homesteads, their assets were their health and labour. These hearth-holds had limited access to non-agricultural income, which undermined their capacity to engage in agricultural activities. The hearth-holds relied on government seed handouts, free ploughing provided by their relatives, and their own labour. The government seed was delivered late into the agricultural season, the free ploughing was done at a time and acreage convenient to the one providing the free service, not necessarily coinciding with the recipient's planning, which increased the single women's vulnerability to climatic variability and the short agricultural season. Over time, the hearth-holds lost assets due to the recurring shocks caused by HIV and AIDS, the volatile socio-economic conditions and Operation Restore Order. Women in these hearth-holds offered labour in exchange for food, which reduced the labour available for the timely preparation of their own land and increased their vulnerability to crop failure. These hearth-holds compensated the diminishing returns of agriculture by diversifying into less risky activities in the locality like working for better-off households. The diversification strategies they followed ensured that they maintained the viability of their hearth-holds on their independent homesteads. They did not have the burden of caring for ill adults or young children. However, the hearth-holds were highly dependent on their capacity to perform work, and ill health or the assumption of a burden of care would push these hearth-holds into Category III. Petronella's experience illustrates a typical category II hearth-hold trajectory.

Case 3: Petronella: Managing agricultural risk through selling her own labour

Petronella was a 57-year-old illiterate widow who was born in Kura village. She lived with an adult unmarried son on the homestead. The well and toilet had collapsed and the buildings were in desperate need of maintenance. Petronella had two head of cattle, which she obtained through an NGO project. She started working on the commercial farms as a teenager. There she met and married a Mozambican. On the commercial farm where they were working, the farmer provided housing, food subsidies and access to a clinic. Petronella and her husband left the farm during the liberation war in Zimbabwe and secured a homestead in Kura with their four children. The husband resumed working on commercial farms and Petronella diversified into local piecework. In 1998, her husband fell ill and died from chest pains. Petronella assumed control of the homestead and remained in Kura. Her three children stopped attending school after the death of their father, as she could not afford to pay for them. Three of Petronella's children married and moved out. Petronella survived entirely on selling her labour. This left her with little time to invest in her own land. In the 2004/2005 agricultural season, she tried to engage in subsistence farming. She used old seed and government supplied seed, which was delivered well into the rainy season, and did not apply any fertilizer to her crop. She hired someone to plough her land but was unable to pay the man. The harvested maize was insufficient to meet the food needs of the hearth-hold. Because during the agricultural season Petronella worked in other people's fields and vegetable gardens, and collected firewood for others in exchange for maize meal grain, she was unable to attend to her own fields. The Kura village head's wife facilitated Petronella's access to the school where she was doing laundry. Petronella occasionally brewed beer to augment her income and also provided healing services to the local community. The high incidence of death, lack of effective health services, drought retrenchment and 'inexplicable misfortune' made an increasing number of people turn to traditional means of solving their problems.

This story reveals a marginal livelihood, sustained by opportunistic decision-making around labour. The move to Kura and diverting from sole reliance on commercial farm employment enabled the hearth-hold to survive the death of the husband. The failure to educate the children after their father's death undermined the hearth-hold's chances of earning remittances, an important source of non-agricultural income for people in the rural areas. In Kura, the widow had access to an independent homestead that enabled her to make autonomous decisions. Petronella's membership of Kura enabled her to access the community and networks through which she gained access to employment and to NGO activities through which she managed to diversify her portfolio further. The resident son complemented his mother's efforts by hiring out his labour. The hearth-hold's trajectory illustrates the importance of physical well-being for category II hearth-holds. The case also showed the potential for non-governmental organizations to break the cycle of poverty in which hearth-holds may find themselves. The portfolio remained vulnerable to the relocation of the households on whom the head depended for work and the hearth-hold having to assume caring responsibilities.

Hearth-holds type III: Vulnerable hearth-holds

The women in this category lived independently on homesteads that belonged to people who had left the villages or died. These hearth-holds depended mostly on transfers from the State, the church or family. Their heads were either ill and/or had a relatively heavy burden of care, as over time they became ill, were hosting and taking care of an ill adult, and/or were taking care of small children. Type III hearth-holds could not produce subsistence, even in a good year. They only invested in agriculture because they obtained the resources from the State or through charity from other homesteads. The burden of care limited their capacity to invest in their own land. Some of the hearth-holds participated in the opportunistic trade of natural forest produce, or did local piecework or commercial farm work. This work left the women with no time to invest in their own land. Type III hearth-holds were vulnerable because they were unable to meet their basic needs. They did not receive remittances, as their children were either too young and/or had failed to leave home (see Table 1).

Case 4: Rita: Destitute divorcee conditionally accepted into the village

Rita was 48 years old in 2005. Her parents divorced when she was young. Rita lived alone on a homestead in Kura that had previously belonged to her parents. She was the village head's stepsister. There was a single hut with a leaking roof on the property. Rita was using the fencing poles for fuel wood, which rendered the homestead prone to the elements, thieves and roaming livestock. Rita had a son out of wedlock in 1980, whom she sent to live with her mother while she moved to the city to secure employment as a domestic worker. In 1994, Rita married and moved to her husband's village. She gave birth to three children and established an independent homestead with the assistance of her husband. They divorced after he married another woman. She returned to Kura with her three minor children. She was frequently too ill (headaches and chest pains) to work and relied on the village head's wife and children to assist her with fetching water, cooking and care. The village head insisted that she return her children to their father.

Rita remained in Kura as she relied on her relatives to assist her in her illness. Her son lost his job during Operation Restore Order and moved in with his mother. Reluctant to assume the extra burden of supporting Rita and her children, the village head gave the son some money and advised him to go and find his own people. The son went, but failed in his bid to claim his birthright to land and returned to Kura. Rita worked as a domestic worker for a teacher and a priest in the local church. She obtained meals from the two workplaces. The work was full time, with time off during weekends and evenings, which left her with little time to invest in her own homestead agricultural production. She also did piecework for other villagers in exchange for food during her time off work. Rita was behind in her Kura village burial society subscription and owed money that she had borrowed to visit her children and two buckets of maize. She spent most of her salary on hospital bills. Kura village gave her access to government provided food relief, as she was ill. Although she had arable land, Rita could not afford any draft so she hand-hoed to prepare her land when she was well, relying on government seed when it was issued. As Rita was either away at work or ill for most of the time, her agricultural efforts were in vain. She harvested nothing in the 2004/2005 season. In May 2005, Rita's monthly portfolio showed a heavy reliance on transfers and borrowing. Even with two jobs and subsidized meals, her income was inadequate to meet her own basic needs.

Rita's constant relocation affected her capacity to stabilize her hearth-holds and accumulate assets. Rita's illness undermined her capacity to sustain her hearth-holds and increased her reliance on transfers. She was accepted into the village on the village head's terms. In order to cope, Rita split her hearth-hold between Kura and her ex-husband's home. Even then, Rita could neither provide for herself nor meet her obligations in the host community of Kura. Rita's decision to abandon her young children in return for care and support from the community reflects some of the desperate choices that hearth-holds afflicted by AIDS and poverty have to make in the communal areas of Zimbabwe. The case also highlights the limits of community support and some of the strategies that overburdened communities use to cope, in this case restricting community membership, which leads to an increase in child-headed households and fostering.

Hearth-holds type IV: Dependent, vulnerable hearth-holds

Type IV hearth-holds do not have an independent homestead. They exist as sub-units of other single women hearth-holds or male-headed homesteads. These hearth-holds were living either as sub-units on a homestead or were split between different locales. For example, a single woman hearth-hold head lived in the urban areas while her children remained on the homestead in the communal areas, or divorced couples where the woman returned to her parents' homestead and left the children under the former husband's care in his village. The women heading these hearth-holds were still of child-bearing age. They did not invest in agriculture as they lacked land and other resources. Their assets were community membership and labour. The latter was compromised by illness or a heavy burden of care. Their portfolios were diversified into dependence on a larger unit, petty trading activities, risky activities like prostitution, and erratic employment at the growth point or commercial farms. These hearth-holds could not sustain themselves without the continuous support of the host domestic unit. The situation was worse when the hearth-hold head was ill.

Case 5: Maria: hearth-hold vainly struggling to construct a viable livelihood

In 2005, Maria was 36 years old. She left school prematurely when her widowed mother could no longer afford the fees. In 1983, Maria married and had two children. The marriage ended in 1990. Maria and her children moved to her widowed mother's residence in Wasara. In 1994, Maria left her children with her mother and went to work in Harare. After three years Maria lost the job after she became pregnant. She returned to her mother's homestead. Maria secured employment as a caretaker for somebody who purchased land in Wasara, but worked and lived in Harare. She moved out of her mother's homestead and had her independent homestead. Maria's employer provided her with agricultural inputs and paid her a monthly wage. The arrangement lasted for eight years. Maria augmented her income by working on commercial farms. She also brewed beer with her mother. In 2005, Maria was evicted by the Wasara village head who accused the homestead owner of settling into the village illegally. Maria moved back to her mother's homestead. Since the demise of her first marriage, Maria had been struggling to establish a viable unit. Being a caretaker had enabled Maria to run an independent homestead for eight years. After that, her hearth-hold remained dependent on her elderly mother who formed the conduit for her access to Wasara village.

The pathway shows the vulnerability of a divorced woman living in her mother's natal village, because this makes her an immigrant with no valid claim to village membership. In spite of all her efforts, Maria remained dependent and vulnerable. Her hearth-hold first progressed from category IV to II, but then degraded to type IV after her eviction. The case shows that even without directly suffering the impact of HIV/AIDS, hearth-holds were vulnerable to impoverishment in communal areas.

Case 6: Cathy: Hearth-hold curtailed by illness

In 2005, Cathy was 23 years old. She was a widow, and a daughter of the village head. Cathy spent 13 years at school. In 2000, Cathy secured work in Harare and lived with her employers but left this residence when she got married in 2001. Cathy was the second wife in a polygamous union. When she married this man, she went to live at the man's homestead in a communal area. The husband was working in town. The marriage produced one son. Cathy's homestead was destroyed by lightning in 2003. She moved back to town, where the husband rented accommodation for her. He died of meningitis in 2003. Cathy and her son returned to her parental homestead in Kura. Cathy initially joined the neighbourhood police in Kura but left when that did not result in formal recruitment into the police force. Cathy took work as a live-in domestic help in the urban area. She lost her employment when the employer emigrated. She returned to Kura and assisted her parents with the agricultural production. She secured another domestic employee job but lost it after two months, when she had recurrent headaches. While at home, she was processing her mother's harvest of maize, shelling and bagging it. She secured another job, which she lost after she suffered a minor stroke. In September, she secured employment as a clerk in Harare but lost that job too after she suffered another stroke. Cathy returned to Kura. She started selling fruit at the local school, but had to stop the fruit business a month later for lack of capital. Cathy asked her father, the Kura village head for land, but he would not give her any, as he believed she might remarry. She used some of her aunt's homestead to grow vegetables for sale. She borrowed some land from her friend in the next village and at the time of this research was clearing it for the 2005/2006 agricultural season.

This pathway pictures a livelihood eroded by illness and mortality. It also shows the importance of communal area residence for hearth-holds to fall back on, and the limits of network support. The woman's opportunities to secure her livelihood were contracting over her life course because of the death of her spouse and her possible exposure to HIV, her responsibility for a young child and the loss of her marital home and assets. Initially it seemed she would recover and accumulate enough resources to establish an independent homestead. However, her bad health incapacitated her, even though she was relatively educated and had networks through which she negotiated employment. Cathy's poor health status made it difficult for her to establish an independent portfolio for her hearth-holds. This was not for lack of trying. The case shows that even networks and kinship support cannot help hearth-holds to surmount chronic illness. Cathy's failure to successfully negotiate an independent homestead in Kura village meant that all returns to her labour accumulated to the host household, which negated her efforts to establish an independent homestead and have autonomy.

Hearth-holds type V: succumbed

The hearth-holds that succumbed to the conditions represented the worst-case scenario for single women. At this point, the hearth-hold has no assets left to protect itself against threats to its livelihood. The following case pictures the circumstances that can overwhelm hearth-holds.

Case 7: Tina: hearth-hold decimated by illness

When I met Tina in 2004, she was 32, ill and bed-ridden, and living in Wasara village. Tina lived with her 9-year-old daughter on her parents' homestead in Wasara. Tina's parents hired a divorced woman to look after her. Tina was born into a well-to-do family and received a good education. She married when she was 20 and had two children. She secured employment as a civil servant, and lived and worked in Harare. Tina and her husband divorced. Tina got custody of the children and moved into her parents' house in Harare from where she continued to work. In 2003, Tina was diagnosed with pneumonia. Her then 6-year-old daughter continued to lose weight and was generally unwell. The child was weak, had a poor appetite and was small for her age. In 2004, too ill to work, Tina and her daughter moved to her parents' homestead in Wasara. Tina's other siblings paid for all her medical expenses and assisted her parents to look after her. In June 2005, the condition of Tina's daughter deteriorated. She was rushed to hospital, where she died. She was buried in Wasara. The daughter's father was too ill to attend the funeral. Tina slipped into a coma shortly after the burial of her daughter. The family transferred her to a hospital in Harare. She died in August 2005.

The case highlights the rapid downward spiral of hearth-holds whose head simultaneously suffers HIV-infection and marital dissolution. Tina's hearth-hold first lost its own individual assets and then had to rely on assistance. Tina's hearth-hold never engaged in agricultural production. Its trajectory underscores the importance of the parental unit, Tina initially relied on her parents' accommodation after the dissolution of her marriage and later on her parents' homestead when she was too ill to work. However, even with the extensive family support and access to medicine, the hearth-hold was unable to cope and finally succumbed to AIDS. Tina's case brings to the fore an emergent consequence of the virus, the illness and death of both young children and economically productive people.

Conclusion

This chapter set out to establish how single women hearth-holds deal with the combined impacts of HIV, AIDS and worsening livelihood conditions in the communal areas of Zimbabwe. Using the hearth-hold as a unit of analysis, it was shown that under the existing volatile conditions, hearth-hold vulnerability cannot exclusively be attributed to HIV and AIDS, but should take into account the land rights and other fundamental linkages. HIV and AIDS do increase the plight of already vulnerable people by increasing mortality, marital dissolution, displacement and erosion of human capital. This implies that interventions that focus exclusively on mediating the impacts of HIV and AIDS will have limited impact in mediating the vulnerability of people in the rural areas.

Through a focus on hearth-holds, it was possible to examine the circumstances of single women outside marriage, not as dependent, but as independent actors in the customary tenure areas. The findings from this focus highlight the need for policy-makers to acknowledge the diversity of domestic units as this determines people's access to livelihood resources. This will improve the effectiveness of policies aimed at improving the lives of women and children currently believed to be the most vulnerable population groups.

The differential application of rules governing land access by local leaders implies that for single women hearth-holds the conditions of acceptance into customary tenure areas cannot be generalized. The trajectories show that in customary tenure areas, even though conditions were worsening, women outside the conjugal unit can successfully consolidate their asset base. This contradicts studies that conclude that women on their own, especially following the end of marriage, face a downward economic spiral. However, although some hearth-holds successfully consolidated their livelihoods through diversification, this alone is not enough to ensure survival. Hearth-holds starting from a poor asset base have limited opportunities for diversification.

The trajectories of single women examined through their life stories, show that, although the importance of land as an agricultural asset had declined for single women in the communal areas, rights to residential land and membership of the community were vital for negotiating access to livelihood opportunities and provided a fall-back position for dislocated hearth-holds. However, this by itself did not guarantee livelihood security. This underlies the need for policy-makers to look beyond access to land when developing capacity building and support mechanisms. Policies should aim to ensure the economic viability of domestic units through improving their access to opportunities to earn an income. These policies include investment in labour-saving devises and initiatives that increase the liquidity of the rural areas so that hearth-holds who have limited access to wages and or remittances can tap into these.

The situation in which adult children increasingly depend on the older generations, questions the normative assumptions about intergenerational support and care relationships. Unemployment and AIDS increase the dependence of adult children on the hearth-holds, which changes children from being a potential source of old-age insurance to a source of insecurity and vulnerability. That adult male children afflicted by AIDS and unemployment increasingly depend on their mothers, challenges the assumptions about gendered resource governance in customary tenure areas. This chapter shows that dependent young and old children do not just pose mobility constraints on hearth-holds but may also undermine its tenure in communal areas. This implies that policies to support poor and vulnerable households should not just target the younger and traditionally considered active age cohorts, but should also target the elderly who in most cases provide support for all other age-groups.

Although networks helped to mitigate vulnerability by increasing hearth-hold's access to information, support and non-agricultural income earning opportunities, they offered little in the way of assisting hearth-hold heads that were ill and/or had contracted AIDS. Afflicted hearth-holds relied on their own kin. This was normally the older generation who bear the brunt of the combined effects of HIV and economic downturn. This questions the effectiveness of policies that aim to mediate vulnerability through community-based social capital capacity building initiatives.

This limits the utility of generalized interventions that give out the same type and amount of resources to vulnerable households. As every case was different, it is important for policy interventions to include the specific local contexts in the design of support programmes. In order to be effective, policies should be as flexible as possible and be based on the specific local conditions.

Note

1   The government of Zimbabwe destroyed the homes, livelihoods, business and shelter of more than 700,000 people in a controversial clean-up operation. The motives were a general concern felt by the government to do something about the chaos and congestion that characterized urban areas, to check the parallel foreign currency market and some viewed the operation a retribution for urban dwellers as they had voted for the opposition party in previous elections. (Action Aid International, 2005)

References

Action Aid International (2005) *Combined Harare Residents' Association, Zimbabwe Peace Project. The Impact of 'Operation Murambatsvina/Restore Order' in Zimbabwe*. National Survey Report. August 2005, www.sarpn.org.za/documents/d0001475/Impact_Operation_Murambatsvina_ Aug2005 .pdf, accessed 13 January 2006

Andersson, J. (2002) 'Sorcery in the Era of "Henry IV": Kinship, Mobility and Mortality in Buhera District, Zimbabwe', *Royal Anthropological Institute*, vol 8, pp425–449

Buvinic, M. and Gupta, G. (1997) 'Female-Headed Households and Female Maintained Families: Are They Worth Targeting to Reduce Poverty in Developing Countries?', *Economic Development and Cultural Change*, vol 45, no 2, pp259–280

Chimhowu, A. and Hulme, D. (2006) 'Livelihood Dynamics in Planned and Spontaneous Resettlement in Zimbabwe: Converging and Vulnerable', *World Development*, vol 34, no 4, pp728–750

Drinkwater, M. (2003). HIV/AIDS and Agrarian Change in Southern Africa. United Nations Regional Interagency Co-ordination and Support Office Technical Consultation on Vulnerability in the Light of an HIV/AIDs Pandemic South Africa, www.sarpn.org.za/ documents/d0000601/Drinkwater_CARE_Sept03.pdf, accessed 15 June 2005

Ekejiuba, F. (1995). Down to Fundamentals: Women Centred Hearth-Holds in Rural West Africa, in D. Bryceson (ed), *Women Wielding the Hoe: Lessons from Rural Africa for Feminist Theory and Development Practice*, pp47–61, Berg, London

Goebel, A. (2005) *Gender and Land Reform: The Zimbabwe Experience*, McGill-Queen's University Press, Montreal and Kingston, Canada

Gregson, S., Anderson, R., Ndlovu, J., Zhuwau, T. and Chandiwana, S. (1997) 'Recent Upturn in Mortality in Rural Zimbabwe: Evidence for an Early Demographic Impact of HIV-1 Infection?', *AIDS*, vol 11, no 10, pp1269–1280

Gregson, S., Zhuwau, T., Ndlovu, J. and Nyamukapa, C.A. (2002) 'Methods to Reduce Social Desirability Bias in Sex Surveys in Low-Development Settings: Experience in Zimbabwe', *Sex Transmission Disease*, no 29, pp568–575

Hansen, K., Woelk, G., Jackson, H., Kerkhoven, R., Manjonjori, N. and Maramba, P. (1998) 'The Cost of Home-Based Care for HIV/AIDS Patients in Zimbabwe', *AIDS Care*, vol 10, no 6, pp751–759

Hartnack, A. (2005) 'My Life Got Lost': Farmworkers and Displacement in Zimbabwe', *Contemporary African Studies*, vol 23 no 2, pp173–192

Huisman, H. (2005) 'Contextualising Chronic Exclusion: Female-Headed Households in Semi-Arid Zimbabwe', *Tijdschrift voor Economische en Sociale Geografie,* vol 96, no 3, pp253–263

IFPRI (1995) 'Divorce and Family Structure in a Changing Environment', *CG Newsletter*, vol 1, no 3, pp1–1

Jackson, H. and Kerkhoven, R. (1995) 'Developing AIDS Care in Zimbabwe: A Case for Residential Community Centres?', *AIDS Care*, vol 7, no 5, pp663–673

Kanji, N. (1995) 'Gender, Poverty and Economic Adjustment in Harare, Zimbabwe', *Environment and Urbanisation*, vol 7, no 1, pp37–56

May, J. (1983) *Zimbabwean Women in Customary and Colonial Law*, Gweru, Mambo Press, Harare, Zimbabwe

MOH (2004) The HIV and Aids Epidemic in Zimbabwe: *Where Are We Now? Where Are We Going?* Ministry of Health and Child Welfare, National AIDS Council, USAID, Harare, Zimbabwe

Mutangadura, G. (2000) *Household Welfare Impacts of Mortality of Adult Females in Zimbabwe: Implications for Policy and Program Development*, Paper presented at AIDS and Economics Symposium organised by IAEN Network, Durban, South Africa

Muzvidziwa, V. (2002) 'An Alternative to Patriarchal Marriage: Mapoto Unions', *Nordic Journal of African Studies*, vol 11, no 1, pp138–155

Nyambara, P. (2001) 'The Politics of Land Acquisition and Struggles Over Land in the "Communal" Areas of Zimbabwe: The Gokwe Region in the 1980s and 1990s', *Africa*, vol 71, no 2, pp253–285

Pankhurst, D. (1991) 'Constraints and Incentives in "Successful" Zimbabwean Peasant Agriculture: The Interaction between Gender and Class', *Journal of Southern African Studies*, vol 17, no 4, pp611–632

Peters, P. (1995) 'Manoeuvres and Debates in the Interpretation of Land Rights in Botswana', *Africa Journal of the International African Institute*, vol 62, no 3, pp413–434

Potts, D. (2000a) 'Worker-Peasants and Farmer-Housewives in Africa: The Debate about "Committed" Farmers, Access to Land and Agricultural Production', *Journal of Southern African Studies*, vol 26, no 4, pp807–832

Schmidt, E. (1992) *Peasants, Traders, and Wives: Shona Women in the History of Zimbabwe, 1870-1939*, Baobab, Harare, Zimbabwe

Scoones, I., Chinaniso, C., Chikura, S., Jeranyama, S., Machaka, P. and Mavedzenge, P. (1996) *Hazards and Opportunities. Farming Livelihoods in Dryland Africa: Lessons from Zimbabwe*, Zed Books, London

UN (2005) Report of the Fact-Finding Mission to Assess the Scope and Impact of Operation Murambatsvina by the UN Special Envoy on Human Settlements Issues in Zimbabwe. Mrs Anna Tibaijuka, www.un.org/News/dh/infocus/zimbabwe/zimbabwe_rpt.pdf, accessed 13 January 2006

UNAIDS (1998) *Zimbabwe National HIV and AIDS Estimates, 1998*, Ministry of Health and Child Welfare, Harare, Zimbabwe

UNAIDS (2003) *Zimbabwe National HIV and AIDS Estimates, 2003*, Ministry of Health and Child Welfare, Harare, Zimbabwe

UNAIDS (2005) *Zimbabwe National HIV and AIDS Estimates, 2005*, Ministry of Health and Child Welfare, Harare, Zimbabwe

UNDP (2004a) *Zimbabwe Millennium Development Goals: 2004 Progress Report,* Harare, Zimbabwe

UNDP (2004b) Zimbabwe Human Development Report 2003: Redirecting Our Responses to HIV/AIDS, Harare, Zimbabwe

Varley, A. (1996) 'Women Heading Households: Some More Equal than Others?', *World Development*, vol 24, no 3, pp505–520

Vijfhuizen, C. (2002) *The People You Live With: Gender Identities and Social Practices, Beliefs and Power in the Livelihoods of Ndau Women and Men in a Village with an Irrigation Scheme in Zimbabwe*, Weaver Press, Harare, Zimbabwe

Wekwete, K. (1991) 'Growth Centre Policy in Zimbabwe with Special Reference to District Service Centres, in N. Mutizwa-Mangiza and A. Helmsing (eds), Rural Development in Zimbabwe, pp187–221, Avebury, Aldershot, UK

Yamano, T. and Jayne, T. (2004) 'Measuring the Impacts of Working Age Adult Mortality on Small-Scale Farm Households in Kenya', *World Development*, vol 23, no 1, pp91–119

Chapter 7

Regional agricultural-consumption regimes and women's vulnerability to HIV in Kenya

E. Wairimu Mwangi

Introduction

Poverty and HIV/AIDS are inextricably intertwined. On the one hand there is the central argument that the experience of AIDS by individuals, households and communities can lead to intensification of poverty (Barnett and Whiteside, 2006; Carter et al. 2007). On the other, is the school of thought that focuses on the converse relationship that poverty, conditioned by gender and economic inequalities encourages the spread of HIV (Gillespie et al. 2007). Within the latter are studies that recognize that large-scale social and economic factors may constrain the opportunities available to individuals and groups and structure their risk of HIV (Craddock, 2004; Kalipeni et al., 2004). These studies in particular focus on economic sources of vulnerability, giving attention to structural components such as access to resources that might place some individuals at risk for HIV. In sub-Saharan Africa, agriculture is the fundamental livelihood activity of most people. A focus on the economic sources of vulnerability would, therefore, not be complete without taking into account the agricultural context. This chapter, set in the context of the AIDS epidemic in Kenya, advances the literature on the economic sources of vulnerability to HIV by empirically assessing how the regional agricultural context may structure risk for some individuals and groups who are systematically marginalized from access to resources. Vulnerability, in this case, is defined in terms of upstream factors, that is whether, and through what pathways, poverty puts people at greater risk of being exposed to the virus (Loevinsohn and Gillespie, 2003; Gillespie, 2008). As noted, the paper focuses on agricultural livelihoods as contexts of vulnerability and in so doing gives attention to what Gillespie and Loevinsohn (2003) refer to as the mesoenvironment, which includes, but is not limited to, plantations and related agricultural industries, local farming systems, and local practices and customs relating to resource allocation.

The discussion in this chapter is based on results of an International Food Policy Research (IFPRI)-funded study documented in an IFPRI/RENEWAL publication titled, *Exploring the linkages between Agriculture and HIV/AIDS: A Multilevel Study of the Impact of Agricultural-Consumption Regimes on Women's Vulnerability to HIV/AIDS in Kenya* www.ifpri.org/renewal).

Background

In Kenya, an estimated 7.1 per cent of adults aged 15 to 49 were living with HIV in 2007 with most cases occurring in the most economically productive age group (UNAIDS/WHO, 2008, p4). As in other parts of the world, in Kenya there are significantly greater numbers of women and girls who are infected with HIV than men. Prevalence among women aged 15 to 49 is nearly 10 per cent compared to nearly 6 per cent among men aged 15 to 54, indicating that women are particularly vulnerable to HIV infection (Kenya National AIDS Control Council (NACC), 2009). Major regional disparities, however, exist within the country, with some regions displaying a higher female to male infection ratio than others (UNAIDS/WHO, 2008).

The statistics above indicate that vulnerability to HIV infection in Kenya, like in most of sub-Saharan Africa (SSA), is gendered (Müller, 2005). Women usually occupy a lower social position in the household, which in turn negatively impacts their negotiating power in sexual relations (Turmen, 2003; Kalipeni et al., 2004). In this study, women's social position is defined on the basis of the two concepts of status and autonomy used in the gender literature to capture the degree of access, control and independence in women's decision-making (Abadian, 1996). In most cultures in sub-Saharan Africa, men dominate decision-making in the household, and their dominance includes their self-perceived 'right' to sexual intercourse, making it impossible for a woman to refuse sex from her husband even if she suspects that he is engaging in promiscuous behaviour (Kalipeni et al., 2004). Women with low level decision-making autonomy in the household are not only at an increased risk of being infected by their partners, but may also find it difficult to translate health enhancing knowledge into preventive action (Reid, 1999).

While women's decision-making autonomy in the household may be influenced by factors such as age (Kritz and Makinkwa-Adebusoye, 1999), family structure characteristics such as marriage systems and number of children (Hindin, 2003), education and employment (Jejeebhoy,1996), Blumberg (1984) views women's autonomy as deriving entirely from economic power. In her gender stratification theory Blumberg (1984) recognizes that economic power derives from a number of structural conditions, each of which provides a degree of control over production and surplus goods. Blumberg thus conceptualizes women's relative economic power in terms of the degree of control of key resources such as income, property, notably land and other means of production. In Kenya, women who have access to production resources and control production income are more likely to have decision-making autonomy in the household (Blumberg, 1984; Mwangi, 2009). Access to resources, however, like vulnerability to HIV infection is also gendered.

Over 80 per cent of women in Kenya live in rural areas where they, as in the rest of SSA, are responsible for over 80 per cent of food production and contribute substantially to cash crop production (UNAIDS, 2006, p12). In addition they are also engaged in livestock production and agro-based income generating activities. While it is clear that women in Kenya are the main agricultural producers and food providers, they are often constrained in access to and control of productive resources. This is particularly the case with access to land (UNAIDS, 2006). Women are disadvantaged in both statutory and customary land tenure systems (Nguthi, 2008). There is no consensus, however, on how much land is held by women in Kenya. Early assessments by Feldman (1984, p71) showed that women owned in their names only 5 per cent of the land. UNAIDS (2006) indicates that the percentage of land owned by women in Kenya ranges from 1 to 10 per cent. It is important to note that while women may not own land in their names, they may have access or user rights. Women's user rights may vary according to specific conditions in different regions, for instance, the social, cultural and economic contexts, as well as the demographic conditions of individual households (Gwako, 1997). Because few women in SSA have land titled in their names, researchers examining the impact of land tenure on women farmers have used indirect measures such as the impact of landholding sizes on women's access rights. Davison (1988) found that in Central Kenya, smallholders with large landholdings assigned a larger percentage to the production of cash value crops, resulting in negative implications for women's access. On the other hand, Zuidberg (1994) found in Burkina Faso that large holdings among smallholders favoured women's access. In Mali, as land became less available, women became workers on family fields instead of farmers in their own right (World Bank, 1995). Researchers have also used more direct measures of women's access rights. Gwako (1997) in his study examining the impact of land tenure on agricultural productivity among Maragoli women in western Kenya measured access rights using the percentage of plot yield in the previous season used or controlled by women.

Land is not the only resource that women in Kenya have difficulty accessing. Women also face limited access to: credit (Saito et al., 1994); agricultural cooperatives (Spring 1995); and extension facilities (Saito et al., 1994; Doss, 2001). Women's limited access to resources results in a situation of economic dependency on men, which in turn increases women's vulnerability to HIV-related risky behaviour (Bryceson and Fonseca, 2005; Dinkelman et al., 2006).

Against this background, this paper seeks to quantitatively assess how the agricultural context in Kenya influences women's vulnerability to HIV infection net of women's social position (defined as women's decision-making autonomy) in the household. The aim, then, is to isolate the effects on Kenyan women's vulnerability to HIV infection of the agricultural context from individual level characteristics such as women's decision-making autonomy in the household. The study involves regional analysis, using districts as administrative units. Kenyan districts vary in relative size, based on the agricultural sector, commercialization of agriculture and employment opportunities. To understand districts as contexts of HIV-related risky behaviour, the challenge is to identify characteristics of potential relevance, which also vary in meaningful ways from one district to the next. In this regard, the focus is on variables that capture agricultural situations that directly relate to women's increased exposure to HIV infection. To capture these variables, the study refers to the agricultural context as agricultural-consumption regimes (ACRs). The term ACRs, while not previously coined, draws from the longstanding literature that examines how agricultural development in developing countries has impacted women's agricultural productivity, and hence their social position in the household (Boserup, 1970; Suda, 1996). ACRs thus encompass the key production-related factors documented in this literature: agricultural commercialization (cash-crop versus food crop production), land tenure, access to credit and access to extension services; ACRs also include household survival strategies that women employ to counter constraints in agricultural production such as opportunities for wage employment, membership in cooperatives and membership in women's organizations.

Conceptual framework

Until recently, HIV studies emphasized rational-action models, focusing largely on 'risk' groups such as military men, truck drivers, migrant workers and prostitutes, with attempts to discern the driving mechanisms of the epidemic focusing on the sexual behaviour of these risk groups (Craddock, 2004). Studies have also given attention to cultural explanations of high prevalence in Africa, focusing mainly on the cultural determinants of the epidemic (Wijgert et al., 2001). A focus on risk groups and risky behaviour, unless carefully contextualized, exaggerates individual agencies and leaves unacknowledged and unexplained the ways in which large-scale social and economic factors structure risk, for individuals and groups who are systematically marginalized from access to goods, services and opportunities (Craddock, 2004). An assessment based on rational behaviour, thus, elides the broader context of power relations, economic necessity and resource limitation within which HIV transmission occurs in SSA. A number of researchers thus advocate for a cultural political economy of vulnerability framework that reflects the understanding of HIV/AIDS as resulting from discursive forces that effectively constrain the opportunities and choices available to individuals and potentially creating conditions of vulnerability for large sectors of regional populations (Craddock, 2004). This approach gives paramount attention to more accurate examination of the social and economic sources of vulnerability and at best can discern the structural components such as employment or access to resources that might place some individuals at risk for HIV (Entwistle 2007).

This study draws particularly from the *vulnerability perspective,* a specific perspective within the political economy framework. This perspective is based on an approach elaborated by Watts and Bohle (1993), which drew largely from Sen's (1981) entitlement theory. According to Sen, entitlement derives from the political and social status a person holds vis-à-vis the household or community, and the impact of this status on the commodity bundle that an individual can access or acquire. Watts and Bohle (1993, p53) extended Sen's entitlement theory and proposed a causal structure, which defines vulnerability through the intersection of three causal powers: command over food (entitlement), empowerment and the structural-historical form of class relations within a specific political economy. Empowerment is the component from which entitlements derive. It focuses on those institutions that regulate access to and control over resources, and examines the rules and rights by which individuals claim social power. Empowerment thus focuses on people or groups denied critical rights in various domains, including the domestic domain (Watts and Bohle, 1993). The political economy accounts for how and why particular patterns of entitlement and empowerment are produced and reproduced in society. The focus then is on the particular mode of production characterizing a particular place and how it is shaped by historical and local contingencies (Watts and Bohle, 1993).

The vulnerability perspective, while initially proposed for the study of hunger and famines and other natural hazards, is applicable to the study of HIV and AIDS because vulnerability to HIV infection, as with vulnerability to other hazards, is a function of class relations and power including gender relations and political relations, and not just a function of biological susceptibility (Gould, 2005). According to Oppong (1998), this perspective takes into account that adverse life circumstances such as hunger and disease do not affect social groups uniformly. In the study of HIV and AIDS, the perspective thus departs from a focus on individual sexual behaviour to a focus on the social, economic and political contingencies that make some groups vulnerable, giving emphasis to issues of differential access to resources.

Expected relationships

The study's general hypothesis is that agricultural contexts in Kenya create regional differences among women, such that those sharing similar social positions in the household face different vulnerability situations. In line with this hypothesis, this chapter's discussion focuses on the following general question and related hypothesis: To what extent does the regional agricultural context (agricultural-consumption regimes) account for the variation in women's vulnerability to HIV infection over and above women's decision-making autonomy controlling for other women's individual and household characteristics. In line with this question, the general hypothesis is that the agricultural context will explain variation in women's vulnerability to HIV infection across districts over and above women's decision-making autonomy in the household.

Methodology

Data
The study utilizes data at two levels: 1) combined individual and household level; and 2) contextual (district level data).

Individual level data
The individual and household level data comes from the 2003 Kenya Demographic and Health Surveys (KDHS). The survey utilized a two-stage sample design. The first stage involved selecting sample points (clusters) from a national master sample maintained by the Central Bureau of Statistics (CBS). A total of 400 clusters were selected from the master frame. The second stage of selection involved the systematic sampling of households. A total of 9,865 households were selected in the sample, of which 8,889 were occupied and therefore eligible for interviews. Of the 8,889 existing households, 8,561 were successfully interviewed. A household survey was undertaken in which information was collected on each member of the household including age, gender and

the person's relation to the head of household. The purpose of the household survey was to identify women between the ages of 15 and 49 who would be eligible for the individual interview. Interviews were completed for 8,195 women. The clusters used in the survey could be matched to their respective districts using district administrative codes.

Additionally, the household data also included administrative codes (district codes); however this file did not have the district names. A separate geographic file contained the district codes and the respective district names. Further preparation of the data thus involved linking the individual and household level files to this geographic file using the common administrative (district level codes) available in both data files. This modification made it possible to identify the district that each household/individual was located in.

District level data

The data collection process for the contextual (district) level was sponsored by the International Food Policy Research Institute (IFPRI). District level data was based on the documented districts in Kenya (70) as of 2003, to allow for consistency with the districts used in the 2003 KDHS. Data were compiled from various sources. These include: 1) the most recent district development plans and district annual reports; 2) the 2005 Kenya Integrated Budget Survey (KIBHS) conducted by the CBS; 3) the Kenya Ministry of Gender and Social Services; and 4) Kenya Ministry of Agriculture. These data were input into SPSS and a column, which included the administrative codes (following the KDHS data above), was created. These codes were used to match the individual-level data above to this contextual-level data.

Measures

Dependent variables

Although more direct measures of HIV risk exist such as multiple sexual partnerships, in this analysis, women's vulnerability to HIV risk is measured using proxy variables. The choice of proxy variables is based on the limitation of using data on self-reported sexual and other behaviours. There is evidence that women tend to underreport and men tend to exaggerate their premarital and extramarital activity (Zaba et al., 2002). Epidemiological studies have also observed a weak association between self-reported risky behaviour and HIV status. For example, a large multi-study of factors determining HIV prevalence in four African cities revealed large numbers of HIV positive women who reported to be virgins or having had only one sexual partner and few episodes of sexual intercourse (Buve et al., 2001).

The first proxy indicator of vulnerability includes a measure of *attitudes toward sex*. This measure is an attitudinal variable for which a respondent was asked to indicate if they were justified to refuse sex if they knew her partner has other sexual partners. Evidence from the literature suggests that women have fewer sexual partners than men, and women with little control over the sexual activities of their partners are vulnerable to infection. The inability of a woman to protect herself, even when she is aware of her partner's risky behaviour assesses vulnerability to risk that derives from a woman's economic dependency on men (Reid, 1999). This variable is used to assess the extent to which economic dependency may prevent or reduce the efficacy of a woman to protect herself from risky behaviour, thus increasing her vulnerability to HIV infection. Given that this indicator assesses risk in terms of a woman's partner having other women, this outcome is limited to married women in non-polygymous relationships. For this variable, women who indicated that they were not justified to refuse sex were considered vulnerable to HIV. A dummy variable was created with women who indicate that they were justified to refuse sex (not vulnerable) as the reference category.

The second proxy indicator is *perceived risk of infection*. Studies have found a positive association between perceived risk and risky sexual behaviour for both men and women (Akwara et al., 2003; Cleland, 1995). The 2003 KDHS included a variable on perceived risk for which respondents were asked to indicate their chance of getting infected with HIV. Background characteristics revealed that the most common reasons women explain the perception risk as low or nil is that they have just one partner or are not having sex. The most common reasons women provide to explain moderate or high perception of risk of infection is that their partners have other partners, or that they are having sex with more than one partner. The data also showed that condom use was generally low for women who indicated having no or small risk. *Perceived risk of infection* thus measures women's vulnerability to HIV infection based on a woman's own sexual behaviour as well as her inability to protect herself even when she is aware of her partner's risky behaviour. The question included four categories of self-assessed risk: no risk, small risk, moderate risk and great risk. For this analysis, based on the distribution, respondents who indicated no risk and small risk were combined into one category, and those indicating moderating and great risk were combined into another category. A dummy variable was created with no or small risk as the reference category.

Main independent variables

The main independent variable is *women's decision-making autonomy*. Five questions about who makes the decisions in the household were used in the data. The questions asked in response to 'Who in your family usually has the final say on the following decision?' were: 1) your own health; 2) large household purchases; 3) daily household purchases; 4) visits to family and friends; 5) what food should be cooked each day. For each of the questions the women were given the following response options: 1) respondent alone; 2) respondent and husband/partner; 3) respondent and other; 4) husband or partner alone. Since in SSA cooking is generally regarded as one of a woman's essential responsibilities within the household, this type of decision-making was excluded from the analysis. Two sets of dichotomous variables were created. In the first set of dichotomous variables, for each question, the variable was coded 1 if the woman had said alone or jointly and 0 otherwise. In the second set of dichotomous variables, for each question, the variable was coded 1 if the woman had the final say in decision-making alone and 0 if the woman did not have the final say. Using these two sets of dichotomous outcomes, two additive scales in which respondents were scored 0 to 4 were created. The first scale measured decision-making autonomy in the case where a woman makes a final decision jointly (joint decision-making autonomy index), and the second scale measured decision-making autonomy where a woman makes final decisions alone (final decision-making autonomy index). The Cronbach's alpha was used to measure internal reliability. For the measures used to create the joint decision-making autonomy index and the final decision-making autonomy index the Cronbach's alpha is 0.82 and 0.78, respectively.

Control variables

The study includes several socio-demographic factors as controls. Women's characteristics include two continuous variables, *women's age* and *women's education* in single years; and two categorical variables, *marital status* and *women's occupation*. The *marital status* variable consists of three categories, *never married, married or cohabiting, divorced/ widowed/separated*, and is measured using a set of dummy variables with *never married* as the reference category. The *women's occupation* variable consists of five categories, *unemployed, working in agriculture, manual labour, clerical/sales or services* and *professional/ technical*. A set of dummy variables was created from these categories, with *unemployed* as the reference category. *Residence* (rural vs. urban) is a dummy variable, with *urban* as the reference category. *Household wealth,* based on an asset index of household ownership on a number of consumer items as well as dwelling characteristics, is a dummy variable consisting of three categories, *high income, middle income* and *low income* as the reference category. While *ethnicity* has been seen as an important control variable due to the cultural implications of risky behaviour, it was not included in the analysis. The decision to exclude the variable was based on the high correlation between the ethnicity variable and the districts. This is consistent with a study by Kabubo-Mariara et al. (2006) on children's nutritional status conducted in Kenya using the 1998 and 2003 KDHS, which found that ethnicity was insignificant due to the high correlation between ethnicity and the clusters used in the KDHS data.

Contextual measures

Table 7.1 *Description and sources of contextual (District) variables*

Variable	Description and sources of contextual variables
Access to credit	Proportion of households in the district that were able to access credit in the past year – *Kenya Central Bureau of Statistics (CBS), Kenya Integrated Household Budget Survey (KIHBS)*
Extension	Ratio of female to male extension agents in the district – *Ministry of Gender and Social Services*
Title deeds	Proportion of households in the district that own title to the land they cultivate – *CBS, KIHBS*
Landholding size	Average landholding size in the district – *CBS, KIHBS*
Women's tenure security	Measured by women's input into agricultural decision-making – *CBS, KIHBS*
Commercialization	Ratio of area under traditional cash crops to area under food crops in the district – *District development plans and reports (most recent)*
Cooperatives	Percentage female membership in cooperatives – *Ministry of Gender and Social Services*
Women's groups	Membership in women's groups as a percentage of district population – *Ministry of Gender and Social Services*
Wage employment	Percentage contribution of wage employment to average household income – *District development plans and reports (most recent)*
GDI	Gender District Development Index (measure of district gender equality) – *Ministry of Gender and Social Services*

Analytical strategy

The study uses multi-level analysis, in particular hierarchical linear modelling (HLM). HLM takes into account that individuals are not isolated but are nested within particular social contexts, in this case districts, and while individuals from the same context differ with respect to their personal characteristics, they nevertheless share the same contextual influences. This technique is also useful in determining whether the study outcome varies significantly across regions and whether this variation can be explained by contextual influences over and above the individual level characteristics.

Model specification

When the outcome variable is binary, the model of choice is the hierarchical generalized linear model (HGLM). In this study, both the outcome variables are binary taking on a value of either one or zero. This kind of outcome requires the application of a special case of the HGLM known as the Bernoulli distribution.

In this analysis, one-way ANOVA also known as the unconditional model (null model with no predictors) is operationalized as the district effect. This model is important in addressing the first question and testing the associated general hypothesis that vulnerability to HIV infection (using both outcomes) varies significantly across districts in Kenya. If significant variation in the outcome variable is identified, then inclusion of covariates at the individual and contextual level can help to identify the source of variation (Raudenbush and Byrk, 2004).

As earlier noted, this study uses two outcome variables for HIV vulnerability. For the first variable, *attitudes towards sex*, the analysis is limited to married women in non-polygymous relationships. The final sample for this variable is, thus, reduced from all the women in the sample, 8,195, to 2,639, based on the 54 districts for which comprehensive data were available. For the second outcome variable, *perceived risk of HIV infection*, the sample consists of all women from the districts for which comprehensive data were available. For this outcome, the final sample is reduced from 8,195 women to 5,355 women.

Results

An overview of the sample descriptive characteristics for socio-demographic factors is presented in Tables 7.2 and 7.3.

The analytical study results are presented in Tables, 13.4, 13.5, 13.6 and 13.7. For each of the tables, the study focuses the discussion of the results on the first column (model 1) and the last two columns (Model 3a and 3b) giving particular attention to the contextual effects. As earlier noted, a more detailed account of this study's analysis is documented in the IFPRI/RENEWAL publication titled, *Exploring the Linkages between Agriculture and HIV/AIDS: A Multilevel Study of the Impact of Agricultural-Consumption Regimes on Women's Vulnerability to HIV/AIDS in Kenya (www.ifrpi.org/renewal).*

Table 7.2 *Descriptive statistics for individual-level predictors (Married Women sample)*

Variable	Mean/ per cent	Standard deviation	N
Joint decision-making (0–4 decisions)	2.1	1.45	2639
Final decision-making (0–4 decisions)	1.1	1.13	2639
Age (15–49 years)	30.64	8.39	2639
Education in years	7.17	3.82	2639
Household socio-economic status			
Low income	39%	0.49	2639
Middle income	21%	0.41	2639
High income	40%	0.49	2639
Occupation			
Not employed	30%	0.46	2639
Works in agriculture	43%	0.49	2639
Manual labour	6%	0.23	2639
Clerical/sales/service	17%	0.38	2639
Professional/technical	5%	0.23	2639
Residence			2639
Rural	87%	0.36	2639
Urban	13%	0.36	2639

Table 7.3 *Descriptive statistics for individual-level predictors (full sample of women)*

Variable	Mean/ per cent	Standard deviation	N
Joint decision-making (0–4 decisions)	1.8	1.59	5355
Final decision-making (0–4 decisions)	1.2	1.39	5355
Age (15–49 years)	28.13	9.48	5355
Education in years (0–26 years)	7.09	3.79	5355
Marital status			
Never married	0.3	0.45	5355
Married/cohabiting	0.6	0.49	5355
Widowed/separated/divorced	0.1	0.3	5355
Household socio-economic status			5355
Low income	0.37	0.48	5355
Middle income	0.21	0.4	5355
High income	0.42	0.49	5355
Occupation			5355
Not employed	0.37	0.48	5355
Works in agriculture	0.34	0.47	5355
Manual labour	0.08	0.28	5355
Clerical/sales/service	0.17	0.37	5355
Professional/technical	0.04	0.2	5355
Residence			5355
Rural	0.83	0.38	5355
Urban	0.17	0.38	5355

Impact on women's vulnerability to HIV infection – attitudes toward sex as the outcome variable

To assess whether women's vulnerability to HIV infection varies significantly across regions, a model with no predictors at either level (individual and district) is estimated. The results indicate that the level two variance component is significant (τ_{00} = 0.424, p<0.001), suggesting that women's vulnerability to HIV infection varies significantly across regions (Tables 7.4 and 7.5). It appears that with respect to the probability of women's vulnerability of HIV infection, in some districts women have a probability of vulnerability of about 5 per cent, while in others the probability of vulnerability to HIV infection is about 40 per cent. This leads to the question to what extent do ACRs explain

Table 7.4 *Random intercept logit models of the attitudes toward sex measure of HIV vulnerability and joint decision-making as the level-1 predictor*

Variable	Model 1	Model 2	Model 3	Model 3	Model 4
Intercept γ_{00}	−1.68*** [a]	−1.32*** [a]	−1.30*** [a]	−1.48*** [a]	−1.49*** [a]
Level 2 variance τ_{00}	0.424***				
Level-1 Variables					
Joint decision-making			1.03	1.05	1.05
Age		0.99	0.99	0.99	0.99
Education in years		0.97	0.96	0.96*	0.96*
Household SES					
Middle income		1.03	1.03	1.03	1.03
High income		0.63**	0.63**	0.61**	0.61**
Occupation					
Works in agriculture		0.63**	0.63**	0.61**	0.61**
Manual labor		0.54*	0.53*	0.52*	0.52*
Clerical/sales/service		0.74	0.73*	0.71*	0.72*
Professional/technical		0.54*	0.53*	0.54	0.54
Residence					
Rural		1.09	1.08	1.15	1.150
Level-2 (Contextual Variables)					
Access to credit				1.02**	1.02**
Title deeds				1.01	1.01
Women's tenure security				0.98*	0.98**
Landholding Size				0.94	0.94
Commercialization				0.94	0.94
Extension (female to male)				0.53	0.54
Cooperative membership (females)				1.01	1.02
Organization membership (females)				0.98**	0.98**
Wage employment				1.02**	1.02**
Gender inequality index					1.01
N	2639	2639	2639	2639	2639
N_j	54	54	54	54	54
[a] log odds coefficient	*p<0.05		**p<0.01		***p<0.001

Table 7.5 *Random intercept logit models of the attitudes toward sex measure of HIV vulnerability and final decision-making as the level-1 predictor*

Variable	Model 1	Model 2	Model 3	Model 4	Model 5
Intercept γ_{00}	−1.68*** [a]	−1.32*** [a]	−1.34*** [a]	−1.53*** [a]	−1.53*** [a]
Level 2 variance τ_{00}	0.424***				
Level-1 Variables					
Joint decision-making			0.93	0.93	0.93
Age		0.99	0.99	0.99	0.99
Education in years		0.97	0.96	0.96*	0.96*
Household SES					
Middle income		1.03	1.04	1.03	1.03
High income		0.63**	0.63*	0.61**	0.61**
Occupation					
Works in agriculture		0.63**	0.65**	0.64**	0.64**
Manual labour		0.54*	0.55	0.54	0.54
Clerical/sales/service		0.74	0.78	0.77	0.77
Professional/technical		0.54*	0.57	0.58	0.58
Residence					
Rural		1.09	1.08	1.15	1.15
Level-2 (Contextual Variables)					
Access to credit				1.02**	1.02**
Title deeds				1.01	1.01
Women's tenure security				0.98*	0.98*
Landholding Size				0.95	0.94
Commercialization				0.94*	0.94*
Extension (female to male)				0.53	0.54
Cooperative membership (females)				1.07	1.01
Organization membership (females)				0.98**	0.97**
Wage employment				1.02**	1.02**
Gender inequality index					0.74
N	2639	2639	2639	2639	2639
N_j	54	54	54	54	54
[a] log odds coefficient	*p<0.05		**p<0.01		***p<0.001

this variability in women's vulnerability to HIV infection across Kenyan districts? After taking into account women's decision-making autonomy and socio-demographic factors at the individual level, at the contextual level (Model 3a), a household's access to credit was found to increase the expected odds of women's vulnerability to HIV infection by about 2 per cent (p<0.01). Similarly, wage employment was found to increase the expected odds of women's vulnerability to HIV infection by 2 per cent (p<0.01). On the other hand, women's land tenure security and membership in organizations was found to significantly decrease the expected odds of women's vulnerability to HIV infection by about 2 per cent (p<0.01). These findings applied for women who made household decisions jointly and those who made decisions alone (Tables 7.4 and 7.5). Additionally, for women who made decisions alone (Table 7.5) commercialization was found to decrease the expected odds of women's vulnerability to HIV infection by 6 per cent (p<0.05). No significant relationship was found between the gender inequality variable and women's vulnerability to HIV infection (Model 3b).

Impact on women's vulnerability to HIV infection – perceived risk of HIV as the outcome variable

This outcome is assessed on the full sample of women. To gauge the magnitude of variation between districts in women's vulnerability to HIV infection, the model with no predictors at either level is estimated (Tables 7.6 and 7.7: Model 1). The estimated results indicate the level-2 variance is significant (τ_{00} = 0.328, p<0.001), suggesting that women's vulnerability to HIV infection, using the measure perceived risk of HIV infection, varies significantly across districts in Kenya. It appears that with respect to the probability of women's vulnerability to HIV infection, some districts have a vulnerability of about 9 per cent, while in others, the probability of vulnerability to HIV infection is roughly 50 per cent.

At the contextual level, after taking into account joint decision-making autonomy and other socio-demographic characteristics (Table 7.6), landholding size and commercialization were found to have significant impacts on women's vulnerability to HIV infection. Landholding size and commercialization decrease the expected odds of vulnerability by about 20 per cent (p<0.01) and 13 per cent (p<0.05), respectively. There was no significant relationship between the gender inequality variable and women's vulnerability to HIV infection (Model 3b).

Similar to the findings for the model that includes joint decision-making autonomy, after taking into account final decision-making autonomy (Table 7.7) – women who make final household decisions alone – landholding size and commercialization decrease the expected odds of HIV vulnerability by 20 per cent (p<0.01) and 13 per cent (p<0.05), respectively. There was no significant relationship between the gender inequality variable and women's vulnerability to HIV infection (Model 3b).

Discussion

In general the results suggest that for both measures of vulnerability, attitudes towards sex and perceived risk of HIV infection, women's vulnerability to HIV infection varies significantly across districts in Kenya. The results also reveal that ACRs explain women's vulnerability to HIV infection controlling for women's decision-making autonomy and other individual-level socio-demographic factors.

For the first outcome variable, to test the independent effects of ACRs, two models, one that included joint decision-making autonomy and the other that included final decision-making autonomy were estimated. The study found that after taking into account women's decision-making autonomy (joint and final) in districts where households had higher access to credit, women were more vulnerable to HIV infection. One would expect the economic benefits deriving from a household's access to credit would be protective for women; however, we find the opposite effect in this case. A possible explanation of this finding is that, first, women traders are more likely to have access to credit (Binate-Fofana, 2009) and women traders are more likely to be exposed to

Table 7.6 *Random intercept logit models of the perceived risk of HIV measure of HIV vulnerability and joint decision-making as the level-1 predictor*

Variable	Model 1	Model 2	Model 3	Model 4	Model 5
Intercept γ_{00}	−1.18*** [a]	−2.10*** [a]	−2.06*** [a]	−2.13*** [a]	−2.13*** [a]
Level 2 variance τ_{00}	0.328***				
Level-1 Variables					
Joint decision-making			1.01	1.01	1.01
Age		1.02***	1.01***	1.02***	1.02***
Education in years		1.02	1.01	1.01	1.01
Marital Status					
Married/cohabiting		2.77***	2.79***	2.81***	2.80***
Widowed/divorced/separated		1.75**	1.76**	1.76**	1.76**
Household SES					
Middle income		0.98	0.98	0.99	0.99
High income		0.96	0.95	0.95	0.95
Occupation					
Works in agriculture		1.02	0.99	0.98	0.98
Manual labour		1.47**	1.36*	1.35*	1.35*
Clerical/sales/service		1.41**	1.37**	1.36**	1.36**
Professional/technical		1.20	1.17	1.17	1.17
Residence					
Rural		1.09	1.06	1.07	1.07
Level-2 (Contextual Variables)					
Access to credit				1.01	1.01
Title deeds				0.99	0.99
Women's tenure security				0.98	0.98
Landholding size				0.80**	0.80**
Commercialization				0.87*	0.87
Extension (female to male)				1.02	1.09
Cooperative membership (females)				1.02	1.03
Organization membership (females)				0.98	1.03
Wage employment				1.00	0.99
Gender inequality index					0.40
N	5355	5355	5355	5355	5355
N$_j$	54	54	54	54	54
[a] log odds coefficient	*p<0.05		**p<0.01		***p<0.001

HIV infection risks (IOM, 2003). More work, however, remains to be done to establish links between women's access to credit, use of credit and HIV/AIDS. Second, the finding may relate to what the access to credit variable captures. This variable is measured as the proportion of households that were able to access credit in the district. Women in SSA have limited access to agricultural credit and therefore household's access to credit may not necessarily reflect women's access. Given that male members of the household

Table 7.7 *Random intercept logit models of the perceived risk of HIV measure of HIV vulnerability and final decision-making as the level-1 predictor*

Variable	Model 1	Model 2	Model 3	Model 4	Model 5
Intercept γ_{00}	−1.18*** [a]	−2.10*** [a]	−2.04*** [a]	−2.10*** [a]	−2.10*** [a]
Level 2 variance τ_{00}	0.328***				
Level-1 Variables					
Final decision-making			1.17***	1.18***	1.18***
Age		1.02***	1.01**	1.01**	1.01**
Education in years		1.02	1.01	1.00	1.00
Marital Status					
Married/cohabiting		2.77***	2.83***	2.85***	2.85***
Widowed/divorced/separated		1.75**	1.39	1.39	1.39
Household SES					
Middle income		0.98	0.98	0.98	0.98
High income		0.96	0.95	0.96	0.96
Occupation					
Works in agriculture		1.02	0.94	0.93	0.93
Manual labour		1.47**	1.28	1.27	1.27
Clerical/sales/service		1.41**	1.25*	1.24*	1.24*
Professional/technical		1.20	1.06	1.08	1.07
Residence					
Rural		1.09	1.09	1.10	1.10
Level-2 (Contextual Variables)					
Access to credit				1.01	1.01
Title deeds				1.00	1.00
Women's tenure security				0.98	0.98
Landholding size				0.80**	0.80**
Commercialization				0.87*	0.87*
Extension (female to male)				1.01	1.07
Cooperative membership (females)				1.02	1.03
Organization membership (females)				0.99	0.99
Wage employment				1.00	1.00
Gender inequality index					0.39
N	5355	5355	5355	5355	5355
N_j	54	54	54	54	54
[a] log odds coefficient	*p<0.05		**p<0.01		***p<0.001

are more likely to access credit than women, agricultural credit allocated to a farming household may not benefit all of its productive members (Saito, 1994). According to FAO (1998), access to credit by male household members may result in credit being diverted to male-dominated production systems at the expense of women's production activities. A household's access to credit may affect women's access to resources such as land, impacting their economic independence and their ability to protect themselves from HIV infection. Substantiation of this finding, however, would require gender disaggregated data on access to credit.

Women living in districts characterized by women's tenure security are less vulnerable to HIV infection and this effect persists, even after taking into account joint and final decision-making autonomy. This finding may suggest that tenure security increases married women's economic independence, which translates to empowerment; allowing women greater control over sexual relations. This finding may also suggest that gender relations in districts where women have secure tenure differ from the relations in districts where women do not have secure tenure. A study examining the determinants of women's decision-making autonomy revealed that in districts characterized by secure tenure, married women had higher levels of joint decision-making autonomy (Mwangi, 2009). Studies have also found that in regions characterized by gender equality, women have increased access to resources and households are characterized by collaborative intra-household decision-making (Roos and Gladwin, 2000). This study, however, can only imply the relationship between women's tenure security and household gender relations; more work remains to be done to concretely establish this relationship.

Still focusing on attitudes towards sex as a measure of vulnerability, this study found that in districts characterized by easy access to women's organizations, women are less vulnerable to HIV infection. This finding is consistent with other studies that have found that membership in women's groups is important for women's empowerment, which in turn has positive implications for women's reproductive and sexual health outcomes (Koenig et al., 2005). The study also finds that women living in districts characterized by a high contribution of wage employment to average household income are more likely to be vulnerable to HIV infection. While one would expect that wage employment would contribute to women's economic independence and thus have a protective effect, this is not the case. This finding may relate to Chapoto and Jayne's (2006) study that showed that non-poor women with business income were more likely to die from HIV-related causes than those with similar characteristics not having business income. Another possible explanation is that because the district-level data on wage employment are not gender disaggregated, the contribution of wage employment to average household income may not necessarily reflect women's participation. Mwangi (2009) used the same data as used in this study to explore the impact of the agricultural context on women's decision-making autonomy in Kenya and found that contribution of wage employment to household income (measured at the district-level) was not significantly associated with married women's decision-making autonomy. This may suggest that in this sample of married women, this variable (wage employment) captures income earned by male members of the household and may not, therefore, translate to an economic advantage for women. If we assume that the contribution of wage employment is through male household members, and a household is largely dependent on wage income for economic survival, wage employment may, thus, increase women's economic dependency, thereby reducing her efficacy to prevent risk of exposure to HIV infection. Rugalema (1999) notes that in rural areas, agro-estates account for about 30 per cent of the formal wage labour. Agro-estates have high seasonal demands for labour and these types of arrangements draw male farmers from their families for extended periods. This separation largely creates situations of dependency of these male farmers on occasional or commercial sex (Rugalema, 1999; Ngwira et al., 2001; Masanjala,

2007). The finding of a positive association between wage employment and women's vulnerability to HIV infection may suggest that women's economic dependency coupled with increased opportunities for males to engage in risky behaviour potentially created by wage employment, increases women's vulnerability to HIV. Concrete conclusions and substantiation of the observed effects of wage employment on women's vulnerability to HIV infection, however, would require the use of gender disaggregated data on wage employment.

For the attitudes towards sex measure, the analysis also reveals that when you account for final decision-making autonomy, cash crop production is advantageous for women and reduces their vulnerability to HIV infection. This finding may suggest that households where women make at least one decision independently are also characterized by more egalitarian intra-household resource dynamics that translate to greater involvement of women in cash crop production. The finding may thus be consistent with the argument that the effects of commercialization on women's wellbeing may depend on the prevailing societal gender relations (Roos and Gladwin, 2000).

Shifting focus to the other indicator of women's vulnerability to HIV infection, perceived risk of infection, the results reveal that at the contextual level, after taking into account women's decision-making autonomy (joint and final), landholding size is associated with women's decreased vulnerability to HIV infection. A possible explanation of this finding is that for this outcome variable, the analysis is conducted on the full sample, which includes widowed, separated and divorced women. For this category of women, landholding sizes may be particularly important because access to land largely depends on availability of land. In situations of land scarcity, the land that widows hold may be reduced or the widow may be deprived of the land that she previously farmed (FAO/IFAD, 1998). It is, therefore, likely that in districts characterized by small landholdings, widowed, divorced or separated women may be forced to turn to risky sexual behaviour, such as transactional sex, to ensure their own survival and that of their families. Rugalema (2004) in his study of agro-estates in Kenya probed into the factors that led to widows settling in commercial settlements rather than their rural homes. It emerged that once a husband has died, the widow and her children become socially and economically vulnerable. Unable to provide for herself and her children, and unable to marshal social and economic support from the extended family, a widow decides to migrate to a commercial settlement, sites that are characterized by a high prevalence of commercial sex.

Another possible explanation of this finding is that in areas where agricultural resources, such as land, are limited, both males and females may be pushed to cyclical migration. Although migration reduces the likelihood of livelihood collapse by allowing family members to earn wage income, it may also promote breakdown of social structures and create opportunities that encourage the spread of HIV. This is particularly the case for males who leave home to find work, become infected and return home to infect women left behind (Kane et al., 1993; Masanjala, 2007). The situation of male migration is especially risky for married women. Kane et al. (1993, pp1261–1265) for instance found that in Senegal, 27 per cent of men who had previously travelled to other countries, and 11.3 per cent of spouses of men who had migrated were infected with HIV, and this prevalence was significantly higher than in the general population. In districts characterized by large landholdings, agriculture may provide a livelihood, reducing the likelihood of households to engage in migrant labour, and thus reduce women's vulnerability to infection. The foregoing discussion on the effects of landholding sizes also potentially applies to the finding of negative effect of commercialization on women's vulnerability to HIV infection. Viability of small-scale cash crop production, for instance, may imply a lower likelihood of household members engaging in migrant labour. While the gender and development literature largely indicates that women have limited access to cash crop production, women may feel less vulnerable to HIV if cash crop production reduces the likelihood of male involvement in migrant labour or other income earning opportunities that exhibit a high correlation with HIV risk.

While there is support for the central hypothesis of this study, that Kenyan districts ACRs explain variation in women's vulnerability to HIV infection over and above women's decision-making autonomy, there are some important limitations. First, the study was limited in the use of direct measures of vulnerability of exposure to HIV infection. There is evidence that women tend to underreport risky sexual behaviour and HIV status. In this dataset, direct measures of HIV-related risky behaviour include sex with multiple partners and lack of condom use during sex with multiple partners. These measures are consistent with biomedical models that generally attribute disease to individual behaviour. These variables, however, do not take into account that some women may be at risk of HIV infection by virtue of the fact that their partners are themselves engaging in risky behaviour. This limitation points to the need to go beyond measures that attribute risky behaviour to individual volition, and incorporate measures that take into account the social context of risky behaviour. Second, the lack of gender disaggregated access to credit and wage employment data limits the ability to understand if the observed effects would have been different if district-level data on the proportion of women able to access credit were available. This limitation also applies to data on wage employment. Third, the commercialization data are limited in that they do not explicitly capture the prevalence of agro-estates or large-scale commercial agriculture. Agro-estates are characterized by a high prevalence of HIV (Rugalema, 1999, 2004; Masanjala, 2007). Comprehensive data that details the prevalence of agro-estates in each district would thus be useful in determining if the effects of cash crop production would differ in regions characterized by a high presence of agro-estates.

Despite the limitations, overall the study makes the following important contributions. First, the study extends the women and agriculture literature to the investigation of women's health outcomes, in particular HIV and AIDS. The findings establish that the challenges women meet as agricultural producers may contribute significantly to their vulnerability to HIV. Second, and related to the previous point, the study extends the literature examining contextual influences on health by allowing a focus on agricultural contexts. The findings that regional ACRs explain women's vulnerability to HIV over and above women's individual-level factors underscores the importance of studying health outcomes in Africa as being enmeshed within the social, political and economic context. In particular, given the dependence of livelihoods in SSA on agriculture, the findings suggest that when examining wellbeing outcomes, we cannot ignore the potential effects of the agricultural context.

In terms of policy, this study's findings suggest that efforts to safeguard women's rights to land, through tenure policy innovation, may be an important component of not only poverty alleviation, but also HIV prevention strategies. In particular, policy efforts need to protect the rights of widows, who are likely to lose their productive assets after the death of their husbands. Increased government commitment to ensure women's, particularly widows, access to productive assets may potentially reduce poverty-related risky behaviour. Additionally, policymakers need to consider other sub-groups, for example, divorced and separated women, who have distinct experiences relating to access to productive resources. This study also reinforces the importance of civic organizations for women's wellbeing and suggests the need to increase support of local initiatives and strengthen women's associations.

References

Abadian, S. (1996) 'Women's Autonomy and its Impact on Fertility', *World Development*, vol 24, no 12, pp1793–1809

Akwara, P.A., Madise, N.J. and Hinde, A. (2003) 'Perception of Risk of HIV/AIDS and Sexual Behavior in Kenya', *Journal of Biosocial Sciences*, vol 35, pp385–411

Barnett, T. and Whiteside, A. (2006) *AIDS in the Twenty-First Century: Disease and Globalization*, Palgrave Macmillan, New York

Binate-Fofana, N. (2009) 'Efficacy of Micro-Financing Women's Rural Activities in Côte D' Ivoire: Empirical Analysis of Women's Livelihood Activities, Productivity and Income', Paper presented at the European Research Conference in Microfinance, Brussels

Blumberg, R.L. (1984) 'A General Theory of Gender Stratification', in R. Collins (ed) *Sociological Theory*, Jossey-Bass, Hoboken, New Jersey

Boserup, E. (1970) *Woman's Role in Economic Development*, Earthscan Publications, London

Bryceson, D. and Fonseca, J. (2005) 'Risking Death for Survival: Peasant Responses to Hunger and HIV/AIDS in Malawi', Paper Presented at the International Conference on HIV/AIDS, Food and Nutrition Security organized by IFPRI, Durban

Buve, A., Largarde, E., Carael, M., Rutenberg, B. and Glynn, J. (2001) 'Study Group on Heterogeneity of HIV Epidemics in African Cities: Interpreting Sexual Behavior Data: Validity Issues in the Multicenter Study on Factors Determining the Differential Spread of HIV in four African Cities', *AIDS*, vol 15, suppl. 4, pp117–126

Carter, R., May, J., Aguero, J. and Ravindranath, S. (2007) 'The Economic Impacts of Premature Adult Mortality: Panel Data Evidence from KwaZulu-Natal', *AIDS*, vol 21, suppl. 7, ppS67–S73

Chapoto, A. and Jayne, T. (2006) 'Socioeconomic Characteristics of Individuals Afflicted by AIDS-related Prime-age mortality in Zambia', in S. Gillespie (ed) *AIDS, Poverty and Hunger: Challenges and Responses*, pp33–55, IFPRI, Washington DC

Cleland, J. (1995) 'Risk perception and Behavioral Change', in J. Cleland and B. Ferry (eds) *Sexual Behavior and AIDS in the Developing World*, Taylor and Francis, London

Craddock, S. (2004) 'Beyond Epidemiology: Locating AIDS in Africa', in E. Kalipeni, S. Craddock, J.R. Oppong and J. Ghosh (eds) *HIV and AIDS in Africa: Beyond Epidemiology*, pp1–10, Blackwell Publishing, Malden, MA

Davison, J. (1988) 'Land and Women's Agriculture: The Agriculture Context', in J. Davison (ed) *Women and Land: The African Experience*, Westview Press, Boulder, CO, pp1–32

Dinkelman, T., Lehvinsohn, J. and Majelantle, R. (2006) 'When Knowledge is Not Enough: HIV/AIDS Information and Risky Behavior in Botswana', NBER Working Paper No. W12418, Social Science Research Network

Doss, C.R.(2001) 'Designing Agricultural Technology for African Farmers: Lessons from 25 Years of Experience', *World Development*, vol 29, no 12, pp2075–2092

Entwistle, B. (2007) 'Putting People into Place', *Demography* vol 44, no 4, pp687–703

FAO/IFAD (1998) 'Uganda, Ghana and Cote D'Ivoire: The Situation of Widows', FAO, Rome

Gillespie, S. (2008) 'Poverty, Food Insecurity, HIV Vulnerability, and the Impacts of AIDS in Sub-Saharan Africa', IFPRI/RENEWAL Publication, Washington DC

Gillespie, S. and Kadiyala, S. (2005) *HIV/AIDS and Food and Nutrition Security: From Evidence to Action*, IFPRI, Washington DC

Gillespie, S., Kadiyala, S. and Greener, R. (2007) 'Is Poverty or Wealth Driving HIV Transmission', *AIDS*, suppl. 7, ppS5–S16

Gould, W. (2005) 'Vulnerability and HIV/AIDS in Africa: From Demography to Development', *Population Space and Place*, vol 11, pp473–484

Gwako, E. (1997) 'The Effects of Land Tenure on Agricultural Output Among the Maragoli of Western Kenya', PhD Dissertation, Washington University at St. Louis, MO

Hindin, M. (2003 'Understanding Women's Attitudes Towards Wife Beating in Zimbabwe', *Bulletin of the World Health Organisation*, vol 81, no 7, pp501–508

IOM (2003) *Mobile Populations and HIV/AIDS in the South African Region: Recommendations for Action*, International Organization for Migration, Geneva

Jejeebhoy, S.J. (1996) 'Women's Education, Autonomy and Reproductive Behavior: Assessing What We Have Learned', Paper presented at the 1995 Conference on the Status of Women and Demographic Change, Honolulu, HI

Kabubo-Mariara, J., Ndenge, G. and Kirii, D. (2006) 'Determinants of Children's Nutritional Status in Kenya: Evidence from Demographic and Health Surveys', Paper Presented at the Center for the Study of African Economies (CSAE) Conference, Oxford, London

Kalipeni, E., Craddock, S. and Ghosh, J. (2004) 'Mapping the AIDS Pandemic in Eastern and Southern Africa: A Critical Overview', in E. Kalipeni, S. Craddock, J.R. Oppong and J. Ghosh, *HIV and AIDS in Africa: Beyond Epidemiology*, pp58–69, Blackwell Publishing, Malden, MA

Kane, F., Alary, M., Ndoye, I., Coll, A., M'boup, S., Gueye, A., Kanki P. and Joly, J.R. (1993) 'Temporary Expatriation is Related to HIV-1 Infection in Rural Senegal', *AIDS*, vol 7, no 9, pp1261–1265

Koenig, M.A., Ahmed, S., Hossain, M., Khorshed, A. and Mozumder, A. (2005) 'Women's Status and Domestic Violence in Rural Bangladesh: Individual and Community-Level Effects', *Demography*, vol 40, no 2, pp269–288

Kritz, M.M. and Makinkwa-Adebusoye, P. (1999) 'Determinants of Women's Decision-Making Autonomy: The Ethnic Dimension', *Sociological Forum*, vol 14, no 3, pp399–424

Loevinsohn, M. and Gillespie, S. (2003) *HIV/AIDS, Food Security and Rural Livelihoods: Understanding and Responding*, IFPRI, Washington DC

Masanjala, W. (2007) 'The Poverty-HIV/AIDS Nexus in Africa: A Livelihoods Approach', *Social Science and Medicine*, vol 64, pp1032–1041

Müller, T.R. (2005) *HIV/AIDS, Gender and Rural Livelihoods in sub-Saharan Africa*, AWLAE Series no 2, Wageningen Academic Publishers, Wageningen, the Netherlands

Mwangi, E.W. (2009) 'Does Agricultural Context Matter for Women's Decision-Making Autonomy', Chapter 2, in PhD Dissertation, The Ohio State University

NACC (2009) Report of the Joint HIV and AIDS Programme Review September 2008, National AIDS Control Council Kenya, Nairobi, Kenya

Nguthi, F.N. (2008) *Adoption of Agricultural Innovations by Smallholder Farmers in the Context of HIV/AIDS: The Case of Tissue-cultured Banana in Kenya*, AWLAE Series no 7, Wageningen Academic Publishers, Wageningen, The Netherlands

Ngwira, N., Bota, S. and Loevinsohn, M. (2001) 'HIV/AIDS, Agriculture and Food Security in Malawi: Background to Action', RENEWAL Working Paper No. 1., The Hague

Oppong, J.R.(1998) 'A Vulnerability Interpretation of the Geography of HIV/AIDS in Ghana, 1986-1995', *Professional Geographer*, vol 50, no 4, pp437–448

Raudenbush, S. and Byrk, A. (2002) *Hierarchical Linear Models: Applications and Data Analysis Methods*, Sage Publications, Thousand Oaks, CA

Roos, D. and Gladwin,C. (2000) 'The Differential Effects of Capitalism and Patriarchy on Women Farmers' Access to Markets in Cameroon', in A. Spring (ed) *Women Farmers and Commercial Ventures: Increasing Food Security in Developing Countries*, pp41–64, Lynne Rienner Publishers, Boulder, CO

Rugalema, G. (1999) *HIV/AIDS and the Commercial Agricultural Sector in Kenya: Impact Vulnerability, Susceptibility, and Coping Strategies*, United Nations FAO, Rome

Rugalema, G. (2004) 'Understanding the African HIV Pandemic: An Appraisal of the Contexts of Lay Explanations of the HIV/AIDS Pandemic with Examples from Tanzania and Kenya' in E. Kalipeni, S. Craddock, J. Oppong, and J. Ghosh (eds) *HIV and AIDS in Africa: Beyond Epidemiology*, pp191–203, Blackwell Publishing, Malden, MA

Saito, K., Spurling, D. and Mekonnen, H. (1994) 'Raising the Productivity of Women Farmers in Sub-Saharan Africa', World Bank Discussion Papers, World Bank, Washington DC

Sen, A. (1981) *Poverty and Famines*, Clarendon Press, Oxford, London

Spring, A. (2000) 'Agricultural Commercialization and Women Farmers in Kenya', in A. Spring (ed) *Women Farmers and Commercial Ventures: Increasing Food Security in Developing Countries*, pp217–342, Lynne Rienner Publishers, Boulder, CO

Suda, C. (1996) 'The Political Economy of Women's Work in Kenya: Chronic Constraints and Broken Barriers', in P. Ghorayshi and C. Belanger (eds) *Women, Work and Gender Relations in Developing Countries: A Global Perspective*, pp75–90, Greenwood, Westport, CT

Turmen, T. (2003) 'Gender and HIV/AIDS', *Gynecology and Obstetrics*, vol 82, pp411–418

UNAIDS (2006) *Property and Inheritance Rights of Women and Girls in Kenya in the Era of HIV and AIDS*, UNAIDS, Geneva, Switzerland

WHO/UNAIDS (2008) *Report on the Global HIV/AIDS Epidemic*, Geneva: UNAIDS, Electronic document, www.unaids.org/epidemic_update.htm, accessed 30 December 2009

Watts, M. and Bohle, H. (1993) 'The Space of Vulnerability: The Causal Structure of Hunger and Famine', *Progress in Human Geography*, vol 17, pp43–67

World Bank (1995) *Rural Women in the Sahel and their Access to Agricultural Extension Sector Study: Overview of Five Countries*, World Bank, Washington DC

Zaba, B., Boerma, J., Pisani, E. and Baptiste, N. (2002) 'Estimation of Levels and Trends in Age at First Sex from African Demographic Surveys Using Survival Analysis', Paper presented at the Annual Meeting of the Population Association of America May 9–11, Atlanta, Georgia

Zuidberg, L. (1994) 'Burkina Faso: Integrated Rural Development for Whom with Whom?' in V. Gianotten, E. Groverman, V. Walgun and L. Zuidberg, *Assessing the Gender Impact of Development Projects: Case Studies from Bolivia, Burkina Faso, and India*, pp49–70, Intermediate Technology Publications, London

Chapter 8

Multilayered impacts of AIDS and implications for food security among banana farmers in Uganda

Monica Karuhanga Beraho

Introduction

The main objective of this chapter is to highlight the differential and multilayered effects of AIDS among banana farming households in the Masaka and Kabarole districts of Uganda. The chapter discusses the differential effects of AIDS – gender, age and life course and, by extension, implications of those effects for food security among different actors. In this chapter, I point out that the effects of AIDS are multilayered in order to illustrate the differential impacts on poor and relatively well-to-do households. The term multilayered is used to refer to the different levels at which one can identify the effects of AIDS. The main 'layers' distinguished in this chapter include: socio-economic status (poor versus well-off), household headship (female versus male-headed households), AIDS status (affected versus non-affected), and the interrelationships between those variables. Lastly, is the layer of geographical location (district), even though the influence of this variable is limited to a few of the above-mentioned variables.

Uganda is a country still relatively reliant on agriculture. The role of the sector in national development and the livelihoods of the majority of Ugandans cannot be over emphasized. However, AIDS continues to cause significant adverse effects to agricultural production and agricultural-based livelihoods. In Uganda, food and livelihood insecurity, increased vulnerability and adverse socio-economic impacts have been identified in many instances as causes and consequences of AIDS. Although achieving self-sufficiency in food production has for long been one of the major food security strategies for government, the situation has been changing and different parts of Uganda are increasingly experiencing food shortages. The Plan for Modernization of Agriculture (PMA) has identified female-headed households and households with large families, women, widows, male youth, and people depending on vulnerable sources of income (e.g. fisher folk and nomads) and small-scale farmers growing only one low-value crop as vulnerable social groups (MAAIF, 2000). With prevailing poverty and high HIV prevalence levels, such vulnerable households are likely to have a lower ability to invest in agricultural production with the likely consequences of reduced production and food security.

The risk of food insecurity has been described as having three dimensions, that is, risk of exposure to crises or shocks, the magnitude or consequences of crises and households' vulnerability to these crises (Bohle, 1993). The latter dimension is determined by the adequacy of a household's capacity to cope with crises. Arguably, a household's asset base or its ability to create new assets may determine its ability to cope with crises. While it has been observed that in times of crises such as those caused by AIDS, vulnerable households begin to sell their belongings or assets, such as livestock, tools, personal possessions or household goods (Gillespie et al., 2001), the magnitude of effects are likely to be different for different social actors. In this chapter we investigate how location, wealth status and household headship modulate AIDS-related effects and household members' capacity to respond to these effects. In addition we examine the implications of these effects to household food (in)security.

Data collection involved the use of both qualitative and quantitative data collection methods. A descriptive survey targeting 543 households (305 in Masaka district and 238 in Kabarole district) was conducted to collect primary data. The survey sought to collect respondents' perceptions of changes in household assets, income and food security status over the period 2002–2005. Additional information was collected from key informants and focus group discussions (FGD) organized separately for both men and women. A total of 15 women's and 15 men's groups were interviewed.

We used both quantitative and qualitative methods of data collection. The household was selected as the unit of analysis. For purposes of quantitative analysis, survey households were categorized into three groups: the first group comprised of male-headed households. The second group consisted of single-female-headed households while the third group comprised of widow-headed households. For analysis, comparisons were drawn between the male-headed and the two types of female-headed households in Masaka and Kabarole districts. In each group of households we categorized well-off and poor households based on variables such as household per capita income, food expenditures and area under cultivation, particularly for main crops. In addition, comparisons were drawn between 'AIDS-affected' and 'non-affected' households. In this study, 'affected households' are defined as households that were directly affected by AIDS and therefore had at least one member known to be HIV-positive at the time of the study or had died from (an) AIDS (-related) illness. Based on key informant information obtained from health personnel, households reporting illness or death due to tuberculosis were included among 'AIDS-affected households'. Households that were not directly affected by AIDS are defined as 'non-affected households' and included those where no member was suffering or had died from illness related to AIDS.

For the purposes of this chapter, quantitative techniques such as descriptive statistics, General Linear Model-GLM (Multiple Comparative Procedure) and nonparametric statistics were used to understand the relationships between different variables. Percentages were used to determine and explain proportions, while means were mainly used to determine differences in household asset ownership and use food adequacy as well as AIDS-affectedness. GLM was used to obtain group means for the following variables: (i) Household (HH) assets by household headship, wealth status and AIDS-affectedness; (ii) mean HH asset change by household headship, wealth status and HIV/AIDS-affectedness; (iii) mean adequacy food score by household headship by district and by household headship; (v) food security status by whether AIDS-affected HH and by district; and (vi) mean HH expenditures by household headship, wealth and AIDS-affectedness. Multiple comparison tests of significance (T-test or Chi Square) were used to assess which group means differed significantly from which others.

It is noteworthy that the adequacy score—a mean rank explaining adequacy of the various food categories for each household was used as a proxy for household food security, which in turn was used as an indicator for livelihood vulnerability. The ranks ranged from 1 to 4 with rank 4 representing the highest adequacy score. The Wilcoxon signed-rank test, T, for matched pairs, was used to compare the mean adequacy food scores of households in the two study areas.

The remaining part of the chapter is organized in three sections. The first section presents the results obtained from the study while the second section presents the implications of HIV/AIDS-affectedness on food and livelihood security of the surveyed households. The last section discusses the key findings and conclusions of the study and implications for agricultural policies and programmes.

Results

Information presented in this section was collected from 541 households (302 from Masaka and 239 from Kabarole districts). Of these, 72.1 per cent were male-headed, 18.7 per cent widow-headed and 9.1 per cent headed by single women. There is a high level of widowhood in the study area with two-fifths being caused by AIDS and the phenomenon being more prevalent among women than men. Categorization by wealth status shows that of the total sample, poor households constituted 69 per cent and well-off households 31 per cent, while categorization by AIDS-affectedness shows that 21 per cent of the households were affected by AIDS. Apart from implications for food security, the data presented are not disaggregated by district. For more information on the differences between the districts, see Karuhanga, 2008.

According to Niehof (2004), the household may be seen as the locus of livelihood generation, with assets and resources forming the basic building blocks upon which it may be able to undertake production and engage in labour markets. However, different households vary in their asset base as well as in their capability to substitute between assets when confronted by change (Reardon and Vosti, 1995 cited in Ellis, 2000). Consequently, the magnitude of the impacts of AIDS on agricultural-based livelihoods are likely to be linked to an individual, household, or community's resource/asset base and eventually on how these resources are managed in the face of AIDS. Arguably, the differential ownership and access to assets and resources by well-off or poor households, whether they are male- or female-headed or by men and women in male-headed households, imply likely differential impacts of AIDS. To have an understanding of the

Table 8.1 *Selected household characteristics by household headship*

Household characteristic	SF-HH (%) N=50 Mean (SD)	Male-HH (%) N=390 Mean (SD)	W-HH (%) N=101 Mean (SD)
Age of Household head*** (years)	43.5 (13.16) [a]	41.6 (13.63) [a]	49.8 (12.03) [b]
Household size	6.1 (2.43)	6.5 (2.70)	5.4 (2.39)
Number of adult equivalents **	3.84 (1.38) [ab]	4.09 (1.54) [a]	3.42 (1.38) [b]
Acreage under banana	0.93 (0.99)	1.23 (1.10)	1.01 (0.98)
Acreage under annual crops[MB]	1.28 (1.43)	1.77 (1.57)	1.40 (1.53)
Total livestock units**	0.44 (0.69) [b]	1.21 (2.71) [a]	0.56 (1.09) [b]
Total land owned in 2005 (acres)**	1.66 (1.45) [a]	3.33 (5.35) [b]	2.04 (1.89) [c]
Education of HH head	(%)	(%)	(%)
Educated*	66.0[a]	82.0[b]	56.0[a]
Not educated*	34.0[a]	18.0[b]	44.0[a]

Source: Household survey, Karuhanga, 2008; a –Annual crops = maize and beans; ***, **,*, implies significant difference at 1%, 5% and 10% levels, respectively. Superscripts with the same letter across the row are not significantly different. SH-HH = Single-female-headed, Male-HH = Male-headed and W-HH = Widow-headed

multilayered impacts of AIDS the results will focus on selected household characteristics and access to key assets of the surveyed households.

Household characteristics

In Table 8.1 we present household characteristics by household headship. The mean age of the household head was 42 years. Female household heads were likely to be older. As can be seen in Table 8.1, the mean age of widowed household heads at 49.5 years was significantly different (p< 0.01) from that of single female heads (44 years) and male heads (42 years). The average household size was about six, of which approximately 2 persons were adults (18 years and above), implying that about two-thirds of household members are dependants. While there was no significant difference in household size, widowed households had significantly (p< 0.05) fewer adult equivalents (mean 3.42) than those headed by single females (mean 3.84) and males (mean 4.09). A higher proportion (p=0.1) of male household heads were educated compared to their female counterparts (Table 8.1). The majority of female-headed households were likely to be less educated, with more dependants and a significantly higher likelihood of being poor and AIDS-affected.

Table 8.2 presents information on selected household characteristics by wealth status. It is shown that household heads in the well-off group were about seven years younger than those in poor households. The well-off households also had fewer household members with the mean household size and mean number of adult equivalents (5.7 and 3.6) being less than the overall sample means (6.3 and 4.0). In addition, a significantly higher (p<0.01) proportion of household heads in well-off households were educated and had capacity to use hired labour compared to household heads in poor households. Therefore, the majority of well-off households was likely to be headed by educated males and had a significantly lower likelihood of being AIDS-affected.

Table 8.3 presents selected household characteristics by wealth status and AIDS-affectedness. It is shown that regardless of wealth status, there was no significant difference

Table 8.2 *Selected household characteristics by wealth status*

Variables	Well-off HH N=167 Mean (SD)	Poor HH N=374 Mean (SD)	Overall N=541 Mean (SD)	T-statistic
Age HH head(years)	38.1(12.4)	45.6 (14.0)	43.3 (13.9)	−5.983***
HH size	5.7 (2.4)	6.6 (2.7)	6.3 (2.7)	3.554***
Number of adult equivalents	3.6 (1.4)	4.1 (1.6)	4.0 (1.5)	−3.693***
Acreage under banana	1.29 (1.29)	1.09 (0.96)	1.15 (1.07)	1.973**
Annual crops acreage[a]	1.93 (1.76)	1.53 (1.45)	1.66 (1.56)	2.742***
Total livestock units	1.02(2.27)	1.02 (2.21)	1.02 (2.37)	−0.000[NS]

	N	%	N	%	N	%	X^2
Education of HH head							
Educated	99	59.3	165	44.1	264	48.8	10.625***
Not educated	68	40.7	209	55.9	277	51.2	
Use of hired labour							
Yes	91	54.5	132	35.3	223	58.8	17.560***
No	76	45.5	242	64.7	318	41.2	

Source: Household survey, Karuhanga, 2008; a –Annual crops = maize and beans; ***,* implies significantly different at 1% and 10% levels, respectively. [NS] implies not significant.

between AIDS-affected and non-affected households with regard to age of household head, number of adult equivalents and use of hired labour (Table 8.3). However, the proportion of educated household heads in affected households was significantly (p<0.01) smaller than that for educated household heads in non-affected households. It is also shown that household heads in poor AIDS-affected households were older with a significantly (p=0.01) higher mean age (50 years) compared to their counterparts in non-affected households (mean age= 44 years).

Access to resources

Access to physical assets

The main household assets accessible to households and discussed in this section include land and family labour, and to a lesser extent, small and large stock. For all the household assets investigated, the two types of female-headed households had fewer assets than their male counterparts (Table 8.1).

Land: While there is almost universal access to land, it is unevenly distributed with the majority owning less than a hectare (2 acres). Household level analysis revealed that single-female household heads owned less arable land compared to widowed household heads (Table 8.1). However, there was no significant difference in crop area cultivated by household headship. Well-off HH had significantly (p=0.05) larger land acreages with the mean acreage under banana (1.29 as against 1.09) and selected annuals (1.93 as against 1.53) being higher among well-off households (Table 8.2). It is noteworthy that landlessness and poverty are not confined to women only. Karuhanga (2008) observed that seasonal variation in access to land as well as the processes associated with women's access to land (that is, access through marriage or male-relatives) increases tenure

Table 8.3 *Selected household characteristics by AIDS-affectedness*

HH characteristic	AIDS-affected mean (SD)	Non-affected mean (SD)	Overall (n=541) mean (SD)	T – Statistic
Age of HH head (Years)				
Well-off HH (n=167)	41.3 (13.8)	37.5 (12.1)	38.0 (12.5)	−1.447[NS]
Poor HH (n=374)	50.1(14.1)	44.1(13.6)	45.6 (14.0)	−3.607[***]
Household size				
Well-off HH (n=167)	5.3 (1.7)	5.7 (2.5)	5.7 (2.4)	0.771[NS]
Poor HH (n=374)	6.7 (2.9)	6.5 (2.6)	6.6 (2.7)	-0.554[NS]
Number of adult equivalents				
Well-off HH (n=167)	3.40(0.86)	3.62(1.46)	3.59(1.38)	0.776 [NS]
Poor HH (n=374)	1.05(0.8)	1.10(1.0)	1.09(1.0)	0.683[NS]
Acreage under banana				
Well-off HH (n=167)	0.84(0.8)	1.37(1.4)	1.29(1.3)	1.953[*]
Poor HH (n=374)	1.05(0.8)	1.10(1.0)	1.09(1.0)	0.428[NS]
Acreage for annual crops				
Well-off HH (n=167)	1.89(2.26)	1.94(1.66)	1.93(1.76)	1.121 [NS]
Poor HH (n=374)	1.70(1.37)	1.48(1.46)	1.53(1.44)	−1.274[NS]
Total livestock units				
Well-off HH (n=167)	0.61(0.94)	1.097(2.93)	1.02(2.72)	0.837 [NS]
Poor HH (n=374)	1.03(2.64)	1.01(2.06)	1.02(2.21)	−0.056[NS]
	N %	N %	N %	X^2
Education of HH head				
Educated	37 31.9	227 53.4	264 48.8	16.883[***]
Not educated	79 68.1	198 46.6	277 51.2	
Used hired labour				
Yes	44 37.9	179 42.1	223 41.2	0.659[NS]
No	72 62.1	246 57.9	318 58.8	

Source: Household survey, Karuhanga, 2008; a –Annual crops = maize and beans; ***,* implies significant difference at 1% and 10% levels, respectively. [NS] implies not significant.

insecurity of individuals in poor households, more so for women. Table 8.3 shows that slightly significant differences (p=0.1) exist among the well-off households with AIDS-affected households having smaller acreage planted with banana compared to those that are non-affected.

*Livestock: M*ale headed households had significantly (p< 0.05) larger numbers of livestock units (mean 1.21) compared to their female counterparts (with single female-headed having a mean of 0.44 and widow-headed a mean of mean 0.56). This result corroborates existing evidence that female headed households are among the poorest and most vulnerable households because of small asset base (MAAIF, 2000). Regardless of wealth status, there was no significant difference between AIDS-affected and non-affected households with regard to area planted with annual crops and total livestock units owned.

Impact on physical assets: Table 8.4 presents change in household assets over the period of study (2002–2005). Female-headed households (majority of which are poor and AIDS-affected) experienced greater asset depletion than male-headed ones. The assets that the two types of female-headed households were likely to own (small

Table 8.4 *Change in household assets by wealth and AIDS status, and by household headship 2002–2005*

Type of asset change	AIDS-affected N=116 Mean(SD)	Non-affected N=425 Mean(SD)	Overall N=541 Mean(SD)	T-Statistic
Well-off HH				
Change in land (n=163)	−0.03 (0.15)	0.11(2.63)	0.09 (2.42)	0.267[NS]
Change in cattle (n=43)	0(0.71)	−1.18(2.87)	−1.07(2.78)	−0.805[NS]
Change in small livestock (n=165)	−0.96(2.89)	−0.87(4.50)	−0.88(4.28)	−0.101[NS]
Poor HH				
Change in land (n=364)	−0.13 (1.67)	0.13 (0.93)	0.07 (1.15)	1.830[*]
Change in cattle (n=79)	−0.81(3.41)	−1.36(4.33)	−1.22(4.09)	−0.528[NS]
Change in small L/stock (n=374)	−1.72(4.03)	−0.35(3.93)	−0.68(4.00)	2.874[***]
Household headship	SF-HH (%) N=50	Male-HH (%) N=390	W-HH (%) N=101	
	Mean (SD)	Mean (SD)	Mean (SD)	
Change in land owned in acres (2002–2005) [**]	1.56 (0.51) [ab]	1.40 (0.49) [a]	1.61 (0.49) [b]	
Change in cattle (2002–2005)	−0.24(0.98)	−0.11(2.15)	0.01(1.17)[NS]	

Source: Household survey, Karuhanga, 2008.[NS] implies not significant; [*],[**], [***] shows variables that are significantly different across the row at the 10%, 5% and 1% levels, respectively. Superscripts with the same letter across the row are not significantly different. SH-HH = Single-female-headed, Male-HH = Male-headed and W-HH = Widow-headed.
N.B: Negative sign implies that the livestock numbers or land acreage decreased.

stock) significantly declined over the period of study. This may imply that fewer assets are depleted to care for sick women in male-headed households or that households experience more asset depletion if the male household head gets infected. While one would need more data to substantiate this conclusion, there is documented evidence to this effect elsewhere (Rugalema, 1999).

Access to labour
Family labour is almost exclusively the main source of labour for agricultural activities. Results in this study show no significant difference in household size and number of economically active individuals per household between the two districts. However, households in Masaka have a significantly higher dependency ratio than those in Kabarole district. Lack of labour due to limited capacity to hire labour or due to reduced household labour as a result of sickness was identified as having significant impact on agricultural production.

In Table 8.1 we showed that widowed households were likely to have less family labour compared to other household types. Results also showed that there was significant difference in the use of hired labour between well-off and poor households (p<0.01).

However, no significant differences were observed between AIDS-affected and non-affected households with regard to hired labour access.

AIDS impact on labour: Ill-health was identified as one of the main causes of reduced household labour with malaria and AIDS being the leading causes of ill health and death. AIDS-related impacts on household labour include poor health, increased care and orphan burden, and loss of income of sick or dead household members (Karuhanga, 2005). While men, women and children participate in AIDS-related care provision, both qualitative and quantitative data showed that the burden of AIDS-related care fell disproportionately on women and girls. The most significant effect of ill health on agricultural production was related to poor agronomic practices for all crops because of reduced household labour (40 per cent). This was followed by a decline in crop yields (39 per cent) and increase in pests and diseases (17 per cent).

Empirical data reveal that AIDS in the household results in a higher reduction of labour productivity compared to reduction caused by malaria and other diseases (Karuhanga, 2008). A significantly higher proportion (p=0.01) of AIDS-affected households reported sick and bedridden productive household members and about twice as many bedridden days than non-affected households. Regardless of wealth status, a higher proportion of AIDS-affected households experienced an adult death than non-affected ones. Focus group information revealed that the impact of a woman's death is more associated with reduced household food security and reduced care of the children, particularly of those below five years of age. However, effects due to the death of a male head are associated with reduced household labour and incomes. Differences in HIV/AIDS-related labour effects were more significant among poor affected households than among their well-off counterparts.

Also noted in the study was that while widowers easily remarried and were able to replace lost labour, most widows did not remarry and therefore experienced labour constraints. Not only did widow-headed households suffer from the loss of the dead spouse's labour, but because in many cases the widows were also HIV infected, they also became less productive. According to Karuhanga (2008), over two-thirds of the AIDS-widows interviewed reported intensifying their own labour to cope with the loss of spousal labour.

It is noteworthy that limited household labour predates AIDS in labour-poor households, also in those headed by old people, women and children. Factors such as the young structure of Uganda's population, the low participation of adult men in agricultural activities and the limited access to child labour due to universal primary education are responsible for causing labour constraints in rural areas (UBOS, 2003). Nonetheless, being AIDS-affected intensifies labour-related constraints in such households.

Access to income

The main source of income was agricultural, from the sale of crops followed by livestock, and to a limited extent, agricultural labour. The majority (87 per cent) reported income change during the period 2002–2005, with two-thirds experiencing reductions. Low yields due to prolonged drought and reduced household labour due to sickness were reported as main causes of reduced household incomes. For those households that reported increased incomes, respondents said that it was due to increased agricultural production, good market prices at the time of sale and engagement in off-farm income-generating activities.

Impact on income: AIDS-related economic effects are reflected in both the incomes and expenditures. With regard to changes in household income over the period 2002–2005, the results show no direct linkage between AIDS status and income changes among the surveyed households. Furthermore, there is no significant difference in the proportion of AIDS households that reported increased or reduced incomes over the same period. The lack of linkage observed between AIDS status and change in household income points to the fact that AIDS affects individuals in all social economic classes (cf. Ainsworth and Semali, 1998; Chapoto and Jayne, 2005).

Table 8.5 presents household expenditure by household headship, wealth status and AIDS-affectedness. It is shown that the relatively well-off households have higher mean values for all household expenditure variables used. Total per capita household expenditure is about three-and-a-half times, total per capita daily food expenditure ten times and the total annual household expenditure three times that of poor households. Furthermore, household level analysis reveals that the two types of female-headed

Table 8.5 *Household expenditure by household headship, wealth status and AIDS-affectedness*

Type of HH expenditure (US$)	SF-HH N=50		Male-HH N=390		W-HH N=101		
	Mean	SD	Mean	SD	Mean	SD	
Annual Expenditure**	473.68[a]	401.58	661.58[b]	604.21	446.32[a]	466.84	
Total per capita expenditure**	0.34[a]	0.26	0.48[b]	0.47	0.36[a]	0.34	
Per capita food expenditure[NS]	0.18	0.21	0.22	0.41	0.17	0.24	

	AIDS-affected N=116		Non-affected N=425		Overall N=541		T- Statistic
	Mean	SD	Mean	SD	Mean	SD	
Annual expenditure							
Well-off HH	1006.42	575.42	1115.47	791.42	1098.53	761.37	0.715[NS]
Poor HH	345.05	236.16	395.32	237.26	383.21	237.68	2.772[*]
Per capita expenditure							
Well-off HH	0.80	0.40	0.89	0.59	0.88	0.56	0.715[NS]
Poor HH	0.22	0.11	0.26	0.12	0.25	0.12	2.772[***]
Per capita food expenditure							
Well-off HH	0.40	0.47	0.45	0.61	0.45	0.59	0.464[NS]
Poor HH	0.09	0.06	0.10	0.07	0.10	0.06	1.384[NS]

Source: Household survey, Karuhanga, 2008. . [***], [**], [*], identifies variables that are significantly different across the row at the 1%, 5% and 10% levels, respectively. [NS] implies not significant. Superscripts with the same letter across the row are not significantly different. SH-HH = Single-female-headed, Male-HH = Male-headed and W-HH = Widow-headed.

households that constituted the largest proportion of poor households have the smallest total annual and per capita expenditure compared to male-headed households.

AIDS leads to an increase in medical expenditure but reduces total per capita expenditure (Karuhanga, 2008). The differences in medical expenditure were found to be more pronounced among poor households (affected and non-affected) than among the well-off, implying that AIDS has limited effects on well-off households. Apart from medical expenditures, there were no statistically significant differences observed in money spent on other household items between AIDS-affected and non-affected households regardless of wealth status. Karuhanga (2008) also observed that among affected households, those reporting an AIDS-related adult death spent more on food than those with an AIDS patient while the latter were likely to spend more on medicines. It is noteworthy that expenditure increases associated with problems that create heightened vulnerability, such as expenditure on curative healthcare or increased food purchases due to inability to produce adequate food for own consumption, should not be mistaken to mean improved wellbeing among affected households.

Implications of AIDS-affectedness for food security

In this study food security was defined as the household's ability to command an adequate amount of required food through any one of a combination of existing sources. The majority of households depend on own production as the main source of household food and the main food crops grown included banana, maize, beans, sweet potato and cassava. Foods that were commonly mentioned as adequate by most respondents (over 60 per cent) included; banana, maize, beans, fruits and vegetables, with fruits and vegetables being the most abundantly available. All household types said that protein foods were in most cases not sufficiently available or inadequate.

Table 8.6 presents mean food adequacy scores by household headship and district. District level analysis reveals significant differences in the mean adequacy food scores (p< 0.1) for the two districts. Kabarole district had a higher adequacy score (2.9) than Masaka district (2.2). For households in Masaka, food adequacy mainly ranged between barely adequate to adequate. The difference between the districts can be partly explained by information obtained from the FGDs, which revealed that between 2004 and 2005 farmers in Masaka district had experienced long periods of drought and other weather-related problems to a greater extent than farmers in Kabarole district. However, the higher economic dependency ratio of households in Masaka (2.8), compared to that of Kabarole (1.8) can be another explanatory factor. Table 8.6 also shows that male-headed households had significantly higher (p<0.01) food adequacy scores than the two types of female-headed households. Single-female headed households had the lowest food adequacy score.

Aggregate scores for each household were also used to categorize households into three groups indicating their food security status.[1] For the sample as a whole, 24 per cent of the households were identified as food secure, 43 per cent barely food secure, while food adequacy scores for about one-third of the households put them in the food insecure category.

---

[1] Food insecure had aggregate scores < 21; Barely food secure had aggregate scores = or > 21 but < 35; Food secure had aggregate scores > 35.

Table 8.6 *Mean food adequacy score by household headship and district*

Mean food adequacy Score	Household Headship[*]			District[*]	
	SF- HH N=50	M-HH N=390	W-HH N=101	Masaka N=302	Kabarole N=239
Mean (SD)	2.33 (0.43)[bc]	2.58 (0.348)[b]	2.45 (0.39)[c]	2.41 (0.57)[a]	2.85 (0.53)[b]

Source: Household Survey, Karuhanga, 2008.[*] Implies significant difference at 10% level. Superscripts with the same letter across a row are not significantly different. SH-HH = Single-female-headed, Male-HH = Male-headed and W-HH = Widow-headed.

More in-depth analysis (see Karuhanga, 2008) reveals that for the sample as a whole, AIDS-affected households were likely to be food insecure, although the evidence is not very strong ($p<0.1$). District level analysis shows that there was no significant difference in the food security status of affected and non-affected households in Kabarole district, indicating no direct link between AIDS and the food security status of these households. For Masaka, non-affected households were more likely to be food secure compared to affected households but the difference was marginal ($p<0.1$), which can partly be explained by factors already discussed above. Household level analysis seems to show a link between household food adequacies and mean household asset status. Households headed by males that performed better in household asset ownership turned out to be more food secure than female- and widow-headed households that had lower mean asset values. The above differences point to the fact that HIV/AIDS is just one among a multiplicity of factors that influence the food security status of a given household and, depending on prevailing circumstances, may or may not be the one producing the most significant effects.

These results show that wealth, gender and being affected by AIDS are key determinants for food security in both districts – the effects are clearly socially differentiated. Better-off households generally access a broader range of resources to mitigate the effects of AIDS than poorer households. Male-headed households in the Well-off HH category, for example, who had access to hired labour and were educated, were likely to have more secure livelihoods and were better able to cope with the effects of AIDS. It is important to bear in mind, however, that some of the differences observed between AIDS-affected and non-affected households are not directly attributable to AIDS but may be associated with other socio-economic or environmental factors. Nonetheless, if those factors are associated with vulnerability, the superimposition of AIDS only intensifies such vulnerabilities.

Discussion and conclusion

As argued in literature, HIV and AIDS impacts are not gender neutral, since they are mediated by social-cultural landscapes (Gillespie *et al.*, 2001; UNDP, 2002). The study found out that gender, wealth status and location influence the way people respond to or cope with the effects of the epidemic.

Key conclusions coming out of the study indicate that well-off households that were mainly male-headed had more physical household assets and income and were more likely to be food secure compared to the other households. However, among the female-headed households, widow-headed households were better off than the single female-headed ones in a number of instances. This may imply that widows from wealthier households may be better off (in terms of resilience to AIDS impacts) than women from poor households. Prolonged drought, followed by reduced household labour due to sickness and pests and diseases, featured as the main constraints to agricultural production as well as causes of declining household incomes. In a situation of AIDS, reduced household labour has significant implications because it impacts on the most important asset of the poor, that is, their time and labour with likely consequences of reduced agricultural production and incomes. With declining incomes, households find it more and more difficult to invest in agriculture, with consequences of reduced production and a high likelihood of household food insecurity. Additionally, AIDS-affected households experience the effects of increased expenditures due to AIDS-related treatment and care. Additionally, although the majority of households reported own production as the main source of household food, the market is increasingly becoming an important source of food. However, in the face of declining household incomes, non-expansion of household assets, small landholdings and other production-related constraints coupled with high AIDS prevalence levels, the capacity of households, particularly female-headed ones, to ensure sustained household food sufficiency becomes questionable.

AIDS exacerbates gender inequalities (Müller, 2005a). The subordinate position of women, the inequalities in access to resources, and the barriers to women's effective control over what they own, have been responsible for women's vulnerability to the epidemic. While AIDS-related health impairment is not gender-specific per se, when superimposed on the debilitation of old age among widows, and exacerbated by other gender-related constraints of limited labour, land and other resources, the resulting circumstances can only lead to increased vulnerability, as qualitative findings in the study illustrate. Conversely, women are not a homogenous group, and the study has shown that women in different households, occupying different positions in the same household or of different wealth status, own different levels of assets and have different life opportunities. Thus, it is relevant to identify the specific resource needs and vulnerabilities of different categories of women.

From the discussion it is clear that a household's wealth or socio-economic status changes in resources over time, and its demographic characteristics substantially influence the extent of the effects of AIDS on the members' livelihood. In the overwhelming majority of affected cases the effects of AIDS are negative and lead to increased impoverishment and vulnerability. However, for some households, the severity of AIDS-related effects are not so great as to be unmanageable, for others there was no impact, while in some cases AIDS produced a positive impact. For example, Appleton et al. (1995), cites case studies showing distress sales of land and labour by the poor to the rich. Others have benefited from the exploitation of cheap labour of widows and orphaned children (UNDP, 1995).

In this study it is also noted that regardless of wealth, gender and age, differences were observed between affected households. This implies that there are other location-specific factors that influence the magnitude of AIDS-related effects and the ability of individuals and households to respond to them. Karuhanga (2008), noted, for example, that affected households that: (i) had close kin capable of providing financial, food or care-related support; (ii) had connections to institutions or NGOs providing AIDS-related care and support or are located in areas served by these organizations; (iii) had access to health services that provided (free) treatment for opportunistic infections and/or ARVs; (iv) were personally known to or have kinship relations with local politicians; or (v) belonged to informal social networks, were better off than affected households that did not have such access or connections. She cites affected households in Mbirizi and Kyazanga in Masaka district, which had more rings of social support (relatives, informal networks, local NGOs and government) than in other villages in Masaka and in Kabarole and seemed to be coping better. For some of these households, this dampened the effects of the epidemic and improved, for example, people's food security or opportunities for orphan education. Comparing the two districts, this study shows that the interaction between the high HIV-prevalence levels and longer duration of the epidemic in Masaka with other location-specific factors like drought, declining soil fertility and pests and diseases, increased the vulnerability of affected households in Masaka district compared to those in Kabarole district.

The results point to the fact that AIDS is just one factor among a variety of factors that make households vulnerable. While AIDS is not the only factor influencing vulnerability and that in some instances other factors may cause more significant effects on people's food and overall livelihood security than AIDS, this study has shown that AIDS seriously exacerbates the livelihood problems of those who get infected as well as their households and communities. At the same time, environmental factors and processes increase susceptibility to AIDS and intensify AIDS-related vulnerability (Müller, 2005b). It is noteworthy that these different factors and processes may converge differently at different points in space or time, creating a very different manifestation of vulnerability for different households and even for individuals within the same household, thus the concept of 'multilayered' impacts.

Livelihoods are complex and the multidimensional nature of the interactions between different factors and processes in the environment, and between and within households complicates investigating them and developing viable solutions that can translate to positive livelihood outcomes. This makes disentangling and dealing with the impacts of AIDS even more difficult. Nonetheless, this study shows that AIDS, whether alone or in combination with other factors, causes differential effects among different actors. This understanding is crucial not only for the development of relevant policies and intervention programmes, but also for ensuring that responses are better designed and targeted to meet the heterogeneous nature of men's and women's needs and vulnerabilities. Furthermore, it is clear that AIDS aggravates the livelihoods of the already poor and vulnerable, hence strengthening a household's asset base and expanding opportunities to diversify activities are likely to assist in protecting a household and its members against external shocks, such as AIDS. Efforts to support vulnerable households could focus on interventions that can (i) increase different actors' ability to increase production and productivity through, for example, increased access to agricultural extension services and credit and other incentives and (ii) increase actors' ability to access quality health information and services (need for increasing awareness on AIDS and other related diseases). This should be in addition to addressing the other broader agricultural constraints identified in the study as well as those related to women's subordinate position.

References

Ainsworth, M. and Semali, M. (1998) 'Who is most likely to die of AIDS? Socioeconomic correlates of adult deaths in Kagera Region, Tanzania', in M. Ainsworth, L. Fransen and M. Over (eds), *Confronting AIDS: Evidence from the Developing World*, European Commission, Brussels, pp95–109

Appleton, S., Balihuta, A., Bevan, P., Mackinnon, J. A., Ssewaya, A. and Ssemwogerere, G. (1995) *Poverty in Uganda in 1994: A Research Report*, Centre for the Study of African Economies (CSAE) [Mimeo]

Bohle, H.G. (1993) *The Geography of Vulnerable Food Systems*, Universität Freiburg, Germany

Chapoto, A. and Jayne, T.S. (2005) *Socioeconomic Characteristics of Individuals Afflicted by AIDS-related Prime-age Mortality in Zambia Policy Synthesis No.10*, Food Security Research project – Zambia. Ministry of Agriculture and Cooperatives, Agriculture Consultative Forum, Michigan State University, www.aec.msu.edu/agecon/fs2/zambia/index.htm, accessed 12 September, 2007

Ellis, F. (2000) *Rural Livelihoods and Diversity in Developing Countries*, Oxford University Press, Oxford

Gillespie, S., Haddad, L. and Jackson, R. (2001) *HIV/AIDS, Food and Nutrition Security: Impacts and Actions*, Paper presented at the 28th Session of the ACC/SCN Symposium on Nutrition and HIV/AIDS 1st May 2001, Geneva

Karuhanga, B.M. (2005) 'Gendered impacts of HIV/AIDS and their implications for food security', *Eastern Africa Journal of Rural Development*, vol 21, no 1, pp137–167

Karuhanga, B.M. (2008) *Living with AIDS in Uganda: Impact on Banana-farming Households in Two Districts*, AWLAE Series No. 6, Wageningen Academic Publishers, Wageningen, The Netherlands

MAAIF and MFPED (2000) *Plan for Modernization of Agriculture (PMA): Eradicating Poverty in Uganda*, Government of Uganda, Kampala, Uganda

MFPED (2004) *Poverty Eradication Action Plan 2004/5–2007/8*, Ministry of Finance, Planning and Economic Development, Kampala, Uganda

MOH and ORC (2006) *Uganda HIV/AIDS Sero-behavioural Survey 2004–2005*, Ministry of Health and ORC Macro, Calverton, Maryland

Müller, T.R. (2005a) *HIV/AIDS, Gender and Rural Livelihoods in Sub-Saharan Africa*, Wageningen Academic Publishers, Wageningen, The Netherlands [AWLAE Series No. 2]

Müller, T.R. (2005b) *HIV/AIDS and Human Development in Sub-Saharan Africa*, AWLAE Series No. 3, Wageningen Academic Publishers, Wageningen, The Netherlands

Niehof, A. (2004) 'The significance of diversification for rural livelihood systems', *Food Policy*, vol 29, no 4, pp321–338

Rugalema, G., (1999) 'It is not only the loss of labor: HIV/AIDS, loss of household assets and household livelihood in Bukoba District, Tanzania', in G. Mutangadura, H. Jackson and D. Mukurazita (eds), *AIDS and African Smallholder Agriculture*, pp41–52, Southern African AIDS Information Dissemination Service (SAFAIDS), Harare, Zimbabwe

Saito, K.A. (1992) *Raising the Productivity of Women Farmers in Sub-Saharan Africa* (Vol. 1), Overview Report, World Bank, Population and Human Resources Development Department, Washington DC

Seeley, J., Sutherland, K., Dey, R. and Grellier, R. (2003) *Mitigation of Gender-specific Impact of HIV/AIDS on Rural Livelihoods*, unpublished report to DFID, Norwich, August 2003

Uganda Bureau of Statistics (UBOS) (2003) *2002 National Census Report,* Uganda Bureau of Statistics, Kampala, Uganda

UNDP (1995) Quoted in *Human Development Report 1997*, Oxford University, New York

UNDP (2002) *Uganda Human Development Report. The Challenge of HIV/AIDS: Maintaining the Momentum of Success,* UNDP, Kampala, Uganda

Chapter 9

Impact of HIV/AIDS on local farming knowledge: differences in the cognitive salience of maize crop pests between affected and non-affected adults and children in Benin[1]

Rose Fagbemissi and Lisa Leimar Price

Introduction

The spread of HIV to farming communities has increased the precariousness of life for millions of smallholders (Jayne et al., 2004). Researchers note a shift towards an increasing number of rural children taking on adult responsibilities (Rugalema et al., 1999; Haddad and Gillespie, 2001; Baylies, 2002; Dewagt and Connolly, 2005; Drimie and Casale, 2008). In difficult contexts such as that of the HIV/AIDS pandemic with its depletive effect on rural livelihoods, agricultural knowledge is a very important resource (Barnett et al., 1995; Bollinger et al., 1999; Haddad and Gillespie, 2001; Dewagt and Connolly, 2005). However, earlier in this decade, the intergenerational knowledge gap was speculated to be profound in the face of HIV/AIDS (Haddad and Gillespie, 2001; Loevinsohn and Gillespie, 2003). An assumed knowledge gap in farming that children orphaned by AIDS may have is of growing international concern (Baylies,

---

[1]A version of this paper was initially published as: Fagbemissi, R.C. and Price, L.L. (2008) 'HIV/ AIDS orphans as farmers: uncovering pest knowledge differences through an ethnobiological approach in Benin', *NJAS*, vol 56, no 3, pp241–259.

2002; Dewagt and Connolly, 2005; FAO, 2005). The Junior Farmer Field and Life School Program, an initiative of FAO in partnership with the World Food Program and other UN Agencies designed to enhance learning in the agricultural domain among these children, exemplifies how serious this issue is being taken in the international arena (FAO, 2005).

The assumption about the loss of knowledge, however, is not yet firmly documented by systematic empirical studies. The study presented in this paper examines maize crop pest agricultural knowledge of children orphaned by AIDS relative to adults in HIV/AIDS affected and non-affected households and children in non-affected households.[2] The study specifically examines girl and boy orphans between the ages of 10 and 14 in comparison to adult men and women in the different kinds of households. Pest knowledge differences were measured through an ethnobiological approach.

The research was conducted in the Couffo region of Benin among the Adja ethnic group. The Couffo region, with an average prevalence rate of 3.6 per cent (UNDP and Ministère de la Santé, 2006), is one of the most HIV affected regions in the country. Maize is the main staple food crop for the majority of the households in the region and is grown mainly for household food consumption. Crop pests are among the most important threats to food security in such a context (Mulder, 2000; Saidou et al., 2004).

Crop pests are well-bounded areas (domains) of agriculture folk and scientific knowledge on which ample research has been conducted (Smith et al., 1984; Jackai and Daoust, 1986; Bentley 1989; Bentley 1992; Setamou et al., 1998; Price 2001; Oerke, 2006; Price and Gurung, 2006). However, HIV/AIDS, with its associated adult mortality, appears to be a threat to agricultural knowledge (Baylies, 2002; Loevinsohn and Gillespie, 2003).

Conceptually, knowledge is situated as an element of culture in this chapter. Culture is learned, thus making it distinct from people's biological heritage and, as such, knowledge is a product of learning (Barsh, 1997; Purcell, 1998; Grant and Miller, 2004). Traditional knowledge is linked to subjective experiences and rooted in the culture, history and biophysical environment of a group (Brosius et al., 1986; Purcell, 1998; Price, 2001). A major assumption in the field of ethnobiology is that language serves as a 'gateway to knowledge' (Price, 2001, p158). Language is a key element in transmitting knowledge across generations, and naming living things allows for communication about them. Naming reflects the cultural importance of different living things, their biological distinctiveness, as well as the significance of their utility (Ellen, 1982; Gatewood, 1983; Brown, 1984; Berlin, 1992; Grant and Miller, 2004; Negash and Niehof 2004; Price and Björnsen-Gurung, 2006).

Naming delineates semantic domains. A semantic domain is defined as an 'organized set of words, concepts or sentences, all of the same level of contrast, that jointly refer to a single conceptual sphere' (Weller and Romney, 1988, p9). According to Price (2001), one

---

[2] A household was labeled 'affected' if it contains at least one child orphaned by AIDS, and 'non-affected' if it contained none such child. The rationale is that our main interest was the children orphaned by AIDS. These orphans were counted in the households where they lived and the presence or not of a surviving parent was recorded.

important aspect to uncovering farmers' pest knowledge is through the salience of items named by the informants. Item salience is generally evaluated by submitting respondents to a free-list exercise. Brewer (1995) tested intracultural variation of knowledge using free-listing, and concluded that this technique is a reliable and strong indicator, and an assessment measure of the respondent's level of knowledge of a specific domain. According to Thompson and Zhang (2006), the free-list be successfully used to evaluate the cultural salience of a group (or sub-group), that is, a group aggregate value can be calculated based on agreement among informants about each item. The present study used Sutrop's Cognitive Salience Index (CSI) to reveal the cultural salience among the Adja people from AIDS-affected and non-affected households (Sutrop, 2001). Data collection was rooted in the following inquiry: 'what are the differences in salience of maize pests between adult and child farmers of the Adja, and what could be the link to HIV/AIDS household status? ' To this end, it was anticipated that 1) child farmers have different maize pest salience indexes; and 2) the differences are linked to their AIDS-orphanage status; 3) gender; and 4) the adult teachers they followed for farming activities.

Materials and methods

Brief description of the Couffo and the study population

Couffo is one of the 12 regions of Benin. The Couffo region comprises six local governments (municipalities). The principal ethnic group is the Adja. They speak a language of the same name. Agriculture and small business are the main occupations of the population. The total maize production in 2004 in the Couffo was 47,741 tons for a total cultivated area of 49,197 hectares (CERPA, 2004). The 2002 population census in Benin (RGPH3, 2002), as well as a census co-organized by IFAD-NGO and Plan International reported a total of 37,372 orphans (children up to age 18), which represents 12.63 per cent of Couffo's population. The present study was conducted in two of the six municipalities, namely Aplahoue and Klouékanmey. Klouékanmey was chosen for the concentration of organizations providing care for AIDS-affected households. Aplahoue was selected for being the locality that has benefited from early and intense sensitization campaigns about HIV/AIDS. The campaigns as well as the care provision institutions did not deal with agriculture.

Sampling and sample size

The main criteria for the selection is first the presence of AIDS-affected households in a given village (that is, villages where AIDS-orphans were identified within farm households), and where AIDS-orphans and non-orphans are involved in farming activities. Children orphaned by AIDS were living with a surviving parent or foster parents. In this study, an affected household is characterized by having a child orphaned by AIDS in residence, irrespective of the infection status of the household members, thus fostering households are included. All affected and non-affected households in the sample were farming households, and adults and children were involved in maize cultivation.

Table 9.1 *Description of the study sample*

Categories of respondents (farmers)	Male	Female	Total
Affected adults	7	8	15
Non-affected adults	7	8	15
Orphan children	24	21	45
Non-orphan children	9	6	15
N = 90			

A community census was conducted prior to the study, yielding 88 AIDS-affected households and 322 orphans. The orphans fell into three categories: fatherless, motherless and having lost both parents (double orphans). Orphans aged 10 to 14 were randomly selected to participate in the study. The choice of the age range of the children was informed by findings from previous studies on agro-ecological knowledge transfer among children (Stross, 1973; Zarger and Stepp, 2004; Setalaphruk and Price, 2007). Fifteen orphans were randomly selected within each of the groups (double, motherless and fatherless). In addition, 15 non-orphans (in non-affected households) were randomly selected. Thirty adult farmers were randomly selected equally from affected and non-affected households. The composition of the sample is given in Table 9.1.

Methods and techniques of data collection

The research proceeded through several steps. First, an exploratory field visit was carried out and consisted of informal discussions with resource persons in the study area. Discussions with researchers such as agronomists and entomologists, and extension agents provided comprehensive information on maize pests in the Couffo region. Later on, focus group discussions were carried out with participants from affected and non-affected households. The information gathered was supplemented by individual semi-structured interviews with key informant farmers. The aim was to understand people's basic terms and conceptualizations of pests in the Adja cultural setting. Initial visits were conducted with some children who were not part of the study sample in order to test and adjust the instrument. As the study consisted of documenting knowledge exemplified by salience among the identified categories of farmers, the sub-domain of pests related to maize was used. The present study used the free listing technique. This functioned perfectly for evaluating group as well as individual item salience based on individual responses.

Free listing

The method is applied through asking informants to list items. Free-listing is a well-studied and well-established method to capture knowledge in a given domain (Romney and D'Andrade, 1964; Henley 1969; Bolton et al., 1980). Three assumptions underlie the method: 'First, when people free-list, they tend to list terms in order of familiarity... second, individuals who know a lot about a subject list more terms than do people who know less...third, terms that most respondents mention indicate locally prominent items...'(Quinlan, 2005, p220).

The standard procedure consists of asking informants to *list the kinds of X* (s)he knows. Free listing was used in this study to account for types of pests. The main tool for the exercise is a list task. List tasks were conducted through oral interviews. The question was this: 'Please name all the maize pests that you know'. The list task technique has been described in detail by Weller and Romney (1988) and Borgatti (1999).

Data analysis methods

Cognitive Salience analysis

Analysis of data from the list task covers two parameters: term frequency and mean position in the individual lists. The tendency for an item to occur at a given position of the elicited lists of terms corresponds to the mean position of a term, while the occurrence of a term across the lists of the informants corresponds to the frequency of that term. The third parameter is the number of subjects (Weller and Romney, 1988; Sutrop, 2001). The combination of frequency and mean position across informants reflects the internal structure of the identified cultural domain and salience. Thus, the basic terms in a domain are the most salient. For the purpose of calculation, the most salient term always named first by all subjects, takes the value 1. The less salient terms have a value declining towards 0. Davies and Corbett (1995) incorporated the mean position of a term in a list in order to strengthen the term frequency parameter. Smith et al. (1995) developed a free-list salience index (see also Smith and Borgatti, 1997), and proposed a formula that captures frequency of mention and position in the list across informants. Sutrop (2001) reframed the salience index into cognitive salience index (CSI) as applied in this paper, whereby the number of items in a list is controlled by using the mean position and can be validly applied with a small sample size. Finally, Thompson and Zhang (2006) note that cultural saliency can be used as a proxy for knowledge of a domain (at the group and individual level). Sutrop's formula to calculate the CSI is as follows:

$$CSI = F / (NmP)$$

With:

F being the frequency of a term (F is the number of the lists where a term is listed);
N being the total number of lists (number of participants);
R_j being the rank of a term in an individual list.

The mean position of a term is calculated as follows:

$mP = (\sum R_j) / F$, hence, the cognitive salience index is rewritten as:
$$CSI = F^2 / (N \sum R_j)$$

The CSI is an integrative salience index that takes into account the frequency of mention and the mean position (mean rank) of items mentioned across informant.

Knowledge differences were evaluated by simple calculation as follows:

$\Delta(CSI) = CSIF - CSIM$, where:
$\Delta(CSI)$ represents the differences in the salience indexes by pest,
CSIF, the salience for females and CSIM that of males.

Understanding the basis for pest salience differences across informants: the Tobit model

The Tobit model was chosen to explore the factors that could explain the differences in the CIS scores. The reason for choosing this model was dictated by the nature of the total individual CSI score, which varies between 0 and 1. Explanations on the model and its use have been reported elsewhere (McDonald and Moffitt, 1980; Amemiya, 1984; Greene, 2003; Rahman, 2005). The model assumes that there is an underlying latent variable, y_i, such that:

$$y_i = \begin{cases} X_i\beta + ui & \text{if } X_i\beta + u_i > 0 \\ / & \text{if } X_i\beta + u_i \leq 0 \\ i = 1, 2, \dots n \end{cases}$$

where:

y_i is the dependent variable (cognitive salience index),
n is the number of observations,
X_i is a vector of independent variables,
β is a vector of parameters to be estimated, and
u_i is an independently distributed error term assumed to be normal with zero mean and constant variance σ^2.

Definition of variables

Previous work on folk/indigenous agricultural knowledge emphasized the importance of the household type and composition on children's knowledge (Foster, 1978; Foster and Williamson, 2000; Haddad and Gillespie, 2001; Zarger and Stepp, 2004). Taking into account the fact that AIDS impacts farm household composition, the present study used several variables to explain the observed variation in pest knowledge, as revealed by the CSI scores. A total of five explanatory (the independent) variables divided into sub-variables were chosen to explain the salience indexes obtained by the respondents. The choice of these variables is based on previous research on AIDS impacts as well as knowledge transmission (Ruddle, 1993; Ohmagari and Berkes, 1997; Bollinger et al., 1999; Rugalema et al., 1999; Baylies, 2002; Loevinsohn and Gillespie, 2003; McMenamy et al., 2005). They are defined below.

Gender is a dummy variable taking the value 1 if female and 0 if male. The literature reports that knowledge and cultural values transmission follow gender lines (Little, 1987; Matthews, 1987; Saito and Spurling, 1995; Setalaphruk and Price, 2007). Age group (agegrp) encompasses the sub-variables agegrp1 for children of 10–12 years, agegrp2 for children of 13–14 years, and agegrp3, which represents the adult group. Children age groups are formed based on the involvement in farming activities in the Adja culture but also, according to previous studies, on the acquisition of agro-ecological knowledge among children (Ohmagari and Berkes, 1997; Setalaphruk and Price, 2007; see also Fagbemissi et al., 2009). Knowledge transmission from adult to children is reported to follow age group division (Ruddle, 1993; Ohmagari and Berkes, 1997; Setalaphruk and Price, 2007). Age is expected to have a positive correlation with the salience indexes. The HIV status was divided into four sub-variables, respectively defined as HivStat1 for AIDS-orphans, HivStat2 for AIDS-affected adults, HivStat3 for non-orphans and HivStat4 for non-affected adults.[3] In the light of the negative effect of AIDS on resources (Haddad and Gillespie, 2001; Baylies, 2002; Edstrom and Samuels, 2007), a negative correlation is expected. This variable was complemented by the household status (Hsstatus). It distinguishes between initial (parental) household and fostering household, and is delineated as Hsstatus1 for children living in their initial households and Hsstatus2 when living in fostering households. The household is termed 'initial' if the child is living with one or both of the biological parents, and 'fostering' if (s)he has moved to another household. It is expected that children living with their own parents have higher salience indexes, and should have a positive sign (Loevinsohn and Gillespie, 2003). The presence of an adult 'teacher' is assumed important in shaping children's indigenous farming knowledge (Ruddle, 1993). This variable is termed here pSuivre, that is, person followed for farm activities. This variable denotes the way knowledge is passed on from an adult 'model' to a child. It is divided into pSuivre1 if the adult teacher is the respondent's own parent, pSuivre2 if it is a fostering teacher and pSuivre3 for those who are with no adult teacher. Finally, the dependent variable cultural salience is termed knowtot, which is the sum of salience indexes of each individual. The variable knowtot is used here as a proxy to reflect how knowledgeable each respondent is (Thompson and Zhang, 2006).

In light of the above defined variables a correlation test was performed using Pearson's correlation. The aim was to test if the variables were linked in order to avoid multicolinearity. The variables that appeared not to be correlated were considered for advanced regression, and were then put in the model. Fitness and heteroscedasticity tests were also done.

Results

The names of maize pests elicited from informants can be found in Table 9.2. A wide range of life forms including birds, rodents, insects and domesticated livestock were elicited. The outcomes consist of results from the Sutrop's CSI calculation that includes individual as well as group aggregate values. The results from the Tobit regression (Table 9.3) substantiate the comparative interpretation of the CSI results.

[3] HIV status was not used as a dummy variable for the analysis in this paper. The variable was disaggregated into sub-variables. To each sub-variable it was assigned a 1or 0 value for a yes or no modality. Each sub-variable was tested with the aim of providing more insights on the diversity in the impact of AIDS affection on pest naming ability among the respondents.

Table 9.2 *Scientific names and damages associated with selected maize pests in the Couffo*

Local name in Adja	English name	Scientific name	Damages caused to maize and other observations	
			Scientific views	Farmers' claims
Abo	Snail	*Achatina fulica*	Snail meat is an important source of protein for the rural poor in Africa. Undomesticated forms of snails are serious pests to crops and seedlings.	Snails suck maize leaves and stems. When they attack the cobs, they make holes in them, making the cobs ugly and reducing their market value. Snails are gathered by women and girls for household consumption, but mainly to be sold for extra income.
Djaka	Rat	*Rattus rattus*	Bush rats are omnivorous and capable of eating a wide range of plant and animal foods. They rank among the world's worst invaders.	Uproot maize seedlings and eat maize cobs and grains. A threat to seed germination. Trapped or hunted by men and boys for household consumption.
Edja	Locust/ Grasshopper	*Zonocerus variegates*	Locust and grasshoppers are insect pests that decimate everything in their path. Locust and grasshoppers are mainly herbivores. Grain, corn, cotton, fruit and vegetable crops are their main targets.	Eat fresh maize leaves. Very destructive when they invade farms.
Egbo	Goat	*Capra hircus*	Household livestock.	Eat maize plants, stems and cobs. Goats are an important asset for smallholders; raised by farmers for extra income.
Ehlin	Red-billed Quelea; African Weaver	*Quelea quelea*	Very prolific, arrive in large flocks wherever grain crops are grown, and eat every seed. Pest control measures have failed against Quelea. Recent discussions are directed towards harvesting Quelea bird as a natural food resource.	Destroy maize cobs and eat the grains. They come in colonies, and can rapidly remove all the grains from the crop. Sometimes hunt them for household food.
Ewan	Borers (Caterpillars/ larvae of moths and butterflies)	*Lepidoptera*	Stem and cob borers are important damaging insect pests, and count as a major limitation to maize production. They can cause incredible yield losses. They encompass several species, with various geographical distributions.	Destroys maize stems, fresh cobs and grains. Make holes in the stems and cobs, making them unattractive and of poor market quality.
Eyin	Bee	*Apis mellifera*	Apis species are insects of the order Hymenoptera which feed on pollen and nectar. Bees are important to achieving sufficient pollination of the plants.	They disturb maize flowers, and sting farmers during weeding and hunting activities.

Table 9.2 *Scientific names and damages associated with selected maize pests in the Couffo (Continued)*

Local name in Adja	English name	Scientific name	Damages caused to maize and other observations	
			Scientific views	Farmers' claims
Eyin	Bee	*Apis mellifera*	Bees are also natural enemies of several other insects found on plant flowers.	
Dedi	Ants	*Formica rufa*	Natural enemies of several insects. Eat other insects and larvae.	They sting farmers during weeding activities.
Hanhan	Millipede	*Trigoniulus corallinus*	Millipedes are a minor pest, but very dangerous when they attack emergent seedlings.	They twine around maize seedlings and suck them.
Hevi	Small birds	Aves *sp.*		They are of various kinds, and they attack maize cobs.
Koklo	Chicken	Gallus domesticus	Common and widespread domestic animal.	Eat maize grains and uproots seed, thus a threat to seed germination.
Takpe	Yellow-necked spurfowl	Francolinus leucoscepus	The birds feed on insects, plants and seeds. Very devastating for seedlings. Also used for human consumption.	Uproots seedlings and eat maize grains. Trapped by farmers for household consumption and also sold on the market.

Source: Fagbemissi and Price 2008

The CSI scores

HIV status and pest naming ability differences between affected and non affected adults and orphan and non-orphan children are depicted in Figure 9.1.

Adults living in affected households and children orphaned by AIDS had higher CSI scores on 10 out of the 12 items compared to the non-affected adults and children. Figure 9.1 further illustrates that AIDS-orphaned children had higher scores than AIDS-affected adults for 5 of the 12 items and had the same score for 4 of the 12 items. AIDS-orphaned children had higher CSI scores for 50 per cent of the items than the AIDS-affected adults. Non-affected adults and their children similarly and over all scored significantly lower than the affected adults and children. The conclusion that can be drawn is that overall children are more like the adults they live with than each other and that the knowledge of children orphaned by AIDS as measured by the CSI is greater than of the AIDS-affected adults.

A disaggregation of the CSI scores by gender and AIDS status was conducted. Figure 9.2 depicts the pest naming ability of boys and girls by AIDS orphan status.

The findings show that boy and girl orphans have higher CSI scores than boy and girl non-orphans. Gender-based similarities are to be found however in the overall pattern for 8 of the 12 items. Regarding the other four items, there are three where orphaned girls had scores and non-orphaned girls did not. For the last item of the four, it was orphaned boys who had a measurable CSI score for which non-orphaned boys did not score at all. The conclusion that can be drawn here is that while AIDS-orphaned boys and girls show a very similar gender pattern in the CSI scoring, boy orphans scored

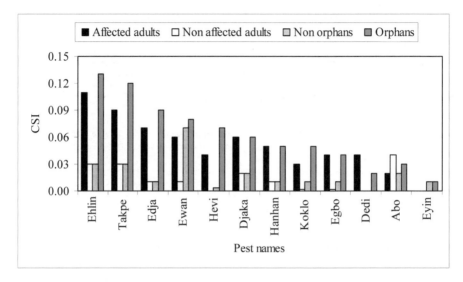

Figure 9.1 *Maize pest naming ability from the most salient to the least salient for adults and children by HIV/AIDS status*

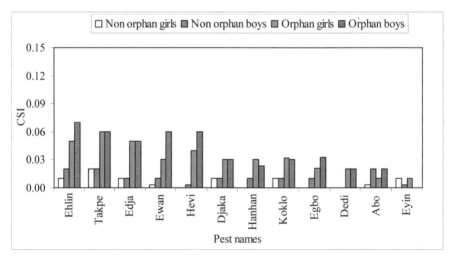

Figure 9.2 *Maize pest naming ability by HIV/AIDS status for male and female children*

higher than non-orphan boys and girl orphans scored higher than non-orphan girls. There are also indications of a gender shifting in knowledge where orphans are acquiring knowledge of pests that are not normally part of the domain of girls or boys who are in non-affected intact families, as evidenced by orphan girls and boys scoring in items that non-orphan children of the same gender do not (4 of the 12 items).

The examination of the CSI scores by gender and AIDS status for adults is depicted in Figure 9.3.

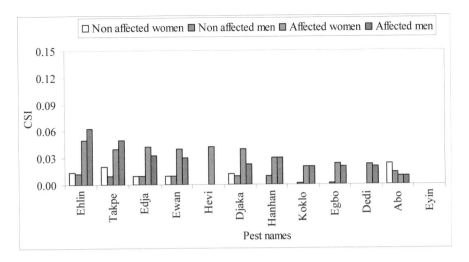

Figure 9.3 *Maize pest naming ability by HIV/AIDS status for male and female adults*

The overall gender patterning does not show a high level of consistency between affected and non-affected adults, particularly for women. AIDS-affected women had CSI scores for 5 of the 12 items for which non-affected women did not score at all. AIDS-affected women scored higher than non-affected women (relative to patterns among non-affected men and women). Affected women also scored higher relative to affected men for three items in comparison to the pattern observed among non-affected men relative to non-affected women. For one item (*Hevi*, generic for small birds) affected women were the only adults who had a CSI score. For one item, both affected men and affected women had CSI scores where neither non-affected men nor non-affected women had a score (*dedi*, which are ants). What we can conclude from the above is that there is also a gender difference between affected and non-affected adult men and women. Affected women have higher CSI scores and know more pests relative to non-affected women. For affected men, the pattern is one of a higher CSI score compared to non-affected men rather than gender differences. For one item only did both affected women and affected men have a CSI score where both non-affected men and women did not. Ultimately, the pattern is one where affected men and affected women have higher scores, but where the affected women are bringing more items into their knowledge domain with salience.

A closer examination of the CSI scores of AIDS orphan children aged 10–14, based on the kind of adult they live with was conducted in order to better understand the role of the adult teacher in the CSI scores the children obtained. To accomplish this, we disaggregated the children's scores into the following categories: 1. AIDS orphans that are still living with the one remaining parent; 2. orphans living in a fostering household; and 3. double orphans who are farming on their own (Figure 9.4).

For 8 of the 12 items, one-parent orphans out-performed orphans in fostering households. Orphans in fostering households had the highest CSI scores on three items (but the CSI scores are still low). Orphans without an adult teacher (double orphan children farming on their own) had significantly lower CSI scores than orphans who continued to reside with the surviving parent. The orphan children without an adult

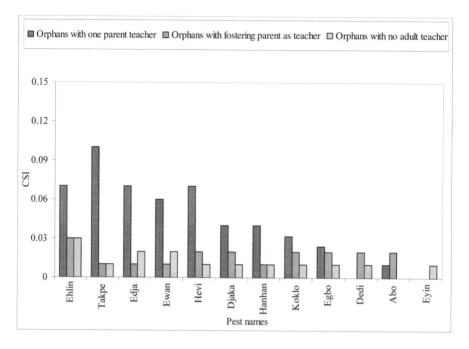

Figure 9.4 *Maize pest naming ability for orphans aged 10–14 by type of adult teacher*

teacher further scored on par or above orphans in fostering households for 5 of the 12 items and lower for 5 of the 12 items. Interesting also, is that the only orphans that listed bees as pests were orphaned children without an adult teacher.

Ehlin (Red-billed Quelea), *Takpe* (Partridge), *Djaka* (rat) and *Ewan* (butterfly pupa/larvae – cob borers) are important crop pests in maize from a scientific standpoint and these items were the most salient. In sum, orphans and affected adults overall have a better ability to name maize pests. It should be noted that the knowledge of children is not fully comparable to that of adults as illustrated by the item *Eyin* (bees) named by only a few children as a maize pest. This item had the lowest salience of all items. The exception to this was that orphans residing with the remaining living parent were like adults in that none named bees as maize pests. For the most serious pests noted above, orphans residing with one surviving parent had the most impressive CSI score performance across all groups.

The Tobit model

Outcomes of the Tobit model are presented in Table 9.3. Results of the analysis show that five variables out of the seven tested had significant correlation with the total CSI (the proxy to respondent knowledge of maize pest in the farm). These factors had different values and explained differently the intra-cultural variation of pest knowledge among Adja farmers. For instance, the parameter *HIV-affected adult* is positively and significantly linked to the total CSI ($\beta=0.132$; $p<0.01$). This means that the proximity of an affected adult is beneficial for an orphan with respect to his/her knowledge of pests.

Table 9.3 *Results of the Tobit model for CSI differences*

Variable	Total Individual CSI Score as proxy for knowledge		
	Coefficient (Estimates)	SE[1]	P>|t|[2]
Age of the respondent[3]	−0.126	0.01	0.219
Gender	−0.016	0.008	0.045*
HIV-affected adults	0.132	0.012	0.000***
Non orphan farmer	−0.022	0.012	0.087*
Own parent as adult teacher	0.016	0.007	0.021**
Fostering parent as adult teacher	−0.01	0.007	0.158
No adult teacher	−0.02	0.008	0.014**
Constant	0.070	0.008	0.000
Log likelihood 172.946			
x^2 (7) 111.81			
Number of observations: 90			

[1] SE = Standard error; [2] Statistical significance level: *=p<0.10; **=p<0.05; ***=p<0.01.
[3] This is the age group1 (children of 10–14 years). The other age groups were eliminated by the multicolinearity test
Source: Fagbemissi and Price, 2008.

This finding is reinforced by the link of the parameter *own parent as an adult teacher* to the CSI differences (β=0.016; p<0.05). From the combination of these two results, it could be inferred that living with, and having his/her own surviving parent as an adult teacher has a positive influence on an orphan's knowledge. Other significant findings were obtained through the negative association of three parameters, respectively *no adult teacher* (β= −0.02; p<0.05), gender (β= −0.016; p≤0.05), and lastly, non-orphan farmer (β= −0.022; p≤0.1). With respect to gender, the coefficient and its sign suggest that the male gender is negatively associated to respondent's total CSI. The age of the child seemed to have no effect on the total CSI (see Table 9.3).

Discussion and conclusion

This study examined knowledge of maize crop pests among Adja farmers in an attempt to ascertain what differences in knowledge are there between children orphaned by AIDS affected adults, and non-orphan children and non-affected adults. Sharp insights can be gained through the use of salience indexes as a proxy for knowledge of a domain. One of the main findings of this study is that children are more like the adults they live with than each other. The results show that individuals (adults and children) living in AIDS-affected households have a better ability to name maize pests than the other respondents. In addition, AIDS-orphans had higher CSI scores relative to all other respondents for the majority of items. This result was not anticipated. One-parent orphan children that continue to reside in the parental home with the surviving parent had higher CSI scores than orphans living in fostering households and double orphans. Overall, orphans dramatically out-performed non-orphans living in two parent maize farming households.

How can we explain the large difference between affected and non-affected adults as well as the fact that affected orphan children have higher CSI scores than affected adults? One explanation for this higher ability in naming maize pests and the saliency of these pests could be the greater dependence on maize for food security for these families coupled with the greater responsibilities children must shoulder in crop production and crop protection (learning from adults and by direct field observation and work), particularly in one-parent affected households. One of the important implications is that the best channel for children to acquire agricultural knowledge is their parents. The huge differences observed in the CSI scores we believe may be poverty-induced differences, revolving around resource mobilization to face agricultural problems in the maize field (Baylies, 2002; Bryceson and Fonseca, 2006). One can distinguish here between tangible and non-tangible resources. Non-affected household members (adults and children) are better off in terms of land, money and hired labour (den Ouden, 1995). People in affected households, however, because of the depletion of their resources by necessity are more dependent on fewer resources. One of the resources they have is their agricultural knowledge (non-tangible resource). In situations of shock and stress such as that caused by HIV/AIDS, knowledge of the agro-ecosystem is a primary resource in building resilience (Barnett and Whiteside, 2006; Gillespie, 2008).

The second major point to note from the results of this study is the relationship of gender to the CSI differences. Affected adult men and women had higher CSI scores overall compared to non-affected men and women. Affected women also had a larger domain and could name additional pests, than non-affected women. Affected women had substantially higher CSI scores than non-affected men as well as being on a par with or surpassing affected men in their CSI scores (except for one item). There are also indications of a gender shifting in knowledge where orphans are acquiring knowledge of pests that are not normally part of the domain of non-affected girls or boys. Orphan girls and boys had CSI scores for items that non-orphan children of the same gender had no scores for (4 of the 12 items). These results may indicate that there is a gender shift in knowledge occurring because the repertoire of women and girls is expanding. For affected boys and men, as with affected women and girls, the salience is deepening (higher CSI scores per item). Affected men and boys, however, are not expanding the domain to include more items identified by females.

We can only speculate that one of the factors involved in the differences we see with regard to gender and AIDS is linked to being either a better-off commercial producer or just a subsistence farmer. In the study region maize is moving from a purely subsistence crop to one with commercial importance. It can be cultivated for the market by those who have sufficient resources to do so. Some studies (Leach, 1994; Fagbemissi et al., 2002; Goebel, 2003) suggest that when a crop gains a commercial value, men tend to dominate in many aspects including skills and knowledge. But commercial farmers can also better afford both labour (for scaring off birds) and inputs (such as pesticides), which might help explain the low CSI scores for maize pests among male and female non-affected farmers compared to those who are affected. Affected households have a real concern for maize as a subsistence crop and they tend to have a shortage of cash and labour (Haddad and Gillespie, 2001). We believe that the expansion of the domain of maize pests by AIDS-affected women and girls is linked to both the greater utility of the knowledge due to the importance of maize for food sufficiency and their expanded active participation and responsibility in the production of the crop and its protection. It can be inferred that since maize is mainly for household consumption, and also, because adults of non-affected households have easier access to inputs such as fertilizer and high-yield varieties, they pay less attention to what happens in their fields, which is reflected in their children's knowledge base (Stross, 1973; Ruddle, 1993). The existence of easy solutions such as pesticides to circumvent certain pest problems, may also negatively impact adults perceiving some of the items as pests, that is, a threat to their maize farm, thus resulting in a lack of salience (Bentley, 1989; Bentley, 1992).

An additional finding is that the field observation data shows that people hunt birds for household consumption and thus birds have a positive utilitarian value (Hunn, 1982) at the same time as a negative utilitarian value as a pest that attacks maize cobs (CERPA, 2004). The two bird pests that fit this assertion are *Ehlin (red-billed quelea) and Takpe (Francolinus leucoscepus)*. These two birds had the highest CSI scores for AIDS-affected adults and orphans. The bird pests that are not eaten, however, have only the cover term of *Hevi* as a name, which is used for all small and difficult to name birds. We thus believe the salience of *Ehlin* and *Takpe* are not only related to them being very destructive pests, but also to their importance as a source of food for AIDS-affected households.

In conclusion, the assumption that HIV and AIDS have a negative impact on the knowledge of children orphaned by AIDS is not supported by the results of this study. AIDS-affected adults had higher CSI scores, and affected women and girls had more pest items in the domain than non-affected women and girls. Affected men and boys while having larger CSI scores than non-affected men and boys did not seem to expand the gender-based aspects of the domain to the same extent as affected women and girls. AIDS-orphaned children had the highest CSI scores. Orphans residing with the one surviving parent in the household of origin scored best followed by orphans in fostering households and lastly, double orphans on their own with no adult teacher. Non-orphans in intact households scored the lowest among the children, and like their parents, very poorly. The results of the Tobit analysis support the observed pattern in the CSI scores: affected adults and children who have their own parent as teacher are shown to have the highest saliency for major pests relative to other subjects of the study.

The expectations from earlier studies that AIDS causes an erosion of agricultural knowledge are not confirmed. One of the reasons may be that the need to secure food for the household through maize farming and the shortage of resources increase the utility of the harvest for AIDS-affected households. We speculate that reasons for the observed difference in scores are that AIDS-affected adults and orphans invest more in their farm in the form of labour and attention, and that utility, necessity and experience have contributed to sharpening their observation skills and increasing their knowledge. The guiding hand of the surviving parent of an orphan, however, is to be valourized. These findings indicate there is a need for careful thinking about the implications of the HIV epidemic for farming knowledge and to engage in further empirical research.

Acknowledgements

We thank the people of the Couffo and the IFAD-NGO for their collaboration in this study. We thank the Dutch Ministry of foreign affairs and the AWLAE programme for providing funds to conduct the research. We are grateful to Patrice Adegbola for discussion and insights on the statistical analyses, and to Achille Kagbahinto for his early contribution to the salience index calculations.

References

Amemiya, T. (1984) 'Tobit models: a survey', *Journal of Econometrics*, vol 24, pp3–61

Barnett, T., Tumushake, J., Bantebya, G., Ssebuliba, K., Ngasongwa, J., Kapinga, D., Ndelike, M., Drinkwater, M., Mitti, G. and Huslwimmer, M. (1995) 'The social and economic impact of HIV/AIDS on farming systems and livelihoods in rural Africa: Some experience and lessons from Uganda, Tanzania and Zambia', *Journal of International development*, vol 7, pp163–176.

Barnett, T. and Whiteside, A. (2006) *AIDS in the 21ˢᵗ Century: Disease and Globalization*, Palgrave Press, New York

Barsh, R. (1997) 'The epistemology of traditional healing systems', *Human Organization*, vol 56, pp28–37

Baylies, C. (2002) 'The impact of AIDS on rural households in Africa: a shock like any other?', *Development and Change*, vol 33, pp611–632

Bentley, J.W. (1989) 'What farmers don't know can't help them: The strengths and weakness of indigenous technical knowledge in Honduras', *Agriculture and Human Values*, vol 6, pp25–31

Bentley, J.W. (1992) 'Alternatives to pesticides in Central America: Applied studies of local knowledge', *Culture and Agriculture*, vol 44, pp10–13

Berlin, B. (1992) *Ethnobiological Classification: Principles of Categorization of Plants and Animals in Traditional Societies*, Princeton University Press, Princeton

Bollinger, L., Stover, J. and Martin-Correa, L.J. (1999) *The Economic Impact of AIDS in Benin*, POLICY Project, Washington DC

Bolton, R., Curtis, A.T. and Thomas, L.L. (1980) 'Nepali color terms: salience in a listing task', *Journal of the Steward Anthropological Society*, vol 12, pp309–321

Borgatti, S.P. (1999) 'Elicitation techniques for cultural domain analysis', in E.J.J. Schensul, M.D. LeCompte, B.K. Nastasi, and S.P. Borgatti (eds) *Enhanced Ethnographic Methods: Audiovisual Techniques, Focused Group Interviews, and Elicitation Techniques. Ethnographer Toolkit*, Altamira, Walnut Creek, CA

Brewer, D.D. (1995) 'Cognitive indicators of knowledge in semantic domains', *Journal of Quantitative Anthropology*, vol 5, pp107–128

Brosius, P., Lovelace, G. and Martin, G., 1986 'Ethnoecology: an approach to understanding traditional agricultural knowledge', in G.G. Martin (ed) *Traditional Agriculture in Southeast Asia*, pp187–198, Westview Press, Boulder, London

Brown, C.H. (1984) *Language and Living Things: Uniformities in Folk Classification and Naming* Rutgers University Press, New Jersey

Bryceson, D. and Fonseca, J. (2006) 'An enduring or dying peasantry: interactive impact of famine and HIV/AIDS in rural Malawi', in Stuart Gillespie (ed), *AIDS, Poverty and Hunger: Challenges and Responses*, DC: International Food Policy Research Institute, Washington DC

CERPA (2004). *La production vivrière en 2004: Départements du Mono et du Couffo. Rapport annuel*, Ministère de l'agriculture, de l'élevage et de la pêche (MAEP), Cotonou, Benin

Davies, I. and Corbett, G. (1995) 'A practical field method for identifying basic color terms', *Languages of the World*, vol 9, pp25–36

Den Ouden, J.H.B. (1995) 'Who's for work? The management of labour in the process of accumulation in three Adja villages, Benin, Africa', *Journal of the International African Institute*, vol 65, pp1–35

Dewagt, A. and Connolly, M. (2005) 'Orphans and the impact of HIV/AIDS in Sub-Saharan Africa', *Food, Nutrition and Agriculture*, www.fao.org/documents, accessed 16 March 2006

Drimie, S. and Casale, M. (2008) 'Families' efforts to secure the future of their children in the context of multiple stresses, including AIDS', IFPRI brief no 7, in the series: *HIV, Livelihoods, Food and Nutrition Security: Findings from RENEWAL Research (2007–2008)*

Edstrom, J., and Samuels, F. (2007) *HIV, Nutrition, Food and Livelihoods in Sub-Saharan Africa: Evidence, Debates and Reflections for Guidance*, IDS, Brighton

Ellen, R. (1982) *Environment, Subsistence and System*, Cambridge University Press, Cambridge, New York

Fagbemissi, R.C. and Price, L.L. (2008) 'HIV/AIDS orphans as farmers: uncovering pest knowledge differences through an ethnobiological approach in Benin', *NJAS Wageningen Journal of Life Sciences*, vol 56, no 3 pp241–259

Fagbemissi, R.C., Lie, R. and Leeuwis, C. (2009) 'Diversity and mobility in households with children orphaned by AIDS in Couffo, Benin', *African Journal of AIDS Research*, vol 8, no 3, pp261–274

Fagbemissi, R.C., Coulibaly, O., Hanna, R. and Endamana, D. (2002) 'Adoption de variétés de manioc et efficacité durable de la lutte biologique contre l'acarien vert du manioc au Bénin', *Bulletin de la Recherche Agronomique du Bénin*, vol 38, pp1–18

FAO (2005) 'Schools for life: Training HIV/AIDS orphans in sub-Saharan Africa. Fighting hunger and poverty with farming know-how and life skills', *FAO Newsroom, News Stories*, www.fao.org/newsroom/en/news/2005/, accessed 2 November 2007

Foster, G. and Williamson, J. (2000) 'A review of current literature of the impact of HIV/AIDS on children in sub-Saharan Africa', *AIDS*, vol 14, pp275–284

Foster, B. (1978) 'Socio-economic consequences of stem family composition in a Thai village' *Ethnology*, vol 17, pp139–156

Gatewood, J.B. (1983) 'Loose talk: Linguistic competence and recognition ability', *American Anthropologist*, vol 85, pp378–386

Gillespie, S.R. (2008) 'Poverty, food insecurity, HIV vulnerability and the impacts of AIDS in sub-Saharan Africa', *IDS Bulletin* vol 39, no 5, pp10–18

Goebel, A. (2003) 'Gender entitlements in the Zimbabwean woodlands: A case study of resettlement', in P.L. Howard (ed) *Women and Plants. Gender Relations in Biodiversity Management and Conservation*, pp115–125, Zed Books, New York

Grant, L.K. and Miller, M.L. (2004) 'A cultural consensus analysis of marine ecological knowledge in the Solomon Islands', *SPC Traditional Marine Resources Management and Knowledge Information Bulletin*, www.spc.int/coastfish/news/trad/17, accessed 15 November 2007

Greene, W.H. (2003) *Econometric Analysis,* Fifth edition, Pearson Education Inc, Upper Saddle River, New Jersey

Haddad, L. and Gillespie, S. (2001) 'Effective food and nutrition policy responses to HIV/AIDS: What we know and what we need to know', *Journal of International Development*, vol 13, pp487–511

Henley, N. (1969) 'A psychological study of the semantics of animal terms', *Journal of Verbal Learning and Verbal Behavior*, vol 8, pp176–84

Hunn, E. (1982) 'The utilitarian factor of folk biological classification', *American Anthropologist*, vol 84, pp830–847

Jackai, L.E.N. and Daoust, R.A. (1986) 'Insect pests of cowpeas', *Annual Review of Entomology*, 31, pp95–119

Jayne, T.S., Villarreal, M., Pingali, P. and Hemrich, G. (2004) 'Interactions between the agricultural sector and the HIV/AIDS pandemic: Implications for agricultural policy', *FAO ESA Working Paper*, no 04-06, www.fao.org/es/esa, accessed 15 November 2007

Leach, M. (1994) *Rainforest Relations: Gender and Resource Use Among the Mende of Gola, Sierra Leone*, Edinburgh University Press, Edinburgh

Little, J. (1987) 'Gender relations in rural areas: The importance of women's domestic role', *Journal of Rural Studies*, vol 3, pp335–342

Loevinsohn, M. and Gillespie, S. (2003) 'HIV/AIDS, food security and rural livelihoods: Understanding and responding', *RENEWAL Working Paper*, no 2, www.isnar.org/renewal, accessed 15 June 2007

Matthews, H. (1987) 'Gender, home range and environmental cognition', *Transactions of the Institute of British Geographers*, vol 12, pp43–52

McDonald, J.F. and Moffitt, R.A. (1980) 'The uses of Tobit analysis', *Review of Economics and Statistics*, vol 62, pp318–321

McMenamy, J.M., Perrin, E.C. and Wiser, M. (2005) 'Age-related differences in how children with ADHD understand their condition: biological or psychological causality?', *Applied Developmental Psychology*, vol 26, pp111–131

Mulder, I. (2000) *Soil Degradation in Benin: Farmers' Perceptions and Responses*. Research Series, no 240, Tinbergen Institute, Vrije Universiteit Amsterdam, Amsterdam

Negash, A. and Niehof, A. (2004) 'The significance of Enset culture and biodiversity for rural household food and livelihood security in Southwestern Ethiopia', *Agriculture and Human Values*, Vol 21, pp 61–71

Oerke, E.C. (2006) 'Crop losses to pests', *Journal of Agricultural Science*, vol 144, pp31–43

Ohmagari, K. and Berkes, F. (1997) 'Transmission of indigenous knowledge and bush skills among the western James Bay Cree women of subarctic Canada', *Human Ecology* vol 25, pp197–222

Price, L.L. and Björnsen-Gurung, A. (2006) 'Describing and measuring ethno-entomological knowledge of rice pests: tradition and change among Asian rice farmers', *Environment, Development and Sustainability*, vol 8, pp 507-517

Price, L.L. (2001) 'Demystifying farmers' entomological and pest management knowledge: A methodology for assessing the impacts on knowledge from IPM-FFS and NES interventions', *Agriculture and Human Values*, vol 18, pp153–176

Purcell, T.W. (1998) 'Indigenous knowledge and applied Anthropology: questions of definition and direction', *Human Organization*, vol 57, pp258–272

Quinlan, M. (2005) 'Considerations for collecting free-lists in the field: Examples from ethnobotany', *Field Methods*, vol 17, pp219–234

Rahman, S. (2005) 'Environmental impacts of technological change in Bangladesh agriculture: farmers' perceptions, determinants, and effects on resource allocation decisions', *Agricultural Economics*, vol 33, pp107–116

RGPH3 (2002) *Troisième recensement général de la population*, Institut national de la statistique et de l'analyse économique (INSAE), Cotonou, Benin

Romney, A. and D'Andrade, R. (1964) 'Cognitive aspects of English kin terms', *American Anthropologist*, vol 66, pp146–170

Ruddle, K. (1993) 'The transmission of traditional ecological knowledge', in J.T. Ingles (ed) *Traditional Ecological Knowledge*, International Development Research Center, Ottawa, Canada

Rugalema, G., Weigang, S. and Mbwika, J. (1999) *HIV/AIDS and the Commercial Agricultural Sector of Kenya: Impact, Vulnerability, Susceptibility, and Coping Strategies*, FAO Research, Extension and Training Division Rome

Saidou, A., Kuyper, T.W., Kossou, D.K., Tossou, R. and Richards, P. (2004) 'Sustainable soil fertility management in Benin: Learning from farmers', *NJAS Wageningen Journal of Life Sciences*, vol 52, pp349–369

Saito, K.A. and Spurling, D. (1995) *Developing Agricultural Training for Women*, The World Bank, Washington DC

Setalaphruk, S. and Price, L.L. (2007) 'Children's traditional ecological knowledge of wild food resources: A case study in a rural village, Northeast of Thailand', *Journal of Ethnobiology and Ethnomedicine*, vol 3, www.ethnobiomed.com/content/3/1/33, accessed 8 January 2008

Setamou, M., Cardwell, K.F., Schulthess, F. and Hell, K. (1998) 'Effect of insect damage to maize ears, with special reference to Mussidia *nigrivenella* (Lepidoptera: Paraglide), on Aspergillus *flavus* (Deuteromycetes: Monoliales) infection and aflatoxin production in Maize before harvest in the Republic of Benin', *Journal of Economic Entomology*, vol 91, pp433–438

Smith, I.M., Chiarappa, L. and Van Der Graaff, N.A. (1984) 'World crop losses: An overview', in R.K.S. Wood and G.J. Jellis (eds) *Plant Diseases: Infection, Damage and Loss*, pp213–223, Blackwell Scientific Publications, Oxford

Smith, J.J. and Borgatti, S.P. (1997) 'Salience counts – so does accuracy: correcting and updating a measure for free-list item salience', *Journal of Linguistic Anthropology*, vol 7, pp208–209

Smith, J.J., Furbee, L., Maynard, K., Quick, S. and Ross, L. (1995) 'Salience counts: A domain analysis of English color terms', *Journal of Linguistic Anthropology*, vol 5, pp203–216

Stross, B. (1973) 'Acquisition of botanical terminology by Tzeltal children', in M.S. Edmonson (ed) *Meaning in Mayan Languages*, pp107–141, Mouton, The Hague

Sutrop, U. (2001) 'List task and a cognitive salience index', *Field Methods*, vol 13, pp263–276

UNDP and Ministère de la Santé (2006) *Stratégies pour l'Atteinte des OMD: Secteur Sante*, Cotonou, Benin, United Nations Development Programme (UNDP) and Ministère de la Santé (MS), www.undp.org.bj/docs/omd/OMD_SANTE_Benin.pdf, accessed 19 August 2009

Thompson, E.C. and Zhang, J. (2006) 'Comparative cultural salience: Measures using free-list data', *Field Methods*, vol 18, pp398–412

Weller, S.C. and Romney, A.K. (1988) *Systematic Data Collection*, Sage, Newbury Park, CA

Zarger, R.K. and Stepp, J. (2004) 'Persistence of botanical knowledge among Tzeltal Maya children', *Current Anthropology*, vol 45, pp413–418

Chapter 10

Adult mortality, food security and the use of wild natural resources in a rural district of South Africa: Exploring the environmental dimensions of AIDS?

Wayne Twine and Lori M. Hunter

Introduction

The environmental dimensions of the HIV pandemic remain little explored, despite the centrality of the natural environment in the livelihoods of the rural poor across Africa (Hunter et al. 2008). Nowhere is the empirical investigation of these linkages more important than in southern Africa, which has the highest rates of HIV infection in the world (UNAIDS, 2008). In South Africa (the setting of this chapter) one in six prime-age adults (15–49 years) is HIV positive (Shisana et al., 2009). The region is also plagued by chronic food insecurity in which the livelihood impacts of HIV may be an exacerbating factor (de Waal and Whiteside 2003; Misselhorn 2005). At the same time, natural resource harvesting makes an important contribution to rural livelihoods in the region (Shackleton et al. 2001). In this context, the extent to which natural resource harvesting might mitigate the impacts of HIV on household food security is a topic worthy of serious scholarly attention, and is the focus of this chapter.

Rural communities across southern Africa make extensive use of wild natural resources such as fuelwood, wild vegetables, wild fruit, edible insects, bushmeat and medicinal plants (Clarke et al., 1996; Letsela et al., 2002; Shackleton et al., 2002; Twine et al., 2003). The levels of use are often substantial; rural South African households consume a mean of 5.3 tonnes of fuelwood, 104kg of edible wild fruit and 58kg of wild vegetables per year (Shackleton and Shackleton, 2004). In the face of difficult economic conditions, these natural resources offer inexpensive alternatives to otherwise purchased goods. The combined direct-use value of these resources averages roughly US$520 per household per year in South Africa (Shackleton and Shackleton, 2004) and is comparable to that of crop and livestock production (Dovie et al., 2002). This constitutes a saving if these resources are harvested without financial cost.

Households also sell a range of raw and processed natural products to earn income (Brigham et al., 1996). Although variable, these incomes are generally modest (Shackleton et al., 2008). Dovie et al. (2002) calculated that households in a rural village in South Africa earned a mean total of US$127 per year from natural resources trade.

Taken together, these varied uses of natural resources constitute a 'rural safety net', buffering households against hardship and crisis (Shackleton et al.; Shackleton and Shackleton, 2004; Paumgarten, 2006). This is especially important in the current era of rising mortality rates among prime-age adults in South Africa due to AIDS (Kahn et al., 2007). A nascent body of research in South Africa is beginning to shed light on how resource use might buffer HIV-impacted households against food insecurity. Kaschula (2008) showed that the use of wild foods may render households more economically resilient, but that households associated with HIV proxies often make less use of such resources, possibly due to labour shortages or stigma. Focusing on children, McGarry and Shackleton (2009) found the highest use of wild foods among children from households characterized as HIV-afflicted, especially among those not attending school. Selling wild foods was also a more common activity among such children. The use of these wild foods improved the children's dietary diversity and protein intake. It is unknown what influence cash savings from resource use might have in shaping food security after an AIDS death, but early evidence from our own ongoing work suggests that households impacted by a prime-age adult death may collect natural resources to supplement previously purchased goods, including food (Hunter et al., 2007).

While these studies suggest important linkages between HIV, natural resource use and food security, they relied on proxy measures, such as presence of orphans or chronic illness or death of a prime-age adult, rather than data on cause of death to identify HIV-mortality impacted households. The study presented in this chapter thus makes an important contribution to advancing knowledge on this topic, since it used mortality data from a rural South African health and demographic surveillance system to identify households that had experienced the recent death of a prime-age adult due to HIV-related causes. This study examined food security among HIV-impacted households, compared to non-HIV-impacted households, with a particular focus on the role of natural wild resources (for example, wild foods) in shaping household resilience following the death of a prime-age adult.

Study setting, data and research methods

Study site

The study was conducted in the Agincourt Health and Demographic Surveillance Site in Bushbuckridge rural municipality, Mpumalanga Province, South Africa. Named after one of the local villages, the Agincourt site consists of 24 villages, comprising over 14,000 households and 84,000 people. Village size ranges from 480 to 6,834 in population. Approximately a quarter of the residents are former Mozambican refugees, most of whom fled to South Africa during the civil war in Mozambique in the 1980s.

The area is typical of rural communities across South Africa, being characterized by poverty and high human densities. Few households are able to support themselves on agriculture alone, primarily due to the shortage of land and declining interest in agriculture as a result of the previous government's forced relocation and separate development policies for black South Africans (Hargreaves and Pronyk, 2003). Due to poor local employment opportunities, a large proportion of adults are migrant labourers, working on commercial farms and in towns and cities across the country.

HIV prevalence in the region, estimated from antenatal surveillance data, was 19 per cent in 1998 (DOH, 1998), while AIDS and TB (often associated with HIV) are the leading causes of death for adults between the ages of 15 and 49 in the study site (Kahn et al., 1999). Furthermore, mortality among young adults increased fivefold in the study site over the decade between 1992–1993 and 2002–2003, attributed largely to the emerging HIV pandemic (Kahn et al., 2007).

In terms of environmental conditions, the area is characterized by poor soils and highly variable rainfall. The underlying geology is primarily coarse granite and gneiss, giving rise to leached, sandy soils. The region is semi-arid, with a mean annual rainfall of 650mm. The natural vegetation is predominantly broad-leaf savannah woodland.

Data sources

Three data sources were used for this study:

1 *Agincourt Health and Demographic Surveillance System (AHDSS)*: Data on the demographic characteristics of Agincourt households and individuals was provided through the longitudinal health and demographic surveillance system of the University of the Witwatersrand/Medical Research Council's Rural Public Health and Health Transitions Research Unit (abbreviated hereafter as the Agincourt Unit). Since 1992, the Agincourt Unit has collected census data at 12–18-month intervals from all households in the AHDSS site. The resulting data are incredibly rich in socio-demographic detail, allowing identification of key household characteristics (e.g. size, male/female headship, age composition, socio-economic status). The AHDSS also provided data on individual mortality, which was crucial for our study design, which required the differentiation between households with different types of adult mortality experience.

2 *Quantitative Survey*: We surveyed 290 households with differing experience of adult mortality, collecting data on food security and use of wild natural resources (refer to household survey and sampling design below).

3 *Remote Sensing:* The state of the local natural environment, in terms of woodland cover, was assessed for the study villages using satellite imagery. Additional detail is provided below.

Household mortality experience

Mortality experience is the primary analytical variable in the study, and the Agincourt Unit's demographic surveillance data were used to identify households that had experienced the death of an adult member during the past two years. Cause of death was obtained from the AHDSS. This is ascertained by the Agincourt Unit through 'verbal autopsies' undertaken for each mortality experience within the study site after each annual census (Kahn et al., 2000; Kahn et al., 2007). Within a verbal autopsy, a trained lay fieldworker interviews the closest available caregiver of the deceased in the vernacular, using a structured questionnaire. The interview transcript is then assessed independently by two medical doctors to assign a probable cause of death. If these doctors' perceptions correspond, the diagnosis is accepted. If they differ, the two doctors discuss the case to try to reach consensus. If no agreement is reached, the interview transcript is sent to a third doctor who has not seen the prior diagnoses. If there is agreement between the third assessment and one of the other two, this is accepted as the most probable cause of death. If consensus can still not be reached between at least two doctors, cause of death is logged as 'ill-defined'. This approach to verbal autopsy was validated locally using hospital records in the 1990s (Kahn et al., 2000), and has recently been revalidated specifically for HIV/AIDS assessment (Kahn et al., 2007). The data from the verbal autopsies thus allowed classification of HIV-related deaths (which are not reflected on death certificates) and other mortality experiences.

The study focused on mortality of prime-age adults (15–49), as this age range represents the period of largest economic contribution to the household, as well as being the ages of those most susceptible to HIV infection. Deaths occurring in this age group over the two years prior to the survey were classified as either HIV-related (abbreviated hereafter as 'HIV death') and non-HIV-related (abbreviated hereafter as 'non-HIV death'). Non-HIV deaths were further classified as 'sudden' (e.g. heart attack, motor vehicle accident) or 'slow' (e.g. cancer). We used these mortality classifications to sample households from three mortality strata: 1. HIV mortality: experienced a prime-age adult death due to HIV-related causes in the two years prior to the survey; 2. non-HIV mortality: experienced a sudden prime-age adult death, where cause of death was not related to HIV, in the two years prior to the survey; and 3. no mortality: experienced no death of a prime-age adult in the two years prior to the survey. Non-HIV mortality households were included in the survey since we were unable to directly address the question of HIV morbidity, due to the cross-sectional nature of the study. More specifically, by comparing households with HIV and sudden non-HIV deaths, we aimed to indirectly capture some of the unique impacts of HIV mortality, which often includes a preceding long period of illness.

Household survey

The survey instrument was developed based upon central literature in the relevant fields, as well as the investigators' previous experience in the Agincourt field site. The instrument focused on: 1. food security; 2. livelihood strategies; and 3. use of natural resources, especially in relation to meeting household food requirements.

The survey's three topical sections were:

1 *Household food security* was assessed using accepted proxy indicators and methodologies appropriate for the local context (see Hoddinott, 1999; Hendriks, 2005). Our choice of methods, based on trade-offs between time, cost, accuracy and the expertise required, was as follows: i) *Dietary Diversity Index* for 99 food

items, including commonly used species of wild foods, recording whether the item was eaten by household members at least once in the last week, month, year, or not at all (Hoddinott and Yohannes, 2002; Swindale and Bilinsky, 2005); ii) *Household Experience of hunger and access to food*, such as number of times in the last 30 days in which the household worried about, or ran out of, food (see Household Food Insecurity Scale (FANTA 2004) or the Food Access Survey Tool (Coates et al. 2003)); and iii) *Coping Strategies* based on frequency of short-term responses to food shortage, such as skipping meals or asking neighbours for food (Maxwell, 1996; Maxwell et al., 1999). All of the above methods were adapted for local conditions through insight gained from three focus groups with local women. The focus group participants assisted in the development of lists of foods eaten locally, as well as coping strategies used when facing food shortages.

2   *Adaptive livelihood strategies*, which are longer term livelihood strategies in contrast to short-term 'coping' strategies, were assessed in the context of food security for all households. This survey section dealt with household livelihood strategies, which relate directly to household food provisioning, including agricultural production, purchasing food and gathering wild foods. Indirect provisioning, such as when resources are used as sources of household income, was also quantified. The role of social capital in livelihoods and coping strategies was assessed in terms of reliance on social networks, such as borrowing food from neighbours, friends or family. Participation in social groups such as women's groups, churches or burial societies was also recorded in the survey's livelihoods section.

3   *Household use of wild natural resources* for: a) direct provisioning of food; b) selling to earn money; and c) saving money through not having to buy commercial alternatives, was recorded. There was a certain degree of overlap between the food security, adaptive livelihood strategies and woodland resource use sections, and this was purposeful to ensure thorough coverage and allow triangulation of the collected data.

The cross-sectional nature of the survey posed a major analytical challenge. For this reason, we asked all households about recent changes in their food security, livelihoods and resource use. For those sampled households which had experienced an adult mortality in the last two years, we also asked carefully phrased questions about changes in food security, livelihood strategies, and use of woodland resources specifically as a result of the passing of the household member.

The survey was conducted by experienced local fieldworkers from the Agincourt Unit. The respondents were typically the female household member primarily responsible for food acquisition and preparation, as well as acquisition of woodland resources. The survey was conducted in May and June 2006, using the dominant local language of the field site (Shangaan).

Woodland cover

The Normalized Difference Vegetation Index (NDVI) was used as an index of woodland cover around villages. Data from Landsat 5 TM images (May 2004) allowed calculation of NDVI in ERDAS Imagine. Such indices are commonly used as indicators of environmental change's impact on vegetation greenness (Wang et al., 2003; Zhou et al., 2003). Chlorophyll absorbs red light and the mesophyll tissues in plants scatter near infrared light – the NDVI is the difference between the values in the red and near-infrared bands divided by the sum of these same values (Tucker 1979). This ratio varies from -1 to 1, and negative values indicate senescent or dead vegetation. Positive values reflect actively growing green vegetation. NDVI values saturate at high biomass (Huete et al., 2002), but preliminary field-work shows that Agincourt, which falls in a semi-arid savannah region, does not contain areas with high enough biomass to approach this saturation point. This provides evidence that the NDVI can effectively proxy for vegetation cover in the region. Tree biomass (for example, fuelwood) and productivity (for example, seed production, stem growth) are also positively correlated with NDVI (Foody et al., 2001; Mutanga and Skidmore, 2004). As such, the availability of natural resources used directly by Agincourt residents (i.e. wild foods, fuel wood) can be effectively mapped with this greenness proxy. For this study, the NDVI was averaged across all 30m x 30m pixels in 1km buffers around each village, giving a mean village NDVI value per village.

Sampling design

The household survey included 290 households. A stratified random sample of households was drawn from the AHDSS database across the three mortality strata as follows: 1. HIV mortality: n=109; 2. non-HIV mortality: n=71; and 3. no mortality: n=110. The third category constituted a control stratum. This sampling frame enabled quantification and comparison of food security and resource use across the three strata. The original intent of interviewing 100 households per category, determined by available project resources, was adjusted since insufficient households met the criteria for the 'non-HIV mortality'. Still, the constraints within this category allowed for increased sampling of the other strata. Selected households were located in the field using their unique identifier number on digital aerial photographs used by the Agincourt Unit in their annual census. This is one example of the benefit of linking with a surveillance site. Indeed, within this project, embedding the work within the AHDSS enabled us to a) draw a random stratified sample from a known population, b) incorporate actual cause of death, rather than HIV proxies, and c) include other household data, such as size and socio-economic status, within the analyses.

As noted, the Agincourt Unit's database provided background on each sampled household's socio-economic status (SES). SES was reflected through a wealth ranking based on household ownership of assets (e.g. appliances) and access to services and amenities (e.g. a water tap in the yard). Household SES score was derived from principal component analysis of the wealth ranking and is a relative value. These scores were then used to classify households into SES quintiles.

Data analysis

Dietary diversity, experience of hunger, coping strategies and resource use variables were expressed as both ordinal and binary outcomes. As an example, inclusion of a food item (e.g. beef) in the household diet was expressed as: 1. an ordinal scale of frequency (at least once in the last week, month, year, or not at all); and 2. as a binary yes/no response for each of these frequency categories individually.

Several steps were taken to calculate a dietary diversity score, reflecting both diversity and frequency of particular foods. First, frequency per food item was converted to a weekly fraction as follows:

1 At least once in the last 7 days (1 week): 1/1 = 1
2 At least once in the last 30 days (30 days/7 days = 4.29 weeks): 1/4.29 = 0.23
3 At least once in the last 12 months (365 days/7 days = 52.14 weeks): 1/52.14 = 0.02
4 More than 12 months ago/never: = 0

These values were then summed for all 99 food items to give an absolute dietary diversity score out of 99, which then incorporated both the range of food items eaten and the frequency of consumption. This additive value was then converted to a proportional dietary diversity score by dividing the absolute value by the maximum possible (99).

Bivariate associations were explored between household food security, adult mortality experience, proximate woodland cover, household use of woodland resources for consumption or sale, and socio-economic status, as well as other relevant household characteristics (for example, household size). Statistical tests included chi-squared test, logistic regression and one-way analysis of variance (ANOVA) with Tukey post hoc test. Multivariate models, such as multifactorial ANOVA, analysis of covariance (ANCOVA) with Tukey post hoc test, multiple regression analysis and multivariate logistic regression analysis, were then estimated to predict food security as a function of adult mortality experience and household use of natural resources, controlling for environmental context and household size and socio-economic status. In these models, only the more commonly used wild foods were considered.

Results

Presentation of results is structured as follows. First, descriptive characteristics of the study households within the three mortality strata are provided. Next, we examine associations between household mortality experience and use of natural resources. Finally, we investigate how adult mortality, household characteristics, use of natural resources and woodland cover intersect to shape food security. Explanations and implications of observed relationships are explored in the final discussion.

Household characteristics

Mean household size did not differ significantly between the three mortality strata, averaging roughly five permanent members. Households with a non-HIV adult death were significantly wealthier, on average, than either HIV-impacted households or 'no death' households. This was true both before the focal adult death (2003) and after (2005). SES score remained static for HIV-impacted households over this period. Most households impacted by a non-HIV death were in the two highest SES quintiles. HIV-impacted households were more evenly distributed across wealth classes, with the poorest class over-represented relative to the 'no death' group (Figure 10.1). By contrast, the majority of households with no mortality had low or intermediate SES, although few were in the poorest category. The odds of a household experiencing an HIV adult death decreased among those with greater SES (Odds ratio (OR) = 0.81, $p<0.05$), while

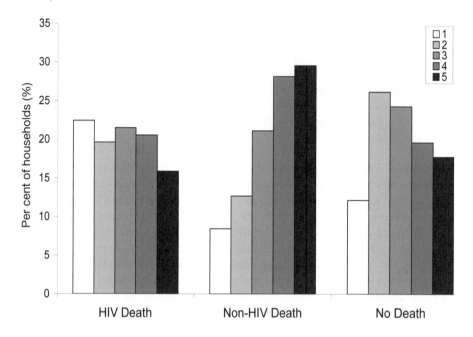

Figure 10.1 *Frequency profile of household socio-economic status classes (1 = poorest, 5 = wealthiest) in 2005, differentiated by mortality experience*

the converse was true for households with a non-HIV adult death (OR=1.43, p<0.01). Household members participated in, or were members of, an average total of roughly three social groups, clubs or organizations, and there was no significant difference in this organizational dimension across the three strata. Membership in social groups was greater among larger households (r=0.20, R^2=0.04, p<0.001) and those with higher SES (r=0.33, R^2=0.11, p<0.001).

Neither time since the death, nor the total number of deaths over the last two years differed between the two mortality strata. However, the role that the deceased had played in providing food for the household differed slightly between the two categories of households. While the deceased had commonly contributed income, tended fields and/or collected wild natural resources in both categories, fewer had contributed income or tended fields among HIV-impacted households, while fewer had collected wild foods among households where the cause of death had not been HIV-related (Table 10.1).

Table 10.1 *The role that the deceased had played in the household economy, with relevance to food security, expressed as percentage (%) of households in which the deceased had played the given role*

Role of deceased	HIV Death	Non-HIV Death
Contributed income	59.6	70.8
Tended food gardens and/or fields	59.6	64.6
Collected natural resources	51.9	46.2

Associations between adult mortality and household use of woodland resources

Use of wild natural resources as a source of food, cooking energy and medicine

Indigenous wild vegetables, fruit and insects were part of the diet of the vast majority of households, with no statistically significant differences in prevalence of use between mortality strata (Figure 10.2). Wild birds, fish and mammals were much less commonly used across all three strata. Although fuelwood was the dominant energy source for cooking across all three mortality strata, a higher percentage of HIV-impacted households (93 per cent) used fuelwood than households having experienced a non-HIV death (85 per cent) or no mortality (83 per cent). Interestingly, there was no significant difference in relative frequency of households using traditional medicine across the three strata.

Most households used wild vegetables and wild fruit more than once a week (when in season), but relatively fewer HIV-impacted households (74 per cent) made frequent use of wild vegetables than households with a non-HIV death (85 per cent) or no death (89 per cent) (Figure 10.3). A 'no death' household was thus significantly more likely to make frequent use of wild vegetables than an HIV-impacted household (OR=2.82, p<0.05). This remained true even when controlling for SES (which decreased the odds of a household using wild vegetables often) and household size (which increased the odds). Neither the time since adult death nor the total number of household deaths experienced was associated with the likelihood of a mortality-impacted household using wild foods.

Despite being less likely to make frequent use of wild vegetables, both types of mortality-impacted households were more likely than 'no death' households to have increased their use of wild vegetables in the last 12 months (HIV death to no death: OR = 0.11, p<0.005; non-HIV death to no death: OR = 0.13, p<0.005). These patterns persisted when controlling for SES and household size. Approximately 30 per cent of households in both mortality strata indicated they relied more on wild vegetables after the passing of their adult member than before. Of the 11 households that indicated they had started eating foods in the last 12 months, which they had not eaten previously, all were households which had experienced a recent adult death (HIV=6, non-HIV=5), and all had started eating wild vegetables. Woodland cover, indexed by mean normalized difference vegetation index (NDVI) in a 1km buffer around each village, exhibited no association with whether households used any given natural resource.

Use of wild natural resources to earn and save money

Few households (14) sold natural resources, but of those that did, 12 (86 per cent) were mortality-impacted households, most of which (7) had experienced a non-HIV death. Natural resource-based products sold included reed mats, marula beer and fuelwood. Because of the low incidence, none of the logistic regression models were significant, but the pattern is certainly of interest and worth additional exploration.

For a total of 13 wild natural resources, significantly more mortality-impacted households indicated they used the resource specifically to save money as compared to those with no adult death (Figure 10.4). At least one of the resources was used to save

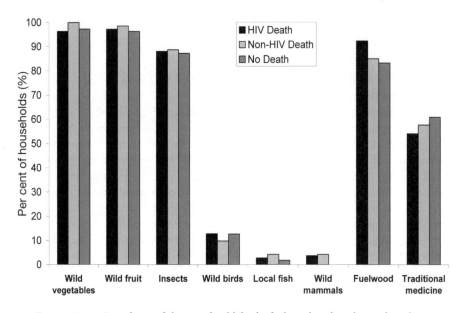

Figure 10.2 *Prevalence of the use of wild foods, fuelwood and traditional medicine across mortality strata*

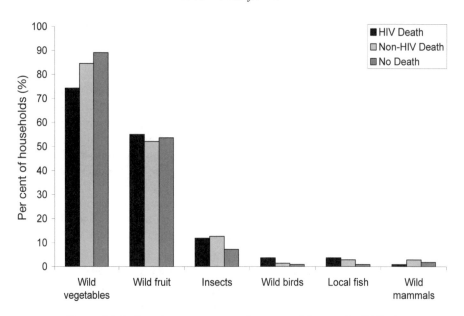

Figure 10.3 *Prevalence across mortality strata of the use of wild foods more than once a week*

money by 32 per cent and 38 per cent of HIV and non-HIV-impacted households, respectively, compared to only 6 per cent of 'no death' households. The resources most widely used for cost savings were grass hand brooms, fuelwood and wild vegetables.

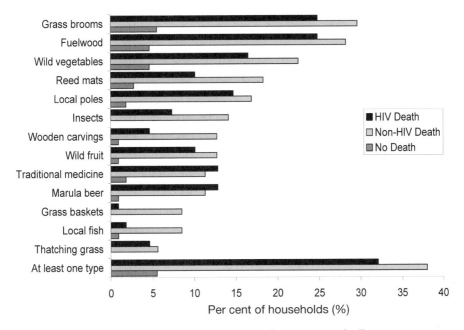

Figure 10.4 *Prevalence of the use of wild natural resources specifically to save money (only those resources for which there was significant variation between mortality strata)*

For all resources except traditional medicine and marula beer, slightly more 'non-HIV death' households than HIV-impacted households used the resource for cash savings. These associations still held when controlling for woodland cover (mean NDVI), and the likelihood of any household using at least one of these resources to save money was greater among those with more woodland cover.

Households were more likely to use at least one type of resource to save money if they had a higher SES (OR=1.28, p<0.05) or had more permanent members (OR=1.10, p<0.05). When controlling for these two factors, mortality-impacted households were still more likely than 'no death' households to use at least one type of resource to save money (HIV death to no death: OR=0.12, p<0.001; non-HIV to no death: OR=0.11, p<0.05). Households in which more time had passed since the adult mortality were more likely to use wild fruit, insects, carvings and reed mats to save money.

The intersection between mortality, poverty, resource use and food security

The final set of analyses reflect the simultaneous associations between food insecurity, death of a prime-age adult due to HIV, poverty, resource use and environmental context, while controlling for household size. HIV-impacted households had significantly lower mean dietary diversity than 'no death' households, net of the other variables (Table 10.2). HIV-impacted households only had lower dietary diversity than non-HIV death households when considering food items eaten over the last year. Poorer households (low SES) had significantly lower dietary diversity than wealthier households for all measures

Table 10.2 *Results of the analysis of covariance (ANCOVA) models for dietary diversity indices across mortality strata. Adjusted means for mortality strata with common superscripts are not significantly different from each other (p<0.05). Values for independent variables are beta coefficients (p<0.05 in bold italics)*

Variable	Food items eaten in the last week	Food items eaten in the last month	Food items eaten in the last year	Proportional dietary diversity score
Model	R^2=0.25 p<0.001	R^2=0.26 p<0.001	R^2=0.24 p<0.001	R^2=0.26 p<0.001
Adjusted means				
HIV mortality	22.6[a]	33.6[a]	58.6[a]	0.259[a]
Non-HIV mortality	23.0[ab]	33.8[a]	60.2[ab]	0.262[ab]
No mortality	25.1[b]	36.9[b]	61.8[b]	0.287[b]
Beta coefficients				
SES	*0.27*	*0.27*	*0.18*	*0.28*
Household size	0.04	0.061	0.11	0.05
Use wild vegetables	0.08	*0.11*	*0.19*	0.10
Use wild fruit	*0.12*	*0.17*	*0.21*	*0.14*
Use insects	*0.31*	*0.26*	*0.24*	*0.30*
Use to save money	0.02	*0.14*	0.01	0.05
Use to earn money	0.02	0.02	-0.01	0.02
Mean NDVI	0.04	-0.04	0.04	0.02

of dietary diversity, and the use of wild fruit and insects was associated with higher dietary diversity. In addition, the number of food items eaten in the last month and year was higher in households that used wild vegetables. Dietary diversity over the last month was also higher in households that used natural resources to save money. Neither woodland cover (mean NDVI) nor using resources for income generation was associated with the household dietary diversity.

Households with no mortality were less likely than HIV-impacted households to have had multiple experiences of hunger (Table 10.3). Wealthier households were less likely to have worried about food or gone hungry in the last 30 days. Households that used wild vegetables and insects were less likely to run out of food, but slightly more likely to run out if there was good woodland cover around their village. Households that used insects were also less likely to have had all three experiences of hunger. Experience of an adult mortality had no significant effect on household coping strategies in the multivariate models. The only model with any significant independent variables predicted a significant decrease in the likelihood of a household skipping meals for a day with increasing SES (OR=0.63, p<0.001).

Discussion

This project was designed to elucidate the role of the use of wild natural resources, especially wild foods, in food security among HIV-impacted households compared to non-impacted households. By taking poverty, indexed by SES, into consideration, and

Table 10.3 *Results of statistically significant multivariate logistic regression models comparing experience of hunger for HIV-impacted households to households with a non-HIV death or no death. Values are odds ratios: >1 indicates an increase in likelihood, <1 indicates a decrease in likelihood (p<0.05 in bold italics)*

Variable	Worried about food	Ran out of food	Went hungry	All three
Model	LR chi²=29.09 p<0.005	LR chi²=36.64 p<0.001	LR chi²=19.60 p<0.05	LR chi²=19.60 p<0.05
Odds ratios (HIV=ref)				
Non-HIV death	1.83	2.29	1.48	1.62
No death	0.78	0.87	0.58	*0.46*
SES	*0.80*	0.77	*0.75*	0.80
Household size	1.02	1.00	1.01	1.02
Use wild vegetables	Dropped	*0.26*	0.92	0.78
Use wild fruit	2.03	2.55	1.31	0.87
Use insects	0.53	*0.33*	0.61	*0.43*
Use to save money	1.71	1.05	1.15	0.92
Use to earn money	3.43	2.99	1.51	1.40
Mean NDVI	1.04	*1.05*	1.02	1.02

comparing HIV-impacted households with those impacted by a sudden non-HIV adult death or no death, we aimed to unravel the nuances between adult mortality, poverty, resource-use and food security.

On the whole, the study suggests that mortality-impacted households are generally less food secure than households not directly impacted by an adult death. However, HIV-related mortality does not appear to necessarily represent a unique form of mortality impact. Within our examination, HIV-impacted households and households who had experienced other forms of adult mortality were similarly impacted by food insecurity. Even so, although not unique regarding general food security, adult HIV-related mortality was associated with lower dietary diversity and food sufficiency, even when controlling for socio-economic status (SES). This is in contrast with Kaschula (2008) who also found lower food quantity security scores in AIDS-afflicted households, but no significant impact on short-term dietary diversity. However, Kaschula only considered dietary diversity within the last 48 hours, whereas this study considered longer periods of time (the last week, month and year), which have been more sensitive to differences in dietary diversity.

Our findings point to the general importance of wild foods, especially wild vegetables, fruit and insects, in the local diet. This concurs with findings of other studies such as Twine et al. (2003) and Kaschula (2008), and accounts for the lack of any discernible difference in the prevalence in use of these resources between mortality strata. One exception is the use of wild vegetables, where households that had experienced an HIV death tended to use these foods less frequently. The lessened consumption of wild vegetables is likely due to the deceased's prior role as resource collector. Indeed, reduced resource collection due to a reduction in human capital in households characterized by AIDS proxies was also observed by Kaschula in her South African research (2008). Nevertheless, in the study presented here some mortality-impacted households (regardless of cause of death) became *more* reliant on wild vegetables after an adult mortality, and in some cases, added wild vegetables as a new item to the household diet. Human resources were less limited in such households and, therefore, collection constraints less likely to be felt.

Central to this study was the question of whether the use of natural resources translated into improved food security for vulnerable households. The consumption of wild foods did, indeed, contribute to dietary diversity. In addition, results suggest that the consumption of wild vegetables and insects mitigated against actually running out of food. As related to mortality, wild foods, especially wild vegetables, played a more important role in the diet of mortality-impacted households than those without such experience. Even so, mortality-impacted households still tended to have less diverse diets than households with no mortality. In this way, the use of these resources did not fully mitigate mortality impacts on food sufficiency. Based on these findings, we conclude that the use of natural resources may be seen as an important component of dietary coping strategies of mortality-impacted households, but not as a fully supportive safety net.

The strong association identified between mortality experience and use of natural resources specifically to save money is also noteworthy and important. Generally, this association points to the broader 'safety net' function (beyond food provision) that natural resources play in rural livelihoods, particularly in times of crisis (Shackleton and Shackleton, 2004). In fact, the use of resources for cost savings was far more prevalent than the use of natural resources for income generation. That said, given the cross-sectional nature of the study, it is not possible to discern the extent to which cost savings through natural resource use actually contributed to economic resilience and/or improved livelihoods more generally.

HIV-mortality impacted households did not appear unique in their use of natural resources for cost savings. However, such a strategy was more prevalent among non-HIV mortality households. In many cases, these households endured the sudden loss of income due to the death of a breadwinner, and the intensified use of natural resources appeared to be a response to worrying about having enough food. In this way, natural resources may provide a short-term coping mechanism for sudden household shocks of this form. Even so, the likelihood of using woodland resources to save money was greater as time passed since mortality, thereby also suggesting a longer term adaptive strategy for many households. The positive relationship between cost savings strategy and local woodland cover may indicate that greater resource abundance enhances the likelihood of levels of use, which afford real cost savings.

Interestingly, greater levels of woodland cover were not associated with more use of wild foods or better food security among HIV-impacted households. As noted in the methods section, woodland cover is not a reliable proxy of particular forms of resource abundance, especially for resources such as wild herbs. It also cannot be used as a direct measure of resource availability around the village, as this is also influenced by factors such as institutional regulation of resource use. That being said, households living in local villages with poor vegetation cover have to invest more time in securing some resources, such as wild fruit or firewood (Giannecchini et al., 2007; Kirkland et al., 2007).

While mortality was, indeed, associated with household food insecurity, our work suggests that *poverty* is central in shaping food security. Poor households, regardless of recent adult mortality experience or woodland cover, were similarly vulnerable. This observation is very important, and echoes the findings of other studies such as Peters et al. (2008), which show that much of the observed hardship associated with HIV is essentially due to preexisting levels of poverty. Even so, mortality experience matters. After controlling for socio-economic status, HIV-impacted households tended to be less food secure than non-impacted households.

In contrast to the conventional view that HIV systematically erodes household capital and causes poverty (Whiteside, 2002; Masanjala, 2007), we found that household socio-economic status (as measured through possessions) had not changed among those impacted by an HIV-related mortality. That is not to say that such households were not worse off financially after the death, but household assets had not noticeably eroded. Of course, it is also possible that two years is not a sufficiently long period to observe mortality impacts on the household asset base.

Finally, this study was cross-sectional in design, which has certain limitations. For example, we were not able to shed much light on the impact of HIV-related illness on household food security *prior* to the death. Longitudinal studies are thus needed to gain greater understanding of the longer term dynamics between adult mortality, livelihoods, environment and food security. Even so, embedding this work within a demographic surveillance site has allowed for the addition of substantial nuance to the examination related to cause of death – allowing disaggregation of mortality to better explore the unique nature of AIDS impacts.

The work presented here, combined with prior work on AIDS mortality and food security, begins to add nuance to our understanding of one among many myriad impacts on affected households. The story emerging is one in which adult mortality exacerbates existing vulnerabilities to food insecurity, primarily associated with poverty. The story, too, involves natural resources, and in this way, we aim to contribute to understanding of the environmental dimensions of the AIDS pandemic. Specifically, we find that proximate natural resources act as a 'safety net', allowing for cost savings and, in some cases, creation of resource-based products sold for generation of household income. With a focus on AIDS, however, the mortality shock to the household is not unique – we find that adult mortality negatively impacts household wellbeing, regardless of its underlying cause. In this way, programmes and policies aiming to enhance food security and/or manage local natural resources, would do best to target vulnerable, mortality-impacted households more broadly, as opposed to a singular focus on those impacted by adult mortality resultant of AIDS.

Acknowledgements

This project was funded by the International Food Policy Research Institute (IFPRI) (grant 2006X110.WIT), via the Regional Network on HIV/AIDS, Rural Livelihoods, and Food Security (RENEWAL). We would like to thank Stuart Gillespie and the IPFRI team, as well as Bruce Frayne and Scott Drimmie (RENEWAL) for their support and assistance. We are grateful to the University of the Witwatersrand/Medical Research Council's Rural Public Health and Health Transitions Research Unit (Wits/MRC Agincourt Unit) for their support with logistics, fieldworkers, data, administration and advice. Barend Erasmus from the Wits School of Animal, Plant and Environmental

Sciences, and Laura Patterson from the University of Colorado assisted us with analysis of the NDVI data. We are grateful to Paul Pronyk of the Rural AIDS Development and Action Research programme (RADAR) for comments and advice on the design of the household questionnaire and sampling. This research was indirectly supported by the Wellcome Trust (grant 085477/Z/08/Z) through its support of the Agincourt Health and Demographic Surveillance System. This research has benefited from the NICHD-funded University of Colorado Population Center (grant R21 HD51146) through administrative and computing support. A write-up grant from the Wits Science Faculty Research Committee is acknowledged. This research would not have been possible without the cooperation of the households and community leadership in the villages of the Agincourt HDSS site, and we are very grateful to them for partnering with us in this project. We would like to especially mention Steve Tollman, Kathy Kahn, Mark Collinson, Paul Mee, Benjamin Clark, Rhian Twine, Geoffrey Tibane, Obed Mokoena, Mildred Shabangu, Zubeida Bagus and Doreen Nkuna, and our team of field assistants. In the Wits School of Animal, Plant and Environmental Sciences, we thank Norman Owen-Smith, Barend Erasmus and Hazel Khanyi for their encouragement, and assistance with analysing satellite imagery and administration. We are grateful to Paul Pronyk of RADAR for comments and advice on the design of the household questionnaire and sampling. At the University of Colorado, we would like to thank Jane Menken for her role as mentor, and Steve Graham and Laura Patterson for administrative support and assistance with NDVI data analysis. In addition, this research has benefited from the NICHD-funded University of Colorado Population Center (grant R21 HD51146). Even so, the content is solely the responsibility of the authors and does not necessarily represent the official views of NIH or NICHD. Finally, this research would not have been possible without the cooperation of the households and community leadership in the villages of the Agincourt HDSS site, and we are very grateful to them for partnering with us in this project.

References

Brigham, T., Chihongo, A. and Chidumayo, E. (1996) 'Trade in woodland products from the Miombo region', in *The Miombo in Transition: Woodlands and Welfare in Africa*, pp137–174, CIFOR, Bogor, Indonesia

Clarke, J., Cavendish, W. and Coote, C. (1996) 'Rural households and Miombo woodlands: Use, value and management', in B. Campbell (ed), *The Miombio in Transition: Woodlands and Welfare in Africa*, pp. 101–135, CIFOR, Bogor, Indonesia

Coates, J., Webb, P. and Houser, R. (2003) *Measuring Food Insecurity: Going Beyond Indicators of Income and Anthropometry*, FANTA, Academy for Education Development, Washington DC

De Waal, A. and Whiteside, A. (2003) 'New variant famine: AIDS and food crisis in southern Africa', *The Lancet*, vol 362, pp1234–1237

Dovie, D.B., Shackleton, C.M. and Witkowski, E.T. (2002) 'Direct-use values of woodland resources consumed and traded in a South African village', *International Journal of Sustainable Development and World Ecology*, vol 9, pp269–283

FANTA (2004) *Measuring Household Food Insecurity*, Workshop R., FANTA, Academy for Education Development, Washington DC

Foody, G.M., Cutler, M.E., Mcmorrow, J., Pelz, D., Tangki, H., Boyd, D.S. and Douglas, I. (2001) 'Mapping the biomass of Bornean tropical rain forest from remotely sensed data', *Global Ecology and Biogeography*, vol 10, no 44, pp379–387

Giannecchini, M., Twine, W. and Vogel, C. (2007) 'Land-cover change and human–environment interactions in a rural cultural landscape in South Africa', *The Geographical Journal*, vol 173 no 1, pp26–42

Hargreaves, J. and Pronyk, P. (2003) 'HIV/AIDS and rural development: Realities, relationships and responses', *Development Update*, vol 4, no 1, pp85–107

Hendriks, S.L. (2005) 'The challenges facing empirical estimation of household food (in)security in South Africa', *Development Southern Africa*, vol 22, no 1, pp103–123

Hoddinott, J. (1999) *Choosing Outcome Indicators of Food Security*, Technical Report, IFPRI, Washington DC

Hoddinott, J. and Yohannes, Y. (2002) *Dietary Diversity as a Household Food Security Indicator*, FANTA, Academy for Education Development, Washington DC

Huet, A., Didan, K., Miura, T., Rodriguez E.P., Gao, X. and Ferreira, L.G. (2002) 'Overview of the radiometric and biophysical performance of the MODIS vegetation indices', *Remote Sensing of Environment*, vol 83, pp195–213

Hunter, L.M., De Souza, R. and Twine, W. (2008) 'The environmental dimensions of the HIV/AIDS pandemic: A call for scholarship and evidence-based intervention', *Population and Environment*, vol 29, no 3–5, pp103–107

Hunter, L.M., Twine, W. and Patterson, L. (2007) 'Locusts are now our beef: adult mortality and household dietary use of local environmental resources in rural South Africa', *Scandinavian Journal of Public Health*, vol 35, supplement 69, pp165–74

Kahn, K., Garenne, M.L., Collinson, M.A. and Tollman, S.M. (2007) 'Mortality trends in a new South Africa: Hard to make a fresh start', *Scandinavian Journal of Public Health*, vol 35, supplement 69, pp26–34

Kahn, K., Tollman, S., Garenne, M. and Gear, J, (1999) 'Who dies from what? Determining cause of death in Africa's rural north-east', *Tropical Medicine and International Health*, vol 4, no 6, pp433–441

Kahn, K., Tollman, S.M., Garenne, M. and Gear, J.S.S. (2000) 'Validation and application of verbal autopsies in a rural area of South Africa', *Tropical Medicine and International Health*, vol 5, no 11, pp824–831

Kahn, K., Tollman, S.M., Collinson, M.A., Clark, S.J., Twine, R., Clark, B.D., Shabangu, M., Gómez-Olivé, F.X., Mokoena, O. and Garenne, M.L. (2007) 'Research into health, population and social transitions in rural South Africa: Data and methods of the Agincourt Health and Demographic Surveillance System', *Scandinavian Journal of Public Health*, vol 35, supplement 69, pp8–20

Kaschula, S.A. (2008) 'Wild foods and household food security responses to AIDS: Evidence from South Africa', *Population and Environment*, vol 29, pp162–185

Kirkland, T., Hunter, L. and Twine, W. (2007) 'The bush is no more: Insights on institutional change and natural resource availability in rural South Africa', *Society and Natural Resources*, vol 20, no 4, pp337–350

Letsela, T., Witkowski, E. and Balkwill, K. (2002) 'Direct use values of communal resources in Bokong and Tsehlanyane in Lesotho: Whither the commons', *International Journal of Sustainable Development*, vol 9, pp1–18

Masanjala, W. (2007) 'The poverty-HIV/AIDS nexus in Africa: A livelihood approach', *Social Science and Medicine*, vol 64, no 5, pp1032–1041

Maxwell, D., Ahiadeke, C., Levin, C., Armar-Klemesu, M., Zakariah, S. and Lamptey, G.M. (1999) 'Alternative food-security indicators: revisiting the frequency and severity of 'coping strategies'', *Food Policy*, vol 24, pp411–429

Maxwell, D.G. (1996) 'Measuring food insecurity: the frequency and severity of "coping strategies"', *Food Policy*, vol 21, no 3, pp291–303

Misselhorn, A. (2005) 'What drives food insecurity in southern Africa? A meta-analysis of household economy studies', *Global Environmental Change*, vol 15, no 1, pp33–43

Mutanga, O. and Skidmore, A.K. (2004) 'Merging double sampling with remote sensing for a rapid estimation of fuelwood', *Geocarto International*, vol 19, no 4, pp49–55

Paumgarten, F. (2006) 'The role of non-timber forest products as safety-nets: A review of evidence with a focus on South Africa', *GeoJournal*, pp189–197

Peters, P.E., Kambewa, D. and Walker, P. (2008) *The Effects of Increasing Rates of HIV/AIDS-related Illness and Death on Rural Families in Zomba District, Malawi: A Longitudinal Study*, IFPRI/RENEWAL, Washington DC

Shackleton, C. and Shackleton, S. (2004) 'The importance of non-timber forest products in rural livelihood security and as safety nets: A review of evidence from South Africa', *South African Journal of Science*, vol 100, pp658–664

Shackleton, C.M., Cousins, B. and Shackleton, S.E. (2001) 'The role of land-based strategies in rural livelihoods: The contribution of arable production, animal husbandry and natural resource harvesting in communal areas in South Africa', *Development Southern Africa*, vol 18, pp582–604

Shackleton, S., Campbell, B., Lotzsisitka, H. and Shackleton, C. (2008) 'Links between the local trade in natural products, livelihoods and poverty alleviation in a semi-arid region of South Africa', *World Development*, vol 36, no 3, pp505–526

Shackleton, S.E., Shackleton, C.M., Netshiluvhi, T.R., Geach, B.S. and Balance, A. (2002) 'Use patterns and values of savannah resources in three rural villages in South Africa', *Economic Botany*, vol 56, no 2, pp130–146

Shisana, O., Rehle, T., Simbayi, L.C., Zuma, K., Jooste, S., Pillay-van-Wyk, V., Mbelle, N., Van Zyl, J., Parker, W., Zungu, N.P. and Pezi, S. (2009) *South African National HIV Prevalence, Incidence, Behaviour and Communication Survey, 2008: A Turning Tide Among Teenagers?*, HSRC, Cape Town, South Africa

Swindale, A. and Bilinsky, P. (2005) *Household Dietary Diversity Score (HDDS) for Measurement of Household Food Access: Indicator Guide*, FANTA, Academy for Education Development, Washington DC

Tucker, C.J. (1979) 'Red and photographic infrared linear combinations for monitoring vegetation', *Remote Sensing of Environment*, vol 8, pp127–150

Twine, W., Moshe, D., Netshiluvhi, T. and Siphugu, V. (2003) 'Consumption and direct-use values of savannah bio-resources used by rural households in Mametja, a semi-arid area of Limpopo province, South Africa', *South African Journal of Science*, vol 99, pp467–473

UNAIDS (2008) *2008 Report on the Global AIDS Epidemic*, UNAIDS, Geneva, Switzerland

Wang, J., Rich, P.M. and Price, K.P. (2003) 'Temporal responses of NDVI to precipitation and temperature in the central Great Plains, USA', *International Journal of Remote Sensing*, vol 24, no 11, pp2345–2364

Whiteside, A. (2002) 'Poverty and HIV/AIDS in Africa', *Third World Quarterly*, vol 23, no 2, pp313–332

Zhou, L., Kaufmann, R.K., Tian, Y., Myneni, R.B. and Tucker, C.J. (2003) 'Relation between interannual variations in satellite measures of northern forest greenness and climate between 1982 and 1999', *Journal of Geophysical Research*, vol 108(D1), pp3–11

Chapter 11

Applying the Farmer Life School approach to support women of poor and HIV/AIDS-affected households in KwaZulu-Natal, South Africa

Kees Swaans, Jacqueline Broerse and Maxwell Mudhara

Introduction

The Farmer Life School (FLS) is derived from the Farmer Field School (FFS), a discovery-based learning strategy developed in the late 1980s in Southeast Asia (du Guerny et al., 2002). In FFSs, the learning process of a group of farmers is situated in the field, and the field is used as the main reference material. FFSs help farmers to gain a deep understanding of ecological concepts, as well as their practical applications. Instead of passive receivers of information and services, farmers are viewed as capable, responsible and sensible entrepreneurs. Although originally developed for integrated pest management for rice farmers in Asia, the FFS is now applied in over 70 countries around the world, in areas as diverse as dairy farming, conservation agriculture and community forest management (Braun et al., 2006).

The FLS goes beyond the agro-ecosystem, and includes human ecology. The central idea is to develop farmers' critical thinking on the relationships between human behaviour and important livelihood issues, making use of their experiential knowledge (Yech, 2003). The first FLS was implemented in Cambodia in response to the rapid spread of HIV and AIDS, and the increasing vulnerability of the rural population to chronic illnesses (Sokunthea, 2002). It aimed to strengthen farmers' understanding of how their socio-economic situation leads to risk-taking behaviour, prevent adverse social and economic effects from HIV/AIDS and other threats, and establish a farmer network to better address social issues in the interest of sustainable livelihoods (Sokunthea, 2002; Yech, 2003).

The FLS differs from other approaches used in HIV-related education in that it combines health-related messages with identifying root-causes of vulnerability to HIV and AIDS, and increasing the resilience of farm households through agriculture-related activities (du Guerny et al., 2002). This may be particularly relevant in the case of HIV and AIDS as the shape of the HIV epidemic is highly dependent on social processes, not by the virus as such, while consequences of HIV-related illnesses and death are shaped by features of agricultural and livelihood systems (Barnett and Whiteside, 2002; Loenvinsohn and Gillespie, 2003). It is perhaps through analysing farmers' lives and their livelihoods that strategies can be developed to prevent HIV infection and mitigate the impact of AIDS.

Despite promises and high expectations, however, there is very little (evaluated) experience with the FLS (Braun et al., 2006). Its potential and applicability in sub-Saharan Africa, with the highest HIV infection rates in the world, are largely unknown. Although the FLS may serve as an educational setting for farmers to shape their future in the context of the HIV epidemic, HIV-related illnesses and death may have a negative impact on participants and the social dynamics of the group and prevent this approach from being effective.

The aim of this study was to gain insight into the strengths and weaknesses of the FLS in the context of HIV/AIDS, by implementing an adapted FLS in Msinga (KwaZulu-Natal), a rural and HIV high prevalence area in South Africa. The paper starts with a description of a case study, after which an assessment is made of the process and impact of the FLS as applied in Msinga. The paper concludes with identifying the strengths and weaknesses of the approach, and presenting the main lessons learned.

Description of the case study

Msinga is one of four Local Councils of the Umzinyathi District situated in the Province of KwaZulu-Natal, South Africa. The soils in Msinga are of poor quality and climatic conditions are adverse. The area has an estimated population of 160,000 people, with population density going up to as high as 1,400 persons per square kilometre. Msinga is a poverty stricken area with few economic resources and little economic activity. As is typical of most communal areas, most males migrate to the urban areas in search of employment. This means that females constitute the majority of the adults. Nearly 70 per cent of the population is illiterate (Msinga Integrated Development Plan, 2005/2006).

Estimated HIV prevalence among antenatal women in Msinga in 2000 was 18.7 per cent and increasing (Msinga Integrated Development Plan, 2005/2006). Recent data at the district level show that HIV prevalence rate has stabilized at almost 30 per cent in 2008 (National Department of Health South Africa, 2009). In the last few years, a network of services has been developed in this area to support people who are infected with HIV or affected by AIDS, ranging from Voluntary Counselling and Testing (VCT), the Mother to Child Transmission Program, home-based care (HBC), ARV treatment and social welfare grants, but there are still many who live out of reach of most of these services (Msinga Integrated Development Plan, 2005/2006).

In 2003, a community-managed health centre in Msinga mobilized almost 150 people from poor and HIV/AIDS-affected households into garden groups to improve food security. Households are said to be more food secure when food availability, access to food, stability of food supplies and quality of food are in balance with each other (Topouzis and du Guerny, 1999; De Waal and Tumushabe, 2003). Since most rural households in Msinga – especially the poor – partly rely on agricultural production for their livelihood (Swaans et al., 2008a), strengthening agricultural capacity was identified as an entry point to prevent HIV infection and mitigate AIDS's impacts. Due to poor quality of land and limited access to water in the area, suitable land was acquired from traditional authorities to form communal gardens near existing water sources (for example, river, water dam, or spring).

The health centre identified households with the help of HBC workers. Women from households taking care of orphans, in particular, were invited to participate. It was expected that a focus on women as care takers and child minders in the family would not only lead to improved food security, but to improved wellbeing of households as well. There was no age restriction. Two groups of 64 and 35 members (group A and B respectively) were newly formed, while one existing garden group of 47 members (group C) was included. Most women had limited to basic farming skills, while some had received previous training in sustainable agriculture. The groups were geographically spread over the sub-district.

Table 11.1 gives an overview of the participants' characteristics, based on a questionnaire that was conducted in May 2004. Information on the personal situation of the households was provided by HBC workers and the chairperson of one of the groups and does not necessarily reflect participants' own responses. Members of the garden groups were predominantly women between 21 and 80 years of age, with a majority (74 per cent) between 30 and 60 years of age (Swaans et al., 2008a). The personal situation of the members varied. Some were HIV-positive or had experienced illness or death in the family, others were looking after orphans, especially in groups A and B. In most cases, members were not aware of their HIV/AIDS status.

An action research project

By the end of 2003, an agricultural NGO and a Dutch university institute established a partnership with the health centre in Msinga. An action-research project was designed to promote secure access to food and increased wellbeing among households participating in the groups through joint collaboration between role players in agriculture and health. The project was structured along the lines of the Interactive Learning and Action (ILA) approach, a multi-stakeholder participatory learning approach to innovation and intervention. The ILA approach comprises four phases: (1) initiation and preparation; (2) collection, exchange and integration of information; (3) priority setting and planning; and (4) project formulation and implementation. A radical openness for the perspectives of the stakeholders implies that the design emerges gradually in conversation with all parties. After phases 1 and 2, a spiral of activities of phases 3 and 4 keeps recurring: planning, action, observation, reflection, replanning, etc. In this way an interactive and iterative, instead of linear, process evolves (Broerse and Bunders, 2000).

The first three phases of the project took place from November 2003 to September 2004. Activities included a context analysis and a base line study. Data were collected

Table 11.1 *Distribution of the questionnaire respondents in each garden group in terms of gender, age, and personal situation of the household*

Garden group	Total	Questionnaire	M	F	15–29	30–44	45–59	60+	HIV-positive	Chronic illness	Recent death	Orphans*
A	64	60	1	59	6	16	22	16	16	9	40	37
B	35	28	1	27	0	12	10	6	6	4	20	19
C	47	41	0	41	3	27	8	3	0	2	12	13
Total	146	129	2	127	9	55	40	25	22	15	72	69

(Columns grouped as: Number of participants [Total, Questionnaire]; Sex [M, F]; Age (years) [15–29, 30–44, 45–59, 60+]; Personal situation of the household [HIV-positive, Chronic illness, Recent death, Orphans])*

*People in Msinga refer to orphans when both parents have died or when the mother has died, not when the father alone has died (emphasizing the role of the mother as caretaker). It is this meaning that is used here.

among group members and stakeholders to assess the impact of HIV and AIDS on people's livelihoods. Although it is difficult to differentiate the impact of HIV and AIDS from other shocks and stresses, the study revealed how they exacerbated poverty and food insecurity (Swaans et al., 2008a). The epidemic touched not only upon 'human capital' (health), but also on financial, social, natural and physical resources; food insecurity featured as a main problem among the households in the study. Moreover, many households lived in fear, denial and hopelessness, while misconceptions and myths around HIV and AIDS were rife, often leading to stigma and discrimination, and limiting health and help-seeking behaviour. The findings indicated that gender-based inequalities, limited access to social grants and ARVs, and the isolated and resource-poor setting, were the main obstacles in terms of access to resources and women's control over sexual behaviour.

Although the need for a diversified and comprehensive programme of development interventions was acknowledged by the groups and the partner organizations, it was decided to focus first on the restoration of the household's resource base and to address psychosocial issues. Especially, the marginalized position of women and the silence surrounding HIV/AIDS were seen as major concerns. Capacity building and organizational development through a process of group-based learning were seen as key ingredients to empower women. The FLS was identified as a potentially appropriate method to be applied during the subsequent phase of project formulation and implementation.

The implementation of the FLS in Msinga

Although the FLS in Msinga was designed according to the main principles and guidelines of the FLS approach (du Guerny et al., 2002; Chhaya et al., 2004), it was adapted to the local context. A curriculum was drawn up from discussions with garden group members and relevant stakeholders, literature review, expert advice and study visits. The FLS usually builds on previous experiences with the FFS, but in this case the approach was new to the participants. A relatively 'short' curriculum was developed as a pilot, inspired by the main concepts of the FLS approach, but with an emphasis on group building through participation and (discovery-based) learning. It was based on a livelihoods perspective, gradually shifting the focus from agriculture to health and

HIV/AIDS, while emphasizing linkages between them. The final format, content and frequency of sessions were discussed with the garden groups before the first session and subsequently adapted. Participation was open to all members.

During the first season weekly sessions were organized with the following topics: introduction and getting to know each other, vision and organization, sustainable agriculture, nutrition and health, illness and care, and experimentation. After thorough evaluation, a combination of technical (related to water access, insect infestations, security and equipment) and institutional problems (related to participation and governance), were raised by the group members (Mweli, 2005). It was decided to continue with the FLS for a second season, but with longer intervals between sessions, and a stronger emphasis on innovations to address technical and social problems through topics such as vision building, problem identification and ranking, strategy development, nutrition, indigenous crops, and HIV/AIDS. At the same time institutional cooperation with the Department of Agriculture and Health was strengthened.

The FLS sessions were constructed according to three key components:

1 The socialization aspect where members came together to socialize and discuss broad issues related to the level of participation of their members and functioning of the executive committee of the group; it aimed to develop leadership and communication skills and to stimulate members to open up to each other and gain empathy for each other's circumstances;
2 The activities where members worked and/or assessed the progress of the crops in the garden. The practical part in the garden served both as a learning process and contributed to food security in kind; and
3 The discussion session where farmers analysed the activities in the gardens and other life-affecting issues with the support of (local) professionals.

Gardens were the cornerstone of the FLS. The size of the gardens for group A, B and C were respectively 2.5, 1 and 2ha. The harvest of the gardens was partly divided among the members for home consumption, some of it was sold by the group and the money was kept in a common account. Groups organized themselves as money saving clubs. They believed that the gardens would generate enough income to make the gardens sustainable without external donations.

To initiate production in the garden, material requirements such as draft power, seeds, fertilizers, perimeter fencing, were provided by the health centre. The agricultural NGO organized the personnel and resources to facilitate the FLS sessions and to conduct regular visits of the garden groups and their activities. It also convened monthly meetings where the stakeholders, including representatives from the groups, met to review and plan FLS activities. The project was embedded within the local context via a platform on HIV/AIDS, which consisted of representatives of governmental departments, the health centre and the municipality. Local departments and organizations also provided professionals to facilitate specific topics during the FLS sessions. The university institute conducted studies on the implementation process and impact. The FLS was organized for two growing seasons. Its main characteristics are summarized in Table 11.2.

Table 11.2 *Main characteristics of the Farmer Life School in Msinga, South Africa*

Size of class	Maximum 25 (two garden groups were split into smaller groups)
Participants	Members of three garden groups, selected by HBC workers and a local health centre based on socio-economic conditions and impact of HIV and AIDS. Mainly women were selected as they are the food providers and caregivers. The FLS was explained in meetings with each group.
Curriculum	The FLS was organized for two growing seasons: • 1st season: Weekly sessions were planned for six weeks. Emphasis was on group-building through participation and learning. Main topics were introduction and getting to know each other, vision and organization, sustainable agriculture, nutrition and health, illness and care, and experimentation. • 2nd season: Intervals between sessions varied from 2 to 6 weeks. Stronger emphasis on innovation development with topics such as vision building, problem identification and ranking, strategy development, nutrition, indigenous crops and HIV/AIDS. After sessions, farmers continued to meet with facilitators to discuss progress and outcomes.
Time and Venue	All participants agreed on when sessions were held. Sessions lasted 2–3 hours. Most sessions took place in the gardens; some took place in community buildings.
Rules	Basic rules/agreements were made among participants and with the facilitators to create commitment: • basic structures/processes of the FLS were not for discussion • choice of topics covered in each session was discussed (broader topics were suggested by facilitators) • participants were requested to come to all sessions; 'catching' up was done in a way of mutual agreement as a rule • no one could be excluded because of lack of attendance • information within the FLS would remain confidential
Facilitation	There were two community facilitators and two researchers (at least one community facilitator and one researcher per session). Profile of the team was: • both men and women • two community facilitators came from the same area as participants, but not same community • various 'technical' backgrounds • all had training in participatory approaches; two had experience as facilitator; two visited a Junior FLS • good interpersonal and literacy skills • local professionals were invited to facilitate specific topics

Assessment of process and impact of the FLS

The main objective of this paper is to identify the strengths and weaknesses of the FLS approach as applied in Msinga in the context of HIV/AIDS. Throughout the project, a team of community facilitators and researchers made extensive reports of the FLS sessions and the field-work for analysis, while interviews were conducted with participants to obtain more insight into the influence of HIV and AIDS on the garden groups. In addition, the overall design, content, expectations and outcomes of the project were evaluated after the first season by an independent consultant through group discussions and interviews with key persons. After the second season, a researcher from the university institute (not previously involved in the project) evaluated the overall process and impact through interviews and focus groups with participants and stakeholders (Swaans et al., 2008b, 2009).

Findings were analysed in terms of key elements of the FFS/FLS approach, i.e. participation, learning and empowerment (Pontius et al., 2000; du Guerny et al., 2002; Braun et al., 2006). Generally speaking, *participation* means 'taking part' and 'getting involved' (Pretty, 1994). It refers to participants' attendance, engagement and role in decision-making. *Learning* refers to technical knowledge and skills on gardening, nutrition, health, social knowledge and skills to communicate and act effectively in interaction with others, and self-reflection and critical thinking about factors that constrain people's lives (Pontius et al., 2000). *Empowerment* refers to increased control over inhibiting factors (Pontius et al., 2000). In this case, we are talking about the empowerment of a group of women in terms of psychosocial aspects (freedom to speak out, self-esteem and confidence), socio-economic aspects (food security and wellbeing), and political aspects (influence on institutional structures and processes) (cf. Page and Czuba, 1999). These aspects closely reflect the various elements of the sustainable livelihoods framework (Carney et al., 1999), although the psychosocial dimension of empowerment has often been neglected in the livelihoods literature (Swaans et al., 2008a). Taking the analytical framework as a starting point, the study examined the impact of the FLS approach as applied in Msinga on participation, learning, the three dimensions of empowerment, and the influence of HIV and AIDS on each of them.

Participation

Participants were positive about the training sessions and appreciated their regularity. According to them this established consistency and encouraged participation. However, when we look at attendance of the FLS sessions during the first season, the number of participants fluctuated greatly. From groups A, B and C, respectively, 45 out of 64 (70.3 per cent), 23 out of 35 (65.7 per cent), and 47 out of 47 (100 per cent) attended at least one session, while 13 out of 64 (20.3 per cent), 18 out of 35 (51.4 per cent) and 28 out of 47 (59.6 per cent) attended three or more sessions. Overall attendance rate during the course varied from 27.6 and 43.4 per cent among the newly formed groups (A and B) to 51.8 per cent in the already existing group (C).

From interviews and group discussions, it became clear that in each group there was a core group of 'committed' members who were consistently present. However, there were also many members who rarely came or not at all. The 'committed' members mentioned that many women, especially among newly formed groups (A and B), expected that orphans would be provided with food, social grants and/or access to education. They were disappointed that the FLS was mainly aimed at capacity building and that these high expectations could not be met in the short-term.

There were also other factors, however, that made participation, even among 'committed' members, difficult. For example, some women were struggling to come to sessions or the garden due to domestic activities, such as taking care of children, and sourcing and preparing food. Many chose to become or remain engaged in other jobs or part-time construction work on local roads, where they received regular wages. Some were not able to attend due to poor health. One of the HIV-infected members said:

I have never been in the garden since it has been planted. Sometimes I do not hear that we have to be there. Sometimes I do, but I am sick and not able to go. I usually suffer from diarrhoea and right now I do not know how big the maize is. I told myself that since I am not able to work in the garden I was going to withdraw.

Others had to take care of ill people in their household. It is usually women who face the extra burden of care.

Also local traditions related to death affected participation. When someone in the community dies, relatives and neighbours are expected to comfort the family of the deceased. Some sessions had to be postponed, as people died almost every week. Even a few group members passed away due to AIDS during the course of the pilot. The chairperson in one of the groups (B) stated that with the loss of members, their determination to participate also dwindled.

Some women left the groups due to stigma. In the communities of the newly formed groups (A and B), the gardens were referred to as 'AIDS gardens'. One woman said:

When this garden was initiated, people refused to join. Others withdrew, because it was said to be for HIV-infected people. We stayed on, because we wanted help. Men walked out of the meeting. They said that those who stayed are HIV-positive.

Resilience to stigma varied across groups. One group (A) was more resolute to continue and seemed less concerned about the gossip. Some women who left the group returned when the garden was doing well. In the other group (B), however, some became too scared to come to the garden, after rumours became hostile and community members tried to damage the crops.

Before the start of the second season, the committees of groups A and B reduced the number of members based on shown interest to respectively, 43 and 17 members, while the size of group C remained the same. In addition, intervals between FLS sessions during the second season were increased to 2–6 weeks. Still, frequency of participation in groups A and B remained irregular, while frequency of participation in group C remained stable with 20 to 25 participants per session.

Learning

Critical reflection during the FLS sessions enabled participants to identify various technical and social constraints, such as limited access to water, pest infestations, damage by goats, unhealthy diets, limited access to markets, lack of money, and problems with governance and participation. Structural solutions were proposed, such as techniques for soil and water conservation, compost making, and the cultivation of vegetables. Other suggestions referred to social aspects, such as saving money as a group, monitoring systems for participation, distribution systems and ideas for marketing, as well as working in smaller groups.

The involvement of (local) professionals helped participants to explore their own knowledge and experience to address some of these problems, while giving access to 'new' knowledge and skills. As expected from adult learning principles, participants tend to remember specific knowledge better when they use it in practice (Pontius et al., 2000). In evaluation sessions, organized at the end of each season, most members still remembered (revived) traditional methods of dealing with pest infestations, information on nutrition, compost making and other farming techniques. Through experimentation they had the opportunity to try out new techniques or different crops, and to sustain newly acquired skills, as some typical reactions show:

> *Manure and compost are better in the garden. We saw that in the experiments we did with spinach, pumpkin and tomatoes.*
> *I did not believe it when you were saying that the spinach could be planted in summer. That is why I wanted to try it. And it has proven you right.*

However, observational and discovery-based learning became more complex when the impact was not immediately visible, local traditions were challenged or when practices depended on others. For instance, it proved more difficult to change unhealthy consumption patterns or cooking practices within households than to change agricultural practices in the garden.

With regard to the topic of HIV/AIDS, learning became even more problematic. Most women were eager for information, but not all of them wanted to share their experiences and talk about it in the group. As HIV/AIDS is related to sex and death, it was considered a taboo. While many questions were raised to local professionals about social grants for people who are taking care of orphans, more specific questions, for example, on 'how you get it', 'the cause of the disease', 'about blood tests', 'how to take care of another person', 'treatment', 'how to behave when infected', were more easily expressed in individual interviews. When women did speak out in group sessions, it was not always appreciated by others:

> *I was not comfortable at all, not at all. She should not have disclosed the cause of the death of her son.*

This was especially prevalent in the newly formed groups who could not build on pre-existing relations between their members.

Although HIV and AIDS remained sensitive topics, participants mentioned in group discussions that the practical and informal nature of the sessions and its relation with nutrition and care helped them to start talking about HIV and AIDS in general terms. The FLS sessions helped the women of the groups to get to know each other better and created an atmosphere in which they could discuss and challenge each other's perspectives. They especially appreciated sessions that included visualization ('pictures'), games ('get to know each other'), song and dance ('vision'), observation ('garden walks') and discovery-based learning ('experimenting'). These methods stimulated group work and creativity, and increased enthusiasm, unity and respect.

Empowerment

Psychosocial aspects

The FLS approach allowed women to participate in planning and implementation, enhancing their capacity to address their own problems, regardless of the low literacy levels within the groups. Participants indicated that they had gained confidence to drive the decision-making process and the activities in the gardens. Women's motivation, confidence and self-esteem were positively correlated with the overall functioning of the group and the garden.

Even though HIV and AIDS were hardly discussed in a personal way, participants opened up and raised questions about the prevention and consequences of HIV infection. Some women who were infected with HIV or affected by the impact of AIDS mentioned in interviews that they were happy they finally had someone to talk to. The sessions enhanced confidence and raised consciousness, as shown by the following statement:

> *When we talk about it (HIV/AIDS) in the garden, there is no stigma. We even encourage each other to go and have a blood test so that we know where we stand.*

One of the facilitators expressed:

> *When we started with the project, only one group [group A] was able to speak with us openly about HIV and AIDS. It was because the HBC workers were already there. (…) And now, you can just go to the groups and talk about it. You don't have to beat around the bush. You can't find that in other communities.*

Although some infected members praised their group's tolerance when they were sick, some members suspected them of being lazy. In the two newly formed groups (A and B), relations and trust were undermined by irregular participation, as a typical comment shows:

> *Some have never been to the garden (…). They don't know how the garden looks like, but sure they will be there when it is time to harvest.*

Other members in these groups were afraid of being associated with HIV and AIDS, which may be another reason why relations were not always optimal. Apart from the sensitivity of the topic, negative attitudes or remarks about those who were infected with HIV or affected by AIDS made some reluctant to speak out.

Socio-economic aspects

In general, members and facilitators perceived the gardens as a success. Access to food from the gardens was ranked as a major benefit. All groups produced maize and beans as the main staple crops in the garden, and experimented with other crops on small plots.

The impact of AIDS on human and financial resources necessitated changes in agricultural practices to reduce production costs, for example, by using organic pesticides, compost making, open-pollinated maize and sorghum breeds. Various options were introduced to enhance nutritious intake throughout the year. These included planting new vegetable varieties or growing vegetables in a season different from the traditional one. One group successfully planted sorghum, as a more nutritious and drought-tolerant alternative to maize – their main staple food (see Box 11.1).

Box 11.1 Innovations identified, tested and/or evaluated during the project in Msinga

i New crops and techniques Innovations were sought to reduce production costs and improve water conservation (for example, organic pesticides, compost making, open-pollinated maize and sorghum varieties (OPVs), seedbeds and mulching). In addition, options were introduced to enhance nutritious intake throughout the year by planting new vegetable varieties (for example, butternut, garlic) or growing vegetables in a different season than traditionally (for example, spinach).

ii Maize variety evaluation Groups compared a Maize OPV with a hybrid and a traditional variety using multi-criteria analysis. Hybrid maize was preferred for its high yields, early maturity and white flour; the OPV for the possibility of storing seed, its ability to dry quickly and its white flour; and the home variety for its low-cost, resistance to lodging, better taste and the possibility of retaining seeds. The varieties performed differently across sites.

iii Sorghum Red sorghum is grown in the area for sorghum beer and is recognized for its tolerance to drought. Because farmers prefer white flour for food, a white OPV sorghum was planted as a more nutritious and drought-tolerant alternative for maize. The early planted sorghum was eaten by birds before maturity, while the grain filling stage of the second sorghum crop coincided with the encroachment of frost. The members realized that sorghum has to be planted early. They are exploring ways of protecting the grain from birds during dough stage.

iv (Traditional) vegetables Various vegetables were grown and evaluated using multiple self-identified criteria. The groups preferred vegetables that produce seeds for replanting, can be planted all year round, harvested at all times, and which are resistant against insects and diseases; quick maturity, taste and nutritional value were also considered important; also crops that could be eaten raw or draw consumers' attention were valued. Groups recalled knowledge about traditional vegetables, and want to plant them on a trial basis.

v Social innovations In addition to technical innovations, the groups came up with various ways to stimulate group participation, to share harvested produce equally, improve communication, etc. Communal farming and the FLS method were also new to the groups involved. One group preferred to work on individual plots, but another preferred communal gardening as it provided new opportunities for knowledge sharing and marketing produce. The FLS was perceived as an important strategy to this.

Despite differences in production, all groups managed to produce food for home consumption and to sell some of it on local markets. One group (C) even succeeded in saving a substantial amount of money. Groups also developed ways of distributing produce among members. Asked how they sold and shared the harvest, the chairperson in one of the groups (A) said:

> Together with the HBC workers, I monitor the sharing and selling. Those members who can walk to the pension pay-out ['public space' in the local area where government officials come to pay out elderly grants each month] are advised to come and buy the maize from the garden at discounted price and resell it for profit. About the sharing, I was marking the book of those who came to work from the time of planting till weeding. I am marking the book again for those who have received a share of the produce.

They took into account that some members were not always physically able to come:

> When people are sick it is understandable when they cannot come to garden (…), when we harvest we will take some portion to them as a group.

However, not all women who were sick shared in the produce, as one of them explained:

> When I was sick and not in the garden, I got nothing. (…). It is just that I was not fit to walk to the garden. It is too far.

Despite their illness, some of these women like to have another possibility to participate in the project. Some already started with their own garden close to their household, hoping to get support for fencing or seeds.

Throughout the season, the groups also faced 'technical' problems, such as the lack of easy access to water, insect infestations, theft, and lack of equipment. The lack of access to water during the winter season made it especially difficult to sustain activities in the garden throughout the year. Most proposed solutions, such as irrigation systems, better conservation, security, and organic pesticides, required a lot of money to develop or time to be applied effectively.

Working together enabled participants to share resources and get access to draft power, seeds, fertilizers and perimeter fencing. However, it also put a bigger claim on social organization and was a source of conflict. Especially in the newly formed groups (A and B) there was confusion about decisions made. For many members it was not clear how much was kept for home consumption, how much was sold, or what happened with the money from selling surplus. Some members did not see the money accruing at group level as a positive impact as it did not directly translate into benefits at the household level. This was partly related to problems with attendance, but the committees were not functioning well either.

Under circumstances of scarce resources and malfunctioning groups, external factors can easily destroy success and morale. During the first season, one of the facilitators remarked:

The members of this group [B] have not managed to grow the beautiful crops like the others. Looking at the beans and maize you can see that they weeded late, the maize looks yellowish and the beans are not in good condition. Maybe it is because of the hail. (…) The group is presently not well motivated. They were destructed by the gossip that the garden was for AIDS.

In addition to food production, some families with orphans were assisted in the form of a social grant or access to education. However, the time frame was too short to address health, education and social welfare problems in a profound way.

Political aspects

Gender relations, lack of access to social services and the isolated rural location made it difficult for women to act upon their needs (see Swaans et al., 2008a). The transformation of the groups into self-managed collectives was one of the main strategies to empower women in the area and address the social breakdown of relations in the community. It helped women to share resources, knowledge, skills and experiences, and to gain easier access to service providers and markets. So far, however, structural changes have been limited due to malfunctioning of the groups, cultural norms and values, and lack of an effective stakeholder network.

All groups wanted to continue with the garden and the FLS sessions. Some individuals saw the garden as a first step towards other activities, such as chicken farming and selling produce to supermarkets. The involvement of local professionals helped in establishing better contacts and relations between participants/groups and service providers. When it came to decision-making and action, however, the newly formed groups (A and B) still depended on the project after two years of implementation. While lack of funding to start up activities and former experiences may have contributed to this, several women argued that the groups were too big and diverse to create social cohesion and decisive action. However, the group that already existed before the project started (C) proves that it is not impossible to establish unity and strong and good leadership.

Although members may have recognized the opportunities for better contacts with service providers, it is questionable whether they are willing to challenge established structures or existing (cultural) norms and values. For example, even though many problems related to HIV and AIDS, such as stigmatization, social exclusion and gender inequality, are 'expressed' through institutionalized rules and behaviour (Douglas, 2004), reflection on HIV and AIDS remained mainly restricted to practical issues, such as access to social grants or how to take care of people who are ill and infected. Moreover, many women felt powerless regarding prevention; in the cultural setting it is men who make the sexual and contraceptive decisions (Swaans et al., 2008a). Inspired by the sessions, some women asked the facilitators to come and talk on HIV and AIDS during the holidays when their husbands were around. This is a clear indication that they want to change their situation, but recognize they cannot do so without reaching out to their husbands.

At sub-district level, the local platform on HIV/AIDS hardly met after some of its key persons left due to other commitments or jobs. It proved especially difficult to mobilize government departments to participate in the project; contacts were often too informal and ad hoc to create strong commitment. Moreover, the diversity in stakeholders also posed challenges in working together. Organizations have specific backgrounds, cultures and traditions, which may come to the surface in interactions (Jasanoff and Wyne, 1998). For example, the agricultural NGO and the local health centre supported the groups from different perspectives, they depended on different kinds of funding, and they used a different type of approach. These differences led to tensions about the followed strategy and tasks, even though these were discussed and agreed upon before the project started. Most stakeholders advocated the re-establishment of a platform to integrate and coordinate HIV and AIDS activities in the area. It is encouraging that the Department of Health wanted to intensify cooperation with existing groups or start a food security project with groups of HIV infected people only, with support of HBC workers and VCT counsellors.

Strengths and weaknesses

The study revealed various strengths of the FLS approach regarding participation, learning and empowerment. Many people, who are usually not reached by service providers, were not only able to participate, but were also very engaged and committed. The practical and informal 'nature' of the sessions made it easier for them to contribute meaningfully. In addition, working together on agriculture and nutrition enabled them to get to know each other, and enabled them to explore and learn more about HIV and AIDS at their own pace. Especially group-based methods using song, dance, visualization and imagination encouraged participants to open up and speak out among others, while experimentation boosted people's confidence and enthusiasm. The practice of conservation agriculture helped them to grow crops with limited means. The FLS as applied in Msinga showed that a welfare-oriented project for women involved in joint agricultural and other activities, providing them with emotional support, could produce food and savings. The group that was formed beforehand became an example of group cohesion and visionary leadership that resulted in positive outcomes.

However, various weaknesses can also be identified. There is a serious problem related to participation. The women who most needed help, because they were sick or had a heavy care load, faced constraints in regularly attending and benefited least. The group-based character and intensity of the programme made it difficult for women who were poor or affected by HIV and AIDS to participate (see also Sokunthea, 2002). To some extent this is acknowledged by the project rules and by the group chairs. However, so far, this has not really led to innovative solutions to resolve this dilemma. The FFS literature acknowledges that women's heavy workload and responsibilities in the household deter their participation in agriculture-focused activities (Fakih, 2003; Rola, 2003); it has been hypothesized that the current modality of FLS, covering wide-ranging topics, such as nutrition, health and social aspects, may have greater potential to attract the women (Balakrishnan and Fairbairn-Dunlop, 2005). However, in a context of high HIV prevalence and many cases of AIDS, a FFS/FLS model that relies heavily on group formation and collective action, might not be feasible. In such a context a mechanism should be developed by which also individual women/households can profit from the knowledge, experience and solidarity built by collective gardening.

Furthermore, problems related to HIV and AIDS, such as stigmatization, social exclusion and gender inequality, are 'expressed' through institutionalized rules and behaviour (Douglas, 2004). Douglas argues that the way people assess risks is rooted in notions of social organization and solidarity, and that change is mediated only through shifts in or challenges to collective values. This may explain why efforts to tackle AIDS and related problems on an individual basis have so far been rather ineffective (Walker et al., 2004). A group-based approach provides the opportunity to challenge deep-rooted values and customary relations between people. However, despite signs of more openness and willingness to share experiences, it remained difficult for participants to talk about HIV and AIDS and to share experiences. This was especially prevalent where groups were newly formed, and could not build on pre-existing relations between their members. Although the results of this study seem to confirm the general belief that human ecosystem analysis can only be implemented successfully when participants are already familiar with agro-ecosystem analysis (Müller, 2005), in the context of HIV and AIDS, other aspects like common ground, trust, safety, confidentiality and respect, seem at least as important. These have not yet received the attention they deserve.

The study also shows the dilemma of the need for targeting women from affected households on the one hand and the importance of decreasing stigma and discrimination on the other. By specific targeting, there is risk of increasing exposure to stigma and discrimination of the women involved, as became clear from statements made by men in the community, the referral to the gardens as AIDS gardens, and the fact that community members tried to damage the crops (see also Swaans et al., 2008b). One might argue that the FLS as a group-based approach excludes others, and is therefore likely to breed hostility and damage social cohesion, the same things that the approach seeks to build, but an individual approach cannot solve this problem. The approach itself needs to get a more open character. Linkages need to be established between various groups and the community – without referring in any way to the HIV/AIDS status of the constituent members, and strategies need to be developed so that others in the community can also benefit (Campbell et al., 2005).

Finally, structural improvement of people's lives has been limited. It takes time to acquire agricultural knowledge and skills and to apply them successfully to reap the benefits. Some suggest that this may take three to five years (Barnett and Grellier, 2003; Bishop-Sambrook et al., 2004). Vulnerable households do not only lack money and time to invest in this, but also lack access to necessary services. In a recent review of FFSs, Braun et al. (2006) emphasize that sustainable, local level, institutionalized gains, can be negated or diminished when surrounding conditions are unsupportive. It seems even more difficult to change practices in relation to HIV and AIDS. Root causes of HIV/AIDS are related to gender and social inequalities, which are deeply ingrained in social norms and values and embedded in institutions and policies (Parker and Aggleton, 2003). Moreover, the diversity of factors that drive the HIV epidemic and the impact of AIDS needs to be matched by a diversity of researchers and service providers, working collaboratively. However, when the various stakeholders have different cultural backgrounds and no history of interaction, the level of trust may initially be low.

Lessons learned

The results suggest that a group-based discovery learning approach such as the FLS has potential to improve food security and wellbeing, while allowing participants to explore issues around HIV and AIDS. The analysis also shows, however, that HIV-related illnesses and death, and the factors that drive the epidemic and its impact, undermine women's ability to participate, the safety and trust required for learning, and the empowerment process. Several lessons can be drawn from this study.

1. *Participation* In an environment of social inequalities, poverty, diseases, deaths and violence – all common in the area – it becomes less likely that people are willing to take risks and engage themselves in a process with uncertain outcomes (see Woolcock, 1998; Campbell et al., 2005). An intervention must bring some kind of 'reward' to the participants, such as a thriving garden, which in turn makes them stronger, as it helps to create a positive self-image, and a project image of which they want to be part. A small successful group can pave the way for a larger initiative that can sway others to get involved. However, a group-based approach may have to be combined with interaction with individuals, particularly women, in the vicinity and privacy of their own home through gardening and counselling. This would minimize the scenario where members who fall sick are excluded.

2. *Innovation and diversification* The FLS provides a good platform for the exchange and integration of information, but there is a need to take account of the diversity among garden group members. This entails more experimentation with different and innovative ways of organizing and sharing work, but also broadening the activities that the FLS undertakes beyond gardens. Dependence on the garden meant that the momentum of the programme could not be maintained off-season when there were no crops in the garden. Alternative activities that can make a change in the farmers' lives and improve food security can be a focal point.

3. *A safe environment for learning* At least as important as shared activities is a feeling of 'togetherness', to reverse the destructive impact of HIV and AIDS on institutions. A 'safe' environment in which participants feel free to express themselves and support each other, can help participants to get to know each other, build trust and stimulate learning (Welbourn, 1995; Campbell et al., 2007). Sometimes, it may be more appropriate to form more homogenous (and small) subgroups, design mitigation strategies for specific vulnerable groups (gender/pro-poor), or target people living with HIV in particular (Müller, 2005; Drimie and Mullins, 2006).

4. *An integrated community-based approach* Besides offering safe-spaces, interventions need to build the power-base of HIV and AIDS affected women to engage actively and collectively with the wider community to raise awareness, and fight stigma and discrimination. It may be difficult however to establish a relationship of trust with those in the community who deny the existence of HIV by stigmatizing others. It may help to focus on what unites people, rather than what divides them. In resource-poor settings, a more general development focus to improve people's health and livelihoods may improve a households' living situation and its relations with other community members. Therefore, the provision of safe-spaces for critical reflection should go along with material and institutional support (see also Cornish, 2006; Hartwig et al., 2006). This can take various forms, ranging from garden projects to improve food and nutrition security – including short-term food assistance (for example, for those with several orphans and few productive adults) – to income-generating activities and micro-credit programmes (for example, Kim et al., 2002; Barnett and Grellier, 2003; Harvey, 2004; Gillespie, 2006).

5. *Institutional collaboration* Interventions, such as the FLS, require strong involvement of all stakeholders, in particular HBC workers, social workers and VCT counsellors, and an integrated approach that includes health, agriculture and social development. The FLS approach should pay more attention to the facilitation of mutual learning and capacity building among stakeholders to bridge the differences between institutions. To achieve impact and innovation over the longer term, changes may be required in larger sets of relationships or institutional arrangements. This involves coalition building and advocacy at the policy level.

Finally, when life more than livelihood comes under threat the effectiveness of the FLS becomes questionable. In that case more immediate support is needed. This requires a technical, social and medical response, whereby individuals can be referred to other service providers when necessary.

Acknowledgements

The authors wish to thank the participants of the garden groups and other relevant stakeholders in Msinga for their time and willingness to share their experiences. We would also like to thank the editors of this book for their feedback on earlier versions. This chapter has been written in the context of a project on HIV/AIDS and food security in South Africa financially supported by the RENEWAL programme of the International Food Policy Research Institute (IFPRI).

References

Balakrishnan, R. and Fairbairn-Dunlop, P. (2005) 'Rural women and food security in Asia and the Pacific: prospects and paradoxes', FAO Regional office for Asia and the Pacific, Bangkok

Barnett, T. and Grellier, R. (2003) 'Mitigation of the impact of HIV/AIDS on rural livelihoods through low-labour input agriculture and related activities', report submitted to DFID, Overseas Development Group (ODG), Norwich, UK

Bishop-Sambrook, C.J., Kienzle, W., Mariki, W., Owenya, M. and Ribeiro, F. (2004) *Conservation agriculture as a labour saving practice for vulnerable households. A study of the suitability of reduced tillage and cover crops for households under labour stress in Babati and Karatu districts, Northern Tanzania*, IFAD/FAO, Rome

Braun, A.R., Jiggins, J., Röling, N., Van den Berg, H. and Snijders, P. (2006) *A global survey and review of Farmer Field School experiences*, Report prepared for ILRI, Endelea, Wageningen, the Netherlands

Broerse, J.E.W. and Bunders, J.F.G. (2000) 'Requirements for biotechnology development: the necessity of an interactive and participatory innovation process', *International Journal of Biotechnology*, vol 2, pp275–296

Campbell, C., Nair, Y., Maimane, S. (2007) 'Dying Twice: A multi-level model of the roots of AIDS stigma in two South African communities', *Journal of Health Psychology*, vol 12, no 3, pp403–416.

Campbell, C., Foulis, C.A., Maimane, S., and Sibiya, Z. (2005) 'I have an evil child at my house: stigma and HIV/AIDS management in a South African community', *American Journal of Public Health*, vol 95, no 5, pp808–815

Carney, D., Drinkwater, M., Rusinow, T., Neefjes, K., Wanmali, S. and Singh, N. (1999) 'Livelihoods approaches compared: a brief comparison of the livelihoods approaches of the UK Department of International Development (DFID), CARE, Oxfam, and the United Nations Development Programme (UNDP)', Department for International Development, London.

Chhaya O., du Guerny., J., Geeves, R., Kato, M., Hsu, L., Cambodian Rice Farmers and Mah, M. (2004) 'Farmers' Life School manual: building regional HIV resilience', UNDP/FAO/World Education, Bangkok, Thailand

Douglas, M. (2004) 'Traditional culture: let's hear no more about it', in V. Rao and M. Walton (eds), *Culture and public action*, pp.85–114, Stanford University Press, Stanford, UK.

Drimie, S. and Mullins, D. (2006) 'Mainstreaming HIV and AIDS into livelihoods and food security programs: the experience of CARE Malawi', in S.R. Gillespie (ed) *AIDS, Poverty and Hunger: Challenges and Responses,* pp283–303, International Food Policy Research Institute, Washington DC

Du Guerny, J., Hsu., L. and Chhitna, S. (2002) 'A development strategy to empower rural farmers and prevent HIV', UNDP South East Asia HIV and Development Project

Fakih, M. (2003) 'Gender mainstreaming in IPM', in CIP-UPWARD (ed) *Farmer Field Schools: From IPM to platforms for learning and empowerment,* p55, International Potato Centre Users' Perspectives with Agricultural Research and Development, Los Baños, Laguna, the Philippines

Gillespie, S (ed) (2006) *AIDS, poverty, and hunger: Challenges and responses*, IFPRI, Washington DC

Harvey, P. (2004) 'HIV/AIDS and humanitarian action', ODI Humanitarian Policy Group, London

Jasanoff, S. and Wynne, B. (1998) 'Science and decision making', in S. Rayner and E. Malone (eds), *Human choice and climate change. Vol. 1: The societal framework*, pp1–87, Battelle Press, Washington DC

Kim, J., Gear, J., Hargreaves, J., Makhubele, B., Mashaba, K., Morison, L., Motsei, M., Peters, C., Porter, J., Pronyk, P. and Watts, C. (2002) 'Social interventions for HIV/AIDS: intervention with microfinance for AIDS and gender equity', Rural AIDS Development Action Research Program, Acornhoek, South Africa

Loevinsohn, M. and Gillespie, S. (2003) 'HIV/AIDS, food security, and rural livelihoods: understanding and responding', RENEWAL Working Paper No. 2, International Service for National Agricultural Research (ISNAR), The Hague

Msinga integrated development plan (2005/2006), www.devplan.kzntl.gov.za/ idp_reviewed_2007_8/IDPS/KZ244/Adopted/Msinga%20IDP.pdf, accessed 1 December 2009

Müller, T. (2005) *HIV/AIDS and human development in sub-Saharan Africa: impact mitigation through agricultural interventions. An overview and annotated bibliography*, AWLAE-Series No. 3, Wageningen Academic Publishers, Wageningen, the Netherlands

Mweli, M. (2005) 'Report on the reflection with support groups and project partners in Umsinga, internal document, Farmer Support Group, Pietermaritzburg.

National Department of Health, South Africa (2009) 'The national HIV and syphilis prevalence survey, South Africa 2008', www.hst.org.za/indicators/HIV_AIDS/antenatal_2008.pdf, accessed 1 December 2009.

Page, N. and Czuba, C.E. (1999) 'Empowerment: what is it?', *Journal of Extension*, vol 37, no 5, http://www.joe.org/joe/1999october/comm1.html, accessed 5 October 2009.

Parker, R. and Aggleton, P. (2003) 'HIV and AIDS-related stigma and discrimination: a conceptual framework and implications for action', *Social Science & Medicine*, vol 57, pp13–24.

Pontius, J., Dilts, R. and Bartlett, A. (2000) *Ten years of building community: from Farmer Field School to Community IPM*, FAO Community IPM Programme, Jakarta, Indonesia

Pretty, J.N. (1994) 'Alternative systems of inquiry for a sustainable agriculture', *IDS Bulletin*, vol 25, pp39–48

Rola, A.C., Jamias, S.B. and Quizon, J.B. (2003) 'Do farmers field school graduates and share what they learn?: Investigation in Iloilo, Philippines', in CIP-UPWARD (ed) *Farmer Field Schools: from IPM to platforms for learning and empowerment,* pp61–62, International Potato

Centre Users' Perspectives with Agricultural Research and Development, Los Baños, Laguna, the Philippines

Sokunthea, N. (2002) *'The Empowerment of Farmer Life Schools: Mobilisation and Empowerment of Rural Communities Along the Asian Highway (route5) in Cambodia to Reduce HIV Vulnerability'*, Project UNDP-FAO/RAS/97/202, Srer Khmer, Cambodia

Swaans, K., Broerse, J., Meincke, M., Mudhara, M. and Bunders, J. (2009) 'Promoting food security and well-being among poor and HIV/AIDS-affected households: Lessons from an interactive and integrated Approach', *Evaluation and Program Planning*, vol 32, pp31–42

Swaans, K., Broerse, J., Van Diepen, I., Salomon, M., Gibson, D. and Bunders, J. (2008a) 'Understanding diversity in impact and responses among HIV/AIDS-affected households: The case of Msinga, South Africa' *AJAR*, vol 7, no 2, pp167–178

Swaans, K., Broerse, J.E.W., Salomon, M., Mudhara, M., Mweli, M. and Bunders, J.F.G. (2008b) 'The Farmer Life School: Experience from an innovative approach to HIV education among farmers in South Africa', *SAHARAJ*, vol 5, no 2, pp52–64

Topouzis, D. and du Geurng, J. (1999) 'Sustainable agricultural, rural development and vulnerability to the AIDS epidemic', UNAIDS Best Practice Collection', FAO/UNAIDS, Rme/Geneva

Walker, L., Reid, G. and Cornell, M. (2004) *Waiting to Happen: HIV/AIDS in South Africa*, Double Storey Books, Cape Town, South Africa

Welbourn, A. (1995) 'Stepping Stones: a training Package in HIV/AIDS, Communication and relationship skills', ActionAid, London.

Woolcock, M. (1998) 'Social capital and economic development: Towards a theoretical synthesis and policy framework', *Theory and Society*, vol 27, pp151–208.

Yech, P. (2003) 'Farmer Life Schools in Cambodia' *LEISA*, no 19, pp11–12.

Chapter 12

Agricultural policy response to HIV and AIDS: Lessons learned from East and Southern Africa

Michelle Remme, Fadzai Mukonoweshuro and Libor Stloukal

Introduction: From a health affair to everybody's business

By the end of the 1990s, it became clear that HIV was more than a health issue and the epidemic was being increasingly recognized as a threat to economic growth and human development (Over, 1992; Brown, 1996; FAO, 1999). In 2000, for the first time in history, the UN Security Council adopted a resolution on a health issue, propelling HIV to the centre of human security (UN, 2000). A year later, the world witnessed another first, when the UN General Assembly held a landmark Special Session on HIV and AIDS (UNGASS, 2001).

At the national level, HIV and AIDS control programmes were moving beyond ministries of health and becoming supra-ministerial coordination structures, which spearheaded the development of national AIDS responses in which multi-sectoralism was a guiding principle. Despite this principle, these strategies continued to focus mainly on biomedical prevention and impact mitigation measures, co-opting other sectors that could contribute to this public health approach, such as education, defence, information, youth and women's affairs (World Bank, 1996). The role of other sectors and private industries remained limited to workplace issues.

It took slightly longer for the severity of the impact on agriculture and food security to be fully acknowledged. Although the Food and Agriculture Organization of the United Nations (FAO) played a pioneering role from the late 1980s in documenting the impacts of the epidemic on agriculture, it was arguably the 2002 Southern African food crisis that proved to be pivotal, as it increased awareness of the multi-sectoral dimensions of the epidemic among governments and international development partners and ushered in the concepts of the 'triple threat' (UN, 2003) and the 'new variant famine' (de Waal and Whiteside, 2003), according to which AIDS greatly accentuated existing food insecurity and governance challenges.

In the late 1990s and early 2000s, the agricultural sector in certain hyper-endemic countries started responding to the epidemic more systematically. This chapter explores these responses in two sections, starting with policy development and then policy implementation. In the first phase of policy development, efforts were made to understand the interactions between AIDS and agriculture, food and nutrition security. Based on a number of studies and research findings, a few countries entered a second phase of formulating policies or strategies to guide the sector's response. In the second section on policy implementation, the chapter relates recent efforts, which have prioritized institutional capacity development, resource mobilization and partnerships for more effective implementation. Throughout the chapter, we discuss achievements, as well as challenges encountered and lessons learned, building on examples from Malawi, Mozambique, South Africa, Tanzania, Uganda and Zimbabwe, where the FAO for several years has been providing technical support to formulate and implement agriculture sector strategies on HIV and AIDS. Finally, the concluding section highlights a number of issues that are yet to be resolved and taken on board within the evolving context of the epidemic.

HIV and AIDS policy development in the agriculture sector

Understanding the interactions between AIDS and agriculture

In order to respond to the threat of HIV and AIDS, it was important to start by developing a solid understanding of how the epidemic is impacting on agriculture and how agricultural practices are affecting its spread (Wiegers, 2008). Generating this knowledge served several purposes over the last 20 years: it provided a justification for strategic action guided by policy and sustained by adequate human and financial resources; it enhanced an informed process of policy-making and programming for more effective action; and it equipped the agricultural sector with the authority of knowledge and experience, thereby asserting its role in national AIDS responses.

A handful of research initiatives, which took the lead in documenting the potential and actual impacts of AIDS on agricultural production systems and rural livelihoods (Gillespie, 1989; FAO, 1989, 1991, 1994; Baier 1997) set the research in motion. In the early studies, particular emphasis was placed on analysing household coping strategies, to guide sectoral interventions and policies in support of affected households (Rau et al., 2008).

Although this body of evidence was growing, it remained limited in scope and did not receive much attention from policy-makers. However, once it became increasingly apparent that the pandemic was also negatively affecting commercial agriculture (Rugalema et al., 1999) and therefore aggregate growth and profit indicators, policy-makers became more responsive to the possible AIDS mandate for the agricultural sector. This accelerated the speed at which studies were conceptualized and carried out, and encouraged policy-makers and donors alike to adopt a development-oriented approach

(IMF, 2004). Indeed, the consensus was growing that HIV was taking advantage of and exacerbating existing development challenges through its systemic impact on poverty, migration, food insecurity and gender inequalities (Topouzis, 1998).

Other studies (commissioned mostly by UNAIDS and UNDP in East and Southern Africa), revealed the adverse impact of AIDS on the workforce and financial resources in the agriculture sector. For example, in Malawi, a research study showed that in 1998 alone, about 66 per cent of staff deaths in the Ministry of Agriculture were AIDS-related (Bota et al., 1999). Similarly, studies in Zimbabwe showed that the epidemic was undermining the ability of institutions to provide services. Institutions such as the extension system were weakening because extension staff were falling sick and dying (Mutangadura et al., 1999). Even then policies remained rigid in terms of providing strategic direction for responding to the multi-faceted impact of AIDS (Mutangadura et al., 2000).

Although most initial studies focused on the impact of AIDS on agriculture, a number of studies did explore the opposite causality: how agricultural practices and programmes were affecting the spread of HIV (Malindi, 2005). Although this so-called bi-directionality was coined and documented in the late 1990s (Topouzis, 1998), these latter interactions have tended to receive less attention from agricultural policy-makers, despite their major implications for HIV prevention.

In the agricultural sector's response, research has played a pivotal role as a critical instrument for policy advocacy. In Malawi, two studies on the impact of AIDS on the agricultural sector's workforce and their susceptibility to HIV infection (Bota et al., 1999 and 2001) were critically important for policy advocacy and buy-in from senior management in the Ministry of Agriculture and other agricultural institutions. It was in fact a network of researchers, academics and technical experts who spearheaded policy advocacy initiatives and the subsequent sectoral policy formulation, which later became part of the Regional Network on AIDS, Livelihoods and Food Security (RENEWAL), under the International Food Policy Research Institute (IFPRI). In Zimbabwe, FAO in collaboration with RENEWAL facilitated the formation of an HIV and agriculture working group among donor agencies based in Harare. Later FAO provided funding to RENEWAL for carrying out a desk review of existing studies and what can be learned from them. One of the recommendations of the desk review was that an agriculture sector strategy for AIDS was urgently required to help streamline the many uncoordinated interventions as well as to set priority areas for intervention (Drimie and Gandure, 2005).

The process of generating knowledge about AIDS and its interactions with poverty, livelihoods, agriculture and food security as well as the active advocacy of individuals and institutions helped create a supportive environment for development of sector specific policies and strategies to address the impact of AIDS.

Agriculture sector policy on HIV and AIDS as an embedded tool

Conducive national frameworks

Early in the epidemic, governments were resistant to develop stand-alone agriculture sector policies on AIDS. In some way, this resistance was justified. Of what use is a strategy or a policy that is far removed from other policy processes and such other instruments. But as time went by, broad development policies and strategies began to incorporate AIDS because it had become too huge a problem to be ignored. This process provided a window of opportunity through which the agriculture sector started to develop sector specific policies and strategies.

At country level, Poverty Reduction Strategies were one of the earliest policy instruments to prioritize AIDS intervention both as a health and a development issue. In these same strategic frameworks and national policy instruments, AIDS was systematically highlighted as a cross-cutting issue to be addressed through concerted, interdisciplinary and multi-sectoral approaches if the ultimate human development objectives and Millennium Development Goals were to be achieved. In fact, certain national development strategies explicitly acknowledged the linkages and interactions between HIV and AIDS and food and nutrition security, such as the Malawi Growth and Development Strategy and the Government of Mozambique's Action Plan to Reduce Absolute Poverty (PARPA II) (Government of Malawi, 2006; Government of Mozambique, 2006). Also, the broader national multi-sectoral policies and/or strategies against HIV and AIDS had specific provisions for what the agriculture sector could do in the 'war' against the epidemic. For example, in Botswana's National Strategic Framework for HIV/AIDS 2003–2009, the Ministry of Agriculture was specifically tasked with outreach to rural communities in behavioural change, support to poverty relief efforts and implementation of food security programmes, particularly those relating to the empowerment of rural women, and to assist commercial farmers' organizations in their development of responses to HIV and AIDS (GoB, 2002).

Recently, within the agricultural sector itself, HIV and AIDS have been integrated into agricultural policy frameworks, in particular in programme-based approaches and/ or sector-wide approaches (SWAps). Existing programme-based approaches, such as Agricultural Sector Public Expenditure Programme (PROAGRI II) in Mozambique, the Agricultural Sector Development Programme in Tanzania and the Agriculture-SWAp in Malawi, have singled out HIV/AIDS and gender inequality as cross-cutting issues that will have to be mainstreamed into the programmes' priority areas and support services if they are to achieve their objectives.

Slow but steady evolution of the agricultural sector's policy response to HIV and AIDS

As the agricultural sector in certain countries sought to respond to AIDS in a systematic manner, the initial focus of this response was on HIV as a workplace issue, to be addressed through health-oriented measures (Topouzis, 2003). In a well-intended attempt to do justice to external mainstreaming, the sector started off by implementing activities to raise awareness and promote behaviour change in rural communities, mostly through health-oriented IEC materials (for example, Malawi, Mozambique and Zimbabwe), in acknowledgement of the sector's unique ability to reach out to rural populations through its extension workers. However, it was soon understood that this is not the comparative advantage of the agricultural sector and that these types of activities should be provided through referrals to the health and community development sectors.

Since 2002, a number of countries in the subregion have developed agricultural sector policies or strategies as they are now referred to since the 'Three Ones'[1] (see Table 12.1). These strategies are generally aligned to the National HIV and AIDS Policy and Strategic Framework, if in place at the time of formulation, and have made clear efforts to guide a comprehensive response from the sector, by enabling internal and external HIV and AIDS mainstreaming processes. They have brought out the need for the sector to address HIV and AIDS in its workplace, but also through its core business. In Zimbabwe, despite initial opposition from the Public Service Commission to have a sector strategy on HIV and AIDS (which was first viewed as duplicating the public sector policy), the Ministry of Agriculture went on to develop its own strategy, realizing that the public sector HIV and AIDS policy focused exclusively on internal mainstreaming and did not touch upon the sector's core business.

In a few countries, HIV and AIDS strategies have been developed for particularly susceptible population groups. In Uganda and Malawi, strategies were formulated to address the specific vulnerabilities of the fisheries sector, (GoU, 2005; GoM, 2007a), whereas in Malawi, the forestry sector simultaneously developed an HIV and AIDS strategy (GoM, 2007b) to tackle similar drivers of the epidemic and mitigate its impact on forestry-dependent groups. Likewise, Zimbabwe has recently launched an HIV policy for the Zimbabwe Farmers' Union to address HIV vulnerabilities faced by the union's employees and members.

Given the work place and health-oriented approach to HIV and AIDS mainstreaming, the external element has been more complex to institutionalize. In order to overcome these inherent challenges, the sectoral HIV and AIDS strategy approach has been an extremely useful instrument to guide key actors as to the implications of mainstreaming for their core work. In Malawi, various stakeholders, such as the National Smallholder Farmers' Association of Malawi (NASFAM), have used the sector strategy to develop their own action plans in line with the strategy's eight strategic pillars.

The process of internalization of HIV and AIDS issues and the subsequent response through the agricultural sector's core business has encountered challenges, but also generated a number of valuable lessons. One lesson learned in the process is that garnering high-level political commitment to addressing HIV and AIDS in agriculture is critical for success. Essentially, the agricultural sector needs to adopt an HIV and AIDS mandate and once it does, the AIDS sector needs to recognize it, particularly the National AIDS Coordinating Authorities and development partners. The former has been achieved in a number of countries, especially those with agricultural sector HIV and AIDS strategies, endorsed at the highest ministerial level, through strategic packaging of knowledge and consultative policy formulation for effective advocacy.

In terms of strategy design, lessons from the 'early birds' include the need to integrate fully costed implementation plans with well-defined roles and responsibilities and a resource mobilization strategy (Economic Commission for Africa, 2006; FAO, 2009b). A solid monitoring and evaluation (M&E) framework and clear coordination

---

[1] The 'Three Ones' Principles are: one agreed AIDS action framework that provides the basis for coordinating the work of all partners; one national AIDS coordinating authority, with a broad-based multi-sectoral mandate; and one agreed country-level monitoring and evaluation system.

Table 12.1 *Agricultural sector HIV/AIDS strategies in selected countries in East and Southern Africa*

Country	Existence of sectoral strategies	Priority Areas	Implementation Status
Malawi	Agricultural sector HIV/AIDS policy/strategy (2003–2008) Fisheries HIV/AIDS strategy (2007–2011) Forestry HIV/AIDS strategy (2007–2011)	(i) Gender, HIV and AIDS mainstreaming; (ii) Economic empowerment; (iii) Food and nutrition security; (iv) Work place support; (v) HIV/AIDS Action Research; (vi) Expanded HIV/AIDS communication; (vii) Community-based support; (viii) Human resources protection and management. (i) Improved policy framework; (ii) Strengthened programme leadership; (iii) Effective programme coordination and partnerships; (iv) Capacity building; (v) Prevention of further spread of HIV infection; (vi) Improved access to HIV and AIDS treatment, care and support services; (vii) Sustainable impact mitigation; (viii) Dynamic research on HIV and AIDS; (ix) Financing; (x) Improved awareness; (xi) Monitoring and Evaluation.	First strategy launched in 2005, implemented and evaluated in 2009. Strategy is currently being revised. Strategy launched in 2008 Implementation in progress Strategy launched in 2007 Implementation in progress
Mozambique	Agricultural HIV/AIDS Strategic Plan (2006–2010)	(i) Prevention; (ii) Advocacy; (iii) Fighting Stigma and Discrimination; (iv) Care and Treatment; (v) Impact Mitigation; (vi) Research, Monitoring and Evaluation; (vii) Coordination of the Sectoral Response; (viii) Institutional Capacity.	Strategic plan launched in 2006, implemented and currently being evaluated before revision.
South Africa	Ministry of Agriculture is leading the development of a sectoral HIV/AIDS strategy		Strategy under development

Table 12.1 *Agricultural sector HIV/AIDS strategies in selected countries in East and Southern Africa (Continued)*

Country	Existence of sectoral strategies	Priority Areas	Implementation Status
Tanzania	Agricultural sector strategy for HIV/AIDS and other chronic diseases adopted in 2006	(i) Empower OVC; (ii) Empower rural widows and female-headed households; (iii) Improve access to and adoption of labour saving technologies and practices; (iv) Increase disposable income and assets among households affected by HIV/AIDS; (v) Improve the food and nutrition security status of HIV/AIDS affected households; (vi) Strengthen social community support for households affected by HIV/AIDS; (vii) Address and prevent property grabbing; (viii) Capacity building of agriculture sector line ministries; (ix) Action-oriented research on HIV/AIDS impact and mitigation for advocacy and planning purposes.	Strategy launched in 2006 Implementation in progress
Uganda	Fisheries sector HIV/AIDS strategy adopted in 2005 Ministry of Agriculture, Animal Industries and Fisheries is currently leading in the development of an agricultural sector HIV/AIDS policy	(i) Reduce HIV prevalence in fishing communities; (ii) Mitigate the impact of HIV/AIDS in the fisheries sector and community; (iii) Strengthen national capacity to coordinate and manage the multi-sectoral response to HIV/AIDS including in fishing communities.	Strategy launched in 2005 Implementation in progress Strategy under development
Zimbabwe	Agricultural sector Strategy Plan on HIV and AIDS (2006–2010)	(i) Strong HIV and AIDS Programme Coordination and leadership; (ii) Capacity building; (iii) Agriculture management and information systems; (iv) Provision of HIV services; (v) Food and nutrition; (vi) Monitoring and evaluation.	Strategy launched in 2006 Implementation in progress

structures have also emerged as critical ingredients in a strategy to enhance focused implementation, M&E and strategy revision for greater impact.

Another lesson is that once an HIV and AIDS policy document (strategy or action plan) is formulated, the next crucial step is to disseminate it to all levels of implementation. In Zimbabwe, after the launch of the strategy, the agriculture ministry facilitated its dissemination to parastatals, agricultural seed producers, agro-chemical industries, farmers' unions, research stations and NGOs specializing in AIDS and agriculture. The strategy document was also distributed in the capacity-building workshops and placed in libraries as a reference. While distribution of hard copies is one important action, dissemination also requires that key stakeholders fully understand and buy into the strategy. One way to facilitate this is to translate the document into local languages, like the Malawi Forestry HIV and AIDS Strategy that was translated into three local languages (namely Chichewa, Tumbuka and Yao). The next fundamental dissemination strategy is to build in sustained and responsive capacity development for key programme staff to ensure that planners, technical specialists, M&E officers and extension workers are fully conversant with the existing policy document and are able to translate it into action in their respective core functions.

Finally, an emerging concern in the formulation of these HIV and AIDS sector strategy is whether or not (and if so, how) to combine the sector's HIV and AIDS strategy with its gender strategy. Since the nature and process of HIV and AIDS and gender mainstreaming are in many ways similar, certain policy responses have found it beneficial and more efficient to address these cross-cutting issues jointly (Elsey et al., 2005). Indeed, there are a number of convincing arguments for a joint approach: the urgent need for more engendered HIV and AIDS responses; the identification of HIV and AIDS and gender as the two cross-cutting issues to be mainstreamed in the agricultural sector; and the human resource reality whereby AIDS focal points are also gender focal points in most agricultural institutions. Incorporating gender within HIV and AIDS strategies has had the advantage of enhancing integrated packaging and tapping HIV and AIDS resources for gender mainstreaming. Although it is evident that AIDS and agriculture cannot be addressed without a strong gender lens, it is worth cautioning that gender equality and women's empowerment have a broader bearing than as a subset of HIV and AIDS. It is therefore critical to consider the conceptual weaknesses and/or confusion that could result, and the implications for the quality of the sector's gender response.

Agricultural sector HIV and AIDS policy implementation

Institutional capacity development

Governments and development partners have always been acutely aware that it is one thing to have a well-written policy or strategy, it is another thing to have such a strategy implemented. A well-written but not implemented policy or strategy is surely worth nothing. It remains as a statement of intent but does not deliver the required services to the people who need them. As such, there was internally and externally generated pressure to ensure that policies and strategies were implemented. In this section, we discuss the process of implementation and lessons learnt from it.

Establishment and staffing of HIV and AIDS Units

Based on the recommendations from national HIV and AIDS control programmes and policies internal to the sector, the agricultural sector in various countries has appointed AIDS focal points or desk officers mainly in charge of guiding and monitoring internal mainstreaming, i.e. HIV workplace activities. For example, the Ministry of Agriculture and Irrigation in Malawi appointed desk officers in all of its eight departments, as well as in its eight decentralized Agricultural Development Divisions. This was not limited to ministries, as agricultural training institutions, private companies, non-governmental organisations and farmer-based organizations also have nominated AIDS focal points.

However, one needs to be aware of the limitations of these focal points who are often junior staff, without the required authority, or the relevant technical capacity to guide colleagues in HIV and AIDS issues, especially beyond what can be done at the work place. In Zimbabwe some of the focal points perceived their new function as an add-on to their existing job descriptions and it was not reflected as a priority in their performance appraisals. But this practice was revised once the strategy had been formulated because it became apparent that implementation would require AIDS focal points with power and authority. In order to guide these departmental focal points, certain agricultural institutions have gone a step further and appointed full-time HIV and AIDS coordinators and established HIV and AIDS committees. In certain cases, units or directorates have been established in ministries of agriculture (Malawi and Mozambique) to spearhead the HIV and AIDS agenda. This represents a major positive change in giving HIV and AIDS the policy and operational importance it deserves.

HIV is considered a 'soft' area in an agricultural sector that typically defines itself through a production function. Where agricultural yields, hectarage, tonnage and heads of livestock are units of measurement, the impact of and interactions between agriculture, HIV and AIDS, usually does not make it to the top of the list of priorities for agriculturalists. This has sometimes resulted in limited political backing of AIDS focal points and committees. In terms of institutional arrangements, it has been observed that HIV and AIDS committees or units are more effective if housed within 'core business' units in the ministry of agriculture, such as agricultural extension, livestock, crop production or fisheries (Topouzis, 2003). The example of Malawi is worth mentioning, as the unit responsible for HIV and AIDS and gender mainstreaming is part of the Department of Agricultural Extension Services, with its own deputy director. There are also AIDS focal points in each of the other seven departments, which meet regularly with the unit in question in a taskforce. The situation is similar in Uganda, in terms of departmental focal points, whereas the Planning Department is the one responsible for coordinating the HIV and AIDS programme.

Capacity Development of staff through training

In-service training Assigning an AIDS focal point or taking on an HIV and AIDS mandate by launching a policy/strategy is not enough to operationalize it into the work of a ministry or even a smaller institution. In several countries capacity building for focal points was prioritized. Officers in agricultural line ministries, as well as agricultural extension workers were trained (Botswana, Lesotho, Malawi, Mozambique, Tanzania, Zimbabwe). For instance, in Malawi, all AIDS focal points were trained, as well as about 15 per cent of agricultural extension and development officers as well as fisheries extension assistants. In Zimbabwe, all focal points attended sensitization workshops as well as training-of-trainers workshops as soon as they were appointed in this new role.

Pre-service training In addition to in-service training, agricultural academic and training institutions have or are revising their curricula to include HIV and AIDS modules, some of which are mandatory in specific study programmes. The Natural Resources College in Malawi (which trains all agricultural extension workers), has adopted a mandatory HIV and AIDS and Gender module since 2002, while Bunda College of Agriculture, which educates most of Malawi's agricultural experts, introduced a module in its extension programme in 2004. By 2005 the human nutrition programme of the same college had adopted a module on HIV and nutrition. More recently, the FAO has supported Zimbabwe to revise the syllabus of agricultural colleges and to incorporate HIV and AIDS in the curriculum for students.

Tools

Besides important efforts to build agricultural sector staff understanding of the linkages between HIV and agriculture, food and nutrition security, there has been an outcry from technical officers at all levels for practical tools to assist in planning, operationalizing, monitoring and evaluating HIV and AIDS programmes within the agricultural sector. In order to respond to this demand, the sector has developed a number of tools for agricultural planners, implementers, monitoring and evaluation officers and extension workers to translate the mainstreaming concept into practical actions.

At the international level, collaboration between the FAO, the International Labour Organisation, the World Bank and the United Nations Development Programme, developed the Socio-Economic and Gender Analysis (SEAGA) materials, aimed at increasing sensitivity towards gender issues, as well as strengthening the capacity of development specialists to incorporate socio-economic and gender analysis into development planning. These materials include handbooks and guides, tailored for field staff, development planners and policy-makers, particularly in the agriculture and rural development sectors. They are regularly revised and updated to respond to emerging issues and have incorporated HIV and AIDS issues. Currently (2009), the FAO is developing a training guide to build the capacity of the agricultural sector in response to HIV and AIDS, which is being pre-tested and refined for further use and adaptation at country level.

In Malawi, the Agricultural Gender Roles Extension Support Services (AGRESS), which is the unit in charge of HIV and AIDS and gender mainstreaming, has developed an engendered and AIDS-responsive Participatory Rural Appraisal (PRA) tool to guide agricultural extension workers when they conduct these community appraisals. At the national level, the same unit has produced a Gender, HIV and AIDS mainstreaming framework for the Agriculture-SWAp.

In Zimbabwe, the HIV manual for the agriculture sector covers topics on the linkages between HIV, agriculture and food security as well as nutrition security. This resource is targeted at equipping senior managers with skills necessary for responding to HIV and AIDS within the core mandate of agriculture. Resource materials are also available for the training of extension workers on the impacts of agriculture, inheritance and property rights, and basic counselling skills for bereaved farmers.

An extremely positive development, which could partially be attributed to the AIDS responses in the sector, is the ongoing shift from a purely production-oriented approach to a more client-oriented approach, which is increasingly participatory, gender-balanced, culturally sensitive and community-based, thereby addressing the existing fault lines, inequalities and concerns that constrain agriculture and rural development. In Malawi, agricultural extension support services are making efforts to take the village as an entry point, rather than separate issues, like HIV and AIDS, gender, crops, livestock, fisheries, etc. With adequate guidance and tools for engendered and AIDS-responsive PRAs, this approach is enabling extension staff to ask the right questions and provide an appropriate package of integrated interventions and technologies.

Resource mobilization

The implementation of a comprehensive actionable strategy, as well as institutional capacity building efforts, all require adequate financial resources. Since most of the sector's policy responses were first viewed as pertaining to the realm of the AIDS' 'sector', and given the considerable funding available at national level for HIV and AIDS over the last decade, resource mobilization efforts have tended to be geared towards the AIDS financial architecture. In certain countries, the bulk of this funding is managed by the Ministry of Health or the National AIDS Coordinating Authorities and in all countries allocations are supposed to be guided by the national HIV and AIDS strategic framework.

However, even where the agriculture, food and nutrition security sector is rightfully acknowledged in national frameworks and objectives for HIV and AIDS, the concomitant financial allocations to these objectives have fallen short (ECA, 2006; World Bank, 2008; FAO, 2009b). National AIDS Coordinating Authorities have been slow or reluctant to fund the agricultural sector, especially through the public sector. Moreover, given the move towards pooled and basket funding, donors are less and less ready to fund the sector bilaterally for HIV-related activities.

While the AIDS sector has been willing to embrace nutrition in principle (UNGASS 2006), very limited resources have actually been invested in incorporating nutrition counselling, care and support or food-based interventions into the comprehensive HIV and AIDS package and Universal Access discourse. Moreover, where nutrition is taken on board, it remains mostly biomedical in nature, through therapeutic and supplementary feeding (for example, food-by-prescription), or as a social welfare intervention by which food packages are provided to PMTCT mothers, ART patients or Orphans and Vulnerable Children (World Bank, 2008; FAO/WHO, 2008; FAO, 2009b).

Despite the increasing recognition that agro-based interventions can play an important role in mitigating the impact of the epidemic, these interventions are generally being funded on a small scale through community-based organisations (CBOs), without simultaneously ensuring that agricultural extension support services can provide timely and adequate technical support to these community responses. As a result, community efforts to strengthen the agricultural livelihoods of vulnerable and affected households are not being optimized (FAO, 2009a).

Two fundamental lessons have been learned in this respect: (i) the agricultural sector needs to mobilize its own internal resources for HIV and AIDS programmes; and (ii) it is necessary that the sector invests more in asserting its role and leadership in a complementary approach to HIV and AIDS, through strategic knowledge generation and dissemination, as well as through ongoing dialogue and involvement in the national AIDS response and its concomitant policy processes.

On the first, certain countries have decided that regular budgets should be allocated for HIV and AIDS within ministries of agriculture as well as all agricultural organisations. In Malawi, at least 2 per cent of every government institution's Other Recurrent Transactions (ORT) is earmarked for HIV (work place) activities. Although there is much debate about whether 2 per cent is enough, what it is to be spent on and how it is monitored, it remains the most effective incentive for staff to work HIV and AIDS programmes and projects. The Ministry of Agriculture, Mechanisation and Irrigation Development of Zimbabwe is now incorporating funding for HIV activities into the annual regular budget of the Ministry. Before the economic downturn in Zimbabwe, it was a government policy that employers and employees contribute (be levied) 3 per cent of their monthly salaries towards the AIDS fund.

The issue of predictability of funding, or lack thereof, is a common lesson in development planning and implementation, requiring predictable medium-term financial resources if policies are to be implemented effectively and sustainably. The move towards SWAps is expected to provide this opportunity for the agricultural sector as a whole. However, its influence on budgetary allocations required to kick-start and sustain HIV and AIDS mainstreaming remains to be seen. In Mozambique, a striking 20 per cent of the PROAGRI II (Agriculture SWAp) budget in 2010 is to be allocated to HIV and AIDS mainstreaming activities. In Malawi, the Agriculture-SWAp has budgeted 2.2 per cent of the total SWAp budget for HIV and AIDS activities.

These are significant steps in genuinely mainstreaming HIV and AIDS into the agricultural mainstream. Yet, until these SWAps are fully operational, AIDS-specific activities are largely expected to be funded through the HIV pool. For this to happen, a closer collaboration and strategic dialogue with National AIDS Coordinating Authorities and Country Coordination Mechanisms are required to enable the sector to access various mechanisms of funding, including funds available under the Global Fund to fight AIDS, Tuberculosis and Malaria.

Partnerships and Coordination

A guiding principle in the global AIDS response, as well as in national HIV and AIDS policies, is a synergetic multi-sectoral approach with strong partnerships and coordination, as no sector or actor can address this epidemic single-handedly. However, this dimension has emerged as a weak link in the chain of the agricultural policy responses, both at international and national levels, as well as with other sectors and within the sector itself.

Partnering with other sectors in the AIDS response

Despite the compelling evidence of the close relationship between food insecurity and HIV susceptibility (Weiser et al., 2007), between food security and treatment adherence and efficacy (Zachariah et al., 2006; UNAIDS, 2008), as well as between food security and resilience to the impacts of AIDS, global and national AIDS responses have not yet convincingly incorporated food and nutrition security into the Universal Access package.

National AIDS Coordinating Authorities and development partners remain focused on biomedical interventions, treatment in particular, and adopt a narrow view of impact mitigation as social welfare interventions for Orphans and Vulnerable Children (OVC). Limited attention is given to a more development-oriented response, which would reduce underlying vulnerabilities that spur the spread of the epidemic and diminish household and community capacity to cushion its impact. This is not only a weakness of the AIDS responses, but it also represents a significant weakness of the agricultural sector in asserting leadership and exemplifying its complementary role to the biomedical and social welfare approaches.

More could be done by the sector within the prevention pillar, for example, to emphasize the need to refocus efforts on primary prevention, by addressing the causes of high risk behaviours, such as gender inequality, food and livelihood insecurity, rather than only attempting to address the symptom of risky sexual practices. Moreover, within the impact mitigation pillar, which typically zooms in on social services for OVC, psychosocial support and safety nets, the agricultural sector could engage with the involved sectors to underline the need for more emphasis on protecting and promoting the sustainable livelihoods of affected households.

Although the agricultural sector's initial health-oriented activities positioned it as a helping hand to the health sector, it has become increasingly clear that the agricultural sector has a unique contribution to make in the response, which is specific to its core business and complements the public health approach. This repositioning actually has the potential to improve the dialogue and collaboration with the health sector and other sectors in the response, so that the agricultural sector is no longer perceived as a subsidiary or competitor, but rather as an equal partner in the national response.

An example of how the agricultural sector can foster collaboration with other sectors and complement their efforts, is the ongoing effort in Southern Africa to enhance a livelihood approach within National Plans of Action for Orphans and Vulnerable Children. Based on the recognition by stakeholders that these policies tend to have limited outcomes and strategies to enhance livelihood opportunities for OVC and their households, the United Nations agencies, led by the FAO, formed the UN and Partners Alliance for Orphans and Vulnerable Children to advocate for effective livelihood-based social protection interventions in national responses. The rallying point is that if these OVC are to become productive adults, especially as most of them are not likely to move beyond primary education, the national plans of action will need to address this gap and prioritize market-responsive skills development and employment. In order to equip these advocacy efforts, the Alliance has invested in the documentation and dissemination of promising practices that have integrated livelihoods within an overall social protection approach.

Coordination within the sector

Based on recent experience, it is now very much understood that an agricultural sector's response to HIV and AIDS calls for strong and ongoing coordination between various stakeholders from the public sector, the private sector, academic and training institutions, farmer-based organizations, NGOs, PLHIV associations, CBOs and development partners, in order to maximize synergies, avoid duplication, share lessons and provide coherent technical guidance to the national response (ECA, 2005; FAO,

2009b). Effective coordination can also assist the sector in its resource mobilization efforts and in overcoming its capacity constraints.

The preferred strategy has been the formation of national (technical) working groups. Zimbabwe's HIV and Agriculture working group, for example, has been instrumental in commissioning research and steering the implementation of the HIV and AIDS strategy for the sector. Again, the Sector-Wide Approach is likely to have a positive effect in strengthening and institutionalizing such coordination mechanisms, as part of the SWAp coordination structures.

Conclusion

The agricultural sector has made considerable efforts to understand and respond to the AIDS epidemic, particularly in the hardest hit parts of East and Southern Africa. In many countries, the development of an agriculture sector response has been rightly approached as an opportunity in a crisis to build on the sector's comparative advantage to remedy long-standing structural problems related to socio-economic inequalities, fault lines and dysfunctions within rural societies. It is now more widely understood that agro-based interventions can (if properly designed and implemented) contribute to reducing HIV transmission and mitigating the impacts of AIDS, while at the same time contributing to broader developmental goals, such as improved food security, reduced gender and social disparities, better management of natural resources, more sustainable patterns of farming, strengthened rural development, broadened scope of livelihood choices for rural people, better workplace conditions, etc.

The questions that remain to be answered are whether these sector responses and strategies have indeed been useful and effective. Despite the challenges encountered, agriculture sector HIV and AIDS strategies have surely proven themselves as useful instruments in engaging the agricultural sector in the national AIDS response, in mobilizing both internal and external resources for the sector to focus on AIDS, and in strengthening the agricultural sector's bargaining power in advocating for comprehensive HIV and AIDS services in rural areas.

However, the question of effectiveness is difficult to answer for a lack of solid efforts to monitor and evaluate actions implemented within the framework of sector strategies. Monitoring and evaluation of agriculture and AIDS responses are still in their infancy, as most strategies from the sector did not develop rigorous frameworks with baseline data and targets. Currently, the monitoring and evaluation indicators being used are those contained in the national 'One Monitoring and Evaluation' frameworks under the UNAIDS 'Three Ones' principle. These were designed from a health perspective and fail to capture the unique contribution that the agricultural sector could make to reducing vulnerability and building resilience among agriculture-dependent groups.

If the sector is to realise its potential in national AIDS responses, it is critical that it develops and refines appropriate indicators to assess the impact of interventions, and that it uses these data to inform a responsive policy-making and programming process that would be equipped to take successes to scale. So far, most agriculture-based livelihood interventions have been implemented on a small-scale, rendering it difficult to demonstrate impact, sustainability, replicability and scalability (ECA, 2005). The need to scale up successful programmes that are only reaching small numbers of people to the national level is at present one of the key issues in the fight against AIDS (Binswanger et al., 2006).

In addition to the various lessons learned from the 'early birds' described in this chapter, countries that would consider following suit would have to be cognisant of the evolving context of the epidemic, as well as the ongoing changes in the agricultural sector.

Recent research findings about the rural context of HIV and AIDS in East and Southern Africa indicate that the intensity of the epidemic is changing. A combination of official prevention efforts and local responses appear to have reduced or stabilized infection rates in many countries in the subregion (UNAIDS, 2009), but the mostly double-digit adult HIV prevalence rates remain high. The remarkably rapid expansion of access to antiretroviral therapy is reducing death rates from AIDS-related causes, allowing people to live longer while remaining active producers (see Table 12.2). The profound long-term consequences that had been predicted for rural labour supplies, commodity production and poverty levels have not come to pass (Chapoto and Jayne, 2008).

At the same time, agriculture remains a major economic sector in most of these countries and continues to sustain large, albeit decreasing, rural populations. The agricultural sector will have to play a critical role in this new context, where increasing numbers of people will live with HIV and remain productive, making it all the more important to improve their food security and nutritional status to enhance treatment efficacy and delay treatment resistance, as well as to delay disease progression for those

Table 12.2 *The evolving context of agriculture, rural development and HIV and AIDS in selected countries in East and Southern Africa*

Countries	Agriculture as % of GDP[1]	Rural population (%)[2]	Adult HIV prevalence (%)[3]	Estimated ART need[4]	ART coverage (%)[4]
Botswana	2	43*	23.9	120,000	79
Lesotho	7	81	23.2	85,000	26
Malawi	34	82	11.9	290,000	35
Mozambique	28	65	12.5	370,000	24
Namibia	8	64	15.3	59,000	88
South Africa	3	41*	18.1	1,700,000	28
Swaziland	8	76	26.1	59,000	42
Tanzania	46	75	6.2	440,000	31
Uganda	23	87	5.4	350,000	33
Zambia	21	65	15.2	330,000	46
Zimbabwe	19	64	15.3	570,000	17

[1]World Bank, World Development Indicators, 'Agriculture, value added (% of GDP)' in 2008, except data for Tanzania and Zimbabwe, which is only available for 2005.

[2] IFAD,Rural Poverty Portal, data for 2006, available at http://www.ruralpovertyportal.org/. Exception: data for Botswana and South Africa are from the FAO website, available at http://www.fao.org/countryprofiles/

[3]UNAIDS (2008) *Report on the Global AIDS Epidemic*, available at: http://data.unaids.org/pub/GlobalReport/2008/jc1510_2008_global_report_pp211_234_en.pdf

[4]Based on UNAIDS/WHO methodology for 2007; WHO/UNAIDS/UNICEF (2008) *Towards Universal Access: Scaling Up Priority HIV/AIDS Interventions in the Health Sector*, Progress Report, June 2008, available at: http://www.who.int/hiv/pub/2008progressreport/en/index.html

who are not yet on treatment. This represents an essential contribution from the agricultural sector to complement efforts by a health sector, which is likely to be even further overstretched with ART roll-out. Additionally, universal access to treatment will represent a significant cost burden on national budgets – and hence on donor funding – underlining the pressing need to invest heavily in prevention (Schneider and Garrett, 2009). In response to this, one of the fundamental strategic roles of the agricultural sector will remain in primary prevention to bring HIV infection rates down by enhancing livelihoods and reducing the vulnerabilities that have been found to lead to high risk behaviour.

Additionally, changes in funding modalities and the overall modus operandi of sectors are likely to have implications for agricultural sector policy responses to the epidemic. Various studies over the years have consistently recommended that HIV and AIDS be incorporated into existing and future agriculture sector policies and programmes. The new harmonized and prioritized Sector-Wide Approaches represent an unprecedented entry point for effective HIV and AIDS mainstreaming, directly embedded in the agricultural mainstream.

References

Baier, E.G. (1997) 'The impact of HIV/AIDS on rural households/communities and the need for multisectoral prevention and mitigation strategies to combat the epidemic in rural areas (with special emphasis on Africa)', FAO, Rome

Binswanger, H. P., Gillespie, S. and Kadiyala, S. (2006) 'Scaling up multisectoral approaches to combating HIV and AIDS', in S. Gillespie (ed) *AIDS, Poverty, and Hunger: Challenges and Responses*, IFPRI, Washington DC

Bota, S., Malindi, G. and Nyekanyeka, M. (1999) *A Report on Preliminary Study for Factoring HIV/AIDS in the Agriculture Sector*, UNAIDS, Lilongwe

Bota, S., Mphepo, M., Malindi, G. and Alleyne, P. (2001) *The Impact of HIV/AIDS on Agricultural Extension Organisation and Field Operations in Selected Countries of Sub-Saharan Africa, with Appropriate Institutional Response*, UNDP/UNAIDS, Lilongwe

Brown, L.R. (1996) 'The Potential Impact of AIDS on Population and Economic Growth Rates', *2020 Vision Discussion Paper 15*, IFPRI, Washington DC

Chapoto, A. and Jayne, T.S. (2008) 'Impact of AIDS-related mortality on farm household welfare in Zambia', *Economic Development and Cultural Change*, vol 56, pp327–374

De Waal, A. and Whiteside, A. (2003) 'New variant famine: AIDS and food crisis in southern Africa', *The Lancet*, vol 362, issue 9391, pp1234–1237

Drimie, S. and Gandure, S. (2005) *The Impacts of HIV/AIDS on Rural Livelihoods in Southern Africa: An inventory and Literature Review*, FAO Sub-regional Office for Southern and Eastern Africa, Harare

Economic Commission for Africa (2006) *Mitigating the Impact of HIV/AIDS on Smallholder Agriculture, Food Security and Rural Livelihoods in Southern Africa: Challenges and Action Plan'*, Economic Commission for Africa, Addis Ababa

Elsey, H., Tolhurst, R. and Theobaldt, S. (2005) 'Mainstreaming HIV/AIDS in development sectors: Have we learnt the lessons from gender mainstreaming?', *AIDS Care*, vol 17, issue 8, pp988–998

FAO (1989) *Potential Impact of AIDS on Food Production and Consumption: Tabora Region, Tanzania Case Study*, FAO, Rome

FAO (1991) *The Potential Impact of AIDS on Agricultural Production and Consumption in Malawi*, FAO, Rome

FAO (1994) *The Effects of HIV/AIDS on Farming Systems and Rural Livelihoods in Uganda, Tanzania and Zambia*, FAO, Rome

FAO (1999) Aids and agriculture in Africa: can agricultural policy make a difference?, FAO, Rome

FAO (2009a) *Livelihood-based Social Protection for Orphans and Vulnerable Children: Promising Practices in Malawi*, FAO, Lilongwe

FAO (2009b) *Final Evaluation of the Agriculture Sector HIV/AIDS Strategy (2003–2008)*, FAO, Lilongwe

Food and Agriculture Organization of the United Nations/World Health Organization (2008) *Nutritional Care and Support for People living with HIV, Country experiences of capacity building from Lesotho, Malawi, Mozambique, Swaziland, Zambia and Zimbabwe*, United Nations Regional Inter-Agency Coordination Support Office (RIACSO), Johannesburg

Gillespie, S. (1989) 'Potential impact of AIDS on Farming Systems: A Case Study from Rwanda', *Land Use Policy*, vol 6, pp301–312

Gillespie, S. and Kadiyala, S. (2005) *HIV/AIDS and Food and Nutrition Security: From Evidence to Action*, IFPRI, Washington DC

Government of Botswana (2002) *National HIV/AIDS Strategic Framework (2003–2009)*, National AIDS Coordinating Agency, Gaborone

Government of Malawi (2003a) *Agriculture Sector HIV/AIDS Policy/Strategy (2003–2008)*, Ministry of Agriculture and Irrigation, Lilongwe

Government of Malawi (2003b) *National HIV/AIDS Policy: A Call for Renewed Action,* Office of the President and Cabinet and National AIDS Commission, Lilongwe

Government of Malawi (2006) Malawi Growth and Development Strategy, Government of Malawi, Lilongwe

Government of Malawi (2007a) *Fisheries Sector HIV and AIDS Strategy (2007–2011)*, Ministry of Agriculture and Food Security, Lilongwe

Government of Malawi (2007b) *Forestry Sector HIV and AIDS Strategy (2007–2011)*, Ministry of Energy and Mines, Lilongwe

Government of Malawi (2009) *National HIV Prevention Strategy (2009–2011)*, Office of the President and Cabinet and National AIDS Commission, Lilongwe

Government of Mozambique (2004) *ProAgri II*, Ministry of Agriculture and Rural Development (MINAG), Maputo

Government of Mozambique (2006a) *Action Plan for the Reduction of Absolute Poverty (PARPA II) (2006–2009)*, Government of Mozambique, Maputo

Government of Mozambique (2006b) *Sectoral Strategic Plan to Fight HIV/AIDS (2006–2010)*, Ministry of Agriculture and Rural Development (MINAG), Maputo

Government of Uganda (2005) *Uganda Strategy for Reducing the Impact of HIV and AIDS on Fishing Communities*, Ministry of Agriculture, Animal Industries and Fisheries, Kampala

Government of Tanzania (2006a) *Agricultural Sector Development Programme (2006–2013)*, Ministry of Agriculture, Food Security and Cooperatives, Dar-es-Salaam

Government of Tanzania (2006b) *Agricultural Sector Strategy for HIV/AIDS and Other Chronic Diseases*, Ministry of Agriculture, Food Security and Cooperatives, Dar-es-Salaam

Interagency Coalition on AIDS and Development (ICAD) (2004) 'HIV/AIDS, Gender Inequality and the Agricultural Sector: Guidelines for Incorporating HIV/AIDS and Gender Considerations into Agricultural Programming in High Incidence Countries', ICAD, Ottawa

IMF (2004) *The Macroeconomics of HIV/AIDS*, International Monetary Fund, Washington DC

Jayne, T., Villarreal, M., Pingali, P. and Hemrich, G. (2004) 'Interactions between the Agricultural Sector and the HIV/AIDS Pandemic: Implications for Agricultural Policy', ESA Working Paper No.04-06, FAO Agricultural and Development Economics Division, Rome

Kwaramba, P. (1997) *The Socio-economic Impact of HIV/AIDS on Communal Agricultural Production Systems in Zimbabwe*, Working Paper 19, Zimbabwe Farmers' Union and Friederich Ebert Stiftung Economic Advisory Project, Harare

Malindi, G.M.E. (2005) 'Revisiting the Agricultural Policy: Through the Gender-based HIV/
AIDS Lenses', Paper presented at the International Conference on HIV/AIDS and Food and
Nutrition Security, 14–16 April 2005, Durban

Mutangadura, G.B. (2000) 'Household Welfare impacts of mortality of adult females in
Zimbabwe: Implications for policy and program development', Paper presented at the AIDS
and Economics Symposium organized by IAEN Network, July 7–8, Durban

Mutangadura, G.B., Bollinger, L., Stover, J., Kerkhoven, R. and Mukurazita, D. (1999) *The
Economic Impacts of AIDS in Zimbabwe*, Futures Group, Harare

Over, M. (1992) 'The Macroeconomic Impact of AIDS in Sub-Saharan Africa', Technical Working
Paper No. 3, World Bank, Africa Technical Department, Population Health and Nutrition
Department, Washington, D.C.

Rau, B., Rugalema, G., Mathieson, K. and Stloukal, L. (2008) *The Evolving Contexts of AIDS and
the Challenges for Food Security and Rural Livelihoods*, FAO, Rome

Rugalema, G., Wiegang, S. and Mbwika, J. (1999) *HIV/AIDS and the Commercial Agricultural
Sector in Kenya: Impact, Vulnerability, Susceptibility and Coping Strategies*, FAO/UNDP, Rome

Topouzis, D. (1998) *The Implications of HIV/AIDS for Rural Development Policy and Programming:
Focus on Sub-Saharan Africa*, FAO/UNDP, Rome

Topouzis, D. (2003) *The Impact of HIV/AIDS on Ministries of Agriculture and Their Work: Focus on
Eastern and Southern Africa*, FAO/UNAIDS, Rome

United Nations (2000) *Security Council Resolution 1308 on the Responsibility of the Security Council
in the Maintenance of International Peace and Security: HIV/AIDS and International Peacekeeping
Operations,* http://www.un.org/Docs/scres/2000/sc2000.htm, accessed 19 January 2010

United Nations (2003) 'Organizing the UN Response to the Triple Threat of Food Insecurity,
Weakened Capacity for Governance and AIDS, Particularly in Southern and Eastern Africa',
Document discussed at the UN's High-Level Committee on Programmes, Sixth session, 18–
19 September 2003, Rome

UNAIDS (2008) Policy Brief: HIV, Food Security and Nutrition, UNAIDS, Geneva

UNAIDS (2009) *2009 AIDS Epidemic Update*, UNAIDS, Geneva

UNGASS (2001) *Declaration of Commitment on HIV/AIDS*, United Nations General Assembly
Special Session on HIV/AIDS, United Nations, New York

UNGASS (2006) *60/262 Political Declaration on HIV/AIDS*, United Nations General Assembly
Special Session on HIV/AIDS United Nations, New York

Wiegers, E.S. (2008) 'The role of the agricultural sector in mitigating the impacts of HIV/AIDS
in Sub-Saharan Africa', *NJAS Wageningen Journal of Life Sciences*, vol 56, issue 3, pp155-167

Weiser, S.D., Leiter, K., Bangsberg, D.R., Butler, L.M., Percy-de Korte, F., Hlanze, Z., Phaladze,
N., Iacopino, V. and Heisler, M. (2007) 'Food Insufficiency is Associated with High-Risk
Sexual Behavior among Women in Botswana and Swaziland', *PLoS Medicine*, vol 4, issue 10,
pp1589–1597

World Bank (1996) *AIDS Prevention and Mitigation in Sub-Saharan Africa, An Updated World
Bank Strategy*, World Bank, Washington DC

World Bank (2008) *Mozambique HIV/AIDS and Nutrition Status Report*, World Bank, Washington
DC

Zachariah, R., Fitzgerald, M., Massaquoi, M., Paluani, O. and Arnould, L. (2006) 'Risk factors
for high early mortality in patients on antiretroviral treatment in a rural district of Malawi',
AIDS, vol 20, issue 18, pp2355–2360

Chapter 13

AIDS and livelihoods: What have we learned and where are we heading?

Stuart Gillespie, E. Wairimu Mwangi,
Anke Niehof and Gabriel Rugalema

Introduction

Three decades into the era of AIDS in Africa, what do we now know about the way in which people's livelihoods interact with the transmission of HIV and with the impacts of AIDS? What determines vulnerability to the virus, and to its downstream impacts? How do people respond, and how can national policies, programmes and external assistance best support local responses, and protect people and livelihoods where and when local capacity is exceeded?

The history of research on AIDS in Africa has moved through different phases, as described in the opening chapter. The last decade has seen an upsurge in the enquiry and understanding of the linkages between HIV, AIDS and food security – more often than not, through the lens of the livelihoods of people affected directly or indirectly by AIDS epidemics. In positioning the work described in this book within the broader literature, we use a simple conceptual timeline that tracks the path of the virus as it affects households, communities and societies (see Figure 1.2 in Chapter 1). We differentiate the stages and types of vulnerability to HIV infection and to the impacts of AIDS. Vulnerability is not only multifaceted, it is also dynamic in the sense that its multiple ingredients are in constant flux – and because people proactively respond to try to reduce their vulnerability. Such responses determine their resilience in the face of concurrent shocks and stresses. Drawing from the findings in the previous chapters of this book, we

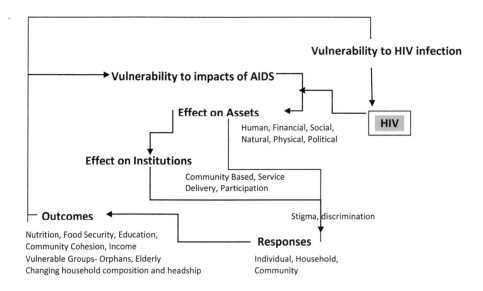

Figure 13.1 *Understanding HIV and AIDS in the context of people's livelihoods*

Source: Adapted from Kadiyala and Gillespie (2004)

can elaborate the timeline and situate the stages of vulnerability within the context of a household's livelihood as depicted in Figure 13.1.

HIV and AIDS both affect, and are affected by, people's livelihoods. The macro context, conditions and trends will, to some extent, determine the vulnerability of different livelihood systems to upstream HIV exposure and to the downstream impacts of AIDS. After HIV has entered a household or community, the type and severity of its impacts on assets – mediated by institutional structures, processes and programmes – will determine the type of strategies that the household adopts. These strategies will differ, among other ways, in terms of their ability to a) reduce people's exposure to HIV and b) increase their resilience to AIDS impacts. Such strategies and responses in turn lead to various outcomes, including food and nutrition security. Finally, Figure 13.1 shows how these outcomes are also inputs – for better or worse – into future vulnerability or resilience. And so the cycle turns.

While there is a burgeoning literature on upstream and midstream vulnerability and responses (of prevention, care and treatment), this is not the main focus of this book. Most of the research presented in the preceding chapters focuses on downstream vulnerability and responses to HIV and AIDS on the part of individuals, households and communities, in the context of rural livelihoods in Africa. These studies further our knowledge of the multiple, overlapping and interacting shocks and stresses affecting households and the diverse – sometimes innovative, sometimes desperate – responses made to these effects.

Socio-economic impacts of AIDS on households and communities

Since FAO first considered the threat that AIDS posed for food security in Africa over two decades ago (Gillespie 1989), many studies have since shown that African farmers are vulnerable to the downstream impacts of AIDS on their livelihoods, as the disease reduces the resources that households can devote to agriculture. Labour loss occurs not only as a result of sickness and premature adult death, but also as a result of its reallocation to nurse the ill, while working capital and income is siphoned off to pay mounting medical bills. The specific levels and types of such vulnerability depend on the characteristics of families, livelihoods and farming systems. Evidence from Southern and Eastern Africa clearly shows that it is the poor and food insecure who suffer greater and more enduring livelihood impacts from concurrent health and economic shocks (Gillespie and Kadiyala, 2005). Chronic food insecurity constrains resilience and forecloses options to adapt to any stress. A full, contextualized understanding of these interactions is crucially important in determining appropriate mitigation strategies.

There are also major intra-household effects, because vulnerability is not homogeneous within households; women and children tend to shoulder a disproportionate share of the burden of AIDS. AIDS-related morbidity generates care needs that place a strain on household resources and compels those who are expected to give care to divert time and labour from productive activities to caring. Since, also in sub-Saharan Africa, in the domestic context women are the main care givers, the burden of care falls primarily on them (Müller, 2005; Nombo, 2007; Du Preez and Niehof, 2008; Karuhanga Beraho, 2008). The 'new variant famine' hypothesis (De Waal and Whiteside, 2003) at micro-level revolves around the culturally underpinned reproductive responsibilities of women. Because of their care duties, women miss out on income-earning opportunities in a situation where the household is already experiencing decline of income and depletion of resources due to illness of previously income-earning adults. As a consequence they can no longer adequately feed their families. When children have to help out and are dropping out of school to do so (Kakuru, 2006; Karuhanga Beraho, 2008), the division of responsibilities and the burden of work in the household have fundamentally shifted, at the expense of women's health, household food security and children's future.

Not only within the household, but also with regard to household composition and headship, AIDS has resulted in significant shifts, changing both the stage and its actors (Niehof and Price, 2007). Household composition is changing more swiftly to adapt to the care needs of returning sick migrants, orphaned children or sick relatives who are abandoned, and to the limits of the resources and the caring capacity of the household (Rugalema et al., Du Preez and Niehof, Nombo, Paradza, in this volume). There are increases in the proportions of households headed by women or orphaned children but one interesting finding is that most households survive (Seeley et al., Rugalema, et al., in this volume).

Though not the subject of this book, it is worth mentioning another major individual-level impact of HIV-related morbidity here – namely, the interaction of HIV with an individual's nutritional status. Nutrition and immunity in HIV-positive individuals can interact in two ways. First, HIV-induced immune impairment and heightened subsequent risk of opportunistic infection can worsen nutritional status.

HIV infection often leads to nutritional deficiencies through decreased food intake, malabsorption, and increased utilization and excretion of nutrients, which in turn can hasten death (Semba and Tang, 1999). Second, nutritional status modulates the immunological response to HIV infection, affecting the overall clinical outcome. Over four decades ago, research started to shed light on this 'malnutrition-infection complex' with the term 'NAIDS' (Nutritionally Acquired Immune Deficiency Syndrome) being coined (Scrimshaw *et al.* 1968). Individuals living with HIV require 10 per cent extra calories if they are asymptomatic, and 20–30 per cent extra if they are symptomatic (WHO, 2003). Nutritional impacts of HIV infection at the individual level will have implications for whole households, especially where income is dependent on manual labour productivity. Moreover, nutrition is a fundamental consideration in *all* aspects of the HIV response – including prevention, care and treatment, as well as mitigation.

Interacting shocks

With regard to other shocks, especially drought, it is worth turning to the hypothesis – first posited during the Southern African drought of 2002–2003 – that AIDS could precipitate famine. The 'new variant famine' hypothesis (de Waal and Whiteside, 2003) posited that AIDS contributed to the crisis in several ways, most notably by reducing the resilience of affected households and limiting their ability to cope with the crisis. As detailed evidence became available, the hypothesis was refined (de Waal, 2007). The role of AIDS in altering livelihood patterns and increasing household-level vulnerability to hunger was identified as significant, especially when combined with other shocks such as drought or market failure.

Other shocks may interact with AIDS. Significant impacts were found to have occurred in many contexts in Eastern and Southern Africa during the food price crisis of 2007–2008 (Gillespie et al., 2009). Nombo's study shows how government policy, in this case, privatization of Kilombero Sugar Estate, can intensify local people's vulnerability to HIV infection and limit their collective ability to respond to the impact of AIDS. Similarly, Paradza's chapter illustrates the knock-on effects that protracted political crisis and economic collapse can have on the effects of AIDS. These two chapters make it clear that in some environments, AIDS amplifies the negative effects of existing social and economic conditions of communities.

Lessons learnt from the studies

In this section, we examine the major themes emerging from the analyses undertaken in the various chapters, and their policy and programming implications.

AIDS, agriculture and land

Set in the context of the AIDS epidemic in Kenya, the chapter by Mwangi advances the literature on the economic sources of a vulnerability to HIV by empirically assessing how the regional agricultural context may structure risk for some individuals and groups, in this case women, who are systematically marginalized from access to resources. In so doing the study gives attention to the upstream sources of vulnerability – that is, the pathways through which poverty may put women at greater risk of being exposed to the virus. Employing multilevel analysis, this study found that these contexts account for regional variation in women's vulnerability to HIV infection over and above women's decision-making autonomy, while controlling for socio-demographic and household characteristics.

Mwangi found that in districts characterized by a high contribution of wage employment to average household income, women were more vulnerable to HIV infection. This may imply greater economic dependency of women on men where wage labour predominates, and/or that female wage labour brings risks, possibly linked to increased mobility of women, or the presence of rural agro-estates where workers were more exposed to HIV. The study by Nombo, discussed below, also shows how the presence of the sugar cane company creates a floating labour force in which HIV prevalence tends to be raised compared to the surrounding population.

Finally, Mwangi found that women living in districts characterized by female tenure security were less vulnerable to HIV infection. Landholding sizes were also associated with decreased vulnerability to HIV. Women were also less vulnerable in districts with easy access to women's organizations, and in districts characterized by dominance of cash crop production. Viability of small-scale cash crop production may imply a lower likelihood of household members engaging in migrant labour thus reducing the HIV risk associated with migration.

The Seeley et al. study, conducted in the Masaka district in Southwestern Uganda, focuses on the impact of the AIDS epidemic on agriculture and seeks to understand why agricultural livelihoods in Africa have not collapsed, despite the widespread suffering caused by the epidemic. The study found a decline in land ownership in HIV+ households, with most households selling land to offset healthcare costs. While the impact of morbidity and death resulted in a significant decline in land cultivated in the medium term, households that did not dissolve generally managed to keep their land in the long term, and pass it on to a new generation to cultivate. They were able to bounce back. Cropping pattern changes were not wholly attributable to AIDS, but were as likely to relate to the prevalence of pests and crop diseases as to labour shortages. Moreover, labour shortages were not necessarily the result of HIV, but often due to work-related migration. Seeley et al. also suggest that studies on the longitudinal impacts of AIDS would benefit from a context-specific differentiated picture that draws attention to the wide variation, within and between households, communities and regions.

Karuhanga's study in Uganda found that ill health was one of the main causes of reduced household labour, and that malaria and AIDS were leading causes of ill health and death. Both qualitative and quantitative data showed that the burden of AIDS-related care fell disproportionately on women and girls. The most significant effect of ill health, and thus reduced labour on agricultural production, related to poor agronomic practices for all crops. In general the results show that wealth and gender of the household head are key correlates of household food security in both districts. Better-off households are generally able to access a broader range of resources to mitigate the effects of HIV and AIDS compared to poorer households. AIDS-affected well-off households did not experience a significant decline in landholding between 2002 and 2005 compared to non-affected well-off households, but for poor households the difference proved to be significant. Male-headed households in the well-off category who had access to hired labour and were educated were likely to have more secure livelihoods and to be better able to cope with the effects of HIV and AIDS. Overall, AIDS was just one among a multiplicity of factors that influence food security status of a given household and depending on prevailing circumstances may or may not be the one producing the most significant effects. But clearly, the superimposition of AIDS on other stresses further intensifies vulnerability.

This is consistent with Twine and Hunter's findings in South Africa that adult mortality-related HIV and other causes exacerbates existing vulnerabilities to food insecurity primarily associated with poverty. Twine and Hunter suggest that HIV-related mortality does not necessarily represent a unique form of mortality impact. Generally, HIV-impacted households and households that experience other forms of adult mortality were similarly impacted by food insecurity; however, the study did find that HIV-related mortality was associated with lower dietary diversity. Mortality-impacted households (regardless of cause of death) became more reliant on wild vegetables after an adult death. Natural resources are potentially an important component of dietary coping strategies of mortality-impacted households, but collection constraints prevent HIV-impacted households from making optimal use of them. The authors conclude that poverty is central in shaping food security, but that the period of two years they covered by retrospective questioning is insufficient to identify the precise ways in which mortality, household assets base, poverty and food security are interlinked.

In several ways the studies provide examples of the importance of land for rural livelihoods in a context of high HIV prevalence. In such a situation, access to land is vital for survival. Examples are single women deploying various strategies to acquire or maintain access to residential and farming land (Paradza); orphans staying on the parental homestead after the death of their parents for fear of losing the land (Du Preez and Niehof); extended family safekeeping the land of their affected relatives (Rugalema et al.); and the retention of land even in dire circumstances (Karuhanga).

AIDS, social capital and social support systems

In her Tanzanian study, Nombo highlights how the shifting macro-economic landscape can undermine social capital and community-based coping systems. Declining economic opportunities makes it more likely that both men and women will migrate in search of income and employment, which in turn destabilizes social structures and family cohesion – thus potentially increasing individuals vulnerability to HIV exposure. In the study area, the privatization of the sugar cane estate in 1998 also deprived many households of customary (though not legal) access to company land, which led to the phenomenon of distant farming. This left those not needed at the distant farm to fend for themselves. Teenage girls left behind may be driven to engage in unsafe sex for food or money for themselves and younger siblings.

The changing socio-economic context, driven by ongoing migration, privatization and distant farming, has affected the ability and willingness of extended family members to assist those who experience AIDS impacts. Socio-economic changes include increased land shortages resulting in economic hardships, which in turn have undermined kinship support. This is accentuated by the fact that economic hardships are concentrated among people with similar livelihoods, which means that people are focused more on their own problems and less on helping others to solve theirs (a similar situation was found in a recent Zambian study by Bond, 2006). Additionally, the increased heterogeneity in the village weakens trust and creates situations that foster a proliferation of witchcraft accusations that permit people to 'make sense' of their dire economic situations and explain diseases like AIDS. In turn, this further undermines social support systems and prevents the emergence of community-based support initiatives.

While Nombo's study looks at the impacts and coping strategies of households and the community in general, Paradza's study in Zimbabwe gives particular attention to single women – unmarried, divorced and widowed women – and investigates the cumulative macro-economic and AIDS-related impacts on the livelihoods of these women in the rural areas of Zimbabwe. This study centres on assessing the impacts on single women that extend beyond the end of marriage. Placing single women's experiences within the broader social, economic and political contexts, the study examines pathways that these women follow to piece together their lives, following the end of their marital relationships. Paradza finds that broader macro-level changes, particularly economic changes, intersect with HIV and AIDS rendering livelihoods of single women 'hearth-holds' more vulnerable over time.

Yet, again, vulnerability does not exclusively relate to AIDS. Moreover, the impacts of change on single women hearth-holds were not uniform across households and depended largely on the extent to which single women could diversify their livelihoods (the latter in turn depending on initial asset base, health of individuals, developmental stage of hearth-holds, access to non-agricultural income, local governance and the specific shocks to which the household is exposed). Contrary to studies that generally conclude that following the end of marriage women on their own face a downward economic spiral, this study shows that in the long-term, in customary tenure areas, women outside the conjugal unit can successfully consolidate their asset base. From this study we cannot conclude that single women have insecure access to land, because rules governing acceptance into customary tenure vary and depend on the local leaders. Paradza also finds that economic constraints and the AIDS epidemic combine to increase the dependence of adult children, undermining a hearth-hold's tenure in communal areas. Dependent adult children were thus a source of insecurity and vulnerability instead of a source of old-age insurance.

Local support networks allowed single women access to information, support and opportunities to earn non-agricultural income. These networks, however, did little to support single women who were ill and/or had contracted AIDS. This finding is consistent with Nombo's study, which found that most support networks have not incorporated AIDS into their objectives and activities, and that their assistance, if any, is short-term and not extended to households that are faced with prolonged sickness, lack of labour or chronic food insecurity.

In their 15-year longitudinal study in Bukoba district, Tanzania, Rugalema et al. track the impacts of AIDS and the responses of individuals and households, to try to better understand the set and sequence of steps and actions that were taken to ensure survival and continuity among households afflicted by AIDS. Focusing on a limited number of households, the study does not seek to identify general trends, but rather seeks to illustrate the differences in outcomes between different households and uncover sources and types of resilience. Extended family networks emerge as pivotal in enhancing the resilience of households to the impacts of AIDS. In particular, fostering of orphans may influence the survival of a household. In this case orphans are fostered in the extended family system and cared for until they are able to lead independent lives; they may stay under one roof or may be forced to relocate from one foster household to another. Fostering orphans is not the only form of support provided by the extended family. The cases provide examples of the extended family safeguarding the land of households of kin of which the adults have died or are not capable of cultivating it, until the younger generation can take over.

The study of Seeley et al. (see above) has shown that households are not static units. AIDS-related deaths negatively impact households but other family members may move in to take the place of those who have died. The study of Du Preez and Niehof in KwaZulu-Natal, South Africa, shows changes in living arrangements largely attributable to TB/AIDS-related illness and death. Inter-household movements of vulnerable or orphaned children occurred when a household affected by AIDS-related morbidity and mortality does not have the capacity to meet the demands for care or – as documented by Paradza and Nombo as well – adult children return to their parental homestead when they are ill and in need of care. Kinship networks are still important, but AIDS induces flux and instability, changes dependency relations between homesteads, threatens safety nets, and undermines relations between partners, particularly those not sanctioned by traditional marriage. At the same time, households and individuals exercise agency in adapting to the emergent care needs as a result of TB/AIDS-related morbidity and mortality by strategically changing living arrangements and moving individuals between households and homesteads.

Vulnerability and response

Overall, we can see that the impacts of AIDS on agriculture (and indeed other sources of livelihood) are not one-time events. They are processes, often hidden and slow-burning. AIDS can exert its effects over a relatively long period of time while rendering other stresses/shocks both more likely and more severe in their effects. Following a shock to household income, households in Malawi affected by AIDS were found to take up to 18 months to stabilize, with a new equilibrium income that was about half the pre-shock income levels (Masanjala, 2006). Similar findings had been reported earlier in Kenya (Yamano and Jayne, 2004). Such limited resilience is likely to increase vulnerability to other shocks. Seeley et al. (this volume) found surviving households in their sample took about 10 years to establish a new stable livelihood base in farming.

Impacts are also context-specific, differing by community and by household in type and degree, and they depend on a range of demographic, economic, and socio-cultural factors and processes – as well as sustained access to effective antiretroviral therapy. Vulnerability to AIDS impacts may be viewed as a function of the type and degree of socio-economic change in relation to the ability to respond to such change. Where there is flexibility and a diversity of possible responses, households may be more resilient. Karuhanga (this volume) found that AIDS-affected households that are well off do not suffer losses of land and livestock. But where response options and resources are limited, households are more vulnerable, since responses taken under duress tend to be costly and unsustainable.

In the AIDS literature, the notion of 'coping' has become a clichéd, catch-all term for such responses. 'Coping' is, more often than not, an externally applied, value judgement that may not correspond to what is actually happening in the present –

and almost always neglects the likely future consequences. Many responses are those of distressed households without much conscious strategy – 'struggling not coping', as Rugalema (2000) pointed out. Responses may have a veneer of coping, but the costs may need to be paid further down the line (for example, a child denied schooling).

The research of Fagbemissi and Price in Couffo, Benin, presents an interesting example of responding to AIDS-induced stress. It highlights the way children orphaned by AIDS use their knowledge on maize crop pests to survive as farmers. Contrary to the assumed AIDS-induced knowledge gap, the children scored higher, not lower, on a salient knowledge scale than adult farmers of households not impacted by AIDS. The researchers attribute this rather unexpected finding to the increased utility of farming for children orphaned by AIDS, as it is the only source of livelihood they have. They speculate that AIDS-affected children (and adult) farmers for this reason invest more time and attention in farming than non-affected farmers, which contributes to their knowledge of local pests. In this case, the children respond to the situation in a way that could strengthen their livelihood, rather than by mere coping.

Many impacts are revealed in actual responses that households and communities make in the face of AIDS. Where households are not subject to additional stresses such as drought, and when viewed over a relatively short reference period (for example, a couple of years), there are indications from the literature, and from these studies, that traditional responses can mitigate the worst effects of AIDS. Often complex factors determine the success of these strategies. These may include the sex, age and position in the household of the ill/deceased person, the household's socio-economic status, the type and degree of labour demand in the production system, the availability of labour support to affected households, other livelihood opportunities, available natural resources, the availability of formal and informal sources of support including credit and inter-household transfers, the length of time that the epidemic has been impacting upon the rural economy, and the existence of concurrent shocks such as drought or commodity price collapses (Gillespie and Kadiyala, 2005). The studies in this book testify to the synergy, specificity and multiplicity of factors that – at the end of the day – determine the ability of individuals and households to respond to AIDS-induced adversity, though initial poverty and a poor assets base clearly reduce resilience.

Policy response

Two studies in the book pay attention to programmatic and policy responses to HIV and AIDS. The first is the study by Swaans et al. in KwaZulu-Natal, South Africa, on a group-based discovery learning approach, the Farmer Life Schools (FLS), to improve household food security and address high HIV prevalence by initiating communal gardens. They conclude that such an approach potentially can improve food security and wellbeing, while allowing people, especially women, to discuss AIDS. The authors recommend: 1. an emphasis on interventions that bring some kind of 'reward' to the participants, for example, a thriving garden; 2. broadening of FLS activities beyond communal gardens; 3. creating a safe environment for learning by formation of homogenous and small groups; 4. using an integrated community-based approach focused on meeting the economic needs of resource-poor communities by garden projects, short-term food assistance, income generating activities and micro-credit programmes; and 5. enhancing institutional collaboration and strong involvement of all stakeholders, including home-based care workers, social workers and counsellors. At the same time, the application of the FLS model is constrained by factors such as the inability of women of AIDS-affected households to sufficiently participate due to care duties, and the mistrust and stigma surrounding HIV and AIDS. The latter led to one of the gardens being termed an 'AIDS garden', which provoked hostility in the community.

In their study, Remme et al. explore agricultural responses to HIV and AIDS in terms of policy formulation and implementation, discussing the challenges encountered and the lessons learned in East and Southern Africa. With regard to challenges they note that though research has played a pivotal role as critical instrument for policy advocacy, it has not adequately enabled evidence-informed policy responses. They attribute this to resources constraints that led to national strategies being based on extrapolations of findings from other countries, thus running the risk of designing locally inappropriate policy responses. Another problematic point is the collaboration between the agricultural sector and the health sector, given the different rationales that prevail in the sectors. The agriculture sector defines itself through a production function and the interactions between agriculture and HIV/AIDS do not usually make it to the top of the list of priorities for agriculturalists (see also Wiegers, 2008a). Finally, they note the lack of rigorous frameworks for monitoring and evaluation of agriculture and HIV/AIDS responses and the lack of funding for agro-based interventions.

On the positive side the researchers find that increasingly in policy frameworks and national development strategies the agricultural sector is recognized as an important partner in AIDS impact mitigation. Partially attributable to HIV responses in the agricultural sector is the ongoing shift from a purely production-oriented approach to a more client-oriented approach that is increasingly participatory, gender-balanced, culturally sensitive and community-based, thus addressing some of the inequalities that constrain agriculture. HIV and gender are being mainstreamed into policy responses. HIV mainstreaming through ongoing capacity building efforts is increasingly visualized as a continuous process rather than as one-time interventions. Practical tools (regularly revised and updated) tailored for field staff, development planners and policy-makers, particularly in the agriculture and rural development sectors to facilitate HIV mainstreaming, are being made available.

Gender

The studies documented in this book reflect the gendered nature of vulnerability to exposure to HIV infection and AIDS impacts. The studies addressing the issues of support and care also show women more than men bearing the brunt of care for ill family and household members and for children orphaned by AIDS. Rugalema et al. (this volume) quote an article in the *New York Times* where AIDS is referred to as a 'grandmothers disease'. Not only are women in the 'grandmother'-phase of life expected to take over care for their grandchildren when the children's parents are ill, dead or no longer to be found (Du Preez and Niehof, this volume), they also have to look after their sick adult children (see above, and especially Paradza in this volume). At the time when these women could expect to be taken care of and supported by their adult children, they have to take up the mother role again. This is a reversal of the 'natural course of events' where parents care for their children to be later supported by their children when they reach old age. It means a break with the traditionally established pattern of reciprocal relations between the generations (Nombo, 2007).

While care giving is more or less universally a woman's job, providing material assistance is usually thought to be men's responsibility, as an extension of their role as breadwinner. However, the studies in the book show that also this is far from self-evident, especially in a context of high HIV prevalence when many people are in need of support. The cases presented in various chapters in the book show that ill adults and orphans are taken in by households in which both men and women try to provide for the basic needs of those under their care by farming or earning cash, while in the case of women-headed households it is women who have to feed and shelter the dependents. Even the support of the extended family tends to be along female rather than male lines. One participant at the 2005 IFPRI/RENEWAL International Conference on HIV/AIDS, Food and Nutrition Security in Durban highlighted this well in pointing out how the 'extended family' in most cases meant 'extended women'. The cases presented by Du Preez and Niehof show what could be called a 'matrilineality of care' (in an otherwise patrilineal society), meaning that care duties and practices in the family are passed along matrilineal lines (mothers to daughters).

In a lot of conventional livelihood studies applying a gender perspective is only done by comparing male- and female-headed households. The studies presented in this book prove this dual opposition to be superficial and – in a context of high HIV prevalence – rather irrelevant. The category of female-headed households is too broad and heterogeneous. Karuhanga found in her study significant differences between single female-headed households and widow-headed households, but also similarities between those two as compared to male-headed households. Paradza's study focuses on domestic units (hearth-holds) headed by 'single' (unmarried, abandoned, divorced or widowed) women. Except for elderly widows who were able to accumulate assets, their different situations are not as related to (non)marital status as to other factors. Far from representing a homogeneous category, Paradza's single women follow different pathways and apply different strategies in responding to AIDS and other crises. In her research in Zambia, Wiegers (2008b) distinguishes several categories of households according to headship (female, male, elderly) and nature of AIDS impact – households with people living with HIV (PLHIV) or with orphans – and compares these types of households with a control group of non-affected households. There appear to be pervasive differences between the categories, also between the two types of female-headed households: those with PLHIV and those with orphans. The latter were doing far better in terms of food production than the former.

The studies make clear that comparisons of purely household-level data, especially when only disaggregated by headship into male and female, are unable to shine a clear light on what is happening *within* affected households with respect to the intra-household division of labour and care giving, allocation of scarce resources, and differential impacts of AIDS morbidity and mortality on women and children. Finally, yet another problem with the notion of 'household coping' (see discussion above) is its implication of intra-household homogeneity of those affected.

The way ahead

Strengthening rural livelihoods

The ways in which HIV and AIDS exacerbate poverty and the factors that condition vulnerability of people to risk of HIV infection and impacts of AIDS add urgency to the 'AIDS plus' agenda. HIV and AIDS are affecting the assets, entitlements and resources people need for sustainably developing and maintaining their livelihood. With regard to rural livelihoods, which are the focus of this book, there are several ways in which policies can help mitigate these effects. For example, policy could reduce migration by incentivizing the adoption of local livelihood strategies in and around the community, extending the growing season through developing small-scale irrigation, product diversification, agro-processing, strengthening existing, and creating new, market linkages, and developing the farm input supply chain. Appropriate policy reform could overcome barriers to participating in agricultural production and marketing by affected households, such as their depleted resource base, their need to be close to home to tend to the sick, loss of key skills and their inability to take on risk. Community-level incentives for inter-household labour exchange could be generated. Finally, an important policy issue is protecting the land tenure and inheritance rights of single women, widows and orphaned children.

Although not addressed in this book, microfinance programmes, especially when targeted at women to support their income-generating activities, may be important for strengthening rural livelihoods, notably those weakened by AIDS. A recent Ethiopian research project that looked into the effects on gender inequalities of microfinance programmes for women investigated the effects of chronic illness. It was found that adult morbidity and mortality, including from AIDS-related causes, led to the reallocation of household labour, increased child labour, and caused women borrowers to default or leave the credit groups altogether (Bekele Haile, 2010). The author of the study wonders about the implications of AIDS for microfinance interventions and whether the epidemic leads to certain groups being excluded from accessing microfinance. The results of another recent study on microfinance targeted at women, in this case in Ivory Coast (Binaté Fofana, 2010), sheds some light on these questions. It was found that the two general microfinance organizations investigated preferred providing loans for trading activities rather than farming, because of the more uncertain returns from the latter. Women themselves also preferred trading to farming because of their limited access to land and agricultural labour. The effects of HIV and AIDS on the policy of the two organizations were not visible, neither could it be ascertained that AIDS-affected women had less access to their services. However, in a special microfinance programme for AIDS-affected women, all women borrowers were lagging behind in paying their instalments. From the focus group discussion with clients of this programme it emerged that diverting the loan for other purposes (for example, medical expenditures) and failure of the business were the main reasons for this. The latter was reportedly caused by frequent illness, but also by the organization's policy to provide the requested loan in phases instead of the whole amount at once, presumably as a precaution for default. This shows that microfinance, though potentially significant, is not an easy option for strengthening AIDS-affected women's income generation and livelihoods.

Strengthening social protection

AIDS epidemics, entwined as they are with multiple stressors affecting livelihoods in Eastern and Southern Africa, imply the need for more comprehensive interventions that are sustainable and that enable families to ensure livelihood security. Given the many and varied challenges, no single intervention can achieve significant or sustained support for wellbeing. This becomes particularly important when looking at the extended time scale of the AIDS epidemic.

Set against the depth and breadth of food insecurity in many countries in Africa, the rationale and scope for an expansion of social protection systems becomes evident. Social protection here refers to institutionalized policies and programmes that protect against shocks and promote livelihoods and the welfare of poor and vulnerable people, thereby building their resilience to such shocks via strengthened and expanded asset holdings and livelihood options. They include both entitlement-based instruments (such as unconditional cash and food transfers, employment guarantee programmes, nutrition programmes, and school feeding) and incentive-based instruments (such as conditional transfer programmes, drought insurance and targeted subsidies).

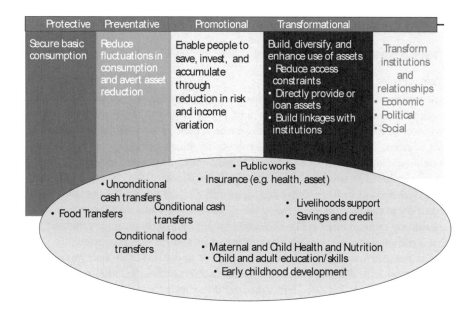

Figure 13.2 *Social protection: objectives and interventions*

Source: Adato and Bassett (2008)

Figure 13.2 presents an asset-based social protection conceptual framework, which was developed by the Regional Network on AIDS, Livelihoods and Food Security (RENEWAL) and the Joint Learning Initiative on Children and AIDS (JLICA) (Adato and Bassett, 2008). The framework demonstrates what social protection can achieve, and how different types of interventions align with different objectives. While preserving basic levels of comfort and human dignity among the sick, social protection interventions may also be the only means of preventing destitution of entire households, and irreversible health, nutrition and education deprivation among children – with lifelong consequences. The different uses of social protection are demonstrated as one moves from left to right, from securing a basic level of meeting consumption needs to transforming institutions and economic, social or political relationships. The programmes in the oval represent a range of interventions that provide forms of social protection. They are loosely placed under the objectives with which they are most normally associated. Although programmes have tendencies to be used to achieve particular objectives, each can be used to achieve any of these bjectives, depending on first, how they are designed (and, importantly, the ability to implement the design as planned); and second, the capacities that people have to take advantage of these design features. A cash transfer programme thus can assist AIDS-affected families by, for example; i) securing basic subsistence for families where illness prevents them from securing a livelihood; ii) keeping children from leaving school because of inability to pay fees or labour needed at home; iii) enabling people to invest in income-generating activities; and iv) increasing the agency of communities where local organizations participate in targeting, monitoring or service delivery.

A new research agenda

Agriculture

There are several topics that could feature on a new agenda for research relating to the agricultural sector. In the first place more has to be known about the implications of national and regional agricultural development policies for rural communities, in terms of effects on social inequality and risk of individuals being exposed to the virus through the adoption of risky livelihoods or behaviours. The extent to which, and the type of conditions in which, AIDS erodes agricultural assets (land, labour, capital and knowledge) need to be further investigated as well. On the flip side of the coin, when one section of the community is losing their assets through sale, another section must be benefiting through buying. How does this dynamic affect community wealth status? What is the emerging relationship between the sellers and the buyers of assets?

More research is needed on the effects of HIV and AIDS, and their importance relative to other health and other non-health factors (such as malaria, tuberculosis, drought, price variability, poor infrastructure) on agricultural decision-making at the household level (for example, land use, crop choice, input use, output marketing). It also needs to be asked how these impacts play out over time and influence overall agricultural sector performance, and the ability of the agricultural sector to serve as an engine of pro-poor economic growth?

Social protection, care and support

Research under this heading has to acknowledge the reality of the highly significant role of households and (extended) family, in particular their female members, in providing first-line support and care to sick individuals and persons otherwise affected by AIDS. The second level of support and care is that of the community, while finally communities need support from appropriate government and non-governmental policies and programmes. Within this framework a number of urgent research topics arise.

Starting at the micro level, a first research question is how to create incentives and opportunities for communities to protect the entitlements of affected households. An option is to enable such households to exchange on fair terms what they have (for example, land they can no longer cultivate) for what they need (for example, food). A second issue is how to support the work of primary care givers by community-based initiatives. Linked to this, the question arises of how the highly skewed gender imbalances in care provision could be redressed and in what ways men could be more involved in providing care and support. Identifying ways of supporting children orphaned by AIDS and orphan-headed households without compromising their integrity and autonomy is another urgent research topic.

About the role of the community in social protection a number of questions come to the fore. Examples of these are the following. What types of community change, innovation and adaptation (resilience) are underway? What is needed to strengthen, sustain or rebuild community resilience in the face of AIDS? What determines an effective community response and what lessons can be learned and applied to scaling up effective responses? How can community collective social action be maximized to fill labour and other resource gaps opened up by AIDS? At least one of the studies in the book (Nombo) presents proof of the limits of community-driven responses to AIDS. When are these limits reached and what community characteristics determine these limits? Finally, important questions concern what is an appropriate balance between government-led (more top-down) social protection policies and schemes and community-led responses and about how national policy and programming can learn from, and scale up, local responses while staying responsive to local conditions and not undermining local agency. How can community-government partnership be facilitated to this end?

A special focus on nutrition

Regarding nutrition much work still needs to be done on the question of what nutrition 'through an HIV lens' looks like and what are the operational implications of rethinking nutrition from this perspective. Another key question is whether nutrition offers an entry point for forging better links between public health and agricultural responses to AIDS, and to other emerging health threats, thus improving both food and health security.

Returning to household and community level there are a number of key questions relating to food and nutrition security of affected households and individuals. How do we balance the need for short-term nutritional support with long-term strategies to ensure nutritional security in affected households? How do we develop and promote linkages between food assistance and livelihood activities and strategies for income security to ensure *sustainable* food security for HIV-infected individuals and their households? How can this be done equitably – for example, ensuring that those who need food and nutritional support (whether HIV-affected or not) have access, and without stigmatizing the beneficiaries? What is the cost-effectiveness of nutrition interventions for people living with HIV and their households and what are the implications for scaling up and sustaining such interventions? Finally, what role does nutrition play in new approaches to social protection in the context of AIDS?

Conclusion

The scale of sub-Saharan Africa's ongoing AIDS epidemics continues to dwarf those in other regions in the world. Despite major advances in treatment access and outreach, HIV and AIDS (the virus and the disease) continue to interact with others sources of vulnerability and stress to jeopardize the livelihoods of millions. Poverty per se may not be the most important factor driving the risk of being exposed to HIV – but without question, it is the poor in these countries, and especially poor women, who are struggling the most with the subsequent impacts of AIDS. If you are a person living with HIV and you are poor, it will be harder for you to sustainably access antiretroviral therapy, it will be harder to find and pay for treatment for opportunistic infections, which (if you are malnourished) will usually be more severe, and it will be harder to ensure any medical treatment is complemented by a diverse and reliable diet. At the household level, poverty will worsen the impacts of other livelihood stresses and shocks, and close down options for effectively responding. At the end of the line, it is women and children who are the most vulnerable.

This book, and other recent studies and papers, have permitted a finer grained perspective of what is happening – and what has happened in the past – as people confront the multiplicity of shocks and stresses that daily threaten their livelihood bases. Such shocks may be social, economic, political, environmental, as well as health-related – but an important conclusion is that they often interact in different ways in different places – and people respond in different ways in different places. Policy and supportive programming needs to grasp such nuance and context-specificity if it is to make a difference.

A properly balanced AIDS response would first seek to stem the flow of new infections via approaches to HIV prevention that cut across all socio-economic strata of society and that are tailored to the specific drivers of transmission within different groups – with particular attention to the vulnerabilities faced by youth and women, and to the dynamic and contextual nature of the relationship between socio-economic status and HIV. Second, care and treatment approaches finally need to take on board the importance of nutrition security for people living with HIV and their families. Third, to better respond to the downstream or post-infection impacts of AIDS-related disease and death, mitigation needs to focus on increasing the resilience of poor and vulnerable households through enhancing local capacity and providing options and incentives for safe livelihood strategies. This in turn needs to be complemented by effective state-led systems of social protection, underpinned by equitable macro-economic growth policies, and gender-progressive legislation and implementation.

References

Adato, M. and Bassett, L. (2008) *What is the Potential of Cash Transfers to Strengthen Families Affected by HIV and AIDS? A Review of the Evidence on Impacts and Key Policy Debates*, Report produced for the Joint Learning Initiative on Children and AIDS (JLICA) and Regional Network on AIDS, Livelihoods and Food Security (RENEWAL)

Bekele Haile, H. (2010) *Targeting Married Women in Microfinance Programmes: Transforming or Reinforcing Gender Inequalities? Evidence from Ethiopia*, PhD thesis, Wageningen University, Wageningen, The Netherlands

Binaté Fofana, N. (2010) *Efficacy of Micro-Financing Women's Activities in Côte d'Ivoire; Evidence from Rural Areas and HIV/AIDS-Affected Women*, PhD thesis, Wageningen University, Wageningen, The Netherlands

Bond, V (2006) 'Stigma when there is no other option: understanding how poverty fuels discrimination towards people living with HIV in Zambia', in S. Gillespie (ed) *AIDS, Poverty and Hunger: Challenges and Responses,* IFPRI, Washington DC, USA, pp181–198

De Waal, A. (2007) 'AIDS, hunger and destitution: theory and evidence for the "new variant famines" hypothesis in Africa', in S. Devereux (ed) *The New Famines: Why Famines Persist in an Era of Globalisation,* Routledge, London

De Waal, A. and Whiteside, A. (2003) 'New variant famine: AIDS and food crisis in southern Africa', *The Lancet,* vol 362, no 9391, pp1234–37

Du Preez, C. and Niehof, A. (2008) 'Caring for people living with AIDS: A labour of love', *Medische Antropologie,* vol 20, no 1, pp87–105

Gillespie, S.R. (1989) 'Potential impact of AIDS on farming systems: A case study from Rwanda', *Land Use Policy* vol 6, no 4, pp301-312

Gillespie, S.R. and Kadiyala, S. (2005) *IIIV/AIDS and Food and Nutrition Security: From Evidence to Action*, Food Policy Review 7, IFPRI, Washington DC

Gillespie, S., Jere, P., Msuya, P. and Drimie, S. (2009) 'Food prices and the HIV response: findings from rapid regional assessments in eastern and southern Africa in 2008', *Food Security,* vol 1, pp261–269

Kadiyala, S. and Gillespie, S. (2004) 'Rethinking food aid to fight AIDS', *Food and Nutrition Bulletin,* vol 25, no 3, pp271–282

Kakuru, D.M. (2006) *The Combat for Gender Equality in Education: Rural Livelihood Pathways in the Context of HIV/AIDS*, AWLAE Series No.4, Wageningen Academic Publishers, Wageningen, The Netherlands

Karuhanga B.M. (2008) *Living with AIDS in Uganda: Impacts on Banana-farming Households in Two Districts*, AWLAE Series No.6, Wageningen Academic Publishers, Wageningen, The Netherlands

Masanjala, W.H. (2006) 'HIV/AIDS, household expenditure and consumption dynamics in Malawi', in S. Gillespie (ed) *AIDS, Poverty and Hunger: Challenges and Responses,* International Food Policy Research Institute, Washington DC, USA, pp57–74

Müller, T.R. (2005) *HIV/AIDS, Gender and Rural Livelihoods in sub-Saharan Africa*, AWLAE Series No.2, Wageningen Academic Publishers, Wageningen, The Netherlands

Niehof, A. and Price, L.L. (2007) 'Etic and emic perspectives on HIV/AIDS impacts on rural livelihoods and agricultural practice in sub-Saharan Africa', *NJAS Wageningen Journal of Life Sciences,* vol 56, no 3, pp139–155

Nombo, C.I. (2007) *When AIDS Meets Poverty: Implications for Social Capital in a Village in Tanzania*, AWLAE Series No.5, Wageningen Academic Publishers, Wageningen, The Netherlands

Rugalema, G. (2000) 'Coping or struggling? A journey into the impact of HIV/AIDS in southern Africa', *Review of African Political Economy,* vol 28, no 86, pp537–545

Scrimshaw, N., Taylor, C. and Gordon, J. (1968) *Interactions of Nutrition and Infection,* World Health Organization, Geneva

Semba, R.D. and Tang, A.M. (1999) 'Micronutrients and the pathogenesis of human immunodeficiency virus infection', *British Journal of Nutrition,* vol 81, no 3, pp181–189

Wiegers, E.S. (2008a) 'The role of the agricultural sector in mitigating the impact of HIV/AIDS in Sub-Saharan Africa', *NJAS Wageningen Journal of Life Sciences,* vol 56, no 3, pp155–167

Wiegers, E.S. (2008b) *Gendered Vulnerabilities to AIDS and its Research Implications*, PhD thesis, Wageningen University, Wageningen, The Netherlands

WHO (2003) *Nutrient Requirements for People Living with HIV/AIDS*, Report of a technical consultation, World Health Organisation, Geneva

Yamano, T. and Jayne, T.S. (2004) 'Measuring the impacts of working-age adult mortality on small-scale farm households in Kenya', *World Development,* vol 32, no 1, pp91–119

Index

academic institutions 200
access
  credit 97, 107–110, 112
  education 39
  food 157
  land 30, 65–66, 80, 121–122, 212–214
  resources 121–126, 182
  treatment 3, 56, 57, 224
accumulated assets 82–85
ACRs *see* agricultural-consumption regimes
adaptive strategies 40–41, 157, 166
adult
  children 80–82, 84–85, 91–92, 215, 216, 218–219
  mortality 10, 153–170, 214
  prevalence rates 2, 3
affected households
  farming knowledge 135, 136, 141, 142, 143, 144–145, 146, 147, 217
  FLS approach 171–189
  food security 118, 121, 122, 124, 125, 127, 128–129, 214
  wild natural resources 154, 159–168
age 138–139, 145, 156
Agincourt Health and Demographic Surveillance System (AHDSS) 154, 155, 156, 158
agricultural-consumption regimes (ACRs) 98–113
agricultural policy 192–204
agricultural production
  epidemic impacts 14, 25
  FLS 173
  food security 117, 118, 124, 128, 213
  participation 220
  women 82–84, 86, 87, 88, 89, 90, 95–115
agricultural research 221–222
agro-ecosystems 146, 171, 185

AHDSS *see* Agincourt Health and Demographic Surveillance System
Amurwon, Jovita 8–9, 13–27
antiretroviral (ARV) treatment 4, 57, 205, 206, 224
ARV *see* antiretroviral treatment
assets
  labour markets 119
  physical 121–123
  prolonged illness 72–73
  resilience 38, 40
  single women 82–85, 88, 91, 215
  social protection 221
  vulnerability 118, 129, 210
attitudes towards sex 100, 103, 105–107, 110, 111
autonomy in decision-making 96–97, 99, 101, 106–107, 108, 109, 110, 111

banana production 10, 24, 117–131
bean cultivation 23, 24
Benin 10, 133–151, 217
Beraho, Monica Karuhanga 10, 117–131, 213–214, 216, 217, 219
Botswana 194
Broerse, Jacqueline 10–11, 171–189
Bukoba District, Tanzania 9, 30–42, 215–216
Burkina Faso 97

Cambodia 171–172
capacity development 198, 199–200, 218
capital
  human 71, 165–166, 174
  lack of 62–63
  social 11, 56, 73–75, 92, 214–216
caring
  adult children 80–82, 216

FLS participation 177, 178, 184
gender 11, 73, 223
household impacts 44, 46, 47–57
labour 124
prolonged illness 71–72, 73
research 222–223
women 73, 78, 80–82, 87, 211, 213, 218–219
see also support
cash crops 15, 97, 111, 112, 213
cassava 24
children 19–20, 56, 66, 133–151, 154, 203, 211
see also orphans
child support grants 49, 51, 52, 54, 55
client-oriented approaches 201, 218
coffee cultivation 23–24
cognitive salience 133–151
collaboration 187, 203, 218
commercial farming 146–147
commercial sex 63, 110, 111
committees 199
communal areas 77–94, 217–218
community level
  coping systems 214
  health centres 173, 184
  health workers 47, 52, 56
  incentives 220
  social capital 92
  socio-economic impacts 211–212
  support 74–75, 87, 88, 222–223
conceptual timelines 209
contextual level 8, 102, 107, 112, 216, 224
continuity 9, 29–42, 45
cooperation 45, 55
coordination 63, 199, 201, 202, 203–204
coping 157, 166, 214, 216–217
Couffo, Benin 133–148, 217
credit 97, 107–110, 112, 220
crop production 22–25, 181–182
cross-cutting issues 194, 198
cross-sectional studies 8, 10, 16, 46, 57, 166, 167
cross-sectoral research 7–8
cultivation 21–25, 49, 52, 213
culture 73, 98, 134, 139, 183
customary tenure 15–16, 78, 91, 214, 215

death
  cultivation impacts 21–22, 25

food security 160
household movement 19–20
labour 30, 124
resilience 32–41
traditions 178
see also mortality
decision-making
  autonomy 96–97, 99, 101, 105, 106–107, 108, 109, 110, 111
  FLS approach 182, 183
demographics 17–21, 48
dependency
  adult children 80–82, 91–92, 215
  economic 97, 110–111
  labour 123
  vulnerability 88–90, 110–111
  women 83, 87, 91, 110–111
desk officers 199
development-oriented approaches 192–193, 203
dietary diversity 156–157, 158–159, 163–164, 165, 166, 214
disability grants 52
discontinuity 9, 29–42
dissolution of households 18–19, 25, 44
distant farming 64, 66, 71, 72, 214
diversification 64, 82–85, 86, 129, 186, 215
diversity 6, 8
division of labour 24–25
divorced women 87–88, 88–89
domestic work 49, 52–53, 55, 87–88, 89, 177, 184
downstream vulnerability 7, 209, 210, 211, 224
drought 24, 212, 217

East Africa 11, 191–208, 218
economic level 68, 69, 72, 74, 81, 95–113
see also socio-economic level
education
  FLS 171–187
  food security 121
  level of 48
  primary 37, 39, 50, 66, 124, 203
  secondary 34, 39, 50, 54
  see also schooling
employment 46, 67, 106, 110–111, 112, 213
  see also labour
empowerment 98–99, 110, 177, 180–184
entitlement-based instruments 221
entitlement theory 98–99

epidemics 6–8, 14, 25, 205
Ethiopia 220
ethnic aspects 64, 69, 102, 214–215
expenditure 125–126, 128
extended family 34, 39, 41, 45, 215–216, 219, 222
extension services 193, 200, 201

Fagbemissi, Rose 10, 133–151, 217
family
    extended 34, 39, 41, 45, 215–216, 219, 222
    migration 214
    single women 90
    social capital 73
    see also kinship
Farmer Life Schools (FLS) 10–11, 171–189, 217
farming knowledge 10, 133–151, 217
female-headed households 118, 119, 120, 121–123, 125–126, 127, 128, 219
see also gender; women
financial resources 4, 193, 201–202, 206
FLS *see* Farmer Life Schools
focal points 199, 199–200
food 30, 33, 68, 69–70, 71–72, 182–183
food security
    farming knowledge 146, 147
    FLS 173, 174, 217
    multilayered impacts 117–131
    nutrition 223
    partnerships 202
    policy responses 205
    social protection 221
    socio-economic impacts 211
    vulnerability 5, 214
    wild natural resources 10, 153–170
foster care grants 51, 52, 55, 57
fostering
    farming knowledge 139, 143–144, 145
    household responses 19, 20, 32, 33, 215–216
    resilience 34, 40
Foster, Susan 8–9, 13–27
free listing 135, 136–137, 140–141
funeral expenses 30, 72
future aspects 220–223

gardens 173–187, 217
gender
    care and support 11, 73, 223

farming knowledge 138, 141–143, 146–147
food security 10, 117–130
heads of households 78–92, 118–130, 213–214, 219
policy responses 198, 200
sexual behaviour 183
social norms 185
vulnerability 96, 218–219
General Population Cohort study (GPC) 15
Gillespie, Stuart 1–12, 209–226
government 39, 41, 183–184, 223, 224
    see also national level
government seed handouts 85, 86
GPC *see* General Population Cohort study
grandmother's disease 39, 218–219
grandparents 33, 35, 38–39, 50, 56
grants 46, 49, 50, 51, 52, 54, 55, 57
group-based learning approach 172–187

heads of households
    changes in 211
    cultivation 21–22, 25
    gender 78–92, 118–130, 213–214, 219
health
    centres 173, 184
    community workers 47, 52, 56
    FLS 172
    policy 191–192, 194, 203, 206, 218
    research 222
hearth-holds 79–92
    see also households
hierarchical linear modelling (HLM) 103
historical aspects 3–5
HLM *see* hierarchical linear modelling
homesteads 45, 88–90
households
    care and support 222, 223
    decision-making 96
    farming knowledge 138, 139
    hearth-hold contrast 80
    inter-relations 45, 55, 56–57, 216, 220
    longitudinal studies 16–25
    mortality and morbidity 43–60
    multilayered impacts 118–130
    policy responses 192
    poverty 224
    resilience 9, 29–42, 215–216
    socio-economic impacts 211–212
    sugar cane 65, 70–73

wild natural resources 155–157, 159–168
women 99–100
see also affected households; heads of
    households; non-affected households
human capital 71, 165–166, 174
hunger 157, 164, 165, 212
Hunter, Lori M. 10, 153–170, 214
hyperendemic countries 2–3, 6, 192

IFPRI *see* International Food Policy Research
    Institute
ILA *see* Interactive Learning and Action
illness
    FLS 180, 182, 184
    labour 124, 213
    microfinance 220
    prolonged 71–72, 72–73, 74, 89–90
    support networks 215, 219
immigrants 85, 89
implementation 195, 196–197, 198–204
incentives 220, 221, 223
income
    access to 124–126
    caring 211
    decision-making autonomy 96–97
    FLS approach 175
    prolonged illness 71, 72
    social grants 46, 49, 51, 55
    vulnerability 30, 110, 216
    wild natural resources 154, 160, 161–163
    women 82, 84, 110
    see also wealth
independence 82–92, 110
indicators 204
innovation 181, 186
in-service training 199–200
institutional level 183–184, 184–185, 187,
    198, 199
integrated approaches 186, 198
Interactive Learning and Action (ILA) 173
intergenerational knowledge gap 133–134
International Food Policy Research Institute
    (IFPRI) 96, 193, 219
Ivory Coast 220

JLICA *see* Joint Learning Initiative on
    Children and AIDS
joint decision-making 105, 106, 107, 108
Joint Learning Initiative on Children and
    AIDS (JLICA) 221

Kabarole, Uganda 10, 117–131
Kabumbilo's family 32–35, 40
Kadiyala, S. 210
Karuhanga 213–214, 216, 217, 219
KCGA *see* outgrowers cane association
Kenya 10, 95–115, 212–213
Kilombero district, Tanzania 9, 61–76, 212
kinship 9, 29–30, 39, 51, 53, 67–68, 90, 92,
    216
    see also family
knowledge 10, 217
Kura, Zimbabwe 79
KwaZulu-Natal, South Africa 9, 10–11,
    43–60, 171–189, 216, 217

labour
    access to 123–124
    assets 119
    community support 223
    death 30, 124
    division of 24–25
    farming knowledge 146
    food security 128
    ill health 213
    inter-household exchange 220
    migration 63
    shortages 24, 71, 72, 213
    single women 85, 86
    social cohesion 68
    socio-economic impacts 211
    see also employment
land
    access 30, 65–67, 80, 121–122, 212–215
    accumulation 84, 85
    cultivation 21–25
    orphans 34
    women 16, 80, 91, 97, 106, 111, 215
    see also tenure
language 134, 198
learning 177, 178–179
leasehold tenure 16
Leimar Price, Lisa 10
livestock 122
living arrangements 47–57
longitudinal studies 8–9, 13–27, 29–42, 167,
    213, 215–216

macro-economic aspects 9, 14, 214, 215
Mailo tenure 16
mainstreaming 195, 198, 199, 202, 218

maize 10, 22–23, 24, 133–151, 181, 217
Malawi 25, 193, 195, 196, 199–200, 201,
   216
male-headed households 118, 119, 122, 123,
   126, 127, 128, 213–214, 219
Mali 97
malnutrition 33, 212
Masaka District, Uganda 8–9, 10, 13–27,
   117–131, 213
Mathieson, Kirsten 9, 29–42
matooke cultivation 23, 24
medical expenses 30, 71, 72, 88, 126, 213
medicine 161, 162
microfinance programmes 220
midstream vulnerability 7
migration
   child 56
   labour 63
   reducing 220
   resilience 35–37
   social structures 67–69, 73, 214
   sugar cane privatization 64, 67–69, 75
   survivors 32
   vulnerability 36, 66, 75, 111, 213
   women 85, 111
mitigation 7, 11, 203, 204, 217, 224
Mkamba village, Kilombero district, Tanzania
   9, 61–76
monitoring and evaluation 195–198, 204
morbidity 9, 14, 43–60, 72–73, 211, 220
   see also illness
mortality
   microfinance programmes 220
   prime-age 10, 20, 32, 153, 154, 156
   privatization 72–73
   South Africa 9, 43–60
   Uganda 13, 14
   wild natural resources use 10, 153–170
   young adults 35, 37, 39, 71, 155
   see also death
movement of people 6, 18–21, 55, 56, 64,
   66, 88–89
   see also migration
Mozambique 196, 202
Mpumalanga Province, South Africa 10,
   154–168
Msinga, South Africa 172–187
Mudhara, Maxwell 10–11, 171–189
Mukagambi's household 38–41
Mukonoweshuro, Fadzai 11, 191–208

multilayered impacts 10, 117–131
multi-level aspects 2, 103, 213
multiple stresses 5
multi-sectoral approaches 191–192, 194, 202
Mwangi, E. Wairimu 10, 11, 95–115,
   209–226, 212–213

national level
   epidemics 6
   policy 191, 193–194, 195, 201, 203,
      204–205, 218, 221–222
   see also government
NDVI see Normalized Difference Vegetation
   Index
networks 45, 56, 89, 92
   see also support systems/networks
new variant famine hypothesis 192, 211, 212
NGOs see non-governmental organizations
Niehof, Anke 1–12, 43–60, 209–226
Nombo, Carolyne I. 9, 61–76, 212, 213,
   214–215
non-affected households
   farming knowledge 135, 136, 141, 142,
      143, 145, 146, 147, 217
   food security 118, 121, 122, 124, 125,
      127, 213, 214, 219
   wild natural resources use 159–168
non-governmental organizations (NGOs) 39,
   41, 87, 175, 184
Normalized Difference Vegetation Index
   (NDVI) 157–158
nutrition 7, 181, 201, 205, 211–212, 223, 224
Nyakato's household 37–38, 40

old-age grants 50, 54
One Monitoring and Evaluation 204
orphans 10, 32–35, 45–46, 56, 133–148,
   203, 217
ORT see Other Recurrent Transactions
Other Recurrent Transactions (ORT) 202
outgrowers cane association (KCGA) 63
ownership 21–22, 62, 213

Paradza, Gaynor Gamuchirai 9–10, 77–94,
   215, 219
participation 177–178, 180, 182, 184, 186,
   200, 220
partnerships 202–203
perceived risk of infection 101, 103, 107,
   108, 111

pests 24, 133–151, 217
physical assets 121–123
policy 11, 75, 91, 112–113, 191–208, 217–218, 220
political economy 98, 99
political aspects 183–184, 195, 199
poverty
  farming knowledge 146
  food security 123, 126, 128, 214
  morbidity and mortality 45
  policy 194
  risk 113, 224
  social capital 73, 74
  socio-economic impacts 211
  vulnerability 41, 224
  wild natural resources 155, 163–164, 166–167
  witchcraft 69
  women 95, 171–189, 212–213
  see also socio-economic level
Poverty Reduction Strategies 194
practical tools 200–201
du Preez, Corrie 9, 43–60, 216
pre-service training 200
prevalence
  Benin 134
  changing intensity 205
  diversity 6
  Kenya 96
  migration 111
  South Africa 43–44, 155, 172
  Tanzania 61, 62, 63
  Uganda 16
  wild natural resources use 162, 163
  Zimbabwe 77
prevention 3–4, 203, 206, 224
Price, Lisa Leimar 133–151, 217
primary school education 37, 39, 50, 66, 124, 203
prime-age mortality 10, 20, 32, 153, 154, 156
privatization 62–63, 65–66, 72–73, 75, 212, 214
production-oriented approaches 201, 218
professional support 175, 178–179, 183
programme-based approaches 194
prolonged illness 71–72, 72–73, 74, 89–90
proxy variables 100–101

qualitative approaches 46, 57, 64–65, 118
quantitative approaches 46, 118–119, 155

rational-action models 98
regional context 10, 95–115, 212–213, 221–222
Regional Network on AIDS, Livelihoods and Food Security (RENEWAL) 96, 103, 167, 193, 219, 221
relocation 18–19, 19–21, 88, 216
Remme, Michelle 11, 191–208, 218
remote sensing 155
RENEWAL see Regional Network on AIDS, Livelihoods and Food Security
research 221–224
resilience
  community 223
  food insecurity 211
  households 9, 29–42, 215–216
  interacting shocks 212
  livelihoods 210
  mitigation 224
  social protection 221
  stigma 178
resources
  access to 121–126
  community support 223
  decision-making autonomy 96–97
  farming knowledge 139, 146, 147
  households 45
  labour markets 119
  mobilization 201–202
  prolonged illness 72, 73
  social cohesion 68
  wild natural 153–170
responses 11, 216–217
risk
  environments 5
  focus on 98
  participation 186
  poverty 113, 224
  sexual behaviour 73, 101, 112, 203, 222
  women 83, 85–87, 97, 100–101, 111, 112
Rugalema, Gabriel 1–12, 29–42, 209–226, Rutayuga's household 35–37, 40

safe environments for learning 186
safety nets 154, 166, 167
saving money 154, 161–163, 166, 182
scalability 204–205
schooling 38–39, 50, 52, 54, 56
  see also education

SEAGA *see* Socio–Economic and Gender Analysis
secondary school education 34, 39, 50, 54
sectoral level 195, 196–197, 202–203
sector-wide approaches (SWAps) 194, 202, 206
Seeley, Janet 8–9, 13–27, 213, 216
semantic domains 134–135
Sen, A. 98
sexual behaviour
    attitudes 100, 103, 105–107, 110, 111
    commercial 63, 110, 111
    risk 73, 101, 112, 203, 222
    social position and power 96, 183
    underreporting 98
short term impacts 9, 14, 223
single women
    experiences 77–94, 215, 219
    headed households 118, 119, 120, 121, 122, 127
    land 214
social capital 11, 56, 73–75, 92, 214–216
social level
    FLS approach 181, 182
    grants 46, 49, 51, 55
    group membership 160
    norms 185
    protection 221, 222–223, 224
    risky behaviour 112
    support 128, 214–216
    vulnerability 61–76, 99, 118
    women 96, 97, 98, 99
socio-demographic factors 102, 103, 104
Socio-Economic and Gender Analysis (SEAGA) 200
socio-economic level
    contextual nature 224
    cultivation 23
    FLS approach 180–183
    gender 73
    households and communities 211–212
    KwaZulu-Natal, South Africa 48
    land shortages 214–215
    social capital 74
    trajectory studies 16–17, 18
    vulnerability 216
    wild natural resources 158, 159, 160, 161, 163, 165, 167
    see also poverty
socio-epidemiological frameworks 5

sorghum 181
South Africa 9, 10–11, 43–60, 153–170, 171–189, 196, 214, 216
Southern Africa 11, 191–208, 218
Ssentongo, Joseph 9, 29–42
staffing 199–200
stigma 174, 178, 180, 183, 184–185, 186, 218
Stloukal, Libor 11, 191–208
street children 34
subsistence farming 15–16, 65–67, 146–147
succumbed hearth-holds 83, 90
sugar cane 9, 61–76, 213, 214
support systems/networks
    community 74–75, 87, 88, 222–223
    extension services 93, 200, 201
    FLS 172
    food security 128
    mitigation 11, 214–216
    professional 175, 178–179, 183
    see also caring 11, 74–75, 128, 172, 214–216, 222–223
    see also caring roles; family; kinship
surplus 83
survivors 32, 38, 144–145, 147
susceptible population groups 195
Sutrop, U. 135, 137
Swaans, Kees 10–11, 171–189, 217–218
SWAps *see* sector-wide approaches
sweet cane 61–76

taboos 179
Tanzania 6, 9, 30–42, 61–76, 197, 214–215
TB *see* tuberculosis
technical problems 175, 178–179, 182
tenure
    customary 15–16, 78, 91, 214, 215
    women 91, 97, 106, 110, 121–122, 213
Three Ones principle 195, 204
timelines 6–7
Tobit model 138, 144–145
training 199–200
transactional sex 63, 66
treatment 3, 4, 56, 57, 205, 206, 224
trust 69, 75, 180, 215
tuberculosis (TB) 46, 49, 50, 51, 55, 118, 216
Twine, Wayne 10, 153–170, 214

Uganda 8–9, 10, 13–27, 117–131, 195, 197, 199, 213–214

United Nations 1, 4, 191
upstream vulnerability 7, 10, 95, 212–213

vegetables 161, 165–166, 181, 214
verbal autopsies 156
village membership 80, 89
vulnerability
  adult mortality 167
  assets 118, 129, 210
  downstream 7, 209, 210, 211, 224
  economic sources 95–113
  food security 5, 214
  gender 96, 218–219
  income 30, 110, 216
  migration 36, 66, 75, 111, 213
  multifaceted 2, 129, 209, 210
  networks 56
  poverty 41, 224
  social change 61–76
  susceptible population policies 195
  timelines 6–7
  women 10, 78, 82–92, 95–115, 128,
    212–213, 215, 224

wage employment *see* employment
Wasara, Zimbabwe 79
water 182
wealth
  food security 118, 119, 120–121, 122,
    123, 126, 127, 128
  heads of households 213
  wild natural resources use 159, 164
  see also income

widows
  assets 121, 122, 219
  disinheritance 38
  food security 118, 119, 120, 127, 128
  labour 123, 124
  land rights 113
  vulnerability 111
wild natural resources 10, 153–170
witchcraft 69–70, 77, 215
women
  caring roles 73, 211, 213, 218–219
  farming knowledge 143, 146
  household heads 118, 119, 120, 121–123,
    125–126, 127, 128, 219
  FLS approach 10–11, 171–189
  infection 3
  land 16, 80, 91, 97, 106, 111, 215
  microfinance programmes 220
  prevalence 43–44
  single 9–10, 77–94
  vulnerability 10, 78, 82–92, 95–115, 128,
    212–213, 215, 224
woodlands 157–158, 161–163, 164, 166
workforce impacts 193, 194, 195
World Vision Tanzania (WVT) 39
WVT *see* World Vision Tanzania

young adults 35, 37, 39, 71, 155

Zambia 219
Zimbabwe 9–10, 77–94, 193, 195, 197, 198,
  199, 200, 202, 204, 215
Zomba, Malawi 25